STREET RODDER'S HANDBOOK

BY FRANK ODDO

Publisher: Rick Bailey; Executive Editor: Randy Summerlin;
Editorial Director: Tom Monroe, P.E., S.A.E.;
Senior Editor: Ron Sessions, A.S.A.E.; Art Director: Don Burton;
Book Design: Donna Sessions;
Production Coordinator: Cindy Coatsworth; Typography: Michelle Carter;
Director of Manufacturing: Anthony B. Narducci;
Photos: Frank Oddo, others noted.

Published by HPBooks
A Division of HPBooks, Inc.
P.O. Box 5367, Tucson, AZ 85703   602/888-2150
ISBN 0-89586-369-3   Library of Congress Catalog Number 86-81201
©1986 HPBooks, Inc.   Printed in U.S.A.
1st Printing

Author Frank Oddo in Bruce Geisler's vintage-tin '29A Ford roadster pickup. Frank found car for Bruce, which he traded '32 roadster for. Car is powered by a blown small-block Chevrolet.

ABOUT THE AUTHOR

Frank Oddo is a veteran street rodder. He remarks in this book that he fell in love with street rodding when he took his first ride in a street-rodded '40 Ford. The only thing unusual about this is he took that ride in the early '50s, and his publicly revealed fascination with high-performance "old cars" has continued unabated for more than 30 years.

Frank Oddo is also experienced in the field of street-rod photo-journalism. He published the first of some 400 articles and columns on the subject in 1968 to begin a career that is in full bloom today. His monthly writings appear in several magazines, the most important being *Street Rodder Magazine.* Just one example of such prolific endeavor is the phrase *fat-fendered* that is today commonly used in reference to 1938—40 Fords of obvious configuration. Oddo coined it in a series of articles published in *Street Rodder Magazine* in 1972 and '73.

Oddo was the first, if not the only, free-lance photographer ever to gain permission to photograph street rods and custom trucks at Disneyland. And he did it three times.

Oddo not only writes about street rods, he's a hot rodder/street rodder through and through. He has built and raced a number of early Ford roadsters at the National Speed Trials on the Bonneville Salt Flats and on El Mirage, the Southern California dry lake that has hosted hot-rod time trials off and on since 1939. Oddo held the Class G Street Roadster record in the late '70s, and he currently campaigns a 217-mph, normally aspirated, gasoline-fed Ford Boss 302 belly-tank lakester at El Mirage and at Bonneville.

But, it is as "Mister Forty Ford"—as *Hot Rod Magazine* once called him—that he is best known to his readership. A title such as that doesn't come easily, but it certainly begins with the long-term ownership of a '40 Ford. Oddo reports that he has not been without a 1940 DeLuxe coupe since acquiring his first in 1955. His current example includes parts from that coupe, and every other he's owned since then, and has appeared in more magazine tech and how-to articles than any other Forty in existence.

Oddo, as one of the charter members of Forties Limited, a Southern California street-rod club organized in 1968, and as associate editor and technical editor of *Street Rodder Magazine,* has been in on the resurgence of modern street rodding from its earliest days. In this enviable position he has not only been there when things happened . . . he has been able to record them for posterity!

ACKNOWLEDGMENTS

Nobody ever built a street rod totally by himself, nor did I write this book by myself. I started down the path more than 30 years ago with two pals in New Orleans: Robert Rider and Lionel Duhon. Later, after I migrated to the West Coast in the early '60s, Jack Garrison, Dick Hendrix and all the guys of the Forties Limited street-rod club took up the reins and kept me interested in street rodding.

Throughout the '70s and '80s my close association with Terry Berzenye of Specialized Auto Repair and Don McNeil of Specialized Auto Components, both of Anaheim, California, and John Hesford of Fast Johnny's Speed Shop in Mission Viejo, California, led to much of the material incorporated in this book. I also owe a great deal to the editors, past and present, of *Street Rodder Magazine.* And finally, to all the guys I've known—and wish I'd known—from the Southern California Timing Association, who put this game on the map in the first place. Thanks for the help.

Frank Oddo
Brea, California
March 31, 1986

Contents

Introduction

Fenderless '32 High Boy roadster is a classic vintage-tin hot rod . . . er, uh . . . street rod. But it says HOT ROD! Find out what these terms mean on page 7; find out how to build your own street rod with this book. Photo by Tom Monroe.

tend to become enchanted by some idealized version of a particular make and model. It doesn't matter that the specifics change many times before the daydream becomes reality.

Be that as it may, the neophyte street rodder certainly knows when he is hooked. The casual interest becomes a desire; his pulse increases when he sees a vehicle that even remotely captures the spirit of his dreams. And, depending upon his mechanical skills and financial wherewithal, the desire eventually becomes goal-directed activity.

There has long been a need for an in-depth, organized book on the major aspects of street-rod building—a book that puts it *all* together. Even though millions of words on the subject have seen print since *Throttle Magazine* started the ball rolling back in 1941, the material has been in the form of one- to four-page articles, few of which were ever collected in a single, usable volume.

Although the contents of this book reflect my judgements about subjects most vital to the street rodder, my opinions, despite being as prejudiced as anyone else's, are based on experience. I have been an active participant in street rodding for a number of years. During that time I've seen many more street rods started than were ever finished. It's my goal in the chapters that follow to lay the groundwork that will prevent your dream from becoming a nightmare.

If you just want a good idea of what the building of a street rod is all about, this book will give you many ideas of how to do it using the modification of vintage cars and scratch-building of fiberglass reproduction cars as examples.

If you've already committed yourself and bought the makings of a street rod, this book will guide you along the way, suggest what to do next, and reduce a lot of difficult choices to a workable few.

What this book won't do is eliminate the need to think creatively. That is the essence of this hobby.

Finally, as we go step-by-step through the potentially confusing process of merging a vintage car or a fiberglass replica and a garage full of late-model automotive parts and after-market street-rod components into a safe, reliable, unique mode of transportation and personal expression, it is my fondest hope that you will enjoy yourself.

The decision to build a street rod is usually the result of many stimuli—the ownership of a street rod by some admired acquaintance, street-rod activity in one's community, or the casual reading of street-rod periodicals. Although the concept almost always comes before the car, the neophyte builder will probably have a certain car in mind. Most of us

From Whence We Came 1

Eldon Snapp's '29 roadster in line at a Southern California Timing Association Dry Lakes meet in the late '30s. When outfitted with modified four-cylinder or flathead V8, Model A's became the prototypical hot rod. The majority of participants merely stripped the fenders from their everyday transportation for one or two runs against the clock.

It is widely held that motorsports began in France with the first organized race—from Paris to Rouen—in 1894. Although the interest and excitement spread quickly to the rest of the world, motorsports in general and auto racing in particular were, by and large, pursuits of the wealthy and their professional assistants. This remained the case until well after the bloody upheaval that was World War I. It wasn't until the 1920s, a time of great expansion in the science of automotive engineering and production, that most younger members of the American middle class could afford a secondhand passenger car and daydream of glory on the racing circuit.

The history of the world may be written in the blood of wars, but the early history of hot rodding is written in the dust of dry lakes racing. The automotive-manufacturing giants and much of the professional racing industry had already picked the industrialized Midwest as their home base. Southern California,

however, with its unique combination of climate and geography, was destined to be the birthplace of the *all*-American autosport of modifying passenger cars for greater speed—*hot rodding*. And, although it is impossible to declare which came first—street rods or hot rods—the early days of our sport was recorded.

Much of what we know comes from a handful of books. The February, 1939 issue of *Popular Science* included 15 photos taken during the last 1938 dry lakes meet. The Southern California Timing Association (SCTA) *Racing News* was published from 1938 to 1941. And the granddaddy of the entire performance magazine genre—*Throttle Magazine*—was published from January to December, 1941. Finally, there are those wonderful early issues of *Hot Rod Magazine*, from 1948 to 1955. The following tidbits of information are passed along for your edification . . . .

THE FATHER OF HOT RODDING

If one man can be given such an imposing title, then by all accounts it must be the revered Ed Winfield. Driven both by economic necessity—his father died when he was five—and a burning desire to learn about mechanical things, Ed started with the science of forging steel. The "Genius of Glendale" began his career in 1909. At the age of eight he secured employment at a local blacksmith shop.

From the smithy, he went to work for a Ford dealer. Then, in 1914 he worked for the nationally prominent race-car and engine builder, Harry A. Miller, in Los Angeles. Ed was assigned duties in the carburetor department of the well-organized Miller complex, which included a foundry and machine shop. It was here that the 15-year-old lad was exposed to all forms of practical automotive engineering. By 1920, however, Ed was more or less in the speed-equipment business for himself, scratch building carburetors and grinding high-lift cams.

In 1921 Winfield started racing his modified Ford roadster at Ascot and other California dirt tracks. No one can say with assurance that this Model T was the first street rod—Ed *had* been working on it since 1912—but it most certainly was the first automobile identified as such. For all practical purposes, 1920 was the beginning of hot rodding as we know it today.

Ed's racing career spanned but a brief six years. Yet, during that time, he built such a reputation for himself and his speed equipment that in 1927 he hung up his driving gloves and devoted full energies to his thriving shop and the production of high-performance camshafts, carburetors and cylinder heads for Ford-based engines.

By the late '20s, most of the Indianapolis 500 cars were running Winfield carburetors. But, as outstanding an achievement as that was, the Winfield name is best remembered by the automotive world for its prominence on the record-setting, cut-down Ford roadsters, which saw double-duty on the streets of Los Angeles and the dusty, dry lakes of Southern California's Mojave Desert.

THE LAKES

The first dry lake to be extensively used by Los Angeles hot rodders was Muroc. Now known as Edwards Air Force Base, and home to the Space Shuttle, it lies some 100 miles north of the Los Angeles basin, just west of Highway 395. For 10,000 years or more, the barren, alkali lake bed served no purpose. Although it could not support plant or animal life, it was often under a few inches of water during the rainy season—a dim and bitter memory of better days. Nevertheless, the lakes is where hot rodding—and not much else—flowered.

In the early '20s Muroc Dry Lake came to life with a vengeance when some unsung performance enthusiasts realized that the 22-mile-long, 10-mile-wide lake bed was nature's gift to the straight-away racer. Not only flat and unblemished except for heat cracks, the surface was hard enough to burn rubber on, yet just slippery enough to keep an out-of-shape race car from digging in and flipping—most of the time—perfect for making Land Speed Record (LSR) attempts.

In the spring of 1924, the well-known Indy 500 race driver Tommy Milton journeyed to Muroc with a 3.0-liter Miller powered racer, a full pit crew and timing equipment. His best speed of 151.3 mph was never recognized by the international powers that be. However, the official Land Speed Record of 145.89 mph was assigned to a "proper" Englishman,

Ernest Eldridge, driving a Fiat on a public road in France on July 12, 1924.

Discouraging as that must have been, the equally famous American racer Frank Lockhart drove a 1.5-liter supercharged Miller to a speed of 164 mph on Muroc in 1927. A valiant effort, but a bit short of the official 171.02-mph record at the time. No matter, by then every Los Angeles kid with a car knew about Muroc. Plenty of them wanted to test their own machines on the dusty lake bed.

When the hot rods hit Muroc in the late '20s pandemonium broke out. With rare exception, there was no significant organization, not even accurate timing. Often 10 or 12 roadsters would tear down the lake bed abreast. Few of the drivers knew where the "finish line" was, much less who crossed it first. Only the front runners could see . . . the also-rans were lost in the murky cloud of alkali dust that swirled about them. Predictably, tragic results were not uncommon.

During the late '20s and early '30s, Muroc played host to unorganized groups of hot rodders from late spring until early fall. Even during the summer months when temperatures on the desert soared to as high as 110 degrees Fahrenheit, hundreds gathered to evaluate the latest modifications made to their creations.

LAKES CARS

By 1930, the Southern California hot rod/street rod, although still a very individualistic automobile, had developed enough common characteristics as to be typified. Almost without exception it was based on the Ford Model T roadster of the early '20s. During the heyday of the Model T—from the end of World War I until the "Crash of '29"—it was standard practice for adult members of the motoring public to buy a brand new car when one needed transportation. A secondhand Model T was considered too worn-out to be a good investment. And trade-ins were offered to the used car market at significant discounts—as little as $25 for a runner! Now, that was a mighty small sum for wheels even in those days. And it put a drivable car into the hands of most any young man with a job.

By 1930 a lot of used circle-track-racing equipment was available. This allowed those so inclined to modify that T roadster engine with a Frontenac or Rajo overhead-valve-conversion head. The Frontenac, built by Louis and Arthur Chevrolet of Indianapolis, had earned an excellent reputation which was enhanced when a Frontenac-equipped Ford racer finished fifth at the 1923 Indy 500. There were many varieties, some including single and dual overhead cams, but few hot rodders could afford even the basic overhead-valve model that cost $115 new. Yet, the head

appeared on street-driven cars that ran at the lakes.

The most popular head conversions among the hot rodders were those manufactured by Joe Jagersberger of Racine, Wisconsin. The *Rajo*—a contraction of RAcine JOe—also came in many versions. The heads that the hot rodders preferred were the valve-in-head Models B and C which were introduced in the mid-'20s. These were equipped with self-lubricating bronze-bushed rocker arms and lightweight adjustable pushrods. The Model C sold new for $85.

The typical hot-rodder's T engine was equipped with a Winfield cam. Although there was a wide variety of carburetors available, the locally manufactured Winfield carb was favored, along with an outside-mount magneto ignition.

The roadster body generally sat atop the frame in *High Boy* fashion. As soon as finances allowed, the car was equipped with a strong gear-shift Muncie transmission and a Ruckstell two-speed rear-axle assembly. The latter was also a more-or-less home-grown product manufactured in Berkeley, California. Worthwhile additions to the Ruckstell axle were Rocky Mountain mechanical brakes. These brakes replaced the Ford transmission brake and operated from the T foot pedal directly to the rear wheels. Needless to say, it was much more reliable than the stock brake system. The final outfitting of a top-notch street T-roadster-cum-lakes-racer was one of the popular brands of racing wire wheels: Buffalo, Phelps, Stewart or House. These installations were more good sense than fad—the original-equipment wood-spoke wheels were likely to snap, crackle and pop during hard cornering.

ORGANIZED RACING ARRIVES

In the spring of 1931, a momentous event occurred—the Gilmore Oil Company Speed Trials. This was perhaps more important than the Milton and Lockhart LSR attempts a few years earlier. It was the first sponsored, organized meet held on Muroc. The man in charge was George Wight, the owner of the already famous Bell Auto Parts. The most significant thing about the Gilmore meet was not the 105-mph record set by Ike Trone in a Riley equipped Model A, but the fact that sponsorship and organization brought a measure of safety and enjoyment for all.

In the months and years that ensued, the hot-rod sport continued to gather new adherents among the young men of Southern California. This was in spite of a general poor public reception that lasted 25 years. Neither the old folks nor The Great Depression could dampen their enthusiasm. They merely worked longer and harder for the money required

Veda Orr's fenderless street deuce first earned honors in 1937 with a 114 mph run. Husband Karl Orr, already one of Southern California's top hot-rod-racing mechanics, was later to open one of the very first speed shops. Car was eventually timed at more than 125 mph. Photo courtesy Veda Orr.

to first buy a used Ford roadster, and then to build it into a hot rod.

HOT ROD, WHAT DOES IT MEAN?

Perhaps this is a good time to define a few terms beginning with *hot rod*. Information indicates that it is a contraction of *hot roadster*. *Hot* refers to the reworking of the original (or replacement) engine in order to achieve an increased level of performance, or more horsepower. The flashy, well-admired roadsters were windowless open cars so generally popular in the '20s and early '30s. They were also reasonable facsimiles of racing cars when stripped of windshields, headlights, fenders and running boards—even more so when the body was *channeled* or dropped down over the frame.

At any rate, Southern Ascot race track, a 1/2-mile dirt oval in Los Angeles, decided to run stock bodied "hot roadsters" one Sunday a month beginning in May 1939. The advertising of such events led to the term *hot rod*. Most entries were Southern California Timing Association (SCTA) members, although the Association disclaimed any official connection.

By the end of World War II, *hot rod* was used to describe any old car owned by a young person and modified for greater speed. It was very definitely a term of contempt.

The term *street rod* didn't come into vogue until the 1950s. In the '30s and '40s, it was assumed that if a young Southern Californian owned a street drivable hot rod, he also raced it at the dry lakes. It wasn't until most hot rods were no longer considered weekend race cars that the street-legal drivability forced the the term *street rod*.

Be that as it may, Muroc Dry Lake was often occupied on summer weekends in the mid '30s by home-built race cars that served as transportation during the week. How did this metamorphosis come about? Not without a great deal of effort.

Labor was the cheapest thing around in those days. A couple of fellows intent on "going to the lakes" would begin by stripping down their roadster as soon as they got home from work on Saturday. Sometimes, they would remove the headlights, even though they might have to drive to Muroc in darkness. They would load up the roadster with tools, spare parts, food and jugs of water for

drinking and for cooling the engine. They also threw in some blankets in case they arrived early enough to get an hour of sleep before the crack of dawn and before the first roar of engines signaled the start of the informal meet.

In 1935, organized speed trials were given a boost when Merl Finkenbinder brought a set of electric clocks to Muroc. The rudimentary timing system was activated when a low transverse piano wire was tripped. The method worked reasonably well, but the wire was periodically broken, bringing the time trials to a halt while repairs were made.

In order to cut down on delays, the starter took a peek under each staging car to verify that all undercarriage components cleared the tripwire. While he was on his knees, the flagman often noted that some overeager racer had relied on excessive usage of bailing wire. Out of these casual examinations came the first safety inspections at the dry lakes races.

SCTA IS BORN

The summer of 1935 also brought the beginning of events that would change the random course of hot rodding forever. Although

Karl Orr opened his speed shop in the Los Angeles suburb of Culver City in 1940. "I built engines and I sold heads, manifolds, cams, carbs and ignitions. And I *sold* them—three or four complete sets a day!" Hot rodding was well on its way. These cars amply reflect the high quality of many pre-World War II street rods. Photo courtesy Veda Orr.

The four-cylinder Ford from late Model T's up through 1934 models was the first mainstay of SoCal hot rodders. As late as 1939—when photo was taken—they were found in street rods and sprint cars. Photo courtesy Frank Baron.

a number of men have been honored with the founding of the Southern California Timing Association, only one was "officially" singled out by that organization during its early days. The following appeared in the November 17, 1940 edition of the SCTA *Racing News:*

BRIEF "AUTO" BIOGRAPHY OF ED ADAMS

Several clubs of the SCTA started when Ed Adams and some of his best friends graduated from high school. They wondered how they could keep track of each other over the years and conceived the roadster club as a solution.

The club grew to 15 members who were soon hopping up their cars. They even timed their cars and held lakes meets long before the association was formed. The roadster club was such a success that soon other clubs formed. The association was formally organized in 1938. Currently there are 28 different clubs in the Southern California Timing Association.

Ed Adams has been president since SCTA's inception. You can see him either running his Cragar Roadster through the traps or on the judges' stand taking down times.

The above clearly demonstrates that the modern world of street rodding owes a sig-

nificant debt of gratitude to Ed Adams and his pals Art Tilton, Vern Hurst, Wally Parks, Jack Harvey, Eldon Snapp, *et al.* I must also add the various law-enforcement agencies located in and around the Mojave Desert and Muroc Dry Lake. On more than one occasion, they emphasized that all dry lakes racing would be halted unless safety and organization were instituted.

A closer look at the formative years of the oldest existing hot-rod organization should be of interest to you, especially if you've ever gazed green with envy at a fenderless High Boy roadster or a chopped-and-channeled coupe.

The first meeting of the fledgling SCTA was held on November 29, 1937, with representatives of the Throttlers Club of Hollywood wielding the gavel. Serious hot-rod-racing business got under way immediately with discussions of ambulance service, club points and trophies. Over the next few months several additional meetings saw not only the Throttlers, Knight Riders, Road Runners, Sidewinders and 90 MPH clubs banding together, but also the Idlers, Ramblers, Gear Grinders, Derelicts and the all-Negro Centuries Clubs making preparations for the first SCTA Lakes Meet in May, 1938.

That the inaugural time trials were a success goes without saying, but it was not with-

out growing pains. At their next meeting, association members decided to further structure things. In addition to such inconsequential debates over outlawing stock Ford V8s unless they could exceed 100 mph, or whether entry fees should be raised from $1.00 to $1.50, it was decided that all coupes and sedans would be banned from SCTA events. Apparently not all hot rods were created equal. In all fairness, the ban was put in effect because closed cars were typically slower than open cars and numerous entries slowed the progress of the meet. The coupe and sedan ban quickly gave rise to the Russetta Timing Association, which accepted closed cars, but frowned upon open cars!

STREET RODDING PROGRESSES

Hot-rod racing on the dry lakes and the accompanying motorsport of street rodding prospered in spite of bickering. However, because of its loose organization, early street rodding is harder to trace.

The typical street rod of 1940 was a much more refined version of its 1930 counterpart. Although few powerplants were based on the Model T block any longer, four-cylinder engines still ruled. For example, of the 95 street roadsters entered in the May 19, 1940 SCTA lakes meet, 48 were powered by fours. Almost all of these were Model A, B, and C

Eldon Snapp and Wally Parks—who later became editor of *Hot Rod Magazine* and co-founder of the National Hot Rod Association (NHRA)—were responsible for the SCTA Racing News Program. Photographed on Sunday afternoon, June, 1941, Wally's roadster is typical of what the pioneers of hot rodding drove. Photo courtesy Eldon Snapp.

The period immediately following World War II saw more customizing of the early Ford body as exemplified by this unknown street rodder's completely filled in and deeply channelled '29 roadster. Four-cylinder engines had all but vanished from the scene by 1946. They were replaced by mildly hopped-up flathead V8s. Photo courtesy Veda Orr.

Fords, and 24 were topped with one of the Winfield flatheads. Forty-five entries, however, were Ford V8 powered. The *bent eight* was on the verge of taking over. The remaining two roadsters were oddballs, powered by a Cadillac V12 and V16, respectively. They were strong runners.

What did that era street rod look like? Following is an accurate description from the March, 1940 issue of the SCTA *Racing News:*

ATTENTION ALL SCTA MEMBERS

Would appreciate any information concerning a stolen black '29 A Ford Roadster. License No. 5F 6318. Equipment included new B block. Motor No. DR24572. Winfield head, 6207, has been milled, twin Winfield S.R. carburetors, bowl numbers BD 5043 and BD 5045, were mounted on Alexander manifold. Also included a 281° Bertrand 5-bearing cam, Set of 16-inch Kelsey Hays black wheels, 700x16 U.S. Royal white sidewall tires on rear, 600x16 U.S. Royals on front. Outside appearance as follows: Black body with no trim, Chevy headlights, two fog lights, black top, fenders and running boards, blue running lights. Anyone with information concerning this car or equipment please contact The Lancers or A.J. Lawley, 1517 S. Berendo St., Los Angeles.

We can only hope that Mr. Lawley got his car back. But what about 1940 prices, you ask? The following advertisement is from the same issue . . .

For Sale: Buick Four in '30 A, V8 wheels, good rubber, new V8 front axle, new 3:27 gears, Riley-ground cam, 7-to-1 compression, 1-7/8-inch exhaust valves, new brakes, '31 steering, ran on dirt track at San Diego, 1940 license plates paid for. Cost over $300 . . . full price $75. Fred Dunn, 240 E. Chapman, Fullerton.

I don't know what kind of brakes Fred had, but hydraulic brakes, although far from common on non-factory-equipped Fords, were being installed by the more safety conscious builders. They were considered to be a significant selling point.

By the way, every street roadster today has to wear a Deuce grille shell, right? Well, believe it or not, Deuce shells were so hard to find as early as April, 1939 that one frustrated individual placed a 35-cent ad in the *Racing News:* "Wanted 1932 Ford V8 Radiator shell in fair if not good condition." Some problems never get better, only worse.

And how's this for a modern day teaser? From the March 1, 1939 *Racing News* . . .

For Sale: '32 V8 Touring—new cut down top, side curtains, good tires, new mains, perfect rearend, new trans . . . . about $125.

Finally, for those who enjoy self-inflicted pain, the following ads from the July 1, 1939 *Racing News:*

For Sale: '33 V8 Roadster. '37 engine and '36 transmission. Milled heads, '38 radio, new paint and top, plenty of chrome. Motor turned 100 last races. $200.

For Sale: '32 V8 Roadster with battery and transmission, less engine and wheels. $60.

TIME OUT FOR WORLD WAR II

Even before the United States became actively involved in World War II, the raging European conflict had its effect on auto racing at Muroc. The eastern "shore" of the dry lake bed had, for quite some time, been set aside as the U.S. Army Bombing Range. As soon as it was apparent to the military that aerial practice was necessary, the hot rodders were told in no uncertain terms to vacate the premises.

The SCTA only scheduled four lakes meets a year and the dates were kept a secret in order to keep spectator attendance—by this time as many as 15,000!—down to a manageable level. So, undaunted, the time trials were shifted from Muroc to nearby Rosamond and Harper Dry Lakes. These alternate sites were similar to Muroc, but not nearly as desirable. The worries about where to race, however, were of minor consequence after December 7, 1941.

World War II certainly left its mark on hot rodding and street rodding. First, there was the general mixing of young Americans from all geographical regions. Transplanted Southern California hot rodders carried with them tales of their passion for modified Ford

John Athan's street roadster, photographed by Veda Orr in front of Karl's speed shop in 1940, page 8, is alive and well today. Although photo was taken in 1979, this is precisely how the roadster looks today. John and pal Ed Iskenderian built the car in 1939.

By 1941, when photo was taken, channelling was well accepted as way of decreasing frontal area to "cheat the wind." Styling had not yet been accepted as the in "street" look. Photo courtesy Eldon Snapp.

By 1950, the '40 Ford—even though considered a late-model car by some—was beginning to be accepted as street-rod material. Tom Eiden, still an active SCTA member, drove his then recently acquired coupe to El Mirage in 1950.

You may not feel this custom '39 Ford coupe, photographed in the early '50s, is particularly attractive with its GM front-end transplant. (Include the author in that group.) Customizing, however, was very popular from the end of the war through the early '60s when vintage tin was still plentiful and there was a strong desire to stand apart from the crowd. Photo courtesy Tom Eiden.

roadsters and coupes, and dry lakes racing. Add to that the fact that a huge number of out-of-state servicemen sailed to the Pacific Theater from the West Coast. Many of these fellows got to see at least some of the famed California hot irons first hand. And so, in the midst of a global conflict, the appeal of the hot rod was strong enough to garner devotees even though the actual pleasures were years in the future. For on December 4, 1942, the SCTA decided to suspend all activities for the duration.

POST-WAR BOOM

It is reported that widespread illegal street racing started in 1945 before the Japanese signed the surrender. Recorded in the blaring headlines of every local newspaper, were the round-ups of "speed-crazed hot rodders" on the streets of the semi-rural outskirts of the Los Angeles metropolitan area. Public reaction was swift and negative. A bill was introduced in the California Legislature prohibiting motorists from increasing the performance level of their cars!

A meeting was held on September 7, 1945 and it was quickly decided that the Southern California Timing Association would resume dry-lakes time trials as soon as practical. In addition, it was also agreed that membership would be offered to outlaw clubs if they agreed to abide by the SCTA's strict rules and regulations. Fifteen clubs with 88 active members constituted the revived Association. Wally Parks, writing in his book, *Drag Racing: Yesterday and Today,* relates the following: "At this same meeting, in recognition of

Art Chrisman, of drag-racing fame, owned this award-winning street rod/custom car that was well known on the streets of Compton, California in 1951. Photos courtesy Art Chrisman.

The voice of Southern California hot rodding before World War II was *Throttle Magazine*. It was a well-done periodical, covering Dry Lakes time trials and West Coast circle-track racing. It didn't survive the wartime upheaval, however.

the outstanding job she had done in keeping SCTA's in-service members in contact through publication of the SCTA *Racing News,* Mrs. Veda Orr was honored with a full membership in the Association, complete with all competition privileges, since she had long before proven her capabilities in dry lakes speed trials."

Veda Orr, the First Lady of the SCTA, had indeed paid her dues. She is also the first lady street rodder. The Orrs, Karl and Veda, originally gained prominence among their peers in the late '30s. Karl's story predates Veda's, however. "I had what you might call a 'speed shop' back in Kingston, Missouri. That was in 1921. I was driving a 'T' with a handmade body and doing some dirt-track racing at state and county fairs. Won some, and lost some. I ran a Rajo head and used the old Zenith carb, modified. We didn't know anything about exhausts, we just ran a big old pipe. Ha, the bigger the better." Karl's mechanical talents, as well as his driving abilities, soon brought him customers who weren't satisfied with the

look-alike, run-alike Model T Ford. "The local mechanic was too busy working on tractors, and when somebody wanted something a little special, he would come to me. I would get it for him and install it."

When Karl migrated to Los Angeles in 1923, he quickly found work in the automotive trades. Almost as quickly he found himself in the local racing milieu. It wouldn't be long before the dry lakes, with their promise of unbridled speed, beckoned him. "In 1929 I bought a '28 roadster, put on an Acme

11

head and went to Muroc. I liked that Acme head, but it sure would knock the rods out quick. So later I got a Winfield 'Red'."

In 1935, shortly after Ed Adams and friends organized the Knight Riders, Karl joined the newly gathered 90 MPH Club. This was an accomplishment considering its difficult membership requirement. In 1936, he married Veda and the two of them began their regular treks to Muroc, Rosamond and Harper Dry Lakes in search of races to run and, after the SCTA was founded, records to break.

And break 'em, they did. One after the other. Not just Karl, mind you, but Veda as well. Too many to list here, but in 1939, Karl pushed Veda's street-legal '32 roadster to 121.62 mph, thereby making it the first Deuce to break 120. Veda herself had driven the car to a 114.24-mph record in 1937. But it wasn't the Orr family records that were important to the hot rodders—it was the Orr family business.

A late '30s line-up of double-duty roadsters on Muroc Dry Lake. Photo courtesy Eldon Snapp.

SPEED SHOPS & SUCH

In the late '30s Karl had begun a very profitable sideline enterprise—converting gasoline carburetors over to alcohol, and rebuilding stock ignition systems into something better suited to the demands of high-compression racing engines. By 1940, however, it was obvious that his craftsmanship was good enough to nurture a full-time business. As a result, his operation became one of the first speed shops to open its doors to the hot-rodding public.

Don't misunderstand. It wasn't an auto-parts store that also sold racing equipment. There were several of those already in existence. Karl's was a bonafide speed shop where high performance was its only reason for existing. Soon, business was good enough for Veda to quit her job at MGM studios and lend her own expertise to the operation. Describing the business, Karl simply states: "I built engines and I sold heads, manifolds, cams, carbs and ignitions. And I *sold* them—three or four complete sets a day. I did a lot of mail order business, too."

When war came, Karl went to work at Northrup Aviation during the day and ran the store nights and weekends. And when Wally Parks and Eldon Snapp donned their uniforms, the SCTA *Racing News* fell to Veda. It had been their joint responsibility since 1938. It became a one-woman newsletter, gossip column and cheering section that forever endeared her to the lakes racers.

THE BOOM CONTINUES

By 1946, SCTA and Russetta were back in full swing, only this time at El Mirage Dry Lake. It would be nice to report that illegal

1935—36 three-window coupe still shows its Ford parentage. Early '50s mild street-rod custom styling with its *tail-dragger* look and teardrop fender skirts has, for the most part, not been revived. Photo courtesy Tom Eiden.

street racing had stopped, but that's just not true. Lakes meets were held with greater frequency than ever before. They often lasted all weekend and continued to draw crowds upwards of 10,000 . . . but apparently all of that wasn't enough.

"A guy could go street racing five nights a week if he wanted to! Hundreds of cars would show up at the Long Beach Traffic Circle. Some would head out Clark Street, others would opt for the highway near the Seal Beach ammo dump." So said Bonneville 200 MPH charter member Otto Ryssman when I interviewed him a few years ago. And, in the midst of apparent chaos, there was organization. On Wednesday nights the street racers gathered at the Traffic Circle in Long Beach;

other communities had their own "race nights." There was such regularity, in fact, that lunch wagons showed up for major events!

Illegal street racing was not always fun and games. Many tragic accidents occurred over the months. SCTA tried, but threats of expulsion simply could not control the thousands of participants. Negative public opinion grew by leaps and bounds. Hot rods and hot rodders, many thought, would forever be outcasts.

ENTER HOT ROD MAGAZINE

If one event were singled out as the most important milestone in the history of hot rodding and street rodding, my money would be on the founding of *Hot Rod Magazine*.

What has survived, and almost in toto, is the highboy. Tom Eiden's version of a Glendale highboy was photographed at the Lakes in late 1950. The '29 roadster body atop a '32 chassis with a Deuce grille shell is basic to much of street rodding today.

The Deuce roadster will always be *The Classic*. This choice example, photographed at the Bonneville National Speed Trials in 1952, wouldn't be out of place at any modern rod run. Photo courtesy Tom Eiden.

The foresight and courage of Robert E. Petersen and Robert R. Lindsay, co-founders of *HRM*, are no-less astounding today than back in 1947 when Petersen and Lindsay each invested $200 in the Hot Rod Publishing Company and set up headquarters on Melrose Avenue in Los Angeles. With help from Bob Lindsay's father—a man with magazine experience—they wrote and photographed the first issue of *Hot Rod*. The initial print order was for 10,000 copies.

They had no network of distribution, so the partners took the magazines to local race tracks and, of course, the dry lakes, and sold them like newsboys. In between sales they took photographs for the next issue.

Within two years, *Hot Rod Magazine* had secured a solid foothold on the nation's newsstands. It was well on its way to becoming the bible of the amateur speed enthusiast. Today it has an enormous circulation, far larger than any other automotive magazine. Even if a smaller percentage of its pages feature prewar roadsters and coupes, and even if SCTA coverage is thin, *HRM* will always be remembered by the faithful as the pioneer organ of the motorsport-with-the-tarnished-name.

LEGAL DRAG RACING IS BORN

With *HRM* now ready to preach safe and sane hot rodding, the next development toward respectability was the quasi-legal use of abandoned air strips for drag racing. In 1949, the Santa Barbara Acceleration Association (SBAA) hosted a reasonably well controlled drag race on a half-mile stretch of private road in Goleta, a small town on the Southern California coast. Three-tenths of a mile was used for the standing-start run; the remainder for shutdown. That's all that was needed in 1949. The SBAA, however, was in the forefront of safe racing with mandatory requirements of seat belt, fire extinguisher, and crash helmet and goggles for open cars.

The earliest drag strip that the casual hot rodder probably recalls is Santa Ana. More properly known as the Orange County Airport Drags and sponsored by the Orange County Racing Association, Santa Ana was for all intents and purposes the first foray into the realm of drag racing for profit. C.J. Hart, a transplanted Ohio street rodder; Frank Stillwell, a local motorcycle-shop owner; and Creighton Hunter, another street rodder, dug deep into their pockets for the money to cover the expenses of one or two drag meets.

The inaugural event was July 2, 1950. Entrants paid $2 to run, while spectators were charged fifty cents to watch. The rest of the story is well known. Over the following nine years, everybody who became somebody in California hot rodding had *some* contact with the Airport Drags, even if only to stand along side the asphalt runway and watch the top shoes of the day burn rubber. With *Hot Rod Magazine* there to promote this "new" 25-year-old motorsport, and with the speed-equipment industry eager to export its products and services beyond Southern California, drag racing took the nation by storm. Street rodding firmly hung on to their coattails.

ROADSTERS GET RIVALS

The typical street rod of 1950 wasn't simply a such-and-such Ford roadster. Graceful Ford coupes and sedans had been around for nearly 20 years. They were making a substantial dent in what had been considered the purview of the "traditional hot rod." A glance at the 1950 *Hot Rod Magazine* index identifies nine roadsters . . . yet five coupes, one pickup and one convertible were also featured. That says something about expanding horizons.

There's not much doubt about the powerplant, however. It was far and away the flathead Ford V8 backed up with either a 1939 Ford floor-shift or a '40 side-shift tranny. The favorite rear end was also a 1940 Ford unit, and even though its stock hydraulic brakes were more or less standard on the better West Coast cars, disc brakes of the Kinmont variety were featured in the May 1950 issue of *HRM*.

Perhaps the biggest influence in the hot-rod world was the car show. In 1948, the SCTA and Robert Petersen's Hollywood Publicity

Associates joined forces to stage the first major public exhibition of hot rods and custom cars. It was a huge success both from a financial and public relations standpoint. In fact, the SCTA made enough money to inaugurate the Bonneville Speed Trials.

Overall changes in hot-rod cosmetics were inspired by car shows. They were subtle in 1950—mild dechroming, *nosing* and *decking*—but the fad marked the first time in hot-rodding history that something besides racing had influenced the sport. That was the good news. The bad news was that the groundwork was laid for much more radical sheet-metal modifications.

HOT RODDING SPORT SPREADS EAST

By the mid-1950s, what was largely a Southern California phenomenon grew to be a full-fledged, coast-to-coast American pursuit. Hot rodding had come of age and street rodding *per se* was asserting an independent identity. The latter's reason for existence no longer depended on dry lakes or drag racing.

During those years of national growth, roadsters and coupes became hotter properties than ever. Two things limited the availability of those cars: WWII scrap-metal drives and post-war *jalopy racing*. When they were finally recognized as predators upon the raw material of the new sport, it was almost too late. Fortunately, the cars that were reasonably new at the outbreak of WWII had been babied during the lean war years. Many were still available at reasonable prices. In 1955, for instance, a 1940 Ford coupe could be purchased for about $100 at most any used car lot. And because a recent high-school graduate could easily earn $40 a week, such a purchase was well within reach.

And reach for them the young Americans did. Sports cars, mostly Jaguars and MGs, were grudgingly appreciated—but never out loud. Their cost, however, meant inaccessibility for the great majority. But a street rod? Now that was horsepower of a different color. The '40 Ford coupe didn't put much of a dent in the average 18-year-old's budget. In fact, there were enough bucks left over to modify the original flathead if it still existed under the hood.

THE FLATHEAD FADES

Just as street rodding was coming into its own, bulk horsepower in the form of stock late-model overhead-valve V8s suddenly became as economical and accessible as the nearest wrecking yard. Not only that, they provided reliable horsepower. And reliability was often what separated street rods from hot rods.

Those who can remember first hand will testify that no matter how "classic" a souped-up flathead looked with its triple carbs, finned aluminum heads with acorn nut covers and chrome-wrapped generator, it was hard to start and harder to cool.

On the other hand, a stock OHV Cadillac or Olds-powered street rod had 'em whipped hands down. As soon as they were painted bright red rather than the factory's dull blue or green, outfitted with finned aluminum rocker covers and a dual- or triple-deuce manifold . . . man, they were accepted by even the staunchest flathead hot rodder. In the mid-'50s *traditional* was a bad word. Street rodding was avant-garde in the truest sense.

That's the way street rodding progressed well into the '60s. If put to the test, one could probably find a street rod with an engine for each American OHV V8 of day. It was a heady time of innovation, and not just in the way of powerplants. More than one stock-bodied coupe or roadster with lines considered untouchable today, underwent drastic cosmetic alterations. As grotesque as many of them appear in retrospect, few voices of challenge were heard back then. Perhaps that's why sometime in the early '60s street rodding inexplicably went underground in favor of go-karts, slot cars, mini-bikes, plastic models and factory muscle cars.

STREET RODDING REBORN

Thankfully, the hiatus was brief. Although *Hot Rod Magazine* continued to expand its market with coverage of a wide variety of subjects including boats, another Petersen publication took stock of itself and ventured back into the street-rod arena. Under the guidance of publisher Tom Medley and with the able assistance of Leroi "Tex" Smith and Bud Bryan, *Rod & Custom Magazine* almost singlehandedly breathed new life into the fading sport of street rodding. And the late '60s marks the beginning of the modern era.

The late '60s—that was a long time ago, but not as long ago as 1920 in terms of a relatively unorganized hobby, it's a substantial block of time. That's why it's astonishing that a street rod that was built in 1987 isn't much different from one built in 1967. Far more—and far better—fiberglass bodies, reproduction frames, and commercial installation kits are now available. Yet, somehow, the basic flavor has remained. Indeed, the cars generally look the same as they did in the late '40s and early '50s. But now, more than ever, emphasis is on detail and quality construction.

If street rodding has lost a little of its individuality—and I think it has—it has also lost its crudeness. Unless one's sole exposure to early street rodding is through car magazines, I must admit that only the street rods featured could be considered class acts.

Much of that is behind us now. Perhaps it's because today's street rod is rarely the sole means of transportation for its owner-builder. In the early days when you had to go to work or school in the morning, you got that turkey running no matter what! Perhaps it's because the builders now have more taste and the financial wherewithal to accomplish their desires. Who knows?

The important thing is that street rodding, after a long and often turbulent history, is here to stay.

REFERENCES

Levine, Leo. *Ford: The Dust and The Glory.* London: Collier-Macmillan Limited, 1969.

Oddo, Frank. "Karl and Veda Orr: Hot Rod Pioneers." *Street Rodder Magazine,* January 1976. pp. 34-37.

Orr, Veda. *Hot Rod Pictorial.* Los Angeles: Floyd Clymer, 1949.

Parks, Wally. *Drag Racing: Yesterday and Today.* New York: Trident Press, 1966.

Parks, Wally, and Eldon Snapp. Eds. SCTA *Racing News,* December 1938—August 1941.

Peters, Jack. Ed. *Throttle Magazine,* January—December 1941.

Post, Dan. *Model T Ford in Speed and Sport.* Arcadia, CA: Dan R. Post Publications, 1956.

Unger, Henry F. "Jallopies Race On The Desert." *Popular Science,* February 1939, pp. 98-103.

Vintage Tin or Repro? 2

Choosing between the many excellent offerings of modern fiberglass manufacture and vintage tin can pose something of a dilemma. One decisive factor, however, is the availability of particular body styles. If your cap is set for a vehicle that's not available in plastic such as this '36 Ford five-window coupe, then start your VT search.

Choosing the right car is no simple task. If you're the aggressive type, you may lean toward a roadster or coupe with traditional racy lines, a stark interior garnished in machined aluminum, and powered by a big-bore V8, chrome-plated fire breather. On the other hand, you may be a more sedate street rodder with a taste for the "good life" and have visions of a moderately powered sedan, sheet metal liberally coated with hand-rubbed black lacquer, and an interior richly appointed in walnut and leather. Or, you may prefer a mix of each.

There's just no telling what any given street rodder really wants. It doesn't matter. What matters is that you get what you really want.

The street rodder of 30 years ago was adamant in his desire to build a car that was first and foremost daily transportation. The fact that he frequently stepped beyond the bounds of reliability in his secondary quest for high performance didn't deter him. He tolerated a temperamental engine that was hard to start and overheated easily.

Times have changed. Today's street-rod builder is far less concerned with daily transportation. His hobby car no longer needs to have a utility overlay to justify its existence; he wants it for its own sake. It has "functional autonomy."

It also has a mandate of perfection. In the glorified '50s, perfection was rarely expected

much less achieved. But today's street-rod builder seriously seeks that elusive goal. He is spurred on by the constant magazine coverage of professionally built turn-key street rods with price tags approaching $30,000! Even more so, the on-site inspection of today's better street rods provides the motivation for new builders.

Down-to-earth, home-built street rods *are* better than ever. Because transportation needs are lessened, builders can take more time on planning, construction and maintenance. The end result is a possession worthy of pride as never before. But you'll never get there without careful, considerate planning of your own.

Planning begins with the basic decision: Build a street rod based on *vintage tin*—an original pre-1949 American production car or light truck—or one composed largely of new-manufacture reproduction parts. Both approaches, different as they are, can be equally satisfying.

At some time in the distant future, the street-rod builder won't have this decision to make. The supply of rebuildable cars in a complete state will dry up. It may take five years, maybe 50 years. Whatever, eventually it'll happen. That's the bad news. The good news is, as the existing supply dwindles and demand increases, newer and better reproductions will come to the market. But for now, more than enough vintage tin is available for the serious rod builder to be faced with a choice.

In this book I limit my remarks to vintage tin that has not already been extensively modified, and those old-timey hot rods and street rods in need of refurbishing and modernizing. Reproduction cars are new-manufacture chassis and body combinations. Most of the repro bodies are fiberglass.

The first consideration in the vintage tin vs. 'glass controversy is that of body style. Availability, condition and price are the most significant factors for those who seek the traditional street rod—fenderless Ford Model A or B roadsters. Although genuine Ford roadster bodies may appear from time to time in the marketplace, the asking prices are nothing short of excessive for the better ones, and ridiculous for poorer specimens.

For example, an original steel 1927—34 Ford roadster body that is in far-less-than-top condition will bring a price at least that of a quality fiberglass body. And unless the buyer-builder is an accomplished metalsmith, the cost of quality repair must be added to the purchase price. The reality of the situation is that most of the available roadster bodies have been picked over for the last 40 years. The cream of the crop is long gone. What is left today is often what was rejected yesterday. Consequently, considerable metalwork is usually required to bring the body up to par.

Another consideration to ponder when choosing between original tin and a reproduction is that a steel body requires the skill of an experienced metal man. I suspect you wouldn't want an amateur to cut your diamonds? On the other hand, fiberglass is far more forgiving. Through practice with fiberglass and related materials, you can quickly become familiar with working it and preparing it for paint.

Not long ago fiberglass bodies were so crude they wouldn't fit original windshield posts, door hinges, trunk handles and the like without major reworking. However, not only will most of the better 'glass bodies readily accept original or quality repro hardware, many are offered with the needed accouterments already installed.

Bottom Line—When price and availability are considered, it's fair to say that a *quality-built* fiberglass repro body is superior to vintage tin. Shortcomings exist only in the eye of the purist or restoration enthusiast for whom genuineness and originality are sacrosanct and whose mind is closed on the subject.

Others, certainly more pragmatic, are less adamant in their demand for originality and tradition. They consider a street rod as any pre-1949 car that can be modified to suit their tastes and personalities. Period. For them, the choice between vintage tin and fiberglass is murky. To a large extent, their final choice must depend on a vintage car that may be available and a reproduction assemblage that can be ordered on a moment's notice.

This obviously calls for a careful consideration of the condition, completeness and price of the vintage car versus the quality and price of a complete fiberglass body and reproduction frame.

Many traditional body styles have been captured in 'glass. Dick Magoo's repro '29 Ford roadster kit is a fine example of what's available.

The repro road is beginning to branch out in a number of directions. To whit: this reproduction 2-1/2-in. chopped-top three-window Ford coupe from Poli-Form Fiberglass Products. The one-piece body features steel reinforcement, polyester-foam-reinforced roof, steel-reinforced doors and deck lid, and a host of other features and options.

'27 Ford Roadster

Owner: Tony Baron

What can you say about a souped-up Model T roadster that was first featured in the May, 1950 issue of *Hot Rod Magazine* with its original builder; in *Car Craft Magazine*, February, 1954 with its second owner/builder; and again in *Hot Rod Magazine*, December, 1958, with its *third owner*? And *don't* say "A race car doesn't belong in a street-rod book!" First off, from whence do you think we came?? And, Tony Baron, the fourth owner, built this car to drive on the street—and that's where it went shortly after I took these pictures on the Bonneville Salt Flats in 1979. But I like them—and the car—so much that I just wanted to share both with you. If these reasons aren't good enough, here's another; Tony's red roadster is unquestionably one of the best restorations of a vintage rod *both in cosmetics and performance* I have ever had the pleasure of seeing . . . and hearing!

That's not a 'glass body. It's a rare steel T roadster that Tony brought back to life. The engine is an Isky cammed Merc of a whopping 325 cubic inches (3-3/8-inch bore X 4-1/2-inch stroke) outfitted with Baron heads and a *four-pot* manifold. (I haven't said "four-pot manifold" in a long time!)

The *Baron* name may sound familiar to you. If you're a student of speed-equipment manufactured in the early post-WWII years you may have heard of *Frank Baron Equipment*.

Yup, Tony's dad. Tony, by the way, still casts a few sets of heads every once in a while. But that's another story.

Tony's car is not exactly what you would call *high tech*, flathead power notwithstanding. The front and rear brakes are 1939 Ford units, which are sightly better than the originals! The rear axle is early Ford/Halibrand. The front axle is an oh-riginal Bell issue with a 2-1/2-inch drop. Oh yes, the steering is a modified Deuce unit. (Hey, I told you this was a restored car!) Every critical vintage part that went into the restoration of his roadster was subjected to the closest scrutiny.

Realize that this car was built to run in the Southern California Timing Association (SCTA) Modified Roadster class as well as cruise the boulevards of the San Fernando Valley. And speaking of the Valley, Tony credits a lot of *Valley* guys with helping him along the five-year path this highboy T took— Mike Scott, Doug Kruse, Ralph Rhodes, Nile Ragusin, Craig Dakins, Jon Bender and Kent Fuller. If you know SoCal street rods, you know these individuals are owed at least that much recognition. How fast did this "antique" go? Thought you'd never ask . . . 136 mph on alky the first time out; 143 the second time around. But now that Tony has a flathead-powered belly tank for the Salt, the legal speed limit in the T will do.

'32 Ford 3-Window Coupe

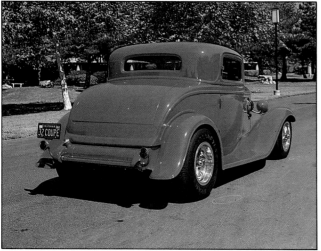

Owner: Mike Maris

Picking a street rod for the cover of this book was not easy. I come across many, many fine cars in the course of my travels through the world of Southern California street rodding. But something about Mike Maris' coupe made it slip to the surface of my thoughts time and again. I think it's because Mike's coupe combines the best of traditional street rodding and high-tech modern rodding. It also combines the best of *owner-built* and *professionally done*. The dichotomy continues when you realize that the hardware incorporated into the three-window Deuce is *full race* . . . yet Mike drives that sucker on the street, "come hell or high water!" In the final analysis, the car is neither 100% vintage tin nor 100% repro. It's the right combination of both.

The body is vintage tin, however, and shows off many hours of hand labor, both in the metalwork and in the paint, that is Ditzler Indian Red. The frame is a reproduction that started out as a pair of Deuce Factory rails. The suspension system is the epitome of what is found under a mid-'80s street rod: four-bars up front, and coil-overs out back—more Deuce Factory parts.

The engine and drivetrain are real grabbers; pro-fessional all the way. There's a Gale Banks turbo-monster small-block Chevy 302 capable of churning out "200-mph" horsepower, a Doug Nash five-speed gearbox to harness all that, and the ubiquitous Ford 9-incher to put it to the ground.

Finally, Mike and upholsterer Al Cooper joined forces on the VDO equipped dashboard and 'hyde interior with out-standing results.

Just A '40
Ford Coupe . . .
But She's Mine

Owner/Author: Frank Oddo

Every street rodder has one car that will always be Number One in his heart of hearts. Against it, all others pale. Sadly, it may not be one that he actually owned and drove. It may have belonged to a neighborhood hot shoe when the dreamer was but 15, or it may be one that he stared at for hours on end at the first car show he ever attended. I believe most rod builders eventually try to bring that eidetic image to life, even if it takes 10, 20 or even 30 years. That's why so many "first rods" are built or commissioned by men who left their teens a long, long time ago.

The Candy Apple Red '40 Ford coupe on this page is my Numero Uno street rod. The pictures are 10-years old, but the quickening of my pulse as I selected them for an egotistical reprise once again reminded me that it is still the car of *my* dreams.

The bad news is that, as it appears here, it no longer exists. The paint faded a long time ago, the Jack Garrison interior wore through on the driver's seat after a mere 17 years, the fourth engine—one Chevy, three small-block Fords—finally gave up the ghost after belching a ring on its umteenth mile, and the buggy springs "bugged" my backside for the last time. The dropped axle and converted '69 Ford disc brakes that served me well for many a year were still going strong, but were sold off.

The 9-inch Ford rear end is still there, but it doesn't recognize itself in the mirror anymore.

The good news is she shall return—not red, no buggy springs, and Jack lives 2000 miles away—better than ever. I didn't get it finished in time to include in the book; now that I'm finished with the book, I can get back on it.

'35 Chevy 2-Door Sedan

Owner: Bob Trawick

One of my all-time favorites is Bob Trawick's mellow 1935 Chevy sedan. I have to admit that when it was first completed in the mid-'70s, only the quality of the work impressed me. It was, as are most cars that are given the best of everything—mechanicals, bodywork, paint and upholstery—an outstanding example of what a street rod should be. At that time, though, most street rods were endowed with lots more flash. The sport was still in its *hard-chrome* stage. And, probably, my personal tastes reflected the era. Since then, however, the soft, earth tones have gained a lot of ground—no pun intended—and Bob's car has grown more beautiful in my eyes.

The front suspension is a much-modified combination in true street-rod style—fresh parallel leaf springs alongside a 3-inch dropped early Chevy axle with Jaguar disc brakes at the ends. The rear suspension is XKE, no more, no less. The powerplant is a stockish and very reliable 327-CID small-block of obvious parentage. The Taup Mohair interior was done by Norm Folwell, and paint and bodywork by Ross McGee.

21

'32 Ford Phaeton

Owner: Vern Williams

Back when Vern was just a teenager, he found this car sitting on a used-car lot in Pasadena. It was to ultimately become the automotive love of his life. The big Ford had just been retired from its duties as a Los Angeles Herald Express Newspaper delivery wagon . . . er . . . delivery phaeton? The year was 1951. And not everyone wanted a phaeton in those days, '32 or not. But Vern couldn't find a roadster, so he settled for the touring car. He paid $145 . . . and never looked back. Vern reports he more-or-less completed the car in 1971, a mere 19 years after its purchase. But the mechanicals indicate that it is a mid-'50s street rod, pure and simple.

The engine is a 1950 Olds displacing a stock 303 cubes. The manifold atop the venerable Rocket is an aluminum Edelbrock with a row of Strombergs. An Isky cam lifts the valves. The stock 10-inch clutch relays engine torque to a 1937 LaSalle floor-shift transmission, then into a '40 Ford rear end.

The stock chassis boasts little more than the '40 Ford juice brakes and a classic Bell Auto Parts dropped axle with a rebuilt spring and Austin-Healey shocks on the front and rear.

Believe it or not, this car was painted in 1961, black lacquer of course, and it looks like the thinner evaporated two months after these photos were taken. Don't tell Vern lacquer doesn't last. About the only metalwork the car has seen, except a few repairs in the early years, is a flat custom firewall.

The interior reflects its period styling with '53 Ford pedals and a '41 Willys steering wheel. The brown vinyl upholstery, done by Eddie Martinez in 1971, belies the fact that Vern still puts several dozen miles on it every weekend. Properly sewn and installed, Naugahyde wears like steel; the "reel steel" of Vern's phaeton, that is!

'27 Ford High Boy Touring

Owner: John Hesford

If you saw John's car before you saw John, you might conclude that the owner/builder was a gentleman of advanced years. After all, a guy in his 30s surely wouldn't build such an old-timey car, would he? Or would he? John, better known locally as the proprietor of Fast Johnny's Speed Shop, poured his heart and one year abuilding it into the little flathead-powered gen-u-wine Ford T touring rod. The powerplant is about as traditional as they come—a stock bore and stroke 1940 issue with an Isky street cam, and Offenhauser manifold and heads. The trans is none other than a '39 Ford with a slightly more modern backup, a Mustang II rear axle. John acquired a 3.73:1 cog to approximate the old flathead 3.78:1 standby.

John's few concessions to 1980s mechanicals—besides the rear axle—include Monroe shocks, Mustang master cylinder and Saginaw steering gear. Just about everything else can be spelled S-T-O-C-K early Ford . . . they way it used to be.

John chose a Bell Auto Parts steering wheel to complement his classic Stewart-Warner gages. Don Geisens of Laguna Hills, CA stitched the tan Naugahyde in an equally classic pattern.

'40 Ford Tudor Sedan

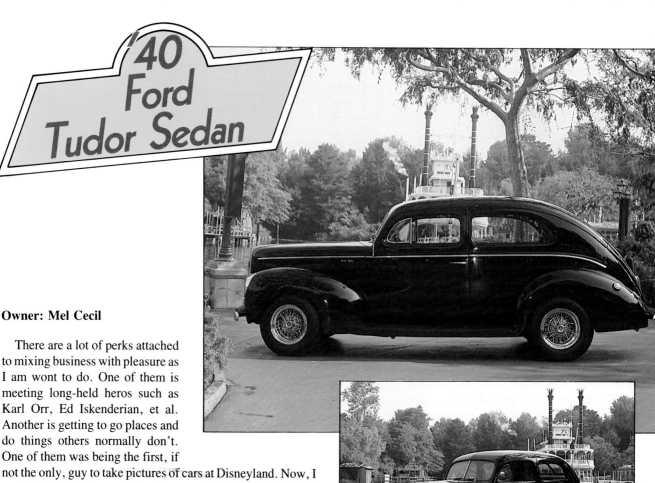

Owner: Mel Cecil

There are a lot of perks attached to mixing business with pleasure as I am wont to do. One of them is meeting long-held heros such as Karl Orr, Ed Iskenderian, et al. Another is getting to go places and do things others normally don't. One of them was being the first, if not the only, guy to take pictures of cars at Disneyland. Now, I can't tell you that came about because I went to high school with Mickey Mouse . . . or even Donald Duck. But I do know a couple of street-rod types who work(ed) for the Magic Kingdom. Even so, that's not why Mel Cecil's black hot-rodded '40, photographed in Disneyland's New Orleans Square, is another of my personal all-time favorites.

I lost my heart to a black hot-rodded Ford—though not nearly as pretty as this one—in my hometown of New Orleans in 1950. But Mel's car . . . well, Mel's car is just the way I like 'em. Beautiful, but low key. You must look at the car intensely to fully appreciate it. Black lacquer tells all and, By Jove, the sheet metal it covers must be picture perfect. This '40's is. It's a big car as street rods go, but that doesn't occur to you. Partially because of the color, but mostly because of the attention to detail that attracts your eye.

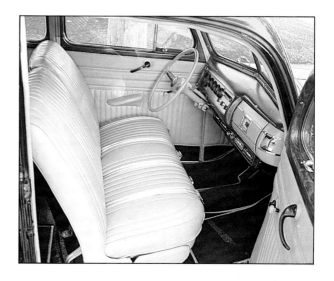

The interior of the car imparts a feeling of luxury as only a big car can with its tastefully appointed Norm Folwell upholstery, Steve Borowitz woodgraining, and Boyd Coddington custom dash. Boyd also had a hand in several other areas of the car—paint and engine, for instance. The powertrain begins with a choice Chevy 283 small-block and Turbo 400 transmission. It ends with a '57 Chevy rear. The something-old, something-new blend of massaged transverse springs, '56 pickup brakes and Mustang steering, work well together with no complaints. All in all, it's a great car!

Vintage Tin, Finding It

Best resource for roddable vintage tin is the more-or-less restored stocker. Usually Model A closed cars are not overpriced. And drive train and accessories and miscellaneous components can be re-sold to another restorer. Caution: Don't reveal that you're a hot rodder when shopping for vintage tin. Some restorers will jack up the price or flatout refuse to sell if they think you're a "dirty-neck hot rodder."

Let's now examine the pros and cons of choosing vintage tin as the basis for your street rod. The first major hurdle is simply finding one. Not just any "old car" will do. Chances are, you want a specific make and model that's in satisfactory condition and at a reasonable price.

But finding one, as relatively easy as that may be in a street-rod-rich area such as Southern California, can be very difficult in other parts of the country. Nevertheless, vintage tin is out there. Even today, more than 50 years after the beginning of hot rodding, old cars still abound. Although they're not there *just* for the asking, if you don't ask, you don't get! So, start looking.

TREASURE HUNTS & WILD-GOOSE CHASES

The best starting place is with your friends and acquaintances . . . and *their* friends and acquaintances. Although it helps, they don't all have to be street rodders. It's surprising just how many folks know the whereabouts of old cars.

Although "old" might be a 1976 automobile to most folks, after a bit of education, they quickly get a handle on what you want and are just as quick to advise you of what they find. Everybody loves a treasure hunt.

Five or six years ago, a friend of mine was downright shocked to learn that his secretary had a '39 Ford coupe stored in a dusty corner of her garage. Her husband acquired it more than 10 years before with the intention of transforming it into a street rod. Unfortunately, he never got around to it. A chat with him that night led to a tentative agreement. The coupe and sundry pieces were trailered away the next Saturday morning after three hours of garage clean-up and the transfer from my pocket to his of two crisp one-hundred-dollar bills!

The easiest hunting, of course, is a diligent perusal of newspaper advertisements and ads in street-rod and antique-car periodicals. Some metro newspapers have ANTIQUES, CLASSICS and RACE CARS sections in the Classifieds that virtually "let your fingers do the walking." After a phone call to verify or investigate the specifics, you may be on your way.

Be an Early Bird—Most sellers advertise cars beginning in the Sunday edition. Usually, that edition is on the stands by Saturday afternoon. So, buy the paper as early as you can. You could be the owner of some fine vintage tin 16 hours before the not-so-slick buyer crawls out of bed gets the paper, then discovers that his "find" is already gone.

Magazine ads are something else. Plenty of cars are offered in the automotive press. Some monthlies seem to excite great enthusiasm in the hearts of its classified advertisers. Prices and descriptions often boggle this reader's mind. From time to time, true street-rod-building material will appear, but more often as not, it seems as if the vehicles advertised were bought new and stored in hermetically sealed garages the following day for the sole purpose of being offered at grandiose prices four or five decades hence. That's my opinion, but nevertheless that's the way the ads read to me.

Cars offered for sale in hot-rod and street-rod magazines are usually already built. Their sale will finance the next car—or house the owner wants to build, and normally won't offer more than passing interest to those intending to build their own. What I'm saying is the ads in car magazines, as opposed those in newspapers, are all too often covered with more than a little "fairy dust." *Buyer beware.*

Swap Meets—One of the most enjoyable ways of searching out basic street-rod material is *window shopping* at auto swap meets, car shows and race events. Swap meets are still

Swap meets are ideal places to shop in a quick and efficient manner, even if you have to drive several hundred miles to get there. You may be able to persuade seller to deliver your purchase for gas money.

There are some real bargains to be found if you are not set on an old Ford. Choice Dodge coupe is a prime example of what you should buy—a complete car that won't take five years just to gather missing parts.

Chevy pickup was photographed in summer of '85 in Southern California, living proof that VT is readily available. Rural areas are rife with old pickups and one-ton trucks that offer the makings of a great rod. Don't expect farmers to sell off their treasures for a hundred bucks.

Saw this one out of the corner of my eye while zipping up the freeway one day. An aspiring Chevy builder could do worse. It didn't have a FOR SALE sign on it, but if you don't ask, you don't get.

not a nationwide occurrence, but they are becoming more widespread every year. They are sometimes held in conjunction with major rod runs and sometimes sponsored by car clubs and local street-rod associations. Whichever, they are always fun to attend, whether you go as a buyer, seller or just a spectator.

Big swap meets such as those at Hershey, Reno and the LA Roadster Show invariably draw high-dollar street-rods from miles around. All is not grim, however, for there are usually an equal number of half-finished rods, stockers, clunkers and other more-reasonably priced *beginner cars* on the auction block. The beauty of such events is that there are competitive/realistic prices. Some cars, however, are there to be shown rather than sold. That accounts for occasional stratospheric price tags.

The beauty of the show-and-sell aspect of automotive events is efficiency. Many potential buildables are on display in one place. Even if you don't find a car that interests you, you can make comparisons. Also, cars you see will spark new ideas for future street-rod-material shopping. And, as you begin to develop comparative-shopping experience, you'll learn one very important thing: *It pays to be choosy.* Resist paying more than you can

Some cars are well represented in reproduction vintage-parts catalogs. 1940 Tudor, although rough and missing a lot of parts, could probably be brought back. Buy catalogs and study them carefully *before* you tender an offer on a basket case. Old cars with legitimate titles come at a premium.

honestly afford. Also, only buy what you want! Don't buy the first or second car that looks as if it *may* satisfy your needs. There's *always* another potential candidate that may be just exactly what you want.

Keep Your Eyes Open—Much less efficient, but often just as much fun as shopping at the swap meet, is cruising with a buddy and looking for that semi-abandoned old car sitting in a back yard, stuffed away in the dark corner of an open garage, stored—and forgotten—behind a fence in an industrial area, or planted in a rural area. Sometimes, what you find will be either an abandoned street-rod project, or one that's slow enough to pass for abandonment. Who knows, you may be able to talk the owner into selling.

Of course, it isn't necessary to cruise, even though it gives you and your buddy an excuse to exercise his street rod. Experienced rod builders develop *selective perceptibility*—an uncanny ability to spot an old car camouflaged in the brush. Develop the habit of keeping an eye open for vintage tin when you're driving.

Wanted: Old Car—If, by some cruel twist of fate you can't find the car of your dreams, there's one last desperate thing you can do—advertise. Don't enter into this lightly however, for there's some danger in placing such an ad. You will be vulnerable to the price gouger. He knows you're anxious because you went to the extreme of advertising, so he figures you must be willing to spend a bundle on the car you want. Right? This is OK if money is no object. However, nobody wants to be "had."

When you finally find what you think may be that "just right" car, you must be able to separate the wheat from the chaff, or accurately appraise the condition of the offered car. And, if it does meet the standards you've set, you then must deal effectively with the seller.

If the Price is Right—For all intents and purposes, the era of the unmodified stocker with an asking price of less than several thousand dollars is gone. It became a thing of the past in the early '70s when high inflation took the country by storm. Sure, occasionally some lucky rod builder stumbles across that legendary low-buck gennie that a soldier off to the wars stored away in an Arizona garage soon after Pearl Harbor. However, if you hold out for such a find, plan on spending most of your days watching other street rodders drive by!

In reality, good-quality vintage tin only changes hands after the owner receives a princely sum. And, like it or not, prices for complete pre-'49 Fords are only going up in the future. Fortunately, a reasonably complete car in good condition will invariably be the most economical car to build in the long run. It's no secret that original parts are very costly. Also, one of the biggest expenses facing the street rodder is the cost of basic metal work. As a result, money saved up front by buying a solid car can be spent on other costly items such as upholstery.

Unfortunately, not every would-be street-rod builder starts with much money. Most find it easier to work on the fender-a-month plan than to accumulate the necessary funds

before beginning the build. They anticipate, justifiably, that their finances will allow them to acquire parts and services on a piece-meal basis over time.

STREET RODS AS AN INVESTMENT

One of my pet peeves is the indiscriminate use/misuse of the term "investment." An investment is defined as "property acquired for future income." It is, in short, expected to reap you a monetary profit. On the other hand, street-rod building is a hobby, profitable only in terms of pleasure. So, spend your money thoughtfully and prudently, but not with the thought that you're making a blue-chip investment. If the latter is of more interest to you, the average bookstore abounds with books on investing. You'll be better off taking advice from the latest copy of *Make-A-Buck Magazine*.

How about those fellows who buy and sell half-finished street rods and boast of profits. I am skeptical of their accounting procedures. I doubt if they've tallied each and every nickel they sunk in the car, or kept records of the hours spent acquiring the needed parts and assembling their most recent "gold mine."

There's no denying that there are a few street-rod entrepreneurs who have the finances, experience and shrewdness to buy street rods at bargain prices and quickly turn over a substantial profit with little or no additional work. They are good businessmen—more power to them. Also, if the average builder wisely purchases an old car, he may recoup most or all of his cash outlay if he's forced into a premature sale. The simple fact

Package deal has all critical parts necessary for building a street rod. Other parts, inclusive of fenders, hood and frame, are as near as your mailbox. If you bargain with sellers shrewdly and intelligently, your chance of making a good purchase is better.

An interesting offer at the '85 L.A. Roadsters Swap Meet was this gen-u-wine early street rod complete with repairable Deuce frame. Lots of work? You bet, and more than a few additional bucks as well. But nothing beats a real steel roadster.

Many more street rods are started than are finished. You may be fortunate enough to stumble across a real "steal" in steel. 1928 Ford Tudor was offered with a TCI repro chassis, Corvette rear end, and Super Bell axle complete with disc brakes . . . for $1000 less than was originally spent!

Supply and demand pushes up asking price of old Fords over comparable "others." But that's OK as long as you are informed. A car such as this Deuce five-window may have a lot of expensive bodywork under the primer; maybe not. Investigate before you invest.

is old cars have a quasi-antique status. As a result, they usually appreciate in value. Additionally, if he put his time and talent into a street rod that's in the mainstream of popularity, he can re-pocket a greater percentage of his original outlay than most hobby-type projects. Try selling an unfinished boat!

Basket-Case Cars—So much for broad economic considerations. Let's get on with shopping for the best vintage tin your money can buy.

When looking at possibles, keep in mind one factor. All of the cars are old. Many parts will be worn, ruined or missing.

For the majority of novice street rodders about to tackle their first car, a vintage-tin *basket case*, which is a disassembled car accompanied by boxes of miscellaneous parts, is most likely what fits their budget. The enthusiastic expectation that they will acquire the missing pieces often encourages them to close the deal on an incomplete package.

Although buying a basket case is usually a good way to go, it has its problems. I can't be there with you as you nose into the boxes that you hope hold the makings of a street rod, so this chapter spells out some of the harsh realities my friends and I have learned over the past 30 years.

Earlier, I spoke of cars in the *mainstream of popularity*. This is important because, not only are popular cars the easiest to sell, more parts—original and reproduction—are avail-

Rust accumulates in the most unexpected places. Chances are no one would have thought to look for it in this seam if hood hadn't been off. Scrape any suspicious places, both inside the car and out.

You can't always remove a fender or even take off a wheel, but never forget there's a lot of potential rust-out up and under the rear fenders. Look carefully.

Never buy an old car without a thorough inspection of the chassis and general underside. The number of potential problems is extensive. They may not deter your purchase, but you should know about their existence.

able for those that have a long reign of popularity. For example, although Chevrolet consistently outsold Ford during the '30s and '40s, ask any Chevy fan how easy it is to find fenders and grilles, much less interior trim.

Another interesting point about Fords: Although 1937 was a very good year for Ford with 1,037,476 passenger cars and light trucks built, and that 1940 was a mediocre year with 638,109 units, it's much easier to find parts for a '40 Ford than a '37! This is due in part to the fact 1940-model cars were newer at the advent of World War II, which brought domestic auto production to a halt for about five years. Cars were garaged or babied through the war years to keep them alive. Consequently, later cars were in better shape after the war. More importantly, they are now favored by street rodders.

I'm not alone in my opinion that cars favored by the early hot rodders—Ford roadsters and coupes of the classic years—were the ones saved from the World War II scrap drives. After all, who would have risked being called unpatriotic for the sake of a Fordor Sedan or a non-Ford of any description?

The point is, as you stand there in some cold, dark garage in Boise, don't deceive yourself into thinking that finding the missing parts you mentally list will be easy. Don't assume that any parts are insignificant. More than one street-rod project has died during the initial build stages because too many parts were unobtainable. *Completeness is the cardinal rule when shopping for street-rod material!* What isn't there when you pack those boxes and you trailer that purchase home, is going to have to be found and paid for later on. Those later purchases—total cost

unknown—can add dramatically to project cost and completion time.

Be Prepared When You Shop—When searching for rebuildable tin, there are some items you should have on hand. Start with a high-powered flashlight. You'll need one when you're in a dark garage and down on your knees peering at the underside of a floorboard! With this in mind, conduct your inspection trips during the day just in case you'll be able to roll the car out into the sunlight. A far more realistic appraisal can be made then.

Another handy-dandy thing to have is a pocket knife. You'll need it to *discreetly* poke into oxidation bubbles. There's no other way to evaluate the extent of under-paint rust. Additionally, a small tool box with the standard assortment of wrenches and screwdrivers may come in handy.

Finally, carry along a shop coat, creeper, small 1-ton bottle jack and jack stand. Don't buy a 45-year-old car without inspecting underneath. It's "buyer beware" all the way.

What Awaits the Seeker—There are two kinds of old cars you'll be looking at: those that have been modified significantly and those that haven't. Of the two groups the latter is certainly the more rare, particularly with open cars, coupes and pickup trucks. The pendulum can swing either way when it comes to sedans.

Let's take a closer look at the rare example—an old car that somehow reached retirement without major surgery. Begin your inspection of what's under the FOR SALE sign by listing the missing bolt-ons.

The ideal car will include original fenders, hood, grille, doors, deck, bumpers, mounting

The insides of doors are almost always rusted. Repairs are difficult and expensive. Missing door and window hardware can be a problem, too.

brackets, bumper guards, running boards, door and deck handles, exterior chrome or stainless trim and interior trim. Otherwise, you may never get your project completed because half of the needed items were missing. If you're not sure what parts are supposed to be there, find out *before* you go hunting. There are too many possibilities for me to provide a parts list for each and every model that could conceivably be turned into a street

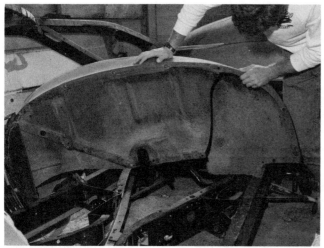

A good inner fender panel is worth its weight in gold. Fatigue cracks, which are common, are relatively easy to repair.

Oh, those pesky rain channels. Enough moisture will have accumulated in most any old car to present a problem. And rain channel is one of—if not the most—difficult areas of all to repair.

rod. Using the list on pages 34 and 35 as a guide, make your own to ensure that you get the needed parts. Do your homework, then take a close look.

The condition of a part isn't necessarily as important as its presence. For example, the door of a late-'30s car may include dozens of impossible-to-find items such as a window crank and door latch to special screws.

Completeness is the primary concern! And yet, completeness is the simplest aspect of a vehicle evaluation. What you see is what you get. If you know what parts should be included with the car, walk around it with your list in hand and take notes. If there are boxes of parts, go through them and make an inventory. Check the list against an antique auto-parts catalog to determine the cost of replacing any missing parts.

After you've satisfied yourself on the completeness of your find, the difficult part begins: evaluating the condition of what's there and guestimating the cost of any farmed-out repairs. Start with the fenders. If they are bolted to the body, look for rust-outs at the beads, points of attachment, and in and around headlight and taillight buckets. Check the inner panels carefully for signs of metal fatigue.

Next, check the exterior body. There are three major areas of concern: drip moldings, lower front and rear quarter panels, and rear deck panel. The first, and usually the most difficult to deal with are the roof drip moldings. These metal stampings that are spot-welded between the roof and side side-panel seam are extremely difficult to repair. So, if the drip moldings are badly rusted and you want to retain them, pass on the car. Or, only consider it for a parts car.

Everybody knows that moisture accumulates behind front and rear fenders. Make a thorough, but discreet, check with your pocket knife.

The next most critical body areas are the lower front and rear quarter panels. These extensions of the fenders are exposed to a lot of road contamination such as salt and water. Through the years the channels inside the body immediately behind the quarter panels accumulate considerable moisture and, as a result, eventually rust away. Carefully inspect these prime areas with your pocket knife. Although replacement body panels are available, you should know the extent of the needed bodywork before you make the purchase, not after the car has been stripped and sent to the metalsmith.

Another major problem area is the rear deck panel. Here, moisture accumulates down in the inner panel where it does its dirty work. As Neil Young said, "rust never sleeps."

Many times the seller will have liberally coated the body with grey primer. This is usually not done deceitfully, but in a misguided attempt to protect the metal. As discussed on page 54, most inexpensive primers are not sealers. Consequently, moisture penetrates through to the metal. Not only that, primer makes it difficult to visually judge the waviness of a panel.

Check the remainder of the body exterior by hand. You don't need the sophisticated touch of the experienced auto bodyman to detect ripples, waves and other expensive-to-repair flaws. Even the more subtle ones are relatively easy to detect by slowly running

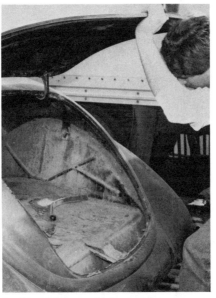

Watch out for spiders, but feel around the underside of the rear deck panel for rust-outs and poor repair work. Inspecting the inside is easy, but rare is the unrestored old car without some problems in this area.

To get a good look at rear floorboards, pull up carpet and remove seat. Floorboards are prime rust areas and expensive to repair correctly.

Integral firewalls are far more important to overall body strength than many early rod builders realized . . . until it was too late! Rare find is body with near perfect firewall. Body such as this should bring top price.

your hands over the sheet metal. If it feels as rough as a corncob, it will take many hours of block sanding to get a smooth, ripple-free surface worthy of paint. Adjust your offer to buy accordingly.

Under the Hood—After you are satisfied with the exterior, take a look under the hood. Unless you're considering hopping up the original power plant—which may be the case with a flathead—chances are you won't care about the engine or its remains. It's a waste of time to check out a powertrain that isn't exactly what you want. In fact, you'll probably be better off if there's no engine at all. It will then be easier to inspect the overall condition of the engine compartment. Check the condition of the interior hood hardware, firewall and inner fender panels.

Inside—Sit behind the steering wheel. If you wondered why I didn't suggest you do this first, it's because there is a magic spell that descends upon a budding rod builder when he takes hold of the wheel. It's too easy to lose touch with reality. All of a sudden you're no longer sitting on disintegrating upholstery that's been home to a tribe of spiders for 10 years, or peering through a dirty and cracked windshield. You're in the car of your dreams.

Even the experienced street rodder can be whisked away on a magic carpet of fantasy when he's behind the wheel. Dented sheet metal straightens out, faded paint suddenly gains depth, and a pitted hood ornament with flaking chrome gleams. So, don't fall for it. Instead, you need the sobering effect of the exterior evaluation before you place yourself directly in the path of temptation.

Begin interior evaluation by pulling up the remnants of the floormats. Scrutinize the sheet metal that lies hidden beneath. Even in the driest climate you'll find far more rust than you expected. But is it all the way through?

The most common floorboard rusting occurs from the scuff plate inward for about

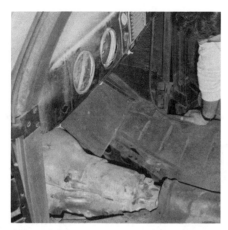

Although late-model tranny was installed in car, no modifications were made to floorboard. Chassis may be another story, however. Make no assumptions.

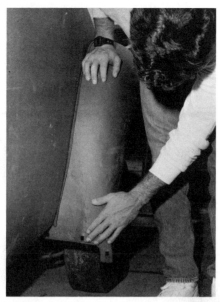

Nothing beats the human hand for detecting surface irregularities. When surveying a potential purchase, take notes. Later when you are mulling it over at home, you'll be better able to weigh factors that will help you make the right decision.

10 inches. If it's only surface scale, chances are you won't have a major repair job. You may even be able to do all of the restoration yourself. To be sure, poke around with your knife.

It is unrealistic to expect a floorboard with no rust, but you have to quantify what's there. Of course, the bigger the hole, the more expensive the repair. And, although excellent replacement floorboards are available, it's still a major repair job. Look for two things: insurmountable difficulties *and* bargaining points. You certainly shouldn't buy a turkey, nor spend one dime unnecessarily.

Roll Underneath—If all looks OK so far, it's time to look at the underside. First, jack up the car and support it firmly on jack stands. Never get under a car that's supported by only a jack. The consequences can be fatal. Check that the car is firmly supported by rocking it. Now, armed with your knife and flashlight, get on the creeper and roll underneath.

Carefully inspect the underside of the car. Start at the lower rear deck panel and slowly work your way toward the firewall. Caked-on grease and road tar are usually positive signs. Oil-based deposits protect the metal frame and floorpan. A dry chassis, on the other hand, won't have this protection. It may be badly rusted. Light surface rust is nothing to panic over, but do some discreet scraping here and there. Look for weak spots or actual rust-throughs in the frame and floorpan. Check in corners and pockets, particularly under the trunk. Rain and moisture accumulate inside the trunk, and those back-end tool compartments in pre-war cars frequently rust through to the underside.

Also check for collision damage while underneath. 'Tis a rare 40- or 50-year-old car

that hasn't been rear-ended at least once. To get the inside story, check the rear of the frame and the underside of the lower rear deck panel for signs of repair. A sign of damage isn't the problem; it's the quality of repair work done 'way back when. Actually, if the car was damaged and repaired from the period of its manufacture until about 1955, chances are the repair work was done with some semblance of care. Normal standards of workmanship were higher in the days before the quicky insurance-company-oriented collision shop. In the '60s, the quality of non-custom body and fender repair fell off dramatically.

If you find repaired damage, look for plastic filler seeping through ice-pick holes, metal wrinkles that were not hammered out—just puttied over—and twisted frame horns that snitch on crude and ineffective attempts to pull them straight.

SIDESTEP SHOT RODS

In all of the foregoing I described an original car, not hot-rodded—a more-or-less stocker, foxtails and Sears seat covers not withstanding. But, no matter how old a car is or the weather conditions it was subjected to while abandoned, the most serious problems found are usually those that resulted from crude modifications, not neglect. Barring the car that is a total rust-out, the hot rodder of old has all too often left a bitter legacy. He may have saved that roadster body from the scrap-metal drive, but he did it on his own terms. That can mean anything from welding the

doors shut to cutting out the floorpan in order to channel the body.

After a careful inspection of the exterior sheet metal as just discussed, let's look at a few problems typically found in hot-rodded cars. One in particular is the rear-wheel openings. When street rodders adopted wide aluminum wheels and rear tires, they suddenly found that the combination wouldn't fit under the rear fenders. Sooo, out came the tin snips! Often, the results were sadly amateurish. Therefore, if you elect to retain those more or less stock fenders, you're going to have to restore them.

Another all too-common sheet-metal headache is from an equally crude attempt to heal rotted drip moldings. This was typically done by slicing off the molding and leading in the seams. Another popular sheet-metal modification during the '50s and '60s was to blank out the side windows and enlarge the smallish rear window of a pre-war coupe. If you don't like such modifications, you may later find out you've bought some expensive body-work.

MODIFICATIONS & MAYHEM

When looking over an old street rod, get to the heart of the matter by removing the hood. Inspect the inner fender panels, firewall and chassis. If the original transmission is still in place, you're lucky. It's a sure sign the engine swap was done a long time ago. This is because one of the most common and frustrating sights encountered in an engine compartment is the gapping holes a past engine-swapper

left in his eagerness to provide clearance for a late-model engine and automatic transmission.

As often as not, excess quantities of metal were removed from the lower part of the firewall and midsection of the chassis. After the damage was done, the holes were crudely patched to keep engine fumes from engulfing driver and passenger. Anything can be repaired. But you must ask yourself, "At what cost?"

Firewall modifications can be a real tragedy. For example, I've never understood the '50s craze to fit the battery into a firewall. Regardless, a lot of firewalls were butchered. Today, most rod builders agree that such a modification should not be done. And the restoration of such a critical panel will drive up the cost of a project. By the way, "critical" is just the right word for many old car firewalls because they served as an integral structural component. Careless metal snipping may have created problems you cannot see, such as increased metal fatigue.

The thought of butchered firewalls calls to mind a modification of similar consequences: the poorly mounted and unsupported late-model hanging clutch-and-brake pedal assembly. If such an installation was performed on a car you are considering, don't think that merely removing it and patching up the holes will correct the problem. It is more than just a question of cosmetics. You may also find stress cracks radiating 6—12 inches from where the cylinders were bolted, and also along the firewall to the body seams.

In general, the cost of repairing a firewall is directly proportional to the amount of metal previously removed, but don't be overly concerned with small holes, of 1/8- to 1/2-inch diameter. Through the years, former owners may have mounted all sorts of things to the firewall. Their repair is tedious, but not expensive. You'll be able to repair most of these even though you're not particularly skilled in metal finishing.

Clear away the cobwebs along both inner fender panels and note what you see and feel. This is a prime area for metal fatigue, but simple welding is often the only fix required. Not so simple to repair are bulges a previous owner might have beat into the panel to provide generator clearance. Firewall-to-distributor clearance was another favorite modification for old-time hot rodders to practice their black art of "ball-peen-hammer metalwork."

POWER CORRUPTS

There's no telling what engine or transmission combination you'll find in an old hot rod. Popular cars, particularly early Ford coupes and roadsters, have been powered by every V8 to come out of Detroit. If it looked as if it made horsepower, the adventuresome would somehow figure a way to shoehorn it in.

Problem engines, however, have traditionally been big Chrysler Hemis and the entire Ford OHV V8 line from the 1954 Y-block to date. Installation of any of these has all too often been an open invitation to a cut-and-hack party. The least you can expect is modification to the lower firewall and fender panels, particularly if the previous builder installed headers.

If the former street rod appears to have been the victim of an unhealthy engine swap, take a peek at the firewall and floorboards from the cockpit side. This is particularly necessary if the engine is still in place, thus restricting your vision from the engine-compartment side. You should know *now* what was done to get the engine installed . . . and what you must undo when it's removed.

Don't be alarmed simply because the frame was altered. What's really important is the quality and quantity of workmanship. Check to see if the X-member or any major part of the chassis has been weakened. Were big chunks crudely burned away or were neat incisions made? Were any strengthening brackets or fish plates welded in that might have prevented stress cracks in hidden areas? Or is there a lack of such precautions that would make you stop and wonder . . . ? And, can the previous modifications be reached for easy repair? Not everybody plans on replacing the frame or even pulling a heavy coupe body off the original chassis for major repairs.

Sometimes you can't see well enough to tell if a chassis was butchered. But, because the original automatic transmission often was installed with an OHV engine, you can imagine what it took to stuff a fat '53 Olds Hydro or '66 Chrysler Torqueflite into a slim prewar frame. There is a brighter side, though. Perhaps the workmanship is good, and best yet, the transmission swapped may be close to what you'd planned on installing.

OTHER CHASSIS & SUSPENSION CONSIDERATIONS

Not only do some rod builders want to retain the original chassis, they may also want the original front suspension, particularly devotees of 1937—48 Fords. If you're among this group, carefully inspect the radius rods, spring perches, axle and spindles. If the radius rods were split, was a decent job done? Or, were the rods heated, bent and twisted out to hook up to big plates welded to the sides of the frame rails? If so, this could mean expensive repairs, or a search for costly replacement parts. In effect, the car would not be complete.

As you continue your inspection, finding at least as many good points as bad ones, I hope, you still can't come to a final judgement without inspecting underneath. As with the stocker, look for excessive rust and rot, but mostly for the ravages of a thoughtless 1950s-era builder who believed old Fords would be around forever.

You'll almost always find that parts of the frame were removed to provide clearance for dual exhausts. It was as if muffler shops of the day couldn't bend tubing to go around anything. They cut the offending frame member away, instead. Most minor alterations won't affect frame strength, although structural integrity is what you must always keep in mind. Nevertheless, crude or excessive cutting can spoil the looks of a chassis, and ours is a hobby that places great emphasis on the appearance of otherwise mundane mechanical components.

I haven't said much about the rear-axle assembly. Whereas front suspensions were often only partially modified with a dropped axle or tubular shocks, even the most casual hot-rod enthusiast quickly learned that the original rear end wouldn't take much power. So, inspect the rear-axle housing, particularly any welded-on brackets, both from a design and an execution standpoint. How are the springs and shock absorbers mounted? Are the brackets for traction bars crudely welded to the frame? Yes, it's true. It seems like *everything* was welded on years ago. Nothing was merely bolted to the frame.

Meanwhile, Back Inside . . . —While sitting behind the steering wheel of an early-era street rod, take a close inventory of the cockpit. Again, forget the condition of the upholstery. If the original seats are still there, are they rebuildable? Replacing them with

Door-hinge areas are another place to check. They get banged about quite a bit through the years, and are sometimes crudely repaired. Look with a critical eye, remembering that every repair will increase total cost.

late-model bucket seats is a possibility, but often at the sacrifice of *proportionality*. The original seat(s) in a coupe or sedan seems to be the only one that "looks right."

Inspect the dash. This has always been a favorite area of modification. The worst situation would be the complete removal of the original and substitution of, say, a 1950 Olds dash. I actually saw this swap in a '40 Ford pickup. Yuk! Forget the gages, you should have *something* to work with depending upon what you plan for the dashboard.

The more interior hardware present, the better off you are. Although many reproduction items such as door handles and window cranks are available, many parts such as window moldings are still swap-meet items . . . and expensive.

Plan on replacing the window glass. Chances are the original glass is *foxed*—turned brown—and is useful only as patterns for the glazier to make new glass.

FILLING IN THE BLANKS

Up to this point emphasis is placed on the condition of what's there, and what it will cost to repair it, be it a basket case or a running car. But, as I've said all along, there is an easy part. It's much more difficult to determine what *isn't* there and what the cost is in time and money to replace the missing components.

If you plan on building a Ford-based street rod, the reproduction parts industry will be a "life saver." And, the situation is getting better for Chevy-based street rods. Not so for everybody else. If you have your heart set on an uncommon street rod, more power to you, but make sure the car has all of its original body and trim components.

Finally, although I've emphasized buying as complete a car as possible—in keeping with the long-term trend of maintaining exterior originality—I haven't spent much time discussing mechanical aspects. The assumption is that you are planning on incorporating modern engineering and reliability into the powertrain, suspension and steering. After all, that's what street rodding is all about. Therefore, you may be better off purchasing a *complete* body and frame with little or no running gear. In that case, you are paying for what you will use, not for the privilege of hauling away the seller's junk.

Remember, it's best to pay a premium for the right car—year, make, model and completeness. In today's street-rodding subculture, the demand for vintage tin far outstrips the supply. Every needed piece that's missing will delay the happy morning you lift the garage door and back that honey out into the street for your first ride.

VINTAGE TIN CHECK-OFF LIST

Parts to look for and inspect when evaluating the completeness and condition of an old car . . . .

FRAME:

Complete, no significant damage	Yes ___	No ___	
Front Horns:	Modified ___	Removed ___	Damaged ___
Front Crossmember:	Modified ___	Removed ___	Damaged ___
Center Member:	Modified ___	Removed ___	Damaged ___
Rear Crossmember:	Modified ___	Removed ___	Damaged ___
Rear Horns:	Modified ___	Removed ___	Damaged ___
Matching Title Papers:			

BODY:

Complete, no significant damage	Yes ___	No ___
Roof Drip Moldings:	Good ___	Rusted ___
Quarter Panels:	Good ___	Rusted ___
Deck Panel:	Good ___	Rusted ___
Fire Wall:	Complete, no significant damage Yes ___ No ___	
Floorboards:	Good ___	Rusted ___
Body trim:	Complete, no significant damage Yes ___ No ___	

FRONT FENDERS: Complete, no significant damage Yes ___ No ___

Front Fender Inner Panels:	Good ___	Damaged ___
Headlight Assemblies:	Complete, no significant damage Yes ___ No ___	
Headlight Rims:	Good ___	Damaged ___
Headlight Buckets:	Complete, no significant damage Yes ___ No ___	

FRONT BUMPER: Complete, no significant damage Yes ___ No ___

Front-Bumper Brackets:	Yes ___	No ___
Front-Bumper Guards:	Yes ___	No ___

GRILLE: Complete, no damage Yes ___ No ___

Grille Guard:	Yes ___	No ___
Grille-Guard Stiffeners:	Yes ___	No ___

HOOD: Complete, no significant damage Yes ___ No ___

Hood-Spring Assemblies:	Yes ___	No ___
Exterior Hood Trim:	Yes ___	No ___
Interior Hood Hardware:	Yes ___	No ___

COWL VENT:

WINDSHIELD-WIPER ASSEMBLIES: Complete, no significant damage Yes ___ No ___

DOORS: Complete, no significant damage Yes ___ No ___

Exterior Trim and Hardware:	Yes ___	No ___
Inside Door Hardware:	Yes ___	No ___
Window Frames:	Yes ___	No ___
Interior Trim and Hardware:	Yes ___	No ___

RUNNING BOARDS: Recoverable, no significant damage Yes ___ No ___

DECK LID: Complete, no significant damage Yes ___ No ___

Deck-Lid Trim:	Yes ___	No ___
Deck-Lid Spring Assemblies:	Yes ___	No ___

As indicated a number of times, purchasing anything other than an old Ford brings with it an even stronger emphasis on completeness. The availability of reproduction parts gets better every year, but has not, and probably never will, catch up to the sheer quantity of what's available—both new *and* used—for early Fords. That's why an even more critical eye with regard to missing parts is required.

VINTAGE TIN CHECK-OFF LIST *(continued)*

REAR FENDERS:	Complete, no significant damage	Yes ____	No ____
Taillight Assemblies:		Yes ____	No ____
Taillight Lens:		Yes ____	No ____
Taillight Buckets:		Yes ____	No ____
REAR BUMPER:	Complete, no significant damage	Yes ____	No ____
Rear-Bumper Brackets:		Yes ____	No ____
Rear-Bumper Guards:		Yes ____	No ____
GAS TANK:	Complete, no significant damage	Yes ____	No ____
DASHBOARD:	Complete, no significant damage	Yes ____	No ____
STEERING COLUMN:	Complete, no significant damage	Yes ____	No ____
FOOT-PEDAL ASSEMBLY:	Complete, no significant damage	Yes ____	No ____
SEATS:	Complete, no significant damage	Yes ____	No ____
WINDSHIELD FRAME:	Complete, no significant damage	Yes ____	No ____
WINDOW FRAMES:	Complete, no significant damage	Yes ____	No ____

4 Repro Bodies

One thing for sure, *repro body* doesn't always mean fiberglass. Experi-Metal's exact replica of the beautiful and rare 1932 Chevrolet roadster is in "original-gage steel." The Sterling Heights, Michigan company reports that it's manufactured on new dies cast from original parts. Car is available with chassis including front and rear independent suspensions with coil-over or fiberglass leaf springs.

Fiberglass: Now there's a material that turned street rodding around in the mid-70s! *Fiberglass* is a word derived from "Fiberglas," a registered trademark of Owens-Corning Fiberglas Corporation. It was coined to describe products Owens-Corning made from tiny spun-glass fibers and plastic resins. As early as 1939, however, Henry Ford had experimented with soy-bean plastics for automotive body panels. And, shortly after World War II, several small-boat manufacturers began experimenting with synthetic plastic hulls. The basic materials used were plastic resins reinforced with a woven glass-fiber cloth. It isn't too surprising, then, that the first complete plastic bodied car was designed and built by the Glaspar Boat Company for a U.S. Army major in 1951. It was premiered at a Los Angeles auto show where it captured

the attention of Detroit's professionals, amateur sports-car builders, racers . . . and the hot rodders.

Vintage-tin roadsters were readily available in 1951 and more coupes were being driven by middle-aged folks than by hot rodders when the Korean War broke out. So, although interested, the boys in T-shirts and blue jeans didn't look into the fabulous potential offered by fiberglass back then. There wasn't much incentive to do so.

Custom sports-car-body builders did, though. The first was the Devin Company of El Monte, California. They were followed by Coachcraft, Kellison Engineering, La Dawri, Track Craft, Victress and other West Coast manufacturers.

It wasn't until the early '60s that street rodders woke up to the fact that fiberglass

roadsterin' would eventually become the wave of the future. This was due largely to the efforts of the late Tex Collins, who founded Cal-Automotive. He began manufacturing and marketing a decent reproduction 1929 Ford roadster body.

Quality wasn't always assumable, though. Many of the early fiberglass creations were of poor quality. In fact, some were so flimsy I considered them to be dangerous. I recall not wanting to spend a single day in one, much less all my street rodding tomorrows. Many of those old repros are still around—and offered for sale by the original buyer. So, you should know what to look at when inspecting a fiberglass body—old or new.

Following is a brief description of how a 'glass body is made.

Molding Fiberglass—Fiberglass is the perfect material for a street-rod body in many ways. It's easy for the non-professional to work with, yet affords high resilience, relatively high strength, is corrosion resistance and light in weight. Best of all, current repros faithfully replicate the early coupes and roadsters. And, although prices have risen to reflect the higher quality, they are within the reach of serious enthusiasts.

Most commercial street-rod fiberglass bodies begin the same way: The manufacturer *pulls* a mold off of an original steel body. Before this is done, the steel body is prepared so it will have a "flawless" surface. Any flaws transfer directly to the *female mold*. Because the mold must be made in sections, molding clay is used to make dams for parting lines. A heavy coat of automobile body wax is then applied and polished to a hard film. After the waxing, a special *parting agent* is sprayed on. The female mold is then built up from the male. This is done by applying several coats of pure resin. The resin contains a high percentage of *catalyst*—curing agent—to make the resin cure quickly.

After the last coat of hot resin cures, the mold builder applies a 1/2-ounce surfacing mat saturated with a slow-curing resin. Mat is used because it's easier to sand should any imperfections have to be removed from the finished mold. The 1/2-ounce mat is usually followed by a layer of 3-ounce mat and one of 10-ounce cloth.

When the body is completely encased in fiberglass, a braced framework is built around the mold to hold each section in its correct

First step in producing a fiberglass body is building one or more molds. Classic T-bucket was the original mass-produced street-rod body.

Long accepted method of producing a street-rod body is hand lamination. Fiberglass mat is laid up right after gel coat is applied. Fiberglass cloth, the primary structural reinforcement, is then laid in.

After 'glass body has cured, it's removed—usually by force—from mold.

Don McNeil of Specialized Auto Components recommends a close inspection of fit with body on chassis, and general fit of doors. If body is "square with the world" and correctly bolts to chassis, doors should fit in jamb with even spacing.

relative positions. This is because the assembly will be jostled about constantly during this process. Also, there must be no hint of sag in the female mold when it's lifted from body.

Imperfections on the inside surface of the female mold must be filled with a mixture of resin and glass fibers, then sanded smooth. With the completion of the female mold, the manufacturer can start building repro bodies.

Basic body-building materials are the same as those used for constructing molds—a combination of spun glass and synthetic resin.

The glass is available to the manufacturer in several forms: mats, cloths and continuous strands. The mat is a fabric made from either chopped or continuous strands of fiberglass bound by resinous adhesives. It varies in weight from a feathery 3/4 ounce to a hefty 10 ounces per square foot. The cloth is woven from continuous strands of fiberglass. It is available in 6—12-ounce weights. Those at the lighter end of the scale—6-, 6-1/2- and 7-ounce cloths—are most commonly used. A very heavy fabric known as *woven roving* is

available when high structural strength is needed, but is not routinely used in the commercial manufacture of street-rod bodies.

Regardless of form, fiberglass only serves as a reinforcement, hence the term *fiberglass-reinforced plastic* (FRP). The other half of the equation is the plastic or synthetic-resin *bonding agent*. The most common resins are polyesters, although occasionally epoxy is used where extra strength is needed or when the fiberglass is to be bonded to steel.

37

Southeastern Automotive Manufacturing of Fort Lauderdale, Florida currently offer no less than six early Ford body styles. These include a 1928 roadster, '30—31 roadster, '32 three-window coupe, '33 Victoria, '34 three-window coupe, '35 pickup, and a '32 Chevy roadster.

Most body manufacturers offer all components required to make complete bodies such as this firewall from Southeastern. It better accommodates Chevy small-block than does original firewall, which is also offered.

BUILDING THE BODY

To manufacture a typical street-rod body, the inside of the female mold is first sprayed with a *gelcoat*. It contains a waxy substance that facilitates the eventual removal of the body shell after it hardens. After the gelcoat *lamination*, or *layup*, begins—the building up of the layers of fiberglass that forms the body.

Body strength depends on the amount of fiberglass reinforcement used. Relative amounts of resin and fiberglass can be varied to meet whatever the manufacturer specificies. Quality is not simply a question of quantity though; the arrangement of the fiberglass fibers is just as important. If all the fibers were laid parallel to each other, there would be great longitudinal strength, but little lateral strength. If, however, the fibers are laid at right angles to each other, overall strength is doubled. Strength is further enhanced when the fibers are arranged randomly. Therefore, the combined strength of bi-directional and randomly arranged fiberglass is preferred for building a street-rod body.

Because major manufacturers of street-rod repro bodies work with the same raw materials and basic techniques, it's easy to assume that there are no significant differences between their products. That's not entirely true. Structural integrity and durability also depends on which of the two major production methods are used: *hand lamination* or *spray lamination*. There are other techniques, but the costs are prohibitive for low-volume manufacturing.

Hand lamination is the oldest and most laborious method of manufacturing fiberglass panels. Varying layers of mat and cloth are used to build the body up from the gelcoat. Resin is applied with a paint brush. This combination of mat and cloth forms easily into the corners and curves of the mold. Mat, which is used first, imparts substance and thickness depending upon how much resin is brushed on. The bi-directional woven pattern of the cloth, which is applied after the mat, gives even strength to the panel.

Methyl ethyl ketone peroxide (MEK) is used as a catalyst to accelerate the hardening of the resin. It induces heat and, as such, must be very carefully and sparingly stirred into the resin at an average rate of 20cc per gallon at room temperature. The manufacturer, however, must constantly monitor shop temperature and adjust the amount of MEK accordingly. Normally, it takes about 30 minutes for the catalyst to harden the resin. During this time, the laminator must work rapidly to eliminate air pockets and gently squeeze out excess resin.

Hand-laminated bodies consisting of up to 65% fiberglass have traditionally been considered the strongest available in terms of the fiberglass-to-resin ratio with a loading of as much as 65% fiberglass.

Spray lamination—*chopper gun*—is faster and less-expensive compared to hand lamination. In spray lamination, a multi-strand fiberglass rope is fed into a spray gun which has a built-in *chopper*. The rope is shredded, or *chopped*, into short strands, mixed with catalyzed resin and sprayed into the gelcoated mold. The coat must be applied evenly or the body will have weak areas.

If you're interested in a fiberglass body, you must choose between hand-laminated or chopper-gun construction. And, although the

One of the largest and oldest of major 'glass manufacturers, Anderson Industries of Elkridge, Maryland, boasts page after page in their catalog of popular body styles and components. Dave Anderson's offerings range from starter bodies that allow you to maximize your own efforts while minimizing the cost, to completely reinforced, ready-to-bolt-on-and-paint bodies.

Harold Ehle's Windsor Fabrication of Battle Creek, Michigan specializes in '33—34 Fords. His sedan deliveries, five-window coupes, cabriolets and Victoria models take a back seat to none. Bodies are oak and steel reinforced with doors hung and latched.

Windsor Fabrication's "standard-door" cars include garnish moldings, dashboard and all inner trim panels. Tack strips and steel window channel is also installed.

Windsor Fabrication's five-window-coupe body is available with or without cowl vent, choice of rumble seat or deck lid, and three firewall choices—stock, small-block Chevy distributor recess or 4-in. full-width recess.

hand-laminated body has been long associated with superior strength and quality, the manufacturers of both types have added a few new wrinkles so that in the final analysis, this traditional distinction simply may no longer be valid.

One quality-enhancing innovation is a vacuum or pressure bag in the mold that squeezes out excess resin and entrapped air. This helps to provide uniform shell thickness and improves the smoothness of the paint surface much like high-production-style

matched molds. Another, and perhaps more significant improvement, is the addition of reinforcement materials to back up the fiberglass mat and cloth. Some manufacturers insert wood between layers of fiberglass—oak, maple and balsa are common. Some use an acoustical foam sandwich; others use strips of previously cured fiberglass. A growing number, however, have gone to steel-tube "birdcages" within the fiberglass shell.

BUYING "USED" 'GLASS

Before I discuss the current fiberglass street-rod bodies any further, let's examine some 'glass offerings of a few years ago. This is no mere walk down memory lane, however. More than one enthusiastic rod builder has purchased a fiberglass body, perhaps "wooded" it, started a chassis and then for one reason or another, abandoned the project. Sooner or later it shows up at a swap meet or in a terse, 10-word ad in the Sunday newspaper. If you encounter either, you owe it to yourself to investigate; it just might be a super deal. But then again . . . .

To determine if the dormant project you've found has a hand-laminated body, check the inside surface. You should detect a coarse, cloth-like texture. The backside of chopped bodies is typically smooth, but shows random 'glass fibers.

Now that you know which body-construction method was used, you have half of the story. Quality is the remaining half. The skill and craftsmanship of the man who

Major option offered by Windsor Fabrication is unique hidden hinges for 1933—34 bodies. Old-timey custom touch has once again become an accepted styling touch. Modification is difficult to do on your own.

actually laid it up and the one who later wooded and fitted it to the chassis is often the difference between something that's worth buying and something that's best forgotten.

The exterior of a body can reveal a lot about both of these fellows and just how conscientious they were. For example, can you see or feel any major surface imperfections? If the body was never painted, are there any air bubbles showing in the gelcoat? Is there any evidence of cracking? Is the gelcoat finish as smooth as a baby's backside—as it should

Another slick custom feature of Windsor Fabrication's body is hinged gas-tank-cover kit. Rather neat, isn't it?

Poli-Form's '27 Track Roadster kit car is billed as "the budget-type kit you can purchase with a credit card . . . or a piece at a time as your budget allows." If you choose the Master Kit, you just supply the engine, transmission, wheels and tires.

Reproduction '29 Ford roadster must be one of the all-time fiberglass champs in terms of popularity with both manufacturers and street rodders. This is Poli-Form's version of the timeless highboy in full splendor. Standard body features steel reinforcement with full floor, finished on underside.

be—or can you see or feel ripples and waves? If possible, shine a powerful flashlight through the shell from the inside. The gelcoat should be opaque with no light shining through. If you detect thin spots in the 'glass, you might want to pass.

A painted and upholstered fiberglass body is more difficult to evaluate, but not impossible. For example, run your hand over the body to check for surface imperfections. Also, check door and deck-lid fit and operation.

One problem often encountered with older, unreinforced and neglected fiberglass bodies is warpage that can be induced by careless storage. One month is what it takes for fresh fiberglass to completely harden. During this period, precautions must be taken to prevent the body from sagging or twisting and taking a set. Otherwise, it will assume a shape that won't be compatible with either the chassis or other components. There's also the possibility of shrinkage. This can range from as little as 1% to as much as 6%, depending on the quality of the resins used.

To prevent warpage and minimize shrinkage, the new fiberglass body should be fitted and secured to the chassis as soon as possible. If this wasn't done, it may be an insurmountable task to right the wrongs. For this reason, avoid a fiberglass body that's been sitting unsupported by either a chassis or major bracing for any but a short length of time.

CURRENT MANUFACTURERS

Since the beginning of fiberglass street-rod bodies, manufacturers have come and gone. Today, there is only a handful who cater to the street rodder. They've solidified their position in the market by turning out high-quality parts. Turn to the back of the book for a listing of these suppliers. The fiberglass-replica bodies and components listed are suitable for street-rod purposes. All are quality products that you can base your car on, but keep in mind that by their very nature, 'glass-reproduction bodies need *fine tuning* before they are ready for paint. Just how much fitting and extra reinforcement will be required var-

ies not only from manufacturer to manufacturer, but from body to body.

Fiberglass bodies, in reality, are *one-off* items with *unique* fitting problems as you'll discover if you install one on your *unique* chassis. Prices vary, too, from $1000 to 10,000, depending on the sophistication of manufacturer and options chosen. All manufacturers provide catalogs that answer typical questions asked by prospective customers.

KIT CARS

In the '20s, an automotive enthusiast with a few loose dollars in his overalls could order all the components he needed to build a speedster. From an ad in an adventure magazine he could convert a Model T frame and engine into an early version of today's street rod. Using goodies from Ed Winfield and friends, lo and behold, he had a *road job* that would run almost as well as a real race car. It could easily whip the daylights out of his neighbor's stocker . . . and scare the devil out of the whole darn town.

The earliest of the modern kit cars is *Fad T* (T-Bucket) styling. This was popularized first by real-life street rodder Norm Grabowski in the famous *Life Magazine* photo taken at a Southern California drive-in and, then, by the character "Kookie" in the TV series "77 Sunset Strip" in the late '50s.

The beauty of kit cars is two-fold: You can save time and money by making one major purchase; and most of the tough fabricating and welding work is already done. As a bonus, a kit car can be purchased at what amounts to a discounted price!

The current crop of kit cars uses high-quality fiberglass bodies. Examples of cars in kit form include not only the 1923 Fad T, but '27, '29, '32 and 1933—34 Ford roadsters, and early '30s Chevy roadsters. As time goes on, more cars will be added as demand increases.

Turn to the Supplier Index in the back of the book for a list of repro-body manufacturers.

NEW STREET-ROD TIN

Not to be outdone by the resin-and-'glass boys, a few bold entrepreneurs have put their capital on the line and have jumped headlong into the street-rod market with "hones'-to-gawd" real steel bodies and components. Although a flegling sub-industry, at least two manufacturers are in full swing, Classic Manufacturing, 2620 West M-8, Lancaster, CA 93536, (805) 947-5460, and Experimetal, Incorporated, 6345 Wall Street, Sterling Heights, MI 48077, (313) 977-7800.

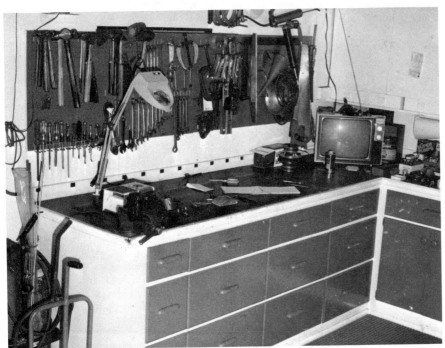

Les Thompson of Costa Mesa, California turned his two-car garage into a workshop that is typical of the family-man street-rod builder who is well-organized, but not a *professional mechanic*. Such a workshop serves many purposes: storage place for the cars, laundry room, and most importantly, a sanctuary where your hobby can be pursued.

There is no option; you must have a workshop to build a street rod. This means converting a part of your living quarters or garage, or renting storage and work space somewhere else. The latter has its advantages, particularly if the rental is in an industrial area. Noise is usually not the problem it can be in a residential area. Of all the difficulties I've encountered in my years of street-rod building, complaints about noise have been the most vexatious!

Rented work areas aren't trouble free. They have their problems, too. First is cost. Every dollar handed over to a landlord is one less for the car. Second, there's a tendency to rebel against paying for the necessary modifications and maintenance of a cold, dark industrial building just because it isn't yours. This, of course, is the age-old dilemma of renters everywhere. But more important than economic considerations, no matter how convenient the away-from-home shop may seem at first, convenience is often only an illusion.

It takes time driving to and from the shop. Tasks that could be done in 20 minutes on impulse suddenly aren't worth leaving the TV set for . . . and, consequently, don't get done. Delays like that can drag out construction time, causing frustration. Then, no matter what you haul to the shop, you'll *always* leave something home. Murphy's Law applies. Either you lock up and go back and retrieve it, or you do without until tomorrow.

For these reasons and more, I heartily recommend the home workshop over all others, unless you are totally without usable space. No matter how quickly that rod can be built, or how little or how much work is farmed out, you'll spend a great deal of time in that shop. In fact, the part of the house which was known as the *garage, carport* or *basement* is where you'll dedicate yourself to completing your self-appointed task—building a street rod.

A good workshop is essential to a home-owning street rodder even though you are minimally involved in the upkeep of your house or family car. In light of today's high cost of professional work, you must be prepared to deal with a multitude of maintenance problems—both major and minor—that naturally occur with time. In the case of a street rodder, however, the shop is not considered a place of labor. It is, in fact, a refuge that usually becomes a source of pleasure; sometimes a secondary hobby.

Where To Put It—There is, of course, only one ideal place to put your street-rod workshop: smack dab in the center of an air-conditioned and heated 800-square foot four-car garage with hot and cold running water. Unfortunately, few of us are that well off. However, you probably have access to at least a single-car garage; maybe a two-car garage. If you are an apartment dweller or similarly "marooned," you must be creative—very creative! Let's take a look at a variety of possible locations from the ridiculous to the sublime. Chances are you will fall somewhere in the middle.

Many street rods have been built under a carport with tools and parts kept in a 6 X 10-foot storage shed in temperate zones such as the rain-soaked Southeast and the sun-baked Southwest. Such facilities are hardly ideal, but as long as there's a concrete slab available for easy mobility, a long enough extension cord and enthusiasm to carry the project through, it can be done.

Just about as trying as the "open-air" garage is the basement or cellar which is partially or completely below ground level and has no auto entry. It may be dark and dingy, damp in the spring, hot in the summer, cold in the winter, and home to a host of creepy, crawly things year round; but as long as heavy components can be removed from its confines with a hoist or willing friends, such a storage area can be used. The work area should have a minimum 8-foot ceiling with pipes and electrical wiring running between the joists and not below. Anything less will detract from a comfortable work area.

If flooding is a threat, make sure interior walls are waterproofed and grades around the house slope away from the exterior walls. Also, make sure the gutters and downspouts are in good condition. If there's any question at all about drainage, install a runoff channel around the footing of exposed walls. You don't want flooded out.

Les paneled the walls of his garage, painted the interior white, and trimmed it in green. This, in conjunction with several overhead fluorescent lights, illuminates work area from corner to corner.

It can be frustrating to organize and store all the small parts you'll need at your fingertips during the build. Shelving loaded with small containers with labels indicating their contents is the proper way to go.

A fiberglass-insulated false ceiling can be built to mask wiring, ductwork and plumbing. It'll also improve lighting. Roll fiberglass insulation between the uprights can be used to minimize the effects of adverse weather—hot, cold or wet—and soften that late-night noise that accompanies a street-rod project.

In short, a cellar can be used as a workshop for a street rod built piecemeal. Final assembly can take place under the carport.

Building a street rod in a narrow ground-level basement or a single-car garage is only moderately more convenient than under a carport, yet many successful street-rod projects have come from such humble surroundings. Not all basements or single-car garages are exactly the same width and length, but 10 X 20 feet is about average. The typical pre-WWII American passenger car, on the other hand, is about 6-feet wide and 16-feet end to end, so not much room is left for workbench, tools, engine and transmission and other major out-of-car components. The rule of thumb is that car storage—even temporary—requires enough space so that one door can be fully opened, and that there's 2-feet beyond its full length. The rest of the space is yours to fill with workbench, tool boxes, shelves, cabinetry and, yes, perhaps a hot-water heater, washing machine and clothes dryer.

The secret to accomplishing something, of course, is to reduce the bulk of the car by

removing bumpers, fenders, running boards and the like for as long as possible. Also, keep the car mobile as long as possible so it can be rolled back and forth or outside while workbench tasks are performed. Beyond this, organization and compactness of your shop facilities are the key to a successful shop.

The next step up the ladder of desirability is the two-car garage. Such a garage is more or less standard on houses constructed over the past few years. It typically started as an empty shell measuring 20 to 22-feet square. Illumination was nothing more than a single 100-watt bulb hung in the center of the exposed-beam "ceiling." Nonetheless, some well-organized remodeling can transform such a shell into an ideal workshop for your street-rod project.

Maybe you're one of the lucky ones whose house has a three-car garage. Such an abundance of elbow room is almost an embarassment of riches, but is a true delight to behold. Then there's the bad news. The problem with a big home workshop is avoiding the temptation to fill it with two or even three unfinished street-rod projects! Don't laugh. I've seen it happen.

For many, the ideal automotive workshop is an existing structure that's completely detached from the house. Quite often, unused outbuildings and, yes, barns can be turned into facilities second to none with regard to space and convenience. One of the most us-

able backyard street-rod workshops I've ever been in is a remodeled stable!

Finally, there's the custom-designed and -built home workshop. I've visited one or two such awesome quarters. Imagine an area spreading over 1200 square feet and equipped the same as a professional shop. Fortunately, such lavish facilities can be left to those who can afford them. We'll set our sights on more realistic horizons that have no less utility.

Likewise, I shall not deal with the potential of club or cooperative shops because they usually don't work. Bitter feelings is the usual outcome, even though the best street rodding is built around the buddy system. Street-rod workshops, like the kitchen, are best commanded by one captain.

PLANNING THE SHOP

Regardless of the location and size of your shop, it should well planned, with an efficient and logical organization of storage, tools and work area. A hobby auto shop, just as its professional counterpart, should have the car at the center of the work area and tools organized in common clusters wherever practical. This is generally called the *U-shaped plan*.

The primary considerations in the placement of major power tools such as the drill press, electric welder and, to some extent, the air compressor, are power supply, clearance and frequency of use. Some electrical tools work best in a corner, some along the wall, and some need clearance on all sides. Another major consideration in planning the placement of tools is the predictable order of their

Paul Dumain, almost as proud of Les' shop as he is himself, shows how Les painstakingly arranged his hand tools ever so neatly in drawers below the work bench.

Note that Les shares space with Mrs. T. Drill press and short steel work bench share area with washer and dryer.

use. Metal fabrication, for instance, proceeds from storage of materials, to cutting, to assembly and to finishing. Fabrication tools, then, should be placed in this order.

Placement of the workbench(es) and tool chest, even if the latter is on a rolling cabinet, is of major importance. I've found that a workbench—no matter how short or narrow—on each side of the car is almost indispensable. The best place for the tool chest is directly in front of the car. Engine work eventually becomes the most frequent task and the hand tools are always within easy reach.

Sketch It—It's always best to work out things on paper. Moving heavy equipment on paper is much easier than to actually do it. Your sketch doesn't have to be fancy, only to scale, usually 1/4-inch to the foot. Remember to sketch in items that will go on the walls and hang from the rafters.

First, draw out the exact floor plan. Include locations of windows, doors, electrical outlets and permanent non-shop equipment such as water heater, wash basin, washing machine and clothes dryer.

Next, make an inventory of the tools and equipment you now own and those you will have in the near future. Make 1/4-scale cardboard cutouts of each. Space them out on the floor plan, keeping in mind the existing electrical outlets and clearance requirements. By the way, leave space for those pieces of equipment you expect to add during the time it takes to build the car.

When you have all the major items positioned, determine where you'll put additional

electric power, special lighting, and a telephone. Pay particular attention to items that may require the services of a professional tradesman. For sure, have a qualified electrician install the 220-volt service and any complicated overhead wiring. And, if you didn't know, the telephone company likes to run their own lines.

While planning, keep in mind that the typical workshop grows through the years and you will have to accommodate new tools and even changing interests. In other words, plan for expansion and stay as flexible as possible.

POWER

Chances are that when you first walk through your shop-to-be, you'll notice that it is sadly deficient in terms of electric power and illumination. More often than not, any changes will be an improvement. It may be that minor additional wiring will make the shop usable. On the other hand, few basements or garages are equipped with 220-volt service. Such service is needed for an arc welder and air compressor.

Older garages usually have two-prong ungrounded outlets, and often even single-service outlets. You don't have to be an electrician to replace the ungrounded outlets with three-prong duplex outlets. Simply shut off the power to the box and replace the old outlets. Run a wire from the grounding terminals of the new outlets to any metal pipe or conduit that leads to the real ground (dirt).

It's possible that your basement or garage has multiple 110-volt circuits. But don't bet on it. A well-equipped workshop should have

Les installed a receptacle strip, small movable fluorescent fixture, and an adjustable magnifying lens close to his vise. Hand tools are within easy reach, too.

43

at least three 110-volt circuits and one 220-volt circuit just for the shop. A washing machine, electric clothes drier or water heater in the shop area should have its own power source, independent from that for shop equipment. Lighting and power circuits should also be independent. Nothing is more distracting than lights that dim when the air compressor kicks in or, worse, go out and leave you in the dark.

The *circuit* is the power line that runs from the circuit-breaker or fuse box to the outlets. Each 110-volt circuit to the workshop—including those for the lights—should be able to handle at least 20 amps. A single 40-amp circuit is barely adequate if several power tools are ganged into it. If more than one tool is in operation at once, the circuit may be overloaded. Likewise, a 220-volt air compressor and small arc welder should be serviced with an internal double-trip 40-amp circuit. There's no excuse for a "blown fuse" in a first-class workshop.

Your local building codes may allow you to do your own wiring, provided you have a permit and have the job inspected afterwards. Otherwise, have it done by a professional contractor. Building-materials stores usually have several different "Home-Wiring-Made-Easy" books in their electrical section. What

they won't have, and what this book provides, is information specifically tailored to your needs as a street-rod builder. However, HPBooks' *Welder's Handbook* does.

Regardless of how many outlets you may have on your walls, you'll still be short one or two in some unanticipated corner, and for sure in and under your car. Heavy-duty extension cords are okay, but extension outlets, either commercial offerings or homemade, are more versatile. Making your own is easy because all materials are available at your building-materials store. All you need is the cord, a 4 X 4-inch metal box and cover, and a pair of duplex receptacles. Once finished, plug the extension into a wall outlet, then take your power to where it's needed.

LIGHTING

For some reason, the home-building industry saves pennies when installing lights in a new garage or basement. Even houses built today with price tags well into six figures will have one naked 100-watt bulb in a cheap ceramic fixture in the center of the garage or on the wall above the laundry area. Such lighting doesn't fill the minimum requirements of a workshop. You'll need all the illumination you can squeeze under the roof.

You simply can't have too much lighting in a workshop. Not only that, lighting is surprisingly cheap. That 100-watt bulb the generous contractor left you draws 1-amp; a fluorescent tube will give you two to four times the light with the same current draw!

The cost of lighting, however, should not be a consideration. You should have ample illumination in your shop for safety. If you can't clearly see what you're doing, you'll be the proverbial "accident waiting to happen." There are more than enough opportunities to skin knuckles, bang elbows and thump your head while building your street rod.

Good lighting is also a necessity and not a luxury for improved work efficiency. Errors are easy enough to make without inviting the gremlins to take liberties.

How much light should you have? A good rule of thumb is two 8-foot 40-watt fluorescent tubes for every 100 square feet of floor space with supplementary incandescent lighting at power tools such as a drill press or band saw. Fluorescent lighting, which produces soft shadows, is good for general overhead lighting. On the other hand, incandescent bulbs are best for pinpoint or spot lighting on power tools. Additionally, you should have several clamp-on reflector lamps and drop lights for undercar and tight areas that nothing else will illuminate.

Can you get your shop too bright? Not really. If the fluorescent fixtures—with

reflectors—are evenly spaced and the walls and ceiling are white, there's no chance of glare. In fact, glare is not a consideration unless one part of the shop is more than three times as brightly illuminated as another.

THE WALLS

Insulation—Depending on where you live, your shop will have uninsulated cement-block walls or frame walls with 2 X 4-inch studs ribbing light-absorbing black-felt lining. Neither is desirable. Masonry walls are porous and should be treated to seal out damp and cold. Not only that, heat will radiate from your body to the walls, even if it's not cold outside.

Plug any holes or cracks in masonry walls. Also, coat their interior surfaces with powder-type block filler and sealer. Follow this up by installing 2 X 2-inch studs, placing them vertically on 16-inch centers on the interior walls. Most building-materials stores carry a special adhesive that works better than nails for securing the studs to the walls.

Even shops in the mildest climates will benefit from insulated walls. Firring or exposed studding is easily insulated with either 3-inch-thick roll or batt fiberglass matting. You can usually wedge it in between the studs and it will stay there. If the fiberglass doesn't have a *vapor barrier*, install 2-mil polyethylene sheeting first to prevent moisture from penetrating.

If insulation from dampness is particularly critical as it is in the Pacific Northwest or Deep South, you may have to go to the added expense of mineral wool insulation blankets. If in doubt, your city or county building department can give you advice in such cases. For more on sealing out dampness, read on.

Paneling—After you've wired your shop and insulated its walls, finish it off with paneling. There is a variety of inexpensive 4 X 8-foot panels suitable for the workshop. Choice depends largely on your bank account and taste, but there are construction considerations.

Half-inch-thick gypsum wallboard backed with foil eliminates the need for the additional polyethylene vapor barrier. It also provides rigidity and additional sound proofing. Some wallboard is also vinyl covered, making it washable—a real plus for a workshop.

Shop-grade plywood, 1/4- or 3/8-inch thick, provides excellent rigidity and is a fine sound-deadening material. Its surface, however, is usually knot-filled, rough and not attractive.

Another low-cost paneling is *pegboard*—perforated hardboard. It is most popular with those who like to hang their tools on the walls. Of the several grades of pegboard, only the

Floor jack—no shop should be without one—*portable* vise, wire wheel—which should have a belt guard—and an oxycetylene set securely fastened to cart, keeps wasted steps to a minimum.

more expensive are rigid enough to resist warping and withstand ordinary use.

Every building materials store has economy 1/8-inch-thick fiberboard panels with at least a dozen different printed patterns. Quality varies from low to decent. Sometimes, finding enough unwarped panels for a project can be a problem.

Somewhat higher in price are 1/4-inch hardboard panels with vinyl or plastic coatings. One of my favorites is off-white plastic-coated panels designed for lavatory usage. They are durable, and can be cleaned with solvents or soap and water. Admittedly, they have an antiseptic look, but the high degree of reflectivity for improved lighting puts them near the top of my list. The hospital atmosphere is easily subdued with posters and pictures.

If you want the ultimate in class, and are willing to pay the extra bucks, there are the better plywoods with a veneer of real furniture wood. There's no doubt that the most beautiful shops are outfitted this way.

Install Wall Panels—Whether you choose wallboard or paneling, installation is fairly simple. Lighter-weight paneling can be attached to the studs or firring strips with adhesive, eliminating the need for nails. If you use nails, special painted ones are available. Or, if the sight of nail heads won't bother you, common box nails will work fine.

Install the first panels in a corner of the shop. Be aware that the corners of a garage or basement usually are not finished with the greatest of care, so are frequently out-of-plumb. To get a satisfactory fit, and to allow for electrical outlets and other projections, hold the panel in position and carefully measure and mark trim points.

Extra framing around water, gas or electric meters may be required. Straight-line cuts and holes are easily made with a power saw or sabre saw, but be sure to use the recommended blades to avoid ripping the panel up. Panels, usually installed vertically, should be secured on all four edges with their intersecting edges beveled slightly for a neat fit. If you install pegboard panels, use fiber washers to space them out from the studs 1/4 inch to make room for the tool hooks.

CEILING

Unlike most other hobby workshops, those for working on a car require considerable room overhead for such tasks as pulling engines. And, if your workshop has living quarters above it, you should soundproof the ceiling. Even if the headroom is sparse, however, you can still fasten 1 x 2-inch firring strips to the joists and install 1/2-inch-thick acoustical ceiling tiles. These tiles come in various sizes

One of the single biggest problems in the home workshop is how to lift an engine. Les and fellow street rodder, Paul Dumain, installed large beam across width of garage, then fishplated it for additional strength. Length of chain and 1000-pound-rated come-along easily lift engine from Les' Chevy-powered '29 one-ton Model A stake bed.

and shapes and can be installed with a special stapler you can rent at the building-materials store.

Even where overhead sound-deadening is not critical, a ceiling or a false ceiling is worthwhile for reflecting light. Inexpensive lightweight panels can be nailed to the joists and painted flat white.

A more creative approach may be necessary if access is required to overhead storage, plumbing pipes or heating ducts. In such a case, you can install an engine removal bar or pipe, then build a suspended ceiling below it. Again, building-materials suppliers offer a wide variety of fiberglass and plastic ceiling panels, installation hardware and, best of all, practical information on how to deal with specific projects.

FLOOR

I suppose that you, like most street rodders, have worked in the dirt on some primordial street-rod task. So, I needn't tell you it ain't no fun! A smooth, crack-free concrete floor is the only way to go. Your creeper and floor-jack will then roll freely without dropping a wheel in a crevice and come to an instant halt. And, although a floor is strictly utilitarian, it doesn't have to be ugly. At least not any more than necessary.

Some guys even go to the trouble of tiling their shop floor. But, after inspecting the

battle scars of 15 years of labor in my shop, I suspect that you could spend an awful lot of time maintaining a tiled floor. Stay with concrete.

Another way to go is to put a good coat of paint on your floor. If you decide to do this, it must be cleaned—maybe degreased. Trisodium phosphate is usually OK for cleaning, but *muriatic acid*—the old-fashioned name for *hydrochloric acid*—may be required to prepare an extra-grimy surface for paint.

Be aware of the dangers of using muriatic acid. Always wear rubber gloves and substantial eye protection. Prevent splatter on yourself at all costs, and the surrounding walls as much as possible.

There are several finishes for concrete floors. The best is epoxy enamel, but there are several acrylic, urethane and latex paints that are adequate. Follow the manufacturer's directions with regard to application. A big roller on a long handle is easiest on the back and knees.

This discussion offers a secondary challenge that should be met with a degree of enthusiasm. How far you go depends only on how elaborate you want your surroundings. Now that we've finished with the walls, floor, ceiling, lighting and electrical service, let's take a look at what a first-rate workshop should contain in the way of tools and equipment.

6 Tools & Equipment

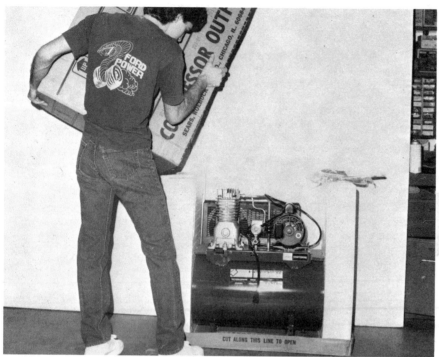

Air compressor is one of the most useful pieces of power equipment in a workshop. Air tools will make your work go much faster.

Once your workshop is ready to go, you must stock it with tools and equipment needed to do the work.

Just as you don't need 1000 square feet of work space, you don't need a full complement of professional tools and equipment. Many special tools and expensive pieces of seldom-used equipment can be rented or borrowed. But, you should have your own set of high-quality hand tools and basic power tools.

HAND TOOLS

There are hand tools of every description. You can easily spend $5000 without duplicating any. So, before you decide which tools to get, ask yourself the following questions about each:

- Should I get the expensive or cheap version?
- How often will I use the tool?
- Is it cheaper to rent, or will an outright purchase cost less in the long run?

- Should I buy each tool individually or should I get the complete set?

These are tough questions. To help with making a decision, following is my response to each question:

Cheap vs. Expensive: To say that these are relative terms is true, but that's a cop-out, so let's get one thing out of the way first.

Starting with the low end of the scale, those bins of low-priced imported items that are found in most auto-parts and handyman stores contain junk. I don't use that word loosely, either. Since I bought a pack of drill bits from one of those "junk bins" 'way back in the early '60s—only to have the first one I used *bend*—I've refused to even accord them the title *tools*. I just call 'em *junk*. If it doesn't have MADE IN THE USA on it, the tool doesn't go in my tool chest.

Most American hand tools are of good quality, but there is often a substantial cost differential between Brand A and Brand B. If you look closely, you can see why. Some

sockets have thicker walls than others—excluding those specially designed and labeled THIN WALL for particularly tight places. Some screwdrivers have stouter shanks and tougher handles. Some ratchets boast better fit and finish. In short, quality shows if you look.

The bottom line: Because your street-rodding project doesn't end on its maiden voyage—you must maintain that creation of yours—consider the long-term. Buy first-class hand tools!

Frequency of Use: You will use each tool from a *basic set* of ratchets and sockets, screwdrivers, wrenches and pliers a thousand times in five years. The question that remains is, just what does the basic tool set consist of?

Buy or Rent: This is tricky, and you may not have the answer even when you find yourself renting something for the second or third time. Nevertheless, you must guestimate when multiplied rental fees will equal the purchase price—and act before then. Also, keep in mind that when you purchase a tool, it's yours. Then, again, you shouldn't spend money on an expensive tool you'll only use once or twice in 10 years.

Individual vs. Set Purchase: Beware of the urge to become a "tool collector." Otherwise, you may not have enough money left for building your street rod. Carefully evaluate each item in a set of tools with regard to frequency of use and unit price. For example, often a set of sockets will contain several items with limited use. With this example in mind, do what the home economists call *comparison shopping*.

First add up the unit prices of everything in the set—call it *$A*. Then add up the unit prices of the pieces you know you'll get full use of—call it *$B*. Compare $A and $B against the price of the complete set which we'll call *$C*.

The answer: If $B and $C are fairly close, and $A is a lot higher than $C, and you get the odd-ball sockets for little or nothing, the set is a good buy.

If, however, $A and $C are close, there's no advantage to buying the complete set. It would be a high price for items that you won't use much. In this case buy only what you need—and when you need it.

Basic Hand-Tool Collection—It's been said that Henry Ford built his tools by hand before he built his first car. Whether this is true or not, it certainly illustrates that you can't build a car without basic hand tools. As for what constitutes the basic set of tools, there is no agreement. It depends on the work to be done.

Putting that aside, most agree that you must have a 3/8- and 1/2-in.-drive ratchet set with shallow sockets and several extensions in the 3—12-in. range. After this comes a set of flat combination wrenches—open at one end, closed at the other. Sizes for sockets and wrenches should range from 1/4 to 1 in. with 1/16-in. increments.

Next, you'll needs at least six pliers, including one Vise-Grip type, one electrical and a needle nose. And, you won't get much accomplished if you don't have at least 12 different screwdrivers; more flat blade than Phillips type. Finally, two each of ball-peen hammers, cold chisels, punches and hacksaws if you are pressed to keep tool costs at an absolute minimum.

Don't take the miserly approach when building your street rod—not if you want it to be any fun, that is. So, rather than see how few tools you can get by with, list what a well-rounded collection should include using the photos and tables as reference. Before you do this, let's take a look at some broad categories of hand tools.

Wrenches: You must have a complete set of open-end, box-end and combination wrenches. These are about as basic as you can get and, even though you may never acquire a ratchet or socket, you could handle about every nut-and-bolt assembly and maintenance task to be found on your car . . . and, you'll find a lot of them.

The handle length of each wrench increases relative to the nominal opening size to allow more leverage (torque) on the larger nut or bolt. The open-end design is for relatively fast work. Their heads are typically angled at 15°, 30° or 60° to the handle to improve access and clearance. Most manufacturers offer a variety of styles with straight and curved, short and long handles, in various head thicknesses. The greater the variety you acquire, the greater the range of applications you can deal with.

A box-end wrench cannot be used with the speed of an open-end but, for given sizes, it can be used to apply more torque. This is because a box-end wrench exerts a force on all six corners of a standard hex head rather than two. There are two basic box-end wrench designs. The *six-point* box-end allows for a new *bite* every 60°; the *12-point* needs half the rotation, or 30° for a new *bite*. Twelve-point box-end wrenches are useful in confined areas where wrench rotation is half of the six-point. However, a six-point box-end wrench is best for applying greater torque because the bearing area of the wrench flat is greater, reducing the chance of rounding off

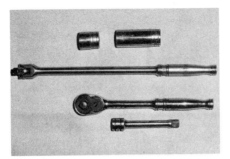

A 1/2-in.-drive socket set is useful for heavy-duty work.

A 3/8-in.-drive socket set is more versatile than a 1/4- or 1/2-in.-drive set. Get as complete a set as possible.

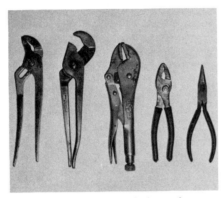

An assortment of pliers belongs in every rod builder's tool collection. Quality tools such as these well-used Vise-Grip pliers, last almost forever. My dad bought the Channellock pliers during WWII!

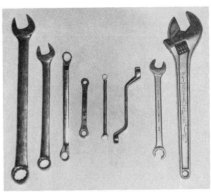

You simply cannot have too many different types of wrenches. No need to buy 'em all at once, but as each task arises; add to your collection as necessary.

the corners of the hex.

Box-end-wrench heads are angled 15° or 30° to the handle to allow for maximum grip and knuckle clearance. Handle shapes and lengths are various.

Real versatility, however, is obtained with combination-end wrenches. These feature a variety of offset and/or angled box-end heads on one end and open-end heads on the other. An experienced tool twister can use a combination wrench very effectively by quickly running the nut down with the open end, then final tightening with the box-end.

Socket Wrenches: Professional mechanics and street rodders thank the Snap-on Tools Corporation for their 1920 invention that revolutionized the knuckle-busting trade. Socket wrenches and their many accessories are indispensable for a wide range of fastener removal and installation jobs.

There are three ratchet drives you should have in your tool chest: 1/4, 3/8 and 1/2 in. These sizes describe the size of square drive that projects from the ratchet or breaker-bar handle. They, of course, match the square

holes in the sockets or extensions. Ratchets are available in a variety of handle lengths from extra-short stubbies to real "pry bars," 1- or 2-feet long that allow maximum leverage. There are ratchets with flex-heads, bent handles, flat handles and plastic handles, but the one with the plain old standard handle is what you'll reach for most often.

The standard 1/4-in.-drive ratchet is about 4-1/2-in. long; the average 3/8-in.-drive is typically 7-1/2-in. long, and the average 1/2-in. drive is about 10-1/2-in. long.

Note: A good rule of thumb to use when using your socket set is: bolt-shank diameter determines drive size. The bigger the bolt, the bigger the drive and vice-versa. For instance, avoid tightening a bolt with a 1/4-in. shank with a 3/8-in.-drive ratchet, or a bolt with a 3/8-in. shank with a 1/2-in. drive. Assuming you apply the same force as you would with the proper ratchet, using one that's too large will over-torque or break bolts. Also, using a ratchet that's too small will break its internal mechanism if you apply a force necessary to tighten the bolt correctly!

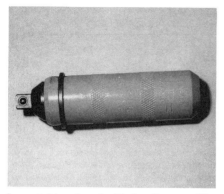

Impact driver is valuable for disassembling old cars when air power is not available. Be sure to use attachments rated for impact use. Driver with screwdriver attachment and ball-peen hammer is used to loosen rusted door-latch screw.

At the "business end" of the ratchet is the socket. As your street-rod-building skills develop and you take on new and different sub-projects, you'll continue to find new and useful sockets that are best suited for doing obscure jobs.

There are four basic sockets in six- and 12-point configurations, just as with box-end wrenches. The standard-length socket is two to three times the nominal size; *deep* sockets are three to five times the nominal size. These, combined with the three basic drives, nominal sizes and configuration varieties, provide a lot of sockets from which you can choose! The best way to deal with the overwhelming variety of sockets is to study the tool catalogs, and when a special job comes up, purchase the special socket.

Screwdrivers: Street rods are not built with nuts and bolts alone. There are always screws with different heads you must contend with. As such, a good complement of screwdrivers is necessary.

The most important thing to remember when using a screwdriver, is that slot or X in the screw head is a definite length, width and depth. Therefore, you shouldn't grab just any old screwdriver just as you wouldn't grab any wrench for installing or removing a nut or bolt. Using the wrong screwdriver could damage it or the screw head.

The cardinal rule is: The screwdriver blade should use all of the available screw-head load-bearing surface. Examine closely the shape of the standard slotted screwdriver. Note that the tip of the blade has nearly paral-

lel sides. *Hollow-ground* screwdrivers have parallel surfaces. Whatever the tip type, it should wedge snugly into the slot.

Most, but not all screwdrivers carry identifying marks. Unfortunately, there isn't a standard identification system or a ready reference for ordinary slotted screws. Sears Craftsman slotted screwdrivers are cataloged by slot dimension and blade length such as 3/8 X 12. Only the slot size appears on the handle. Snap-on, conversely, stamps a code on the handle, such as SSD 8, which is useless for quick identification.

Therefore, the guy under the car is left with the trying experience of shouting *big, little* or *medium* to his partner who's handing him the tools. Ultimately, he must develop an eye for screw-slot sizes so that, at a quick glance, he'll be able to choose the screwdriver that will give a snug fit. Fit, by the way, is particularly critical on old, rusted screws, the likes of which are found on old, rusted cars.

The situation is better with regard to Phillips and Pozidrive screws. Once you learn what a No. 0, 1, 2, 3, and 4 Phillips or Pozidrive looks like, you can ask for a specific screwdriver.

Pliers: The choices are bewildering. There are at least 35 different styles of pliers from which to choose! Those listed at right should be adequate enough to get the job done. Caution: Pliers are near the top of the list in terms of readily available low-cost imports. As with other hand tools, use top-notch American-made brands. Among other problems, the two halves of imported cheapos have an annoying way of slipping past the detents and pinching fingers!

Gas-welding outfit is indispensable piece of equipment for any rod builder. Get one with two-stage regulators. They will better maintain delivery pressure. Most sets come with hose, torch, cutting attachment and small selection of tips. Oxygen and acetylene bottles can be rented or purchased outright. Ask salesman at your welding-supply store for a recommendation.

BASIC HAND TOOLS (Sizes in Inches)

WRENCHES
Box-End—Standard 12-Point Flank Drive:
1/4 & 5/16, 3/8 & 7/16, 1/2 & 9/16, 5/8 & 11/16, 3/4 & 7/8, 13/16 & 7/8, 15/16 & 1.
Standard Open-End:
1/4 & 5/16, 3/8 & 7/16, 1/2 & 9/16, 5/8 & 11/16, 3/4 & 7/8, 13/16 & 7/8, 15/16 & 1.
Combination—Standard 12-Point Flank Drive:
1/4, 5/16, 3/8, 7/16, 1/2, 9/16, 5/8, 11/16, 3/4, 7/8.
Adjustable, Standard Thin Jaw:
4, 6, 12.
Open-End Flare-Nut:
3/8 & 7/16, 1/2 & 9/16, 5/8 & 3/4.

RATCHET & SOCKET SETS
1/4-in. Drive:
  Ratchet:
  Standard Handle (4—5-in. long)
  Long Handle (6—7 in.)
  Long Handle, Flex Head
Six-Point Sockets:

Standard	Deep
1/8	1/8
5/32	
3/16	3/16
7/32	
1/4	1/4
9/32	
5/16	5/16
11/32	11/32
3/8	3/8
7/16	7/16

1/2	1/2
9/16	9/16

18-in. Speeder Handle
X, 6, 14 Extension Bars
Universal Joint

3/8-in. Drive
  Ratchet:
  Standard Handle (7—8-in. long)
  Long Handle (10—11-in. long)
  Long Handle, Flex-Head
  Six- and 12-Point Sockets, Standard and Deep
  3/8, 7/16, 1/2, 9/16, 5/8, 11/16, 3/4, 13/16, 7/8
  15-in. Speeder Handle
  3, 6, 12 Extension Bars
  12-Point Flexible Sockets, Standard Length:
  7/16, 1/2, 9/16, 5/8.

1/2-in. Drive
  Ratchet:
  Standard Handle (10-in. long)
  Speeder Handle (20-in. long)
  Breaker Bar (18-in. long)
  Sockets: 6-Point:

Standard	Deep
5/8	5/8
11/16	11/16
3/4	3/4
7/8	7/8
13/16	13/16
15/16	15/16
1	

1-1/16
1-1/8
1-1/4

SCREWDRIVERS
Slotted
1/8 X 2, 1/8 X 4, 1/4 X 1-1/2, 1/4 X 4, 1/4 X 6, 1/4 X 8, 1/4 X 12, 3/16 X 4, 3/16 X 9, 5/16 X 1-3/4, 5/16 X 6, 3/8 X 12
Phillips
#0 X 2-1/2, #1 X 3, #2 X 1-1/2, #2 X 4, #2 X 8, #3 X 6, #4 X 8

PLIERS
Interlocking Pliers: 6 and 12 in. with plastic grips and jaw heads set at 45° to provide easier access to obstructed areas.
Combination Jaw Slip-joint Pliers: 6 in. with plastic grips.
High Leverage Diagonal Cutting Pliers
Needle-Nose Pliers: 6-in. straight and bent nose, with plastic grips.
Vise-Grip pliers: 7 and 10 in.

HAMMERS
Ball-Peen: 8 and 16 oz.
Brass Tip: 16 oz.

PUNCHES & CHISELS
Flat Chisels: 5/16, 7/16, 1/2.
Center Punches: 5, 6, 7.
Pin Punches: Point sizes 1/8, 3/16, 1/4

MISCELLANEOUS HAND TOOLS & EQUIPMENT

Ratchet-Head Torque Wrench; 30—200 ft-lb.
Tap & Die Set; 1/4—1/2 UNC and UNF threads.
Hack Saw: Heavy-duty 12-in. model with front-end grip and blade tensioner. Maintain a good supply of high quality blades in all major varieties.
Taper-Bit Screw Extractor Set: Should contain at least 1/8, 9/64, 7/32 and 5/16 in. sizes.
Brake-Adjusting Tools: (Check tool catalogs for items designed for specific brakes.
Bolt-on Type Axle Shaft Puller: Required to break loose Ford and GM axle shafts.
Scrapers: Tool chest should contain several scrapers and putty knives with 1, 2 and 3 in. blades.
Electrician's Wire-Stripping and Crimping Tool.
Extra Deep C-Clamps: At least four each of 6-in. capacity.
Crankshaft-Damper Puller.
Measuring Tools: 35-blade combination master feeler-gage set in standard sizes with extra brass blades for electronic ignitions; 25-ft measuring tape.

Files: High-grade alloy steel; minimum set should include 6- and 12-in. round files, bastard cut; 6-, 8-, 10- and 12-in. mill files, bastard cut; 6- and 10-in. triangular files, bastard cut; 6-, 10- and 12-in. half-round, bastard cut. File handles *must* be installed on every file.
Tube Cutting and Double Flaring Tools: Set should include tubing cutter and small bender.
Tool Storage Units: Tool chests and roller cabinets should be of high quality and as large as possible. They can never be too large.
Hydraulic Floor Jack: High-quality US-made, minimum 2-ton lift capacity and 24-in.-lift; steel wheels with ball bearings; rear swivel casters; and removable handle.
Hydraulic Axle Jack (Bottle Jack): High-quality US- made, minimum 1-ton lift capacity and 4—5-in. lift.
Jack Stands: Minimum of four heavy-duty stands with tripod base; 2-ton minimum load capacity; ratchet type preferred.
Creeper: Washable finish, ball-bearing casters.
Creeper Seat: Built-in tool tray and large-diameter caster wheels.

Steel Chain Hoist: Minimum 2000-lb capacity.
Safety Equipment: Clear polycarbonate face shield; flexible mask impact goggles with polycarbonate lens. Heavy-duty dry chemical fire extinguisher suitable for Class A, B, and C fires.
Bench Vise: Heavy-duty model, 4—5-in.-wide jaws that open at least 6 in.; swivel base that rotates approximately 160°.
Parts Washer: Small, inexpensive portable parts-washing bins are available in many auto-parts stores. Use with non-flammable solvent.
Standard Oxyacetylene Gas-Welding Outfit: Basic gas-welding set should include torch, cutting attachment, regulators, hoses, strikers, goggles, tip cleaners and a variety of welding and cutting tips. Two-stage regulators are preferable over the single-stage type. They deliver constant gas flow to torch within a wide range of cylinder pressures without the need to make constant adjustments to compensate for dropping cylinder pressures. However, if your budget is limited, single-stage regulators will work.

Heavy-duty electric sander/grinder is handy when doing chassis repair and modification, bodywork and general fabrication.

A small piece of equipment often overlooked—until needed late one night—is a drill-press vise. This inexpensive tool is an effective safety device.

Miscellaneous Hand Tools: As you can see from the preceeding list, *miscellaneous* includes a variety of tools. The specifications are self explanatory, so there's no need for elaboration. Of course, there are many more hand tools that would be nice to own, but start with those listed. As you progress through your project, you'll quickly discover which additional tools are worth having even though they may not be *basic* or *necessary* in the strictest sense.

POWER TOOLS: ELECTRIC

I'm sure I don't have to sing the praises of electric power tools. I can't imagine that anyone would trade his electric drill for a brace and bit, or a bench grinder for a rough-cut hand file. Or even a power hacksaw for a hand hacksaw (for those with a fat pocketbook). But for those of us on a limited budget, some power tools are far more necessary than others power tools.

At the top of the list are power drills. You'll need three: one each with a 1/4-, 3/8- and 1/2-in. chuck. A heavy-duty Black and Decker, Craftsman and Skil—to name some top-notch brands—will last a street rodder many, many years. Economy power drills, even those with good brand names, usually won't live through the construction of one street rod.

The same is true of grinders, both hand held and bench mounted. The heavy-duty models will withstand considerable use; inexpensive ones won't. If you buy the best, chances are you'll never have to buy another one.

POWER TOOLS: PNEUMATIC

You'll find, soon after you start your ground-up assembly, that there aren't enough minutes in each of those precious weekend hours, even with ratchets or speeder handles. Eventually, you'll conclude that you're not only working too slow, you're working yourself and the tool too hard.

Professional mechanics solve both problems by using quality pneumatic tools. 'Tis a rare shop indeed where the most prominent noise isn't the staccato breep . . . breep . . . breep of the impact wrench or air ratchet.

Most street rodders are aware of the time-saving feature of pneumatic tools. Few, however, know that with minimum care, air tools are amazingly durable, outlasting their electric-powered counterparts four to one. And, they are economical!

To design a pneumatic-tool system for your workshop, determine the needs at both ends of the air hose. Start with the types and demands of the air tools, then buy an air compressor that will supply the needed volume. Or, buy an air compressor and add the appropriately rated tools to your collection as you need them.

Either way, determine what is needed in the way of tools now . . . and in the predictable future. A pneumatic system is a permanent, long-term fixture in the shop and, although most of the components are not expensive—as power tools go—the cost is far from insignificant.

Compressor—The compressor is the most expensive item in a pneumatic system. It's also the most difficult to choose, so consider it first. Portable compressors suitable for home-shop use come in a variety of models. Common ratings are 1/3, 1/2, 3/4, 1, 1-1/2, 2, 3, 4 and 5 horsepower.

Usually, the lower-rated compressors are powered by a 110-120-volt electric motor. Bigger compressors are almost always powered by a 220-240-volt motor or gasoline engine. Then there's the compressor itself.

After you become accustomed to air tools, you'll wonder how you ever got along without an air compressor. Adequate wiring is a must to run such power equipment.

Air tools such as an impact wrench and *butterfly* ratchet, will reduce project down time by 25%. Always use impact sockets and accessories with impact wrench.

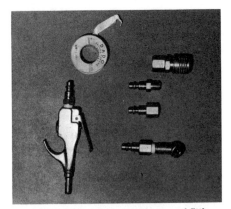

A handful of *quick disconnects* and fittings are a must when working with air tools. Use teflon thread sealant to prevent air leakage at threaded joints.

These have single- or twin-cylinders. Compressors with two cylinders normally require a minimum of one horsepower for efficient operation.

Horsepower notwithstanding, the most important compressor specification is its volume—standard cubic feet per minute (scfm)—at a given pressure—pounds per square in. (psi). Typical portable units are delivery rated at odd-ball figures such as 1.7, 2.7, 3.2, 3.4, 6.4, 7.3, 7.8 or 9.3 scfm. About the next biggest non-stationary compressor is rated at 15.3 scfm. Pressure ratings run from 40 to 175 psi.

Naturally, more power is needed to deliver high volume and pressure, but as pressure demands increase, volume delivery drops. Therefore, many units have dual ratings, such as 7.8 scfm at 40 psi and 6.3 scfm at 90 psi.

Another major consideration is the air-storage tank. Like most tanks, air-compressor tanks are rated in gallons. The 7-1/2-gallon

compressors that are frequently on sale are too small for the automotive workshop. A 12-gallon compressor is better, but 20—30 gallons is best. In other words, when you are considering air supply, the more the better.

A 1-1/2-horsepower compressor delivering at least 7 scfm should be the minimum for your workshop. These units almost always require a single-circuit 220-volt line. Thanks to the big merchandising chains, compressors in this range are readily available and reasonably priced.

Air-system horsepower, as with street-rod horsepower, costs money. That's why you should anticipate your current and future needs before you make a purchase. To do that well means you should understand the volume and pressure demands of the pneumatic tools you are planning to purchase.

Probably the first air device that comes to mind is a paint spray gun. High-quality, professional-type siphon-feed guns suitable for applying automotive paints and primers need 5—16.5 scfm at 40—90 psi. Reasonably good siphon- or pressure-feed guns need 3—9 scfm at 35—50 psi. Non-bleeder types—which are not practical for auto painting—can get by with as little as 1—3 scfm at 20—50 psi. Nevertheless, when you're dealing with air power, delivery is all-important.

Pneumatic Tools—Of major interest, however, are the many air ratchets, impact wrenches and drills advertised with air compressors. Working with these tools is a real pleasure and, since they'll outlast their electric counterparts four to one in an industrial setting, they should last "forever" in your workshop!

Maintenance of most air tools is very simple. All that's usually required is a few drops of special oil each time an air tool is used and a moisture-free air supply. If these considerations are met, your air tools will last many, many years; if not, the best tool will wear and rust internally.

Most auto-shop air tools require 8 scfm or less. Only very large ones such as a 1-in.-drive air wrench or heavy-duty sander/grinder require a substantial air supply, or 12—20 scfm. Of those, only the sander/grinder will be useful in your shop. But, with a 20 scfm demand—requiring a 5-horsepower compressor—it's impractical for most home workshops.

Generally speaking, any tool in the 7—8-scfm range will have no air-supply problem. In fact, most useful tools use 4 scfm or less. That means a 1-1/2—2-horse compressor is easily capable of performing most street-rod building chores.

A main advantage of air tools is that over-extending them usually doesn't cause any

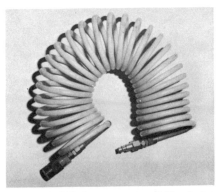

All types of air hoses are available, but a perma-coil type is particularly handy for bench work because of its self-stowing feature.

Pay attention to personal safety. A mask and goggles are a must for lung and eye protection.

Although I'm not a big fan of sand blasting, small portable Sears unit is handy for cleaning those vintage parts.

Air-drive grinders and polishers are sweethearts to work with, but be sure your air compressor has enough capacity for them before you buy one or the other.

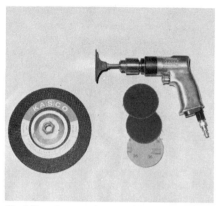

Air drill motors can be used for long periods without overheating and, therefore, are useful for performing many tasks. Don't forget to put in a few drops of the prescribed oil with each use.

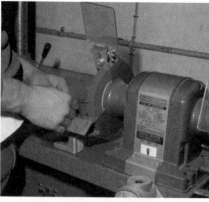

No street-rod workshop should be without a heavy-duty bench grinder. You should also have a selection of grinding wheels and wire wheels.

damage. Once the tool reaches its capacity, it just blows air past a built-in safety valve. The exception to the rule is the air ratchet. If overextended, it's possible to strip the internal gears. Follow the rule of thumb I gave with regard to hand-ratchet size versus bolt size when using a pneumatic ratchet.

Note that the maximum *working* demand of air tools is not necessarily a *constant* demand. Many tools have built-in regulators to reduce the air supply (power) for light-duty jobs. Also, most air-tool manufacturers offer add-on in-line regulators for tools not originally equipped with regulators.

Beware! Continued use of air tools is addictive. Once you become accustomed to them, you'll never want to pick up a hand tool again. About the only drawback I can think of is that the world outside could care less about your speed and efficiency. The breep . . . breep . . . breep of the air ratchet, particularly late at night, tends to generate neighborhood hostility!

WORKBENCH

It's been said that the workbench is the most indispensable item in a workshop. Although I can't go quite that far, I believe that you should invest in a substantial workbench immediately after you purchase the basic hand and power tools.

There are many types of true workbenches. You can either build a workbench or purchase one. A bench can be built out of a solid, uncut door, or you can convert an old wooden or metal office desk. Several manufacturers

offer bench-leg kits with plans for building the top and shelf.

Plans for workbenches abound in craft and do-it-yourself wood-working magazines. Sears, Montgomery Ward and J.C. Penney are a ready resource for light- to medium-duty workbench assemblies that come unassembled. And, major tool-supply houses stock a variety of workbenches.

The best deals, however, are often found in used industrial workbenches. Good leads for these can be found in the newspaper classifieds under Tools and Machinery. For example, I bought my favorite bench for a very reasonable price from the surplus yard of a large Southern California aircraft manufacturer. Wise buying is easy, too. It's hard to go wrong on a used workbench. Look 'em over and rock 'em a bit to judge their steadiness. If one isn't to your liking, move on to the next one.

Workbench heights range from 30 to 34 in., and widths from 24 to 30 in. Lengths are equally as variable. Available space often dictates width and length maximums, but bench height should be determined by what suits you. The working surface should be at your hip joint so you can work comfortably without bending over.

If possible, position the workbench lengthwise in the shop with a minimum of 18-in. clearance at each end. If you have gobs of room, move the bench away from the wall so you'll have access to it from all sides.

Once in place, avoid using your bench as storage place for tools. No matter how large

its working surface, keep permanent space-stealing equipment off. Some industrial-arts references caution you to not permanently attach a vise or grinder to a general-purpose bench. Regardless, I have broken both rules. The impact is lessened, though, because I have two benches. You may find that space in your shop is so limited that you must use your best judgement and compromise the ideal.

The bench should be level in all directions; so level that a marble placed in the center of the work surface won't roll off. There should be ample electrical and compressed-air outlets within reach. The bench top or working surface should either be of tough end grain wood or one of the many available durable synthetic industrial materials. A sheet-metal surface is OK. Just make sure you place a rubber mat on top if you repair any electrical appliances on the bench.

Lighting over the bench is important. Ideally, a bench should have a full-length fluorescent light overhead plus one or two incandescents nearby that can be clamped on for close work.

Finally, because a bench occupies considerable floor space, use the dead space above and below it for storage. Just leave enough foot and head room for comfortable working.

Lock it Up—Now that you've done such a great job of outfitting your home workshop, don't forget to put it under lock and key. Otherwise, your valuables will "grow legs." Put a stout lock on the door to protect all those expensive goodies!

Begin vintage-tin street-rod project by setting car in your shop and methodically take it apart. Start with major components such as a door, but don't disassemble them until you're ready to work on each.

OK. You followed the advice given in preceding chapters and you took the plunge. Right? You also bought an old car and are ready to turn it into a street rod. There it sits, more-or-less in the middle of the driveway. Now, what do you do?

Start by removing all the junk that has accumulated over the years from the car. Vacuum out those cobwebs, dirt and critters that thought they found a permanent home. This is where a shop-type vacuum cleaner comes in handy. Then give your old car the bath of its life. After all, it hasn't had one in years. Scrub it well. While it's drying, inspect it closely. I hope you won't be disappointed by what you purchased after your inspection. It does happen, though. That's why recision clauses are put in contracts. None here, though. What you see is yours.

Consider how far you will go on your project. Are you going to completely rebuild the car, or will you settle for an engine and transmission swap? If you take the easy way out and do a light restoration job, remember that simple projects have a way of growing.

As you progress, you'll find that one thing invariably leads to another. That is, if you install a highly modified engine and heavy-duty transmission, you must install an equally healthy rear axle. Or, if you change the steering gear, you may have to change the steering column and/or steering linkage. And, if you install power disc brakes on the front, you should go with better brakes at the rear. That's the way the story goes whenever you set out to build or modify anything. It's called the *snowball effect*. Like a snowball rolling downhill, a street-rod project tends to grow as it "rolls" along.

Now that you're committed, set your ratchet to OFF and plan the disassembly.

Teardown—Disassembling an old car seems simple enough. You just take it apart, clean up and repair all the pieces, then screw 'em back together after the engine- and driveline-swap modifications are completed. It's that simple. Unless you aren't well organized—you'll lose half of the small parts. And unless you have a "perfect" memory, you'll forget how and where some of them go back

together. There are other pitfalls. Rendering a car immobile is one; insufficient storage and work space is another.

PARTS STORAGE

After you've organized your immediate work area, set up *long-* and *short-term* storage areas. If your long-term storage is under the fabled shade tree, you'll need to cover everything with heavy-duty plastic sheets. If you bought a complete car, you will have loose fenders, bumpers and the like to store. They must be stored in a *secure,* dry area.

If you have the room, install sturdy shelving for storing small parts. Good used heavy-duty industrial shelving is often available through salvage yards and second-hand industrial-equipment auctions. Most any size or height will do—they are adjustable. Just avoid flimsy, light-gage shelving that's frequently on sale at discount hardware and building supply stores.

TAKE NOTES

Get yourself a large bound notebook. Collect several tin cans and boxes; a lot of small ones are better than a few big ones. Get two boxes of clear-plastic sandwich bags and a fistful of shipping tags. Many bolts and nuts on your old car are for unique applications and should be marked accordingly. Although you may want to replace them, some items may not be available new, used or repro, so try to remove and store each as if it's the only one in existence. Count on it. If you get careless and lose or ruin any part, it will be irreplaceable!

TAKE IT EASY!

One of the best ways to turn an old car into a street rod is not to immediately disassemble *everything.* The *gung-ho* approach where the builder rips the body off the chassis in the first week is fine. But, don't do this unless you know exactly what you're going to do and how to do it *first,* particularly if you don't know which engine and transmission you're going to use. Instead, keep the basic body and frame intact down to and including a working front and rear suspension. This not only retains mobility, but will later allow you to do some easy exploratory engine- and power-train swaps.

Disassembly can't always take place under ideal conditions. Nevertheless, don't discard *anything* you'll replace until its replacement is *in place.* It's frequently easy to forget what a part looks like when it comes time to fabricate or purchase another.

TAKE IT APART

Disassemble Body—Once you've centered your car in the work area, begin disassembly by removing the bumpers, bumper guards and brackets *as a single unit.* Keep these and other major subassemblies in one piece for as long as possible. Even bumpers, as simple and uncomplicated as they may seem at first, can be confusing when all the nuts, bolts and brackets are dumped loose in a box. Replace all bracket-to-body attaching nuts and bolts in the bracket ends and hand-tighten.

Make notes and take photos of anything that you're likely to forget six months or more from now. Sketch or trace bumper brackets. Many are similar in appearance, but are specifically designed for left or right, front or rear, or deluxe or standard models. Put loose nuts or bolts in a plastic bag; *tag the bag.*

Lightly wire brush rusted areas, then spray-paint them with cheap enamel from an aerosol can. Don't worry about the color and *don't use primer.* Unfortunately, far too many rodders think ordinary primer is a protective coating. Not so! On the other hand, cheap enamel is an excellent surface sealer that's easily removed when necessary.

Next, remove the hood, all four fenders and running boards. Remove, clean and store

the chrome trim items. Keep the hood-latch assembly and headlight buckets intact. Outdoor storage is OK for major sheet-metal parts, but before you put them outside, hose off any mud that was missed when you washed the car, and then allow everything to dry. Again, wire brush and spray-paint bare metal with enamel. If the fenders or hood were primed, but not painted, lightly sand the primer before enameling.

With that done, drain and remove the fuel tank. The tank may have to be shifted to one side and twisted slightly before it drops out. As soon as you figure out the combination, write it down in your notebook. The more notes you make now, the fewer mistakes you'll make when the car goes back together. Drain any gasoline from the tank, then blow out the remaining vapor. A gas tank that's been drained, but not purged of gasoline vapor is the most dangerous. Use compressed air for this. Or, *blow* out the vapor using a vacuum cleaner. Afterwards, seal the outlets with duct tape, not masking tape.

Next, remove the seats and floormats or carpets. Again, return all nuts and bolts to their holes or bag and tag them. Don't store seats or any upholstery outside. If you're out of indoor storage, borrow an unused garage

corner from a friend, relative or neighbor. To repeat: Keep the seats out of the weather at all costs. And even though stored indoors, cover them. Old shower curtains work well for this.

Remove Engine & Transmission—After you've completed the preliminary body disassembly and cleaned and stored all bits and pieces, turn your attention to the engine and transmission. Access to them will be easier now that the surrounding sheet metal has been removed.

If you'll be reusing the original engine as is, read the following section, then return to the following paragraph. However, if you are going to replace or rebuild it, proceed as follows.

Remove the battery and drain fluids from the radiator, engine and transmission. Then disconnect all hoses, lines, wiring and linkages. You can now remove the radiator, engine and transmission. Store the radiator in a safe place even though you don't plan on reusing it. I'll get back to it when we look at the cooling system, Chapter 22.

Don't Kill a Good Mill—Storing an engine that will be used at a later date as-is involves more than throwing a piece of plastic over it to keep off dust. Otherwise, moisture will enter through open valves, rusting valve seats and

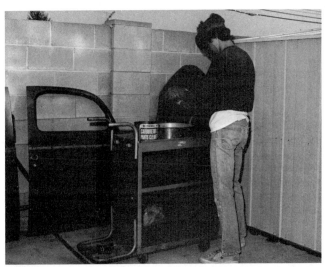

Major problem faced by every rod builder is storage. And the smaller the workshop, the more storage area you'll need. No matter what you have available, you'll soon fill it to capacity.

Although not always critical, clean greasy parts before storing them. Tag and bag *everything* you can't immediately re-identify.

cylinder walls. Gasoline in carburetor bowls evaporates, leaving behind a thick varnish-like residue. "Old" oil, with its accumulation of acids, attacks the bearing and bearing-journal surfaces it was supposed to protect.

If you expect your engine to immediately start after sitting idle for the duration of your project, then treat it like the expensive piece of equipment it is. Start by draining the oil and removing the filter. Refill the crankcase with fresh detergent oil and a polymer additive such as STP. The lubricant must cling to the rings. Install a new filter. Now, run the engine long enough to circulate the clean oil throughout. Then drain the coolant while the engine is still warm.

Remove the carburetor and drain every drop of fuel. Liberally squirt light machine oil or gun oil in the passages and pour some in the bowls. Finally, seal the carburetor in two plastic bags and store it.

Now, remove the distributor, water pump, fuel pump, spark plugs, intake and exhaust manifolds, and core plugs, commonly known as *freeze plugs*. Spin the crank a number of times and force air through each water-jacket opening in the block and heads, and intake and exhaust ports. This will ensure that the water jackets are as empty and dry as possible. Compressed air eases this task, but you can also use the old vacuum cleaner.

Rotate the crank some more and, while doing so, squirt oil into the intake and exhaust ports. This will rustproof the valve seats and faces. After this, pour fresh oil into each

cylinder to get a good coating on the walls and piston rings. It isn't necessary to remove the valve lifters, but pour oil over them.

After this profuse oiling, spray a liberal dose of demoisturizer, or water-dispersant oil, such as DOM, CRC or WD-40, into the ports and cylinders. Immediately replace the spark plugs and tape up the lifter valley, intake and exhaust ports. Duct tape, commonly called *racer's tape* or *200-mph tape,* works best for this. This will keep out dirt and moisture, and seal the demoisturizer in the engine. Finally, loosen the rocker arms enough to close all the valves. This seals each cylinder and minimizes valve-spring load.

Disconnect the battery, drain oil from the engine and manual transmission—fluid from an automatic—and pull out the engine and transmission as one unit.

Once out, separate the transmission and engine. Set the engine on a dolly or mount it on an engine stand. Bolt on the valve covers—if it's not a flathead—and intake manifold. Put it in a clean, dry spot, and wrap it well with plastic sheets or heavy-duty trash bags. Unless you are going to rebuild the transmission, wrap it up as well. You can forget about the engine and transmission for now, knowing they'll be in good condition come installation time.

What if your engine isn't worth saving? Maybe you'll have to pay someone to haul it away! But, if you're going to rebuild the engine or transmission that came with the car—or one you've acquired along the

way—you should still protect it from rust and corrosion. This is best done by leaving the engine or transmission assembled. The grime and crud will do a fair job of inhibiting rust. Further protect it by draining the fluids and drying it out. Then seal the engine or transmission in plastic sheets or bags.

BACK TO THE CAR

After all of the foregoing is squared away, buy or design and build a stout tow bar if you don't already have one. You'll need this for towing your car to various shops before it can move under its own power. Even if you have access to a car trailer, it's often easier to flat tow.

The first place to tow your prize is to a steam cleaner. Find one that shows more than a passing interest in doing a careful and thorough job. Tell 'em a little about your project and how important it is to you. Practice doing this now because many rod builders have learned the hard way. Most shops—steam cleaner, sandblaster, metalsmith or painter—don't care enough to do more than an average job. If it's top-quality work you want, let your enthusiasm rub off on them! Then, spend the time and money to get the car sparkling clean before you go any further.

When you get your car back home, carefully look it over. If you made the right purchase, you won't be disappointed or disenchanted with what you see with her "makeup" off.

8 Original Frames

Street-rodded '40 Ford frame is ready for driveline and body components.

The modern street-rod frame—main chassis component that supports the body—is a true hybrid. Its function as the body platform—original or repro body—must remain unhampered. However, it must be significantly modified in order to handle a big V8 or V6 and the accompanying drivetrain. Also, if an independent front or rear suspension is in the plans, the frame must be changed to accommodate mounting of either. The frame is, in short, the bridge between the old and new which is the essence of street rodding.

In the early days of street rodding, before World War II, builders recognized that the straight and narrow open-channel Ford Model T and A frame was hopelessly inadequate for even the moderate horsepower developed by hot four bangers and luke-warm flathead V8s. They were quick to note that the curvaceous 1932 frame with its substantial K-member was a major departure from the simple rails and 90° crossmembers that preceded it. Alert backyard builders were equally quick to acquire a '32 frame no matter what model body was slated to top it off.

The early hot rodders realized that a frame for a hot rod must handle increased loads and stresses. Even then, designing and fabricating a car frame was far more complex than building a hot engine. Yet the wiser old timers did their best to compensate for lack of technical expertise by using the most modern hardware

available. You must do no less. You owe it to yourself and your passengers to put the safest, most reliable frame possible under your vintage roadster or coupe body.

If you have or will elect to use a reproduction street-rod frame, turn immediately to Chapter 9. There's no need to learn how to inspect, repair and modify a production chassis. If you detect a hint of encouragement in my words, you're right. I've done a major chassis rebuild a time or two, and believe me, saving up the bucks for a repro frame is easier than slaving over a twisted, rusted piece of iron that has outlived its usefulness! You know what you have, so you be the judge.

FRAME TYPES

Before you can make an objective decision as to what constitutes a safe and reliable frame, you should know your options—at least theoretically. There are several types of original frames found under the typical street rod. First, those supporting the more primitive models—1920s through early '30s—are the straight twin-channel-rail type described above. These stock frames were inadequate when they were five or 10 years old. Today, such a frame is *totally* inadequate, regardless of how *mint* or fresh it may appear.

As for the '32 Ford frame, it's a classic beauty both in form and function. Today, it and its 1933—34 brothers are elderly, so

consider their structural integrity open to question. I'll discuss inspection later, but the biggest problem with early frames—even though some incorporate rudimentary triangulation—results from excessive twisting due to inadequate torsional stiffness of the unboxed, channel-section rails. On an uneven road surface, this twisting can adversely affect the integrity of the body and the stability of the car.

Generally speaking, Ford frames didn't reach a level of sophistication needed for street rods until the mid-'30s. Design-wise, the 1935—48 frame is a double-wall, full-perimeter type with triangulated—X-member—inner sections. They are *swayback* designs, which means that the section under the passenger compartment dips closer to the ground. It was then, as now, a good compromise, with regard to weight and size versus strength.

It is true some other American manufacturers improved their frame designs a few years earlier. It wasn't until the 1935 Ford appeared that hot rodders could rest easy. From then through 1948—generally accepted closing date for modified cars that carry the designation street-rod—unaltered Ford frames are structurally adequate. Of course, the ravages of time and amateur post-factory modifications can void this desirability.

Although I won't encourage you to build a frame from scratch, following are some design factors you should be aware of. X-braced frames of the mid-'30s were a belated recognition of basic structural engineering; that is, triangulation is the key to rigidity. Triangulated frame members provide much more torsional frame rigidty than square or rectangular members.

Another point of major significance is that an open-channel frame must have a very large crosssection to provide even mediocre rigidity. *Boxing* a channel section, which is closing in the open side of the channel with a steel plate of equal or greater thickness, increases the strength of the member *several hundred times*.

Body Mounting—A frame and body are separate structures that must be free to move relative to each other, although slightly. Consequently, a body should be mounted to a frame with *soft* mounts to isolate it from the frame. This is done by placing rubber pads on the frame, setting the body on the pads, then

Chassis builder Jim Kirby checks squareness of frame. Measure it diagonally from opposite corners and/or factory holes both ways. If two dimensions are the same, frame is square. If jack stands are square and level, there should be no gaps between stands and frame.

Diagonal measurements between the two reference points should be within 1/16 in. If not, frame should be straightened. Depending upon severity of frame tweak, you may be able to re-work it at home with a few rented tools . . . or you may have to farm it out.

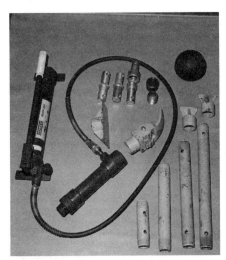

If you are only dealing with a minor *diamond*—out of square—and a few dents and ripples in the rails, you should be able to get frame back in shape at home with a rented tool such as the Walker Body-Jak.

Many street rods have fiberglass bodies. Consequently, a super-strong frame is required. Why? Unlike original steel bodies, fiberglass bodies add little or nothing to the overall strength of the vehicle. If you doubt this, ask a roadster owner whose car doors pop open every time he crosses the railroad tracks; or at worst, the poor soul who has to replace cracked windshields with regularity. So, forget an open-channel frame if you're going to use a 'glass body.

If you purchased vintage tin, decide whether or not the original frame is repairable. If it is, clean it up, find any problems, get replacement parts and practice repair techniques. If the frame isn't repairable, or if you've concluded that the repro frame is best for you, you then must pick and choose among the growing list of manufacturers and their wares.

If you're dealing with the remnants of an original frame, you may regret it before the

attaching them together with bolts through the rubber mounts.

Furthermore, although engine and suspension attachments must be extra strong, they should be mounted to the frame with rubber bushings or, as is more popular, urethane bushings. They should never be mounted directly to a frame. The classic cross-leaf buggy spring jammed into, and U-bolted to, the crossmember leaves much to be desired. An age-hardened rubber engine-mount *biscuit* isn't so hot either.

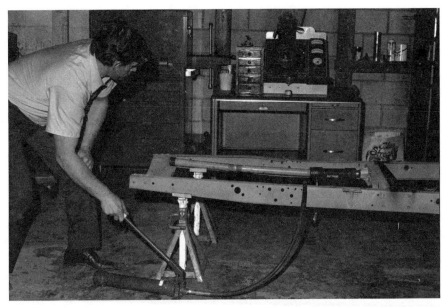

Using a Body-Jak to straighten frame: It doesn't do the straightening; it merely holds frame in square while you do the work. Care should be taken not to overstress frame and break loose any rivets.

While held in position, repair work, hot or cold, can proceed. Terry Berzenye prefers cold hammering because heating can warp frame unpredictably.

project is completed. If so, "bail out" sooner, rather than later. The longer you stew over the dilemma, the more costly—both in time and money—your unusable frame will become. I don't want to sound too gloomy, though. Not all original frames are refugees from the scrap heap . . . just a lot of them.

Model T Frame—First, I'll stick my neck out and say that *all* Ford Model T frames in existence and unattached to an original Model T are junk. Do anything you want with the one you have . . . except put it under your

street rod. A wide variety of replacement frames is available. Few are true reproductions—for reasons stated earlier in this chapter. Most are fabricated from a combination of rectangular and round tubing. A few duplicate the original specifications, but most have *kicked-up* rears, making them suitable for a variety of rear suspensions. So, if you are building a Model T-based street rod, think 100% reproduction.

I almost recommend doing the same if your car will be Model A based. The stock Model A is better than the Ts, but it was still a ladder-type design with two straight open channel side rails approximately 100-in. long. Three crossmembers—front, center and rear—are riveted to the side members with each corner reinforced by gusset plates or brackets. Front and rear crossmembers serve as spring mounts. Separate body-support brackets are riveted to the side rails.

Model A Frame—All Model A passenger-car frames are basically the same, although there are three slightly different designs. Only 200 of Design A were manufactured in late 1927. Design B was standard for all 1928—29 models. Design C, which incorporated a few new body bolt holes, was used from late 1929 until the end of production in early 1932.

Model A frames were built from 3/16-in.-thick steel. Thanks to rust, you may find yours to be a tad thinner. Even if not rusted, an original Model A frame is so old and inadequate for handling the loads imposed by a modern engine, the amount of work required to bring one up to par would justify going to a repro frame in nearly every case.

Nevertheless, you may be one of those rod builders who has a nice Model A frame and is willing to put the extra hours into it, particularly if you're planning to build a channeled roadster or coupe rather than a High Boy. And, since massaging this sinfully simplistic frame design into a suitable street rod structure is a time-honored pursuit, you should know about two of the more important construction options—*kicking* the rear and *boxing* the rails.

Of course, common sense dictates that nothing will be gained by jumping headlong into a major frame modification before you know what front and rear suspension you will use. You should also know what you want the car to look like. But, if you are contemplating the traditional buggy-sprung rear—cross-leaf spring—and a super-low look, a *kicked* frame is one way to get there.

Kicking the frame up in the rear—sometimes called *Z-ing*—allows the body of the car to be dropped as low as practical and still retain the Model A buggy spring.

In this operation, the frame is cut just forward of the rear axle. A new section of channel is spliced into each side rail. This is done so the rear quarter of the frame, inclusive of the rear crossmember, which houses the transverse spring, is repositioned 5—8-in. higher than the forward three quarters. Although this severely reduces trunk volume, it provides ample spring clearance over the rear axle.

Boxing the rails, as mentioned earlier, greatly increases frame strength. It all but eliminates sagging and twisting of the side rails.

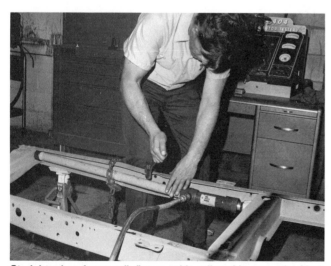

Straightening frame-rail flange with adjustable wrench: Modifications such as adding boxing plates, new engine and transmission mounts, or cosmetics such as hole filling, should be done on a reasonably sound, completely square chassis.

There is enough demand for channelled Model T's or A's to encourage several chassis manufacturers to include Z-ed repro frames as special-order items. If you have an old chassis, Model A patterns and instructions are available from Don McNeil's Specialized Auto Components.

Many original frames have had indignities heaped upon them such as a front- or rear-*horn chop*. Fortunately, some components manufacturers offer reproduction frame horns. This repair section is available from Progressive Automotive as are fronts and rears for 1932 and 1933—34 Ford frames.

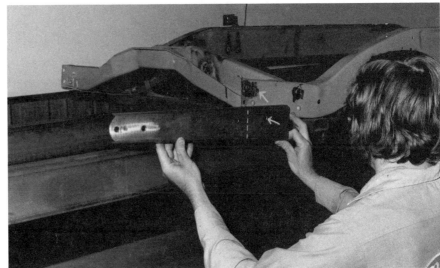

Replacing missing frame horns is relatively easy if you're a moderately skilled welder who can follow instructions. Horns are spliced onto rails to return frame to original condition.

The operation is quite simple. Make a cardboard pattern of the frame area to be boxed, then transfer the pattern to sheet stock—usually 1/8-in. thick. Cut out the steel and weld it in. If you don't feel like making patterns and cutting out steel blanks, several street-rod-component manufacturers catalog precut boxing plates that need only minor trimming before you can weld them in place, page 63.

'32 Ford Frame—The 1932 Ford frame is a tough one to deal with. For almost as many years as the sport is old, the Deuce frame has been the favorite means of support, not only for the classic Deuce body shell, but fenderless Model A roadsters and coupes as well. When it was still a teenager, the stock frame was plenty adequate for hopped up flatheads. However, by the time it had reached its "majority" and early OHV-engine swaps were applying higher loads to its handsome 1/8-in.-thick rails, metallurgical deficiencies began to show up.

There was another problem, too. The original K-type crossmember couldn't handle the longer and larger automatic transmissions. As a result, out came the hacksaws and torches—a practice that's about as old as hot rodding. Many frames were butchered to make room for the massive automatics. Once clearance for the transmission was achieved, the K-member was, as often as not, too flexible and unstable. Crude chunks of angle iron were often welded to it in an attempt to restore stiffness.

Nevertheless, the 1932 frame was a big jump forward from its weak-sister Model A frame, even if it still had no rearward support designed in. Although this latter problem was solved the very next year, no frame has ever

supplanted the Deuce for sheer grace and beauty in the misty eyes of the tradition-bound street rodder.

However, the value some street rodders place on an original frame is unrealistic. It isn't a rare work of art. It's just an assembly of mass-produced stamped-steel rails and crossmembers that have now been faithfully—for the most part—reproduced. The desirability of an "original" should not be confused with that of an original body. An original 1932 Ford steel body in most any condition will justify the economic cost of its restoration. It *is* a rare work of art.

But the frame is an important piece of working hardware which shouldn't be clouded with sentimentality. Most of the original '32 Ford frames that aren't in use should be sold to the purist restorer who will unleash no more than a 65-horsepower flathead within its confines.

1933—34 Ford Frame—What I said about the '32 Ford frame also applies to the '33—34 frame. Like the Deuce frame, when it was introduced it was a significant improvement over what had gone before—it was the first Ford frame with a true X-member. And, although it hasn't nearly the charisma of original Deuce rails, there are still those who take great pride in pointing to a clean factory-built frame. If it's near perfect, I'll go along with the program. If it isn't, you will be ahead in terms of effort, time and money if you save up for even a bare-bones repro.

1935—48 Ford Frame—I do an about face with the 1935—1948 Ford frames. These frames are well designed and built. Aside from those that have rusted away or have been

totally butchered—and many have—a '35—48 Ford frame is easily repaired if the body is removed. Repairs can then be done at a moderate cost by a skilled welder. There are, however, some original frames on the market that may be better than the one that came with the car.

Prices for average-condition 1935—38 frames are usually higher than those for 1939—42 frames. However, a choice 1939—40 frame will bring a pretty penny. Post-war models—1946 through 1948—are usually the least expensive. But, they are the least likely to be ruined.

Other Frames—Admittedly, I've left out non-Ford cars and frames. Of course, the variety is astronomical. After all, some 5000 different marques have been produced in the U.S. alone since the 1890s. Some have been in production for more than 50 years! Then there are the old foreign roadsters or coupes that can be converted into street rods. There's no end to potential street-rod candidates.

No, when it comes to the specifics of converting this or that to a street rod, we must lean on the traditional Ford choices for the most part. As for the rest, and there are some terrific possibilities, you must settle for "glittering generalities" of clean-up, inspection and repair.

BODY DOLLY

Whatever frame you start with, clean it thoroughly. To do this, you must lift off the body. That means further disassembly and, unless you have or build a *body dolly*, immobility of the body proper. A body dolly is nothing more than a small frame with wheels on which you set the body and can roll it around. Read on for how to build a body dolly.

Caution: If you have a *woodie*, removing the body from the frame can result in disaster. Most old woodie bodies are very weak so that when unsupported, the wood can break and the metal permanently deform. So, great care must be taken to provide adequate support for the body *prior* to any disassembly beyond removing the fenders and doors. Some builders, in fact, don't risk removing the body. Instead, they do the frame-restoration job with the woodie body left in place.

A body dolly is worthwhile regardless of how big or heavy the body is. After all, if you remove it from the frame, you must wrestle with all that sheet metal one way or another. However, if you followed my advice in Chapter 7, you've already removed and stored the hood, doors, seats, deck lid, fenders, running boards, gas tank, engine and transmission. The body is much lighter now that these components have been removed.

A crude but effective body dolly for a roadster or similar lightweight can be made from 2x4s. If yours is heavier, such as a four-door sedan, better use some well-seasoned 4x4s. Measure the length of the body from the firewall to the rear deck panel, and the width of its base. Build a slightly longer and slightly narrower rectangular frame using long carriage bolts for fasteners. Put flat washers under the nuts. Bolt a caster of adequate capacity on each corner and you're pretty much in business. It'll take a few hours and a little money to do it right, but you'll never regret having the dolly once it's done.

Remove Body—Now, the tough work begins. Find all of the body-attaching bolts and remove them. Don't be surprised if a few are reluctant. Chances are the body bolts have been rusted in place for as many years as the car is old. To help with loosening them, squirt some penetrating oil or light oil such as WD-40 on each and let it soak for several minutes. When you think you've removed them all, try lifting each corner of the body two or more inches.

When lifting, don't strain too hard. It's likely that you overlooked one or two bolts, cables or other things that pass through the body and frame. Find the problem and correct it before trying again.

Once the body is free, you should be able to lift each corner. Once you're satisfied it is ready to come off, put some drinks in the refrigerator and call at least three friends—five if your car is a sedan. Ask 'em if they'd like to come over and "hoist" a few. You needn't tell them that the "few" is a few hundred pounds.

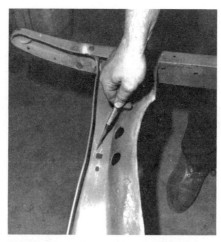

Check frame for cracks such as those radiating from mounting holes. Repair by welding. Consider adding doubler to area to prevent cracks from reoccuring.

You know what to do next: Once everybody is in place, pick up the body, carefully step over the frame rails and carefully lower it onto the dolly. Padding and contour-cut 2x4s placed under the mid-section and other unsupported locations will help prevent sagging and stressing. Convertibles and roadsters will greatly benefit from some interior 2x4 bracing and guy wires. The idea is to help the body, particularly 'glass, retain its shape and still be mobile. Now, roll the body out of the way, preferably to the farthest corner of the shop. We can now have a close look at the frame.

Chances are you won't be terribly impressed. Maybe just depressed once you see how much damage occurred to your frame over the years. You can now decide whether to run to the phone and order a repro frame . . . or enlist the services of a professional welder. However, if the frame is bad, you should have known before now. So, if you are going to continue with restoring the original frame, it's time to clean that ugly thing.

RESTORE FRAME

Inspect Frame—There are several ways you can go about it, but first remove all suspension components, brake lines and the many bits and pieces of hardware attached here and there. Prop up the frame on four jack stands and closely inspect it from one end to the other for telltail signs of collision damage. Check for cracks, splits and other irregularities. Make notes in your car diary of anything you must remember. Look closely between and behind double-wall sections. Once

you've checked the top side, flip the frame over and check again.

You won't be able to detect every flaw, but certainly the major ones. Once they're marked and neatly listed in your diary, you can contemplate them at your leisure. All of this thoughtfulness, of course, is merely a systematic way of determining what must be done to restore your frame to its factory-fresh state. This must be done before any modifications are made to fit the engine and mount the new front and rear suspensions.

Note: Don't take the frame down to bare metal until you're ready to start work on it. Otherwise, the bare surface will rust and you'll have more work to do.

Remove Rust—When you're ready to begin the clean-up in earnest, decide whether you will rent or purchase sandblasting equipment, farm out the sandblasting job or, if you have a Redi-Strip derusting franchise business in your area, cart your frame to that worthy establishment.

In descending order of effectiveness, I have no doubt that the Redi-Strip electrolytic-derusting process is the most efficient method of all. This is such a boon to the street rodder that I've devoted a substantial part of Chapter 24 to the process.

If you can't take your frame to a Redi-Strip facility for one reason or another, your only option is sandblasting. This is unfortunate because there's no way for a sandblaster to get around every corner and into the many nooks and crannies. However, whether it gets Redi-Stripped or sandblasted, your frame is ripe for immediate re-rusting. Therefore, make preparations for coating the frame with a preservative *before* you take the frame to the rust-removal "palace."

Prevent Rust—If immediately after rust removal, you can begin repairs and/or modifications, spray the entire frame with a de-moisturizer such as D-0-M or WD-40. A substantial coating is good for several weeks if it doesn't rain every day. If, however, you're uncertain when you can begin repairs and/or modifications, or you expect the frame will be exposed to excessive moisture, give it a healthy coat of primer and a light sealer-coat of inexpensive lacquer. Don't use enamel! It's too hard to remove or paint over.

Before you preserve the frame, though, inspect it closely. Pay particular attention to obvious stress areas—areas on the frame where high-load components mount, such as the steering, suspension, engine and transmission. Metal fatigue is caused by dynamic forces pulling, bending, twisting and compressing the frame over a long time period.

Re-Inspect—Check closely around the rivets. Cracks frequently begin just under

If frame is too severely damaged to take on the repair job yourself, send it to a professional for evaluation and repair. Such was the case with this Deuce Tudor that suffered a blow on the left front axle. Frame gage indicates driver's side is too low.

Heat is applied to deformed area while car securely chained in frame alignment machine. Then . . .

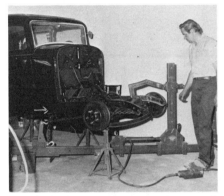

. . . hydraulic pressure is exerted on rail. More heat may have to be applied.

rivet heads and radiate outward. After you've found the cracks, don't lose track of them. Make a few annotated sketches in your trusty notebook and after you have given the frame its temporary preservative job, mark them with a daub of red paint.

With the exception of a few tiny cracks under rivet heads and similar high-stress points, finding many of the predictable problems in an old frame won't require the deductive abilities of a Sherlock Holmes. Big ragged holes testify as to their exact location. But sometimes a frame can be in bad shape literally. Sometimes? Make that many times! Damage is not always obvious, either. Often, a frame is twisted only 1 in. or so out of alignment. But that is plenty even if you can hardly see it.

If yours doesn't quite "look right" and you suspect that it is indeed out of shape, don't

panic. Just start looking for a good body-and-frame man—not just *any* body-and-frame man. There's one in every collision shop that caters to fast-buck insurance work. You need a skilled craftsman who sincerely appreciates fine automobiles and who is ready and willing to work on one. These fellows are around, and usually their reputations are well known within the street-rod community.

As you might imagine, old Fords, with their soft and unsupported frames, are particularly vulnerable to heavy frame damage even from a relatively minor collision. The lack of an X-member in the Ts, As and Bs means that they're almost wide open in the center. Even a moderate blow can upset the side-to-side alignment of the frame . . . and everything attached to it.

The reason you need more than a casual tradesman to do a frame alignment is because he must have a thorough mastery of sophisticated frame equipment. The basic instrument is a precision frame gage—a unit composed of two cross bars moving in opposite directions through a center assembly. The gage has a sighting pin in the exact center of the assembly, and when three or more are hung from a frame, the operator can read the degree and direction of misalignment.

Diamond—The first thing the frame man will do to a suspect frame is run a *diamond* check. A diamond-shaped frame—one that is out of square—is not always easy to see. The center section must be true so the remainder can be compared with it. So the alignment man checks for a diamond condition by setting up his special gages, one just behind the front crossmember, and one just before the rear crossmember.

With a square frame, the center pins in the sighting bar of one gage will align with the pins in the other gage. If the frame is *not* square, the line of sight will be at an angle to the frame centerline, and the center pins in the other gage will be to one side of the line of sight.

As you can imagine, the diamond check is particularly useful for early Ford frames if the car was ever struck broadside or on a front or rear corner. Improper modifications to the crossmember make things worse, of course, but even normal, troublefree driving for 40 or more years is likely to distort the frame. Builders of 1937—48 Ford-based street rods have less of a problem. These heavy X-membered cars are much less prone to the condition.

Other checks the frame specialist should make include one for twist of the central section; one to ascertain that the full length of the frame conforms to the original center; and level—flatness of the overall frame.

Datum-Line Check—Another critical test of frame trueness is the *datum line*. Here the height of each frame rail is measured by sighting across the top side of the gage cross bars and reading against a vertical scale. Finally, measurements are taken to ensure that the front- and rear-suspension radius rods or lower control arms are correctly positioned and that any suspension crossmembers are of the correct width. Problems here can create problems with front- or rear-wheel alignment later.

A precision frame gage, however, only tells the frame man what's wrong and how much. The machine that corrects frame-alignment problems is the frame aligner. It's a rather large machine that steadies one frame rail while it exerts a force on the opposite rail.

FRAME REPAIR

Ordinarily, a frame can be *pulled*—straightened—cold, but occasionally heat must be applied. Unfortunately, once a riveted frame has been damaged, it cannot be fully restored. The rivet holes are stretched at the time of impact. Consequently, one way to keep a once-damaged frame in proper realignment is to heat and hammer down the loosened rivets and then weld the crossmembers to the frame rails while the frame is supported by the frame-alignment machine. Another, more expensive way would be to completely disassemble the frame by drilling out the rivets, weld up the rivet holes, redrill them, then re-assemble the frame using new rivets.

Frame alignment isn't just for the wreck-damaged street rod. It is also good for a frame that will receive substantial repair or modification. I'll discuss that later. For now, let's take a look at—and start working on—some of the "shot"-rodder-caused frame damage you may encounter.

The first step is to place the frame securely on four jack stands, each adjusted to the same height. You'll also need about six large C-clamps and several hefty Vise-Grip locking pliers. Four 6-ft lengths of heavy-wall 1 X 3-in. rectangular tubing will also come in handy.

The next thing to do is find a smooth, level area on your workshop floor. This part of rod building is literally from the ground up, so you must have a level surface on which to place the jack stands. In short, don't build in a new problem by welding your frame on a floor that's uneven due to low spots or settling cracks. Make sure the jack stands are positioned in the same places across from one another and that the frame remains level.

With help from a friend, measure diagonally from both front and rear corners of the frame. The diagonal measurements will be equal if the frame is perfectly square. When measuring, it's very important to measure from the same reference points on both side rails. The best points are factory bolt holes or rivets. That's because the rails were stamped originally, and those are the only holes you can depend on being in exactly the same location on both sides.

Both diagonal measurements should be within 1/16-in. If not, you already have a diamond problem and, depending upon its magnitude, you may have to seek the services of that professional frame-alignment man before you go further.

With the frame sitting on four leveled jack stands, you shouldn't be able to slide a sheet

of typing paper between it and any of the jack stands. If you can, or worse, if you can see daylight between any of the two, the frame is "tweaked," or twisted. The amount of twist will determine the effort required to reduce it. A minor gap—and that is defined as up to 1/8 in.—can be corrected at home when you're welding in new crossmembers.

If the gap is really bad, you may be better off getting it pulled back into alignment before you do any welding. Welding alone will make things worse. Adding stiffness to a tweaked frame such as when boxing, Z-ing or replacing crossmembers, makes realignment much more difficult.

Welding—Once you've determined that your frame is square enough to proceed, begin welding—electric welding, that is (wire feed, Heli-arc or arc welding). Frame material is too thick for gas welding. If your frame is in average condition, there are a number of operations you should undertake. Because such operations vary with regard to the danger of introducing misalignment, start with the simplest—*hole filling*. Normally, filling holes won't tweak the frame.

Filling holes will afford you safe passage through unraveling the metallurgical mysteries of your particular frame. For example, 40 different steel alloys were used in the manufacture of the Ford Model A car! There's no telling what might be lurking in the crystalline innards of the frame you have!

Installation of a repro front or rear crossmember, or a replacement X-member, is trickier than filling holes, but still relatively easy on frame alignment—if you follow the up-coming advice. The same goes for tubular engine mounts and rear-suspension coil-over-shock mounts.

Probably the most critical operation—in terms of potential frame warpage—is welding in boxing plates. Nevertheless, to be on the safe side, you should ensure against warpage any time you apply high heat to the frame.

The best way to repair or modify a frame is with an accurate holding fixture—*frame jig . . .* period! Unfortunately, you probably don't have access to one. And, you can't run to the frame-alignment shop every other week. Therefore, you'll have to use a little ingenuity. To help prevent warpage, position something heavy on the front and rear of the frame before you do any welding. If heavy enough, this will keep the frame from lifting off the jack stands or shifting around when you are welding, pounding or grinding on it.

Although crude looking, a rear-axle assembly or old engine block chained to the frame on each end will work fine.

Replace Crossmember—Replacing a stock front or rear crossmember with a new repro or one designed for an independent suspension

Original frame modified for street-rod use will have some unnecessary holes. Large ones should be filled by welding. Holes 1/2-in. or smaller, however, can be repaired with special brazing rod that melts at about 800F, which means less distortion.

Abrasive discs are used to remove scale and rust, smooth torch cuts and welds, and round off sharp corners.

Countersink frame holes to provide bevel on which to build up braze, lead or putty when filling. Stick lead and plastic body fillers work well on small holes.

Use paste tinning compound to remove oxides, then heat and apply lead with gentle flame to minimize distortion.

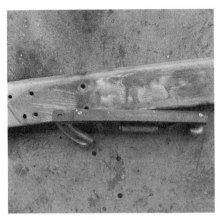

Body file is used to smooth areas filled with lead.

Master street-rod builder, Boyd Coddington, recommends stick lead to fill minor frame imperfections after brazing.

When using plastic filler to fill holes in frame, tape back side to prevent *drip-through.*

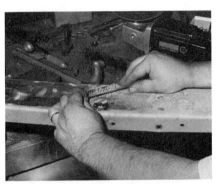

Hardened plastic is shaved flush with *cheese grater.* Follow by smoothing with #36 open-coat paper on sanding block.

is common practice. But, removing the old crossmember is time consuming. Also, the longer you work on it at one sitting, you will probably apply more heat or force than you should. So, before you remove any major frame component, trim two pieces of rectangular tubing slightly longer than the frame width and clamp them on the top and bottom of the rails. Next, cut out a section from the center of the old crossmember. With the load lessened on the side rails, burn or grind off the rivet heads and drill them out. You should now be able to remove the remainder of the crossmember with relative ease. During this operation, make sure the side rails are held firmly in place.

With the frame rails clamped and loaded, make the necessary measurements and trim the replacement member to size and shape. By the way, a certain amount of gentleness is necessary when a new frame section is being fitted.

I am not going to try to teach you how to weld or work metal at this time. And I really don't have to; at the end of the book, you'll find a complete listing of in-depth HPBooks on this and other pertinent subjects. However, I should mention the fact that the amateur frame builder's most common mistake is trying to use a welding rod that's too big. The consensus of professional opinion is that 1/8-in. rod is just about right—approximately the same diameter and thickness of the material welded. And, if you are not sure about the correct welding heat range, don't experiment on a good part of your frame.

Practice welding on an old crossmember or other metal scrap cut from the frame. And, of course, we are talking about electric welding. Don't even think about gas-welding your frame.

After you've finished welding, don't remove the clamps before the welds have cooled enough to touch.

Boxing—Boxing an old frame is one of the biggest headaches with regard to maintaining frame alignment. Keeping the front and rear of the frame loaded will lengthen the time required to complete the job, but will minimize frame warpage.

As described earlier in this chapter, boxing plates can be cut from steel sheet stock. Or, pre-cut plates can be purchased from one of several street-rod-components companies that catalog them. Before you start welding in the boxing plates, hand fit them in the channels to make sure the frame flanges are flat and there are no apparent interference problems. Gentle heating and some hammer work may be in order.

Reinforced aluminum-oxide grinding discs are made of several layers of material and grit bound in one-piece construction. Discs are designed to grind and shape metal. Eye protection is a must.

Original decades-old early Ford chassis, rebuilt and modernized, offers viable approach if you wish to minimize cost and are not afraid to replace bucks with labor. This is Pete & Jake's update of a Model A frame.

and around the rear crossmember. The plates should be fitted part way into the opening of the frame-rail C-section. Push in the plate so about half of the top and bottom edges of the plate are exposed. This will allow you to lay in a substantial fillet weld along the edges of both pieces of material.

When everything looks right, start welding from the *center* of the plate, skipping back and forth toward the ends. Lay 8-in. beads at a time—no longer—changing from side to side of the frame. This will balance out any warpage.

Depending on your skill as a welder, you may be able to do the whole job without turning over the frame, but that's needlessly cutting corners. When somebody looks at the finished job, chances are he will look at the bottom side edge. So, for maximum neatness and ease of welding, flip over the frame to do the bottom. This means repositioning the ballast, but it will be worth it.

Make sure the welds are cool before you unload or move the frame. If you take your time, you should be able to do all the foregoing work without warping the frame significantly. Nevertheless, when all major frame modifications have been completed, check frame alignment.

Conclusion—The cost of straightening a badly damaged frame, even one as simple as the typical early Ford, can be several hundred dollars. A frame that is found to have a minor tweak or one that has been warped by careless welding can be made right for less. Even so, it's worth it, although a hundred-dollar bill ain't chicken feed. So, take precautions to ensure that what you do is done right.

The key here, as everywhere else in the construction of a street rod, is patience.

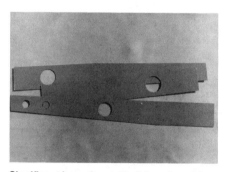

Significant boon for rod builder who wishes to update original chassis is the boxing-plate kit. Again, several manufacturers including Specialized Auto Components and Progressive Automotive offer kits complete with instructions for a variety of early Ford frames.

Typically, a frame is boxed between the front crossmember and the start of the X-member, and in the area of new crossmembers. Boxing the full length of older rails is not normally done for street-rod applications. The danger of distorting the rails is too great. *Fully boxed* is a common term, however. It usually refers to boxing that begins just behind the front crossmember, goes to the firewall area, around the center crossmember,

Once you're satisfied with their fit, determine if there are any places on the inside frame rail where you will bolt brackets or components. If so, weld in nuts or small sections of 1/4-in. plate. Later, you can drill and tap the plate with the desired thread. If, however, you elect to weld in pre-threaded fasteners, remember that heat distorts the threads. This means that the threads must be *chased* before you can run a bolt through—at least by hand. Consider also that it's easier to fill in unwanted holes before you begin the boxing process.

Tungsten inert gas—*TIG*—welding is best for installing boxing plates with minimal chassis distortion. Using conventional homeshop arc welder is possible if you proceed slowly and deliberately.

ABRASIVE-DISC GRITS

Refinishing Operation	Abrasive Type	Recommended Grit
Removing rust, scale and paint.	Open coat	16, 24
Grinding welds.	Abrasive wheel	
First-step metal conditioning.	Closed coat	24, 36
First-step featheredging.	Open coat	80, 100
Second-step final finish.	Closed coat	220, 320

Open-coat sanding discs are available in grits from #16 to #120. The disc backing is 50% to 70% covered with abrasive grains to prevent clogging. Discs that have smaller grit numbers are coated with abrasive that is more coarse and more widely spaced than those with larger numbers. Open-coat discs are designed to remove paint and to grind down welds, as well as lead and other soft materials that clog the abrasive and reduce cutting efficiency.

Closed-coat discs have very-coarse (#16) to extremely fine (#320) abrasive. The abrasive particles are as tightly packed together. Closed-coat discs are designed for work where the ground-off particles will not clog the disc. In general metalwork, an open-coat disc is used first to remove metal, then a closed-coat disc is used for final smoothing.

If reproduction frames were not available, chances are that more than one early Ford body would languish unsupported in the corner of a garage. This repro '32 chassis was built around Roy Fjastad's Deuce Factory rails.

Repro Frames—Reasonable facsimiles of original frames began auspiciously about 15 years ago when the pioneers of today's street rod industry began manufacturing the parts necessary to restore original frames.

Predictably, the first repro frame parts were for the '32 Ford. As mentioned earlier, its K-member took the brunt of punishment handed out by well-meaning, but unknowing hot rodders of an earlier day. One of the first replacement components to hit the scene was Dick Hendrix' "Chassis In A Box"—a bolt-in *X-member* for the Deuce. The kit—packaged and mailable, hence the name—was designed so the rod builder could bolt its 1/8-in. mild-steel channel sections into the frame following removal of what was left of the original center section. Although the fore members were somewhat longer than their stock counterparts, they fit in the position of the original K-member. The transmission cradle, however, was moved rearward and the rear members, which had no counterparts in the original frame, bolted to the side rails through existing holes.

Along about the same time, Jerry Kugel of Kugel's Komponents in Whittier, California,

Much, if not all, of the previous chapter can be skipped if you elect to use a reproduction frame. If that's the case, this is the chapter for you.

The reproduction-frame industry, which followed closely on the heels of the reproduction-body industry, is a blessing to the street rodder. Whether the average fellow realizes it or not, repro body and frame manufacturers—most of 'em street rodders themselves—breathed life back into a stagnant sport.

Tube Frames—The frame end of the repro street-rod business began with basic tube frames built for Fad Ts back in the late '50s. These are not reproduction frames. But, they are more than adequate for the task at hand—safely supporting the body, engine, driveline and suspension components.

A tube frame may or may not be strong enough for a supercharged V8. Fortunately, most street-rod builders can judge what's excessive horsepower for a given frame. If there's any question, the manufacturer will make recommendations.

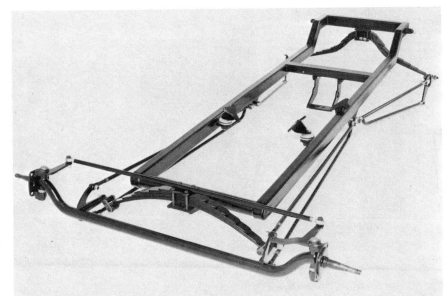

California Custom Roadster's fine example of traditional T-bucket frame is manufactured from 2 X 3-in. rectangular tubing with 3/16-in. wall. Rear frame rails kick up to achieve maximum practical lowness.

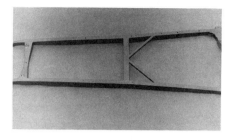

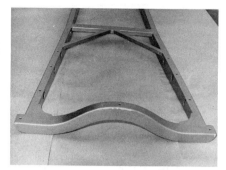

Excellent Model A repro built by Ed Moss of TCI Engineering fame was one of the first street-rod frames for other than the Fad T. When I first met Ed he was building them part-time all by his lonesome. TCI, one of the largest street-rod-component manufacturers in the country, offers frames in any stage of construction with a variety of crossmembers and body brackets.

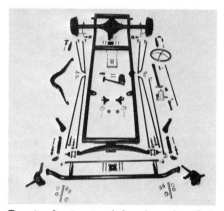

Beauty of a street-rod chassis such as California Custom Roadster's offering is more than the fact that it is new. It can also be ordered in kit form with all matching support bracketry—and a number of components—from a single source.

started marketing precision-formed reproduction front frame-rail sections. Jerry's replacement rails were designed to accept the Jaguar independent front-suspension. Regardless, with or without the special crossmember and fancy cat's paws, they are near-exact duplicates of the Deuce front horns that took such a beating during the early years of the '32's popularity.

Front horns weren't the only mangled members of the stock '32 Ford frame. As popular as it is today, the *High-Boy Deuce* sitting tall and mighty atop a full-length frame wasn't always the street-rodder's favorite. If the truth be known, the channeled roadster—cut down as low as it could go—was what our forebears considered the "in thing." If that seems strange, just recall the ride height of everything else in the '30s and '40s.

Channeling, of course, is an extensive operation. It entails cutting out the floor pan,

dropping the body over the frame and moving the body hangers up. The floorpan is then rewelded back in. The driver and his passengers, in effect, sit right on top of the frame. Unfortunately, the channeling of a '32 Ford was not done without *dehorning* (bobbing) the back end of the frame—the last 18—20 in. were unceremoniously chopped off.

That's what they used to do. All that changed in the early '70s, when the High Boy look caught fire on the West Coast. More than one old-timey "channel job" underwent yet another change—an *uplifting,* if you will. During the mid-1970s and when the need for back side refurbishment became apparent, Alan Maas began manufacturing exact duplicate rear frame horns in his shop in South Gate, California. These repro frame horns neatly fitted to a bobbed Deuce frame. Unfortunately for us, Alan has gone on to other things.

Progressive Automotive of Baltimore, Ohio established their reputation by way of independent front-suspension kits. Frames are available with Mustang independent front suspension and triangulated, rear suspension coil-over-shock units for many popular Ford and Chevy bodies.

Variation on Progressive Automotive theme is their Pro Street '34 Ford chassis with rear of frame narrowed to accept extra-wide tires. Axle is narrowed 9-in. Ford, suspended by TCI coil-over-shock shocks and located with the Progressive bar and bracket system. Similarly styled frame is also available for '32 and '35—48 Ford and '31—32 and '34—35 Chevy Standard bodies.

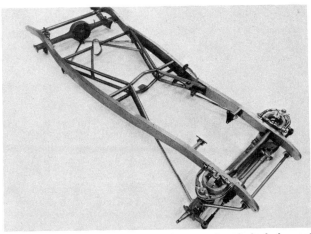

Complete Linken 1933—34 Ford repro chassis includes extra frame triangulation with integral drive-shaft hoop, urethane-bushed engine mounts, and transmission, master-cylinder and brake-pedal mounts.

Linken Manufacturing, Ltd. coil-over suspended frame provides support for Ford Model A pickup.

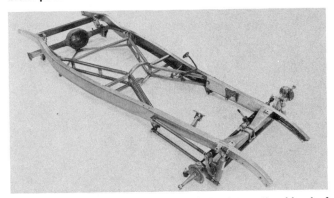

Linken's reproduction Deuce frame is an interesting blend of boxed rails and double-tube X-member construction.

As exemplified by Specialized Auto Components' rolling advertisement, most popular street-rod chassis incorporates mild to major variations on original theme.

Don McNeil's Specialized Auto Components reproduction 1933—34 Ford frame is designed with the needs of the rod builder in mind.

Two men are primarily responsible for the really big jump forward in repro frames. They are Ed Moss of TCI Engineering, who is the man who brought us the first successful repro Model A frame, and Roy Fjastad of the Deuce Factory, who set the street-rodding world on its ears with his reproduction 1932 frame rails.

By the time the former circle-track race-car builder Ed Moss brought his Model A frame to market, there were enough patch pieces and crossmembers available to completely refurbish either the Model A or '32 frame. Using the pieces, many a rod builder spent hours welding on a sad frame in an effort to bring it back to life. But, Ed Moss changed all of that in one fell swoop. His labor of love was a dimensionally exact duplicate of Henry's 1928—31 frame, but fabricated from 2 X 4-in. mild-steel rectangular tubing. The fully boxed frame deviated from the original in other ways as well, particularly since it in-corporated a redesigned K-member that stretched out rearward in the direction of the rear crossmember. It was, and is, a product for the street-rod market. Rod builders loved it from the start.

It wasn't long after the TCI frame was publicized that another former race-car build-er woke up the street-rod fraternity. Roy Fjas-tad jumped in feet first with perfect replicas of the 1932 right and left frame rails, precision die stamped on a 1000-ton press. This was expensive mass production just like the big boys do it, hence the company name, "The Deuce Factory."

Ed and Roy ventured where others had peeked, but feared to tread. And, what must have seemed like real gambles at the time ultimately proved to be wise business moves. Today, they and their colleagues have given the street-rod sport the kind of future it never would have had otherwise.

See Supplier Index at the back of book.

10 Engines

Louisiana-based Bill Schmidt's *three-quarter-race* flathead is a prime example of nostalgia rodding. Modified early Ford power plants remain part and parcel of the contemporary street scene. So much so that new parts such as aluminum heads and intake manifolds are available. Photo courtesy Don Winn.

If there's one item that could be credited for bringing street rodding into existance, it was the demand for more power—speed! In the early days of hot rodding, speed was the only thing that mattered. Of the countless worn-out Model T and A roadsters that fell into the hands of young men with mechanical talents, a goodly number of them received some kind of high-performance modification. Such modifications ranged from the installation of a bigger carburetor all the way to dual overhead-cam conversions.

TRADITIONAL STREET-ROD ENGINE

Within a few years of the introduction in 1932 of the Ford flathead V8, engine swapping became—and has remained—the primary interest of the street rodder.

In the decade following the appearance of Henry's pride and joy, nearly all vestiges of the Models T, A, B and C four-cylinder engines were gradually eliminated in favor of the *bent eight*. And, when that was accomplished, the focus of hot rodding was on the flathead V8 going from 21- to 24-stud heads and the addition of rudimentary, but effective, commercial *speed equipment*.

As Henry and staff improved the flathead and displacement grew from 221 cubic inches in 1932 to 255 cubic inches for the '53 Mercury, engine swapping was relatively simple. The only true swap, of course, involved the popular 1923—27 Model T and 1928—31 Model A chassis. And, because the original four-cylinder cars used completely different engine and transmission mounts, the art and practice of engine swapping was born.

Early swappers had it relatively easy. They only had to fabricate new front engine supports and bolt or weld them to the frame rails. And, since it wasn't practical to use the Model T or A transmission with the flathead—bolt patterns were different—the equally improved transmission was installed with the engine as a single unit. Of course, that meant that a rear mount had to be fabricated and the wishbone split. Also, a new clutch linkage was required, a throttle linkage devised, and

on and on . . . . Finally, when a legal exhaust system was deemed necessary, street rodding proper had arrived.

It wasn't until the early '50s that engine variety began to spice up the lives of street rodders. Oldsmobile, Cadillac and even Studebaker V8s suddenly looked interesting. Within a few years, the mighty Hemi had made its debut. And by the middle of the decade, the small-block Chevy entered center stage. Today, one or two of the old favorites are very much with us, but the rules of the game have changed. Brute horsepower is, in many cases, not as important as it once was. Instead, driveability is far more important.

ENGINE-SWAP CHOICES

Like everything else in the wide, wide world of street rodding, you have a vast array of power plants from which to choose. Big-city wrecking yards are full of more or less modern engines for you to sniff out.

Unfortunately, the majority of modern American engines may not excite you. Many are low on power and long on emissions-control paraphernalia that even mechanically astute hobbiests can't come to terms with. Leave some smog widget off and the engine may run so poorly you'll have some sleepless nights. Worse, the engine may not start! On top of all this, modern engines have low compression, retarded cam timing, impossible-to-adjust carburetors, and equally impossible ignition systems. For these reasons and the fact that newer engines are more costly, you may decide to simply pass them by unless you're interested in mini-engines. I'll discuss these later.

Rather than get into a lot of details about smog engines with the bottom line of "who wants one anyway?", let's go to the known favorites: 1965—72 Chevy and Ford small-block V8s and, to a lesser extent, small-block MoPars, and a few selected big-block models from here and there . . . plus the engine that started it all, the Ford flathead V8.

There's no question. The small-block Chevy is the street-rodder's favorite engine, bar none! Flathead lovers read from the Book of Tradition and worship at the shrine of the 59AB. Ford small-block street rodders are equally proud of their Henry heritage, and have a strong desire to keep it all in the family. MoPar rodders brag about engineering

Small-block Chevy is the street-rod builder's all-time favorite. It's been installed in about 60% of all street rods built since the early '60s. Note *ram's horn* exhaust manifold. Although not the best for performance, engine installation is usually easier.

One problem sometimes encountered in the installation of the small-block Chevy is interference between rear-mounted distributor and firewall. Not so in spacious early-'30s engine compartments.

Significant advantage of using small-block Chevy is the high-performance equipment available for it, both new and used. Not only that, everything from specially machined accessory-drive pulleys to motor mounts to headers can be mail ordered for all early Ford installations.

Bow-Tie small-block does not fit inline-six engine compartment quite as well as it does early Fords', but GM fans love it so much that minor installation problems are tackled with relish.

innovation and superiority. Regardless, the small-block Chevy V8 is installed in more street rods than all other engines combined! I did some research in 1985 and found that approximately 60% of all street rods in existence were small-block Chevy powered. I wasn't surprised. So, let's start with it.

Small-Block Chevy V8—The small-block Chevy was introduced in 1955 as a 265 cubic inch, 90°, overhead-valve V8. It had a 3.75-in. bore and 3.00-in. stroke. The two-barrel-carb version developed 162 horsepower at 4400 rpm and 257 pound-feet of torque at 2200 rpm; the four-barrel version developed 180 horsepower at 4600 rpm and 260 pound-feet of torque at 2800 rpm. From the beginning, it was apparent that the little V8 was a *high winder* rather than a *stump puller*. And,

because more drag races have been won with rpm than brute torque, that suited the hot rodders of the day just fine.

Two years after its debut, the Chevy V8 was boosted to 283 cubic inches, then to 327 in 1962, 350 in 1967, and 400 cubic inches in 1970. In 1967 a short-lived 302-cubic inch version was slipped in and a 307-cubic inch version was introduced in 1968. All models were well received, with the exception of the 400-cubic inch engine. It never gained much of a following among enthusiasts because of the subtle but significant performance reductions required by the expansion of the block to a displacement never envisioned by the original designers.

Kurt Thorson's '36 Ford five-window coupe seems to have swallowed small-block Ford he shoehorned in. Normally Ford engine does not install easily because of deep front oil sump, but Thorson replaced stock oil pump with Weaver Brothers' external dry-sump oil pump, eliminating need for deep-sump oil pan.

My cherished small-block Ford powered '40 coupe almost never came to be once I realized that considerable firewall surgery would be required. I think it was worth it to "keep it all in the family."

Ford 351C squeezed into Deuce coupe: Although installation is difficult, engine is popular among FoMoCo fans. Terry Berzenye's lavishly chromed Cleveland should attract even more converts.

Small-block Chevys and Fords aren't the only answer. Consider potent late-'60s/early-'70s 350-CID Buick. Adaptable V8 is light, compact, has rear oil-pan sump and front-mount distributor.

Today, the 350 reigns supreme due to its superb performance potential, but the 283 ranks quite highly because of its fabled good mileage. Complete engines of every caliber are readily available, though, and the tremendous supply of aftermarket equipment of every description, both new and used, promises to keep the small-block Chevy in the majority of street rods for many years to come.

Not only is the small-block Chevy an outstanding performer, this performance is contained in a package that is almost the same size, shape and weight as the Ford flathead V8—the engine it replaced in 90% of all street-rod type cars ever built. Where it differs, the nod is in favor of the Chevy!

Small-Block Ford V8—Not *all* street rodders grab the Chevy and run, however. There is a significant percentage who choose to install the often awkward small-block Ford V8. They maintain that, after all, it is Henry Ford's products that form the backbone of street rodding, and as such they should be outfitted with power by Ford. And who can argue with them? Certainly not I.

The FoMoCo small-block series—the 221-260-289-302-351-cubic inch Windsor castings—is technically described by the company as being the skirtless, thin-wall, 90° V family. The outstanding feature of Ford's version of the 90° V design is its compactness and lightweight features; of course, it shares with its crosstown rival. Like most overhead-valve V8s of the last 25 years, the small-block Ford block is *oversquare*—bore-diameter dimension is greater than stroke.

Ford was the first company to develop precision thin-wall casting techniques to control warpage and bore misalignment, and they made the most of it in their early ad copy. When the high-performance 289 was introduced—it was rated at 271 horsepower—it was shrewdly pointed out that the engine weighed only 480 pounds.

The lightweight block is available in a variety of displacements in 40-cubic inch increments, ranging from the minuscule 221 all the way to the 351 Windsor. The *Windsor* designation differentiates the small-block-based 351 from the 351 cubic inch *Cleveland* cast at the Ford foundry in Cleveland, Ohio, or 351W and 351C, respectively. The Windsor engine weighs closer to 500 pounds, but that's lighter than the 580-pound small-block Chevy. Because of its 1.30-in.-taller block, the 351W is slightly bulkier than the 289/302.

Finally, there's the Boss 302 with its solid-lifter cam, forged pistons, and canted-valve, large-port cylinder heads. Standard in the 1969 and '70 Boss 302 Mustangs, these engines are in short supply. The high-revving Boss 302s are also expensive due to the high demand for them.

The standard 302 is more plentiful than the 351W and, when mildly modified, is more than adequate for the average street rod. This brings up the major problem with the small-block Ford, which is not its performance potential. The problem is the small-block Ford's front-mounted oil pump and front-sump oil pan. This makes it much more difficult to install in the 1933—48 Ford than the small-block Chevy.

Most small-block Ford engine-to-early-Ford chassis swaps require the Bronco oil pan. With this setup, the oil-pump pickup and oil-pan sump is moved rearward, just behind the center of the engine. Installations in the Model A and 1932 Ford are not quite as difficult as in later models. Another approach is to relocate the firewall sheet metal rearward; however, the Ford-based street rod can have modern Dearborn power, and I confidently expect that the number—which is now about 15%—will grow.

In favor of the small-block Ford, it has a front-mounted distributor. This makes for better packaging and easier servicing. Also, pre-'65-1/2 small-block Ford five-bolt bell-housings have plenty of room in early Ford transmission tunnels.

351C Ford—The "big" small-block Ford is a bit less popular with Ford rodders than the small blocks. Three major versions of the 351 Cleveland exist: two-barrel carb, the four-barrel carb, and the Boss. As desirable as the high-performance Boss is, its availability is so limited as to be insignificant. The regular production 351C sports large cylinder heads very similar to the fabled Boss 302.

Although the 351C block is a true thin-wall casting and has the same bore spacing and head-bolt pattern as the Windsor series engines, it doesn't have a separate die-cast aluminum timing-chain cover. Instead, the timing-chain cover is cast integral with the block. Coolant is routed from the heads through the block to the radiator, rather than from the heads and through the intake manifold.

Other Engines of Interest—Although not used in the numbers of those just described, there are a few relatively modern V8s that street rodders have been partial to. For instance, the 400/455 Olds is fairly popular, a smattering of MoPars keeps their marque afloat even if the variety runs from the 318 to 440 CID. And, the Ford FE family, which includes the truck rodder's favorite 390, still shows up under an early hood every once in a while. So, for those who wish to be different, here are a few more choices which have found a suitable home betwixt street-rod fenders:

Small-Block MoPar V8—If all you wanted was a lightweight, compact V8 that swapped easily and produced more than its share of

If maximum horsepower is not your top priority, a modern power plant with ease of installation may be for you. Long-running OHC FoMoCo 2.0- and 2.3-liter four bangers have found homes in early Henrys from Model A's to '40 pickups. You'll have your power, too, if engine is turbocharged.

1927 Dodge is fitted nicely with early '70s 340-CID Dodge. Fit is superb, with performance to match. Small-block MoPars are fine for early Ford installations, too.

horsepower, you'd be hard pressed to find a better engine than Chrysler's long-lived little one. Unfortunately, the engine is hardly considered by early Ford builders at all. The nod of popularity comes from early MoPar rodders even though it is a worthwhile choice if you dare to be different.

Big-Block Chevy—The big-block has found a home in about 5% of the street rods currently on the road. This engine is for those who like brute horsepower. Introduced in 1965 and available in its early years in both 396- and 427-cubic inch versions, the big-block Chevy has never failed to satisfy the ego of any rodder who could afford to regularly replace rear tires.

Contributing in large part to the big-block's awesome power is its cylinder-head design: canted valves and efficient intake and exhaust ports. The valves are tilted away from each other, a design that minimizes bends in the ports, thus increasing intake- and exhaust-port flow.

Dimensionally, the adaptability of the big block is surprisingly good; it's only 1 in. wider and 1/2-in. longer than the flathead! It is, of course, heavier than the flathead, weighing in at about 685 pounds compared to the late flathead's 569 pounds.

Big-Block Olds—The monster Oldsmobile is another one of those anomalies in an age where high miles-per-gallon quotients are supposed to be so important. Admittedly, the 455-cubic inch Olds won't drink fuel quite as greedily in a light street rod as it will in its natural habitat, but still . . . . Regardless, quite a few street rodders will go to the trouble and expense of installing the potent Olds.

Big-Block Pontiac—The same applies to the big Pontiac V8s. Mickey Thompson put the marque on the high-performance map some years ago. As a consequence, a small but faithful percentage of rod builders will always have a warm spot in their hearts for the "Big Chief."

Ford Flathead—A few years ago, and to everyone's amazement, it was realized that the Ford flathead V8 had simply refused to die. It is, in fact, used by about 7% of the street-rod builders! That's a substantial number. Building a modern flathead, however, is fraught with danger. First and foremost, even though many are still available, few blocks are worth the usually high asking price.

Before you purchase either a 1946—48 59AB or 1949—53 8BA Ford or Mercury flathead, demand a money-back guarantee based on having the block thoroughly de-rusted and completely Magnafluxed by a competent automotive machine shop. Indeed, if you find a virgin block—they appear on the market from time to time—spend the extra money and save yourself considerable time and grief. All internal parts and speed equipment you may want are currently available for the venerable gran'daddy of street-rod engines.

Mini-Engines & Mileage Squeezers—When gasoline prices began their dramatic rise in the early '70s, more than a few voices of doom were heard. The chorus flatly predicted the demise of auto sports, both professional and amateur. That, of course, didn't occur. But changes have been felt. Although prices have stabilized or have fallen, premium unleaded fuel still sells at a "premium."

Although not your everyday street rod, classic Depression Era Buick is as rod worthy as a Depression Era Ford. Because of shorter overall length and oil-sump and distributor placement, Buick V6s are becoming popular.

Bent sixes of every persuasion have gained a significant following since the mid '70s.

FoMoCo V6 powers Lee Kelly's beautiful '34 Ford five-window coupe. Modern V6 engines, when fitted with aftermarket ignition, *adjustable* carb and an RV cam, retain most, if not all, of their original fuel economy, but improve in the power department.

Even though the rallying cry of hot rodders has always been, "There's no substitute for cubic inches!", some street rodders have forsaken the mega-inch, macho-torque engines of the '60s Muscle Cars for smaller power plants. Although they represent a minority—about 5%—I would be remiss if I failed to recognize their needs.

Of course, street-rod power-plant *downsizing* is more than merely installing a small-displacement engine. For reasonable acceleration from the stoplight or when you want to pass an 18-wheeler on the highway, the engine and transmission should be sized to the weight of the car in terms of torque at the flywheel.

If you accept the current advertising, you'd believe that every car produced is a high-performance, economy model with superlative luxury. Maybe yes, maybe no. But there *are* many true economy cars on the market. And they have something to offer to you if you'll take a close and thoughtful look.

Statistically, the average weight of a small modern car is about 2300 pounds, averaging one cubic inch of displacement for every 20 pounds. In terms of *SAE net-rated torque,* the average lightweight chalks up one foot-pound for every 23 pounds of curb weight. And although these are not hard-and-fast rules, the figures are surprisingly consistent across manufacturer lines and have been for several years.

SAE Ratings—As late as 1970, an engine's SAE net horsepower and torque was determined on the dyno under ideal conditions with no power-robbing accessories attached to the engine such as an alternator, power-steering pump or air pump. Consequently, the resulting figures were not representative of normal operating conditions; engine-output figures were inflated. Nevertheless that was what was used in advertising copy.

In 1971, however, the California legislature started a "Truth in Advertising" campaign that put severe limitations on horsepower and torque claims that could be made. Eventually, the only horsepower ratings quoted nationwide were those obtained with all accessories connected and with the automatic spark advance in operation. By 1974, the published ratings were decreased even more because by then the manufacturers had to indicate how much power was available at the driving wheels.

This is not to say that actual horsepower and torque developed by modern engines has not actually dropped since the early '70s. Hardly. Emissions controls, low compression, and retarded ignition timing have all but destroyed the concept of high performance—except in advertising copy. So, whether you're considering mini-engine or a modern, de-tuned V8, don't be misled by published horsepower and torque figures.

Drive Line—A quick word about matching a transmission to a small engine: Remember that the smaller the engine—in terms of displacement and torque production—and the heavier the car, the more you need a good *manual* transmission. Three-speeds are OK, four-speeds are better. And, if you can come up with a five-speed, great! For good driveability, you simply need all the torque multiplication you can get. Most mini-engine automatic transmissions don't get the job done. Transmissions are covered in detail in Chapters 11 and 12.

You must also consider the rear-axle ratio. Chances are you know that better mileage comes with a *taller*—lower numerical—gear ratio. Be forewarned, however; it is easy to go too tall, particularly with a mini-engine. Overwork a little engine and mileage will suffer. Economy of operation is a question of torque output versus weight. Arriving at a satisfactory compromise requires a little homework on your part. Use some of the following information to help compute a rear-axle gear ratio.

Finally, if you want to maximize the mileage of your street rod, you must look beyond using a V6 or overhead-cam four-banger. You must also come to grips with the frontal area and side profile of your car—in short, its *streamlining*. There's a world of difference between the streamlining of a pre-1948 street rod and a modern economy car.

Streamlining—Automotive streamlining is not the easiest thing to quantify on paper. If it were, the manufacturers wouldn't need wind tunnels, bits of yarn and computers to achieve acceptable aerodynamics. So don't even try.

You can, however, roughly calculate the frontal area of your car with a straight-on front-view photograph.

The frontal area of a '29 High Boy *body*—no fenders—is about 16 square feet; a Deuce High Boy, a square foot or so more. A full-fendered '40 Ford coupe is nearly 25 square feet—a veritable billboard! True economy cars such as the Honda Civic are down to about 18 square feet, and sports cars such as a Ferrari or Lotus are as low as 16 square feet. If yours is a High Boy, don't get carried away. Most of the aerodynamic drag is created by the wheels, not the body.

A full discussion of streamlining and how to achieve it could fill a book. However, let's just discuss power-plant considerations at this point. So, if you decide to build an "econo-rod," choose an engine that displaces at least one cubic inch for each 20 pounds of vehicle weight, and at least one foot pound of SAE net rated torque for every 23 pounds of vehicle weight. Therefore, if you estimate that your car will weigh 2500 pounds, the engine should displace no less than $2500 \div 20 = 125$ cubic inches and the engine should develop a minimum of $2500 \div 23 = 109$ pound-feet of torque.

ENGINE SHOPPING

When shopping for a street-rod engine, assume that you *must* completely rebuild whatever you purchase. Regardless of how good it looks on the outside, completely disassemble, inspect and rebuild it. Otherwise, you'll end up pulling it out so you can do what you should've done in the first place.

With that said, let's get on with the search for a good rebuildable power plant. The best resources for the engines I've discussed are your friends and acquaintances, swap meets and, of course, wrecking yards. Let's first take a look at the possibilities afforded by the latter.

Wrecking-Yard Engines—The trend among metropolitan automotive dismantlers is to specialize. For instance, some wrecking yards feature only GM products, others FoMoCo or MoPar. Still others deal exclusively in imported cars and parts. Not only that, because their primary customers are commercial repair shops—shops are mostly concerned with relatively late-model cars—many wrecking yards deal with vechicles no more than 10 years old. What this means is a bit more resourcefulness may be necessary if you're interested in a good, rebuildable mid-'60s or early '70s engine. You can all but forget a flathead in decent condition. However, a big-city wrecking yard is the best place to look for a low-mileage, late-model mini-engine.

For anything else, begin your search in non-specialty wrecking yards that are best found in rural or semi-rural areas. Usually two or three will be within a reasonable distance from your home.

There are two reasons these are good places to start: First, a few telephone calls can be used to find suitable candidates, or indicate the scarcity thereof. You'll also get an idea of

Chevrolet's contribution to V6 brigade is hardly out of contention. Rod builder Boyd Coddington installed this 90° 200 incher in a customer's chassis. Engine weighs 328 pounds, but produces 155 horsepower and 180 lb-ft of torque.

If it's power you want . . . how about a Chrysler Hemi? One of the finest American V8 designs short of the overhead-cam engines, its appearance in a street rod is rare. Why? It's big and heavy.

the going rate for your desired engine. Prices quoted should not be considered a baseline, however, but rather a top-dollar figure. The true baseline is *free,* or next to nothing! Yes, there are freebie engines out there. I've even had them delivered to my house!

The second reason is that when found, the engine will very likely be complete—often with transmission attached. And best of all, it may still be in the donor car. The value of completeness should be apparent from earlier discussions. But, the desirability of finding an engine still in the car may not be apparent. Think about it though . . . .

An engine still in the car will probably be protected from the elements, especially if the car has its hood and air cleaner in place. Also, you'll be able to check the mileage on the odometer, stick a finger in the exhaust pipe, and look for damage suffered in a front-end collision. In short, you can better evaluate the condition of an engine that's still in place.

It doesn't even matter whether the yard pulls the engine or they allow you to do the dirty work. You either save time and effort, or you get to pocket—with their permission—those little bits and pieces of hardware that could save you bucks later on down the road.

Swap-Meet Mills—The next step up the ladder of cost-conscious engine shopping is the swap meet. At big swap meets, you'll find a fairly good selection of popular engines; dozens of Chevy small-blocks, several small-block Fords, and a smattering of everything else.

The main advantages of touring swap-meet aisles includes lower price, occasional home delivery of your purchase, and the availability of engine accessories at little or no extra cost. The most significant disadvantage is you'll seldom get *return privileges,* something that nearly every wrecking yard tosses into a package deal. Still, the ability to haggle over prices from the driver's seat—and that's exactly your position as buyer at the swap meet—is a significant factor. You can bet the seller doesn't relish toting that 1/4-or-so ton of cast iron back home.

The Good-Buddy Deal—Street rodding is not a hermit's hobby. Very few practitioners go it alone. Everybody has buddies and friends, so look to them first and foremost when it comes time to actually *buy* an engine. Let's face it: Street rodders are, by their very nature, horders of what the ill-informed often call *junk*. You've probably heard it at one time or another: "When are you going to get rid of these junk cars, junk parts and junk engines!" It is true, though, if you've been into street rodding for long, that you'll have accumulated what I call *surplus inventory*. Fortunately, you can usually be persuaded to part with some of it.

The advantage of buying from a friend or acquaintance is a fair, often well-below market price. Not only that, *most* rodders will not knowingly sell a friend an engine that's not rebuildable. This is not to say you shouldn't exercise prudence; it's just that if you can't trust your friends, you'd better move to another neighborhood.

The major pitfall of buying an engine from an acquaintance is that it may not be complete. You should, therefore, familiarize yourself with what goes with the engine you plan to install.

STOCK OR MODIFIED?

Although the quest for speed was the original motivation of street rodding when the sport was young, modifications made for the sake of speed alone are now relatively insignificant. Nevertheless, few street rodders would consider installing a completely stock engine.

The modified power plant is simply the heart and soul of any street rod, regardless of whether you are taking the traditional path or are planning a car as modern as tomorrow. Questions to address in this respect concern the degree and type of modifications you should contemplate.

First, last and always, the cardinal rule for a street-rod engine is *reliability*. No matter how powerful, beautiful or economical, an unreliable engine doesn't belong in a street rod. The overly zealous pursuit of high performance will lessen reliability proportionally. So, guard against temptation as you peruse speed-equipment catalogs. The attempt to maximize horsepower has lessened the drivability of more street rods than anything else.

A moderate-weight street rod—2000—3000 pounds—rarely benefits from more horsepower than the typical bone-stock 300-cubic inch V8 can produce in *pre-smog-control guise*—valve timing is roughly comparable to what was stock in 1965. Such valve timing is now called *RV* or *mileage* timing, which is in the neighborhood of 240° duration and 0.425-in. lift. Mild? You bet. Not only that, a 600-cfm four-barrel carburetor has two primary and two secondary venturis that can be adjusted both to the lean or rich side to compensate for altitude changes—it's all the carburetion that's needed. An ignition system capable of operating at 6500 engine rpm will top off the engine requirements.

The engine specifications in the above paragraph basically describes the engines I've run in my 2800-pound street coupe over the past 20 years. I use a hydraulic cam with an automatic transmission and a mechanical cam with a manual four-speed. It works for me.

Is my engine down on power? No! I love high-performance as much as the next guy. In fact, you'll find me in my race car at Bonneville every August and on El Mirage Dry Lake for every SCTA meet. But I depend on my *street* coupe for transportation, usually racking up 1500—2000 miles a month. And that means I need a smooth, tractable and, above all, *reliable* engine.

Of course, not many street rods are driven as much and as hard as mine. And when the demand for fire-up reliability is decreased to once or twice a week and there's a lot of time in between for maintenance, you can tolerate a more radical engine. So, if your car will see limited service, you can "reach for the moon" when it comes to engine modifications. But, if your desires are more mundane, keep them to a minimum.

Automatic Transmissions **11**

Regardless of automatic-transmission make and model, shift-reprogramming kit will provide significant boost in performance and durability departments.

Few street-rod builders seriously considered the use of an automatic transmission back in the '50s. In fact, the Hydra-matics, Powerglides and Ford-O-Matics of the day were more often the butt of a bad joke than anything: "Slip 'n' slide with Powerglide, Hydra-Mush and Ford-O-Slush!" The custom-car buff, of course, always on the lookout for something a little different, found the early automatics worth the time and effort, particularly in really low channel jobs. Clutch operation can be a bear when you're almost sitting on the floorboards.

By the early '60s, however, street rodders took another look. It wasn't that automatics improved that much. It was the gradual change in street-rod driving habits . . . fewer and fewer cars were built with the intention of drag racing. Street rods were becoming a legitimate form of family recreation. As such, they were driven more and more by the distaff side of the family who have always favored the convenience of the automatic tranny.

To be sure, the relative merits of the modern automatic versus the new manually shifted transmissions is a question not yet decided. That's why many new cars have both as an option. But today, even in the absence of hard figures, you'd be safe in assuming that the large majority of street rods powered by a V8 are backed up by an automatic transmission. And, inasmuch as automatic transmissions are far better than ever, it's equally safe to assume that their use will increase as time goes on.

INSIDE THE AUTOMATIC

Although the automatic transmission has been with us since before World War II, only in the past 10 years has its performance *and* economy potential been reached. Indeed, some passenger-car and light-truck manufacturers now provide a heavy-duty towing warranty *only* with automatic transmissions. Sounds good. However, if you choose an an automatic, it becomes the most complex single component in your street rod.

That's not a problem, though, for I have no intention of teaching you how to rebuild an automatic transmission. We'll just take a quick "cook's tour" so you'll at least have an understanding of what goes on in that aluminum cornucopia between the engine and the driving wheels.

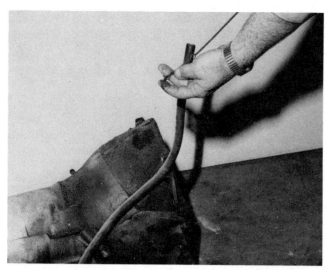

Don't buy an automatic that's too-far gone for an economical rebuild. Dale Cromwell of Specialized Auto Repair in Anaheim, California, says to check the condition and color of the fluid. If it is completely black or you see any metal flakes in it, pass.

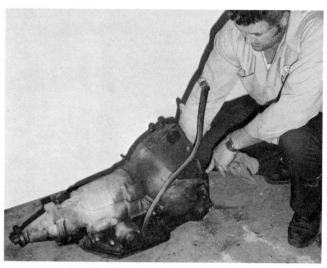

Another thing to check an automatic for is excessive input-shaft end play. With the torque converter removed, grasp the shaft and pull it back and forth. If you can move it in and out a noticeable amount, chances are there is major hard-part damage.

The transmission—automatic or manual—multiplies engine torque and delivers it to the differential via the drive shaft. The workings of a *manual* transmission and clutch is relatively easy to understand. The automatic, although it performs the same function, isn't so easy. It does its work through fluid pumped under pressure to the torque converter and through valves and orifices to clutches and bands.

Let's take a quick look at the anatomy of the basic automatic transmission and the three major systems: torque converter, hydraulic system, and clutch, band and gear system.

TORQUE CONVERTER

The torque converter, that fat, round reservoir of dark red fluid that installs between the engine and transmission, is a sophisticated *fluid coupling*. Fluid couplings contain within them *propellers* and *vanes*. One, the *impeller*, is a driving member that when rotated develops fluid pressure and flow. This fluid pressure and flow causes another component within the coupling—a driven member called the *turbine*—to rotate. The *stator*, a freewheeling fluid propeller, redirects fluid flow in the direction of rotation at low engine rpm as it leaves the turbine, thus assisting the rotation of the impeller and multiplying torque approximately 2:1.

Although there is no direct mechanical connection in the converter, it is to the remainder of the automatic transmission what the pressure plate and friction disc are to the manual transmission. The torque converter, however, is attached to the engine crankshaft

through a flexible driving plate. The *flex-plate,* as it is often called, is *not* a flywheel. Conventional engines equipped with automatic transmissions do not have true flywheels. The converter assembly fills the roll of the flywheel.

HYDRAULIC SYSTEM

The lifeblood of an automatic transmission is the 15—20 quarts of low-viscosity, red hydraulic fluid pumped throughout its die-cast veins and arteries. The heart of the system is the oil pump, usually located just behind the converter. It runs when the engine is running at crankshaft speed.

An automatic with this much crud in its pan will probably cost so much to rebuild that you should move on. Chances are you'll find one that's in better condition for about the same price.

The pump supplies the torque converter and transmission with pressurized fluid. It also routes fluid through the transmission cooler, which is normally in the engine radiator. Heat is transferred from the fluid to the engine coolant. Accessory fluid-to-air coolers are sometimes used to supplement or replace the radiator cooler.

One of the pump's major functions is to supply pressurized fluid to the valve body—the brain of the transmission. The valve body contains most of the various transmission control valves and a multitude of check balls and other bits and pieces. The job of the valve body is to shift the transmission automatically or manually by operating the clutches and/or bands.

GEAR SYSTEM

The muscles of the automatic transmission are the various planetary gear sets and hydraulically applied multiple-disc clutches and operated clutch pistons, servo pistons and brake bands.

The planetary gear train in the automobile has been with us since the days of the Ford Model T transmission. Basically, it consists of an internal ring gear and a central, or *sun,* gear mounted on a shaft with three or more planetary pinions encircling it and meshed at all times with it and the ring gear.

Clutches drive the various members of the planetary gear set, while bands hold the members. Both, of course, are hydraulically applied. The particular arrangement of the clutches and bands determines the gear ratios.

POWER FLOW

When running, the engine spins the torque converter and turns the input shaft. The input shaft of the typical automatic is splined to the forward-clutch cylinder, which engages the forward ring gear. This, in turn, rotates the forward planetary pinions on their shafts. In low gear, torque is transmitted from the planetary pinions to the sun gear.

In second, however, the sun gear is locked to the transmission case by an intermediate band. Force applied by the ring gear causes the planetary pinions to encircle the stationary sun gear. The sun gear rotates the planetary-pinion carrier which is splined to the output shaft and, thereby, transmits torque to the differential.

In high gear, the forward-clutch cylinder is engaged, and the input shaft drives it, causing the forward ring gear to transmit torque to the forward planetary pinions. Because the reverse-high clutch is also engaged, the pinions cannot rotate and torque is transmitted directly—1:1 ratio—to the output shaft and on to the differential.

In reverse gear, the forward clutch is released, the reverse-high clutch is engaged, and the rear ring gear rotates in a counter-clockwise direction. When in reverse, gear reduction is approximately 2:1.

WHICH TRANSMISSION TO CHOOSE?

This, obviously, is the most critical question. If you've chosen a popular V8, you'll have up to three or four different transmissions that will fit to the back of the block. Of the many different automatics built since the mid '60s, most of them would be good choices for a street rod except for their size and weight. Also, some are more expensive than others—with no appreciable increase in usefulness to the non-racing street rodder.

The best street-rod automatic is one that is most compatible with the particular engine chosen. That is, it and all the accessories must fit with perfection. Absolutely no modification of the bellhousing, grinding of the starter base, or reworking of the flexplate should be necessary. And, it must be equal to the task in terms of ability to withstand engine torque.

Obviously, such a transmission is the one that the factory installed with the engine. Beyond that, it should be light and generally fit your car's chassis without major modification to either transmission or chassis. Anything less than near perfection can easily result in needless headaches.

For GM Engines—General Motors produces or has produced more than a dozen passenger-car transmissions since the introduction of the small-block Chevy. Fortu-

nately, that number can be reduced to a more manageable number.

CHEVROLET POWERGLIDE

The cast-iron-case Powerglide, used in Chevrolet passenger cars and light trucks through the early '60s, dates back to the mid-'50s. It's a basic torque converter/two-speed automatic transmission with one hydraulic-controlled planetary gear set. The case is approximately 28-1/2-in. long and the dry transmission weighs a little more than 200 pounds.

The torque converter is a conventional unit with an impeller, turbine and stator. The planetary gear set and hydro-mechanical clutch assembly serves all driving ranges of the transmission with its single planetary gear train and single clutch assembly.

The hydraulic system has both a front and rear pump, and a conventional valve body with the necessary passages and components to permit the required hydraulic pressures to be delivered at the proper time. The front pump is the larger of the two and is used in starting, at low road speeds and in reverse. The rear pump is turned by the output shaft to generate hydraulic pressure at higher speeds and for push starting.

A pressure-regulator valve—vacuum-modulator valve in D range—predetermines the pressure with the valve body. A normal valve operated by external control linkage directs pressure to the proper clutch and band.

As you'll see, there's a Powerglide that's superior to the original V8 cast-iron offerings. I've already said, though, that the best transmission is the one that was originally installed with the engine. And, inasmuch as so many 1955—62 Chevy V8s will yet be installed in street rods, you may want to follow this advice to the letter. If you choose to do so, investigate the high-performance and re-programming kits available for the older cast-iron 'Glides.

The Light One is the Right One—The aluminum-case Powerglide, introduced in the 1962 327, is used in a wide range of 1963—73 Chevrolets. It weighs approximately 150 pounds, and case length is 28-5/8 in. The 1962—64 versions have shorter tail shafts than the later V8 versions. The gear portion of the aluminum Powerglide is a two-speed compound planetary set with a first-gear ratio of 1.82:1 in the light-duty version, and 1.76:1 in the heavy-duty version. High gear is, of course, 1:1.

The shift from low gear to direct drive is automatic. The vehicle speed at which the shifts occur is determined by the interaction of the output-shaft-driven governor and a throttle valve controlled by the accelerator pedal. Thus, the car launches with both the

torque converter and the gear-box multiplying torque. As vehicle speed increases, the gear box upshifts to direct drive, leaving only the torque converter for any speed-torque changes required. Torque-multiplication ability of the converter multiplied by the planetary-gear reduction allows an overall torque multiplication of 4.5:1.

The planetary gear set is beefier in the aluminum-cased Powerglide, but one of the most significant advantages for the rod builder is the nearly 70-pound weight savings it has over the cast-iron version. Using this tranny in older than 1962 blocks can be a hassle, however. For one thing, the starter mount is on the block, whereas it is mounted to the cast-iron transmission case in earlier applications. Beyond that, there are several different lengths and output-shaft-spline counts with regard to the cast-iron and aluminum cases. If you haven't already fabricated the drive shaft, this presents no particular problem. If you have, however, parts to match the back side are easily found in the wrecking yard. Nevertheless, there can be many a delay in fitting things before all components—block, starter, flexplate and case—are compatible.

TURBO HYDRA-MATIC 350 & 350C

These transmissions can be found in a great many 1969—84 GM automobiles. The factory installed them when light- and medium-duty service was anticipated. The TH 350, an extremely popular and very street-roddable transmission, is a fully automatic three-speed consisting of a compound planetary gear set, four multi-disc clutches, two roller clutches and a band to provide the required friction elements to control the planetary gear set. The 1983 series TH 350C has a four-element hydraulic torque converter and a planetary gear

Turbo 350—it's about 28-in. long and 14-in. wide—is found behind more small-block Chevys than any other transmission. Performance-wise, it's not quite as desirable as the Turbo 400.

Cockpit view of Turbo 400 (left) and Turbo 350 (right) shows that whereas the 400 is wider in the gear area, it's not quite as bulky in the valve-body area. If you like GM horsepower in healthy doses, use the Turbo Hydra-matic 400. This beefy transmission measures 28-5/8 in. from end to end, plus either the short (4 in.) or long (9-1/2 in.) tailhousing. Transmission is 13-in. wide, not including the modulator.

Kenne-Bell adapter plate will adapt Buick, Olds or Pontiac Turbo 400 to Chevy block. These Turbo 400s cost less than their Chevy counterparts.

set. C indicates converter clutch, which provides mechanical lockup under cruise conditions for improved fuel economy. Case length is approximately 27.5 in. plus a 5.75-in. tailhousing. Dry weight is approximately 125 pounds.

The friction elements couple the engine to the planetary gears through fluid pressure, providing three forward speeds and reverse. The three-element torque converter is of welded construction (as opposed to the old bolt-together Powerglide design) and consists of a driving member, a turbine and a stator assembly. When required, the torque converter supplements the gear assemblies by multiplying engine torque.

The converter-clutch assembly consists of a conventional three-element torque converter with a converter clutch. The converter clutch is splined to the turbine assembly and, when operated, applies against the converter cover to provide a direct coupling of the engine to the planetary gears. When the converter clutch is released, the assembly operates as a conventional torque converter.

The basic TH 350, however, is the one to use behind most GM V8s in street rods. In general high-performance terms, only the case seems to be the weak link, and even then only under truly severe conditions. If there is the possibility of a choice, 1970 and later TH

350s are the most desirable because of an improved front pump. Early pumps tended to force fluid out of the trans because of higher pressures developed during high-rpm operation.

About the only significant fault you might find in the TH 350—and in most automatics—is the fact that they use fluid accumulators to delay and soften shifts. Therefore, whenever high performance is desired, install a shift-programming kit so shifts will be more positive. Transmission durability will also improve.

TURBO HYDRA-MATIC 400

Hydra-matic transmissions were the first domestic automatics, premiering 'way back in 1939. The earliest, and all the subsequent Hydra-matics, had four forward speeds until a three-speed version was available on several 1961 Pontiac models. The modern three-speed TH 400 has been used in heavy-duty applications on all 1966—81 GM products. It is a fully-automatic unit consisting of a three-element torque converter and a compound planetary gear set. Three multiple-disc clutches, two one-way clutches and two bands provide the friction elements required to operate the planetary gears. One of the major differences setting the TH 400 apart from most other transmissions is the *sprag*

clutch—a one-way clutch that takes the place of additional bands. It rotates freely in one direction and locks up in the other.

The torque converter, multiple-disc clutch and one-way clutches couple the engine to the planetary gears through fluid pressure in specific combinations to provide three forward speeds and reverse.

External-control connections to the transmission include: manual linkage to select the desired operating range, engine vacuum to operate the vacuum modulator, and an electrical signal to operate an electric-detent solenoid. The vacuum modulator is used to sense engine torque to the transmission automatically. The vacuum modulator transmits this signal to the pressure regulator, which controls line pressure, so that torque requirements of the transmission are met and correct shift spacing is obtained at all throttle openings. The detent solenoid is activated by an electric switch at the carburetor.

When the throttle is opened sufficiently to close this switch, the solenoid in the transmission is activated, causing a downshift at speeds below 70 mph. At lower speeds, downshifts can occur at lesser throttle openings without the use of the electric switch.

In the Chevy and Cadillac versions of the TH 400, forward gear ratios are 2.48:1 in first, 1.48:1 in second and 1.1:1 in third. Some transmissions, however, have a low gear of 2.97:1 and a second gear of 1.56:1. Case length is approximately 28.5 in. plus either a 4- or 9.5-in. tailhousing. This transmission is relatively heavy and bulkier than the TH 350. It is, however, the automatic transmission almost always used with big-block Chevys and many high-performance small-blocks.

There are in fact, some high-performance buffs who unabashedly claim that the TH 400 is the best automatic tranny ever built, bar none. It certainly is a heavy-duty transmission, requiring only minimal shift-programming for even racing.

Variable Pitch Turbo-Hydros—Beyond the differences in gear ratios, bellhousing configuration and tail-shaft length, there is one variety of TH 400 that deserves further scrutiny—the 1965—67 Buick, Cadillac, and Olds TH 400 that came with a *variable pitch* stator in the torque converter.

The stator assemblies in these TH 400s have vanes that are operated in one of two angles—26° maximum and 18° minimum. The higher angle gives greater redirection of the fluid and increased torque multiplication for maximum performance. You don't get something for nothing, though. It also reduces the efficiency of the converter because "slip" is higher. However, low angle makes the torque converter more efficient for cruising and overall fuel economy.

A solenoid is used in early TH 400s to change stator-blade angle. In most installations, the solenoid is activated by a signal from a switch at the carburetor. In others, the solenoid is activated by the brake-light switch.

Apparently, the powers that be during that period decided that this refinement was neither needed nor cost effective; the variable-pitch stator was dropped. All 1968 and later TH 400 transmissions came with stationary vanes set at a compromise angle of 23°.

As so often is the case, however, high-performance manufacturers didn't let matters be. Sometimes their very livelihood depends on retrieving and updating goodies from the past as well as developing new performance-oriented modifications. That's exactly what happened with the variable-pitch stator.

Several years ago, Kenne-Bell Performance Products of Upland, California, developed a strictly street Switch-the-Pitch conversion kit. It consists of a new converter-pump assembly and a rebuilt and modified torque converter for *all* TH 400 transmissions. The kit can be installed by any competent transmission shop and is a worthy addition to the TH 400.

TURBO HYDRA-MATIC 700-R4

This relatively new transmission debuted in the 1982 Corvettes. It was later installed in the 1983—84 Camaro and Firebird lines. Many of these vehicles are in wrecking yards around the country, and since any Chevy V8 is grist for the street-rodder's mill, these later engines and attached transmissions will find a home under a vintage hood. Beyond that, virtually any transmission originally installed in a Corvette is considered "highest-performance" and is, therefore, well worth being considered, particularly '84 and later. Earlier 700-R4s had teething problems.

General Motors transmission engineers originally set out to develop a gear box that

All Turbo 400's are not created equal. Big 1965—67 Buicks, Cadillacs and Oldsmobiles use a *variable-pitch* stator in the torque converter. This gives low-rpm stall speed for cruising and high-rpm stall for better accelaration.

was truly versatile—one with a low first gear that could get a car or light truck moving, but with built-in overdrive that would take over to deliver good gas mileage for cruising down the Interstate.

The TH 700-R4, although a fully automatic transmission with all the expected innards, has one or two surprises. It has a torque-converter clutch (TCC). Yes, a real clutch. The pressure plate is operated by hydraulic pressure created by the fluid in the rotating converter. The friction pad binds under this pressure to a surface on the converter cover.

The general operation is almost identical to that of a conventional clutch in a manually shifted transmission, but it has all the convenience of an automatic transmission. For instance, the 700-R4's clutch provides a mechanical lock-up between engine and transmission. The torque converter couples engine power to the transmission's planetary-gear sets, five multiple-disc-type clutches and two sprag clutches and band to develop four forward speeds with ratios of 3.06:1 (first), 1.67:1 (second), 1:1 (third) and an overdrive of 0.7:1 for fourth.

Gear-ratio changes are fully automatic relative to the car's speed and engine torque. The onboard computer selects the correct gear ratio for maximum efficiency and performance at all throttle openings. This is why the transmission hasn't found favor with street-rod builders: the need for an onboard computer. But, you can bet that as *avant garde* rod

builders gain familiarity with the intricacies of the automotive computer, the overdrive feature will begin to appear on street rods.

The TH 700-R4 functions best when subjected to a few, but significant, aftermarket modifications such as those pioneered by the Southern California-based high-performance transmission specialist, Art Carr.

AUTOMATICS FOR FORD ENGINES

Although Ford hasn't built as many different transmissions in the past 20 years as has GM, those suitable for street-rod applications number about the same. Let's look at each.

FORD C-3 DUAL-RANGE

The popularity of the FoMoCo V6 in many lightweight fiberglass street rods is undisputed. Many of these transplants use the C-3 automatic transmission.

The C-3 is used behind the V6 up through 1979. It consists of a conventional torque converter, compound-planetary gear train, two multiple-disc clutches, one-way clutch and a hydraulic-control system. The C-3 features a drive range that gives fully automatic upshifts and downshifts. The main control, however, incorporates manually selected low and second gears.

FORD C-4 DUAL RANGE

The Ford C-4 automatic has been used in medium- and light-duty applications beginning with the 289 small-block in 1965 on

Most common automatic transmission found behind Ford small-block is C-4 Dual Range. It's been used in medium- and light-duty applications for more than 20 years, and continues to be the favorite among true-blue Ford street-rod builders.

New offerings out of Dearborn such as automatic overdrive transmission (left), holds a lot of promise for the future. C-4 is at right.

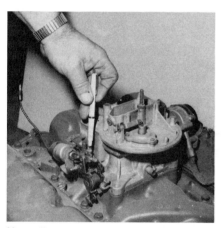

Use adjustment for passing gear on conventional C-4 for throttle-pressure adjustment on overdrive tranny. Activation is by means of a tubular-type linkage—not cable—because pushing force is required.

Mid-section of automatic overdrive is somewhat larger than C-4. As a result it can be ruled out for many existing cars. However, it can be used for a car that's under construction.

approximately 28-in. long and dry weight is a miserly 110 pounds.

FORD C-5 DUAL RANGE

With the continuing trend toward V6 engines, and particularly the increasing popularity of the late Ford 171-cubic inch (2.8-liter) V6, I should mention the C-5 that was introduced in 1982. If you're using this engine, consider the C-5.

As in the case of its C-series brothers, the C-5 is a fully automatic three-speed that allows first and second gears to be selected manually. The planetary gear set is the same as that used in the C-4 except for a few minor changes. The C-5, however, does incorporate major differences in the hydraulic system and it uses a different valve body. For instance, at speeds below 25 mph, the transmission immediately shifts to low gear to accommodate the lower torque of the smaller engine.

FORD C-6 DUAL RANGE

The Ford C-6 was originally used in medium- and heavy-duty passenger cars and pickup trucks with 351C 4V, 351M, 400, 427, 428 and 429-cubic inch engines. In recent years, it has also been used with the 302. As with all dual-range automatic transmissions, the C-6 is designed for both automatic and manual shifting. It, too, consists of a conventional torque converter, compound planetary-gear set controlled by one band, three disc clutches and a one-way clutch. Case length is approximately 29 inches and weight is about 140 pounds.

Forward speed gear ratios are the same as the C-4 except for reverse, which is 2.18:1. The C-6 uses a low-and-reverse plate clutch instead of the low-and-reverse *band* used in

through and including the 302, 351W and 351C. It has also been used behind a variety of engines not commonly associated with street rods such as the 351M, inline sixes, the 255 V8 and even some four bangers. Although there are other possibilities, this is the automatic best suited for a street rod if you're going to use a 289/302/351W or 351C 2V engine.

Internally, the C-4 is similar to the C-3, and to the early two-speed and three-speed Ford-O-Matics. In the mid '60s, however, the company began calling it the *SelectShift Cruiso-O-Matic Transmission*. It is essentially the same as those preceding it, except that the main-control assembly was revised to incorporate a first and second gear that could be manually selected if the driver so chose. It has a con-

ventional torque converter, compound planetary gear set, two multiple-disc clutches, a one-way clutch and a hydraulic-control system. Even the gear ratios are similar to the older three-speed Ford-O-Matics, with a 2.46:1 low, 1.46:1 second and 1.00:1 high. The C-4 reverse is 2.2:1.

When in Drive, the transmission will upshift automatically to intermediate and then to high as the throttle is depressed from the idle position. Conversely, the transmission will downshift automatically as vehicle speed drops to 10 mph. The driver can also force a downshift from high to intermediate at speeds below 65 mph by applying full throttle.

The C-4 has been offered on all Ford products with the aforementioned powerplants through the mid '80s. The aluminum case is

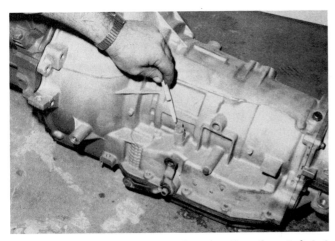

Small but important point to note is re-location of neutral-start switch. It's above shifter arm in overdrive tranny.

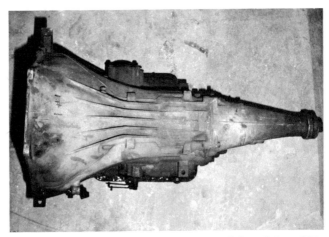

Tough Ford C-6 used behind big-block range in length from 28 to 33-1/2-in. long, and are approximately 14-1/2-in. wide. They weigh about 150 pounds, which is heavy for most street rods.

the C-4. Valves in the hydraulic control system are also similar to the C-4, but in no other way should the C-6 be equated with its smaller brethren. And that's the rub. Typical street-rod use simply doesn't demand a powerhouse transmission.

Still, inasmuch as the 351C 4V is a reasonably popular engine, regardless of the difficulty of installation, and many are equipped with the C-6, the additional bulk and weight can be tolerated. Therefore, if you are planning something like a *working* classic pickup, and are willing to do the extra work needed to make the installation, the 351C 4V/C-6 is a tough combination to beat.

FORD FX-MX, FMX

These transmissions, similar to the old Cruise-O-Matic, re-appeared in 1969 after a brief hiatus. They have been offered on a limited basis up to the present.

Featured is a drive range that provides fully automatic upshifts and downshifts, and manually selected low and second gears similar to the dual-range transmissions. Gear ratios, however, are different with a 2.40:1 low, a 1.47:1 second and a 1.00:1 high. Reverse is 2.00:1. The FMX is a little bulkier than the C-4 and should not be considered for high-performance use. It has a cast-iron case and is heavier than the aluminum-cased C-4. Nevertheless, it can be found behind a few 302s and 351Ws and will undoubtedly find its way into some street rods.

FORD AUTOMATIC OVERDRIVE

The Ford automatic overdrive appears to be the V8 transmission of the future. This four-speed unit, introduced in 1980, incorporates integral overdrive. The transmission will start

Ford automatic overdrive will bolt to any six-bolt-bellhousing small-block or 351C.

and remain in low gear when selected manually. In the 3 position, it upshifts automatically through the entire three forward speeds. In the D position, the transmission automatically selects the appropriate time to shift into overdrive.

In third gear, which has a ratio of 1:1, 40% of the engine torque is transmitted hydraulically through the torque converter and 60% is transmitted mechanically. This *split-torque* gear train is said to reduce hydraulic losses usually associated with a torque converter. When the transmission is in overdrive or fourth gear (0.67:1 ratio), all torque is transmitted through the direct-drive input shaft. This full mechanical lockup completely bypasses the torque converter and eliminates the usual torque-converter slippage.

Ford automatic overdrive will work as long as a flexplate matches torque converter. No re-balancing of flexplate is normally required. Same engine plate and starter can be used.

The most significant advantage of the automatic-overdrive transmission is that it allows lower engine speeds for greater fuel economy. The big disadvantage is that this transmission is relatively new and, consequently, expensive. In short, the wrecking-yard asking prices may defeat the bottom line economy when the four-speed overdrive transmission is compared to the run-of-the-mill three-speed C-4.

CHRYSLER TORQUEFLITE

Where the other two of the "Big Three" seem to have spent a lot of time designing a different transmission for every occasion, Chrysler has kept their offerings to a manageable three. Two of these three are suitable for street-rod use.

MoPar 904, for small-blocks only, is considered a light-duty transmission. It is approximately 31-in. long, 14-in. wide and weighs a little over 100 pounds.

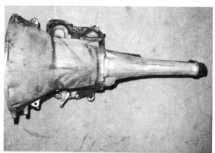

The MoPar 727, for both big- and small-blocks, is nearly 35-in. long, and 14-in. wide. Length, however, is not usually a significant problem in street rods. Width is what causes the grief.

The first TorqueFlite was introduced in the 1956 Imperial, a real monster of a car when most American cars were monsters. It was originally encased in cast-iron, but through the years it underwent several modifications, one of which is an all-aluminum, one-piece die-cast case first used in 1962.

The heavy-duty 727, used from 1966 to date in Dodge, Plymouth and Chrysler passenger cars equipped with 318-, 340-, 360-, 400- and 440-inch engines, is in the same league with GM's Turbo 400 and Ford's C-6—bulletproof! If you're power crazy and have gone to a blown Hemi, this is the transmission for you. The 904, which has been used in light-duty applications from 1970 to date behind the street-rod-popular 273s and 318s, is an excellent choice.

There are no surprises here; early models of these transmissions combine a conventional torque converter with a fully automatic three-speed gear system. Later models—from 1978—use a lock-up torque converter almost exclusively except in heavy-duty applications and a few oddball California smog engines. The transmission proper consists of two multiple-disc clutches, a one-way clutch, two servos and bands, and two planetary-gear sets to provide three forward speeds and reverse: first is 2.45:1, second is 1.45:1, and high gear is the old standby 1.00:1; reverse is 2.21:1.

The hydraulic system consists of a front pump and valve body with all the necessary valves except the governor. The A-727 is the longer and heavier of the two at 34.5 in. and 138 pounds. The A-904 is 30.5-in. long and weighs a skimpy 105 pounds.

SHIFT-PROGRAMMING THE STOCKER

The automatic transmission was designed to cater to the luxury needs of the mass market. As such, it shifts gears without any fanfare, smoothly and softly. This is great if you're not a performance buff and don't miss the minor concussions of a four-speed.

If, after your car is running, the shifts seem too mushy, the cure lies in the valve body—that part of the transmission that determines the shift points and the hydraulic pressures triggering them.

Gradual shifts are not the only irritant, either. There is the questionable stock design parameter called *gear overlap*. This is where one gear is engaged slightly before the previous gear is fully released. The intentional state of being in two gears at the same time makes for a smoother shift, but it generates a lot of unwanted heat. The Ford C-series, the MoPar TorqueFlites and the Powerglide all exhibit this condition to one degree or another.

The solution is the transmission shift-programming kit. There are several types manufactured by a number of companies for every domestic transmission built in the last 25 years. You pays your money and you takes your choice. They all offer about the same performance.

A shift-programming kit minimizes overlap by speeding the release of the previous gear and hastening the application of the next one. There is no hesitation or delay in either upshifts or downshifts. Typically, the shifts are firm, but not unpleasant.

Most of the kits contain modified separator plates, spool valves and pressure-regulating springs. They can usually be installed without even removing the transmission from the car. Generally, if you can change the transmission filter and fluid in-car, you can install a shift-programming kit in-car.

Be advised. Don't use a competition shift-programming kit for street use. Shifting will be too harsh. Only install a kit designed for high-performance *street* use.

MANUFACTURERS OF AUTOMATIC-TRANSMISSION HIGH-PERFORMANCE KITS

A-1 Automatic Transmissions
7359 Canoga Ave.
Canoga Park, CA 91303
818/884-6222

Art Carr Performance Transmission Products
10575 Bechler River Ave.
Fountain Valley, CA 92708
(714) 962-6655

ATI Racing Transmissions
6747 Whitestone Rd.
Baltimore, MD 21207
800/656-2872

B&M Automotive Products
9152 Independence Ave.
Chatsworth, CA 91311
213/882-6422

Fairbanks Racing Automatics
336 Elm St.
Stamford, CT 06902
203/327-9530

Kenne-Bell Performance Products
1527-K W. 13th St.
Upland, CA 91786
714/981-6006

Mr. Gasket
4566 Spring Rd.
Cleveland, OH 44131
216/398-8300

TCI Racing Transmissions
815 E.H. Crump Blvd.
Memphis, TN 38126
901/526-0321

TransGo Inc.
2621 Merced Ave.
El Monte, CA 91733
213/283-0245

Turbo-Action
1535 Owens Rd.
Jacksonville, FL 32218
904/751-3101

One of the finest manual transmissions available, although not often seen in street rods, is Doug Nash Engineering five-speed. Street version of this racing gearbox is housed in an aluminum case. Optional extension housings and input shafts are available for GM, Ford or MoPar applications.

If you're like most street-rod builders, you quickly and easily came to a decision as to which engine you're going to use. But, you're not sure about the transmission. So, let me make the decision easier for you.

To repeat from the previous chapter, your best choice in a transmission is the type that was installed by the factory with the engine you selected. More than one street-rod builder has experienced grief with a mis-matched transmission, flywheel, flexplate, starter or clutch assembly. The apparent simplicity of the back of an engine block and front of a bellhousing can be deceiving. The mere fact that the major components can be bolted together doesn't ensure that the two will work together. Hence, the reason for installing the original factory engine/transmission combination.

Unfortunately, such a quick and easy answer begs the question when it comes to manual transmissions. It still leaves the builder uncertain about too many details, to say noth-

ing of the problems that may not have occurred to you. Before you attempt to seek any in-depth answers, however, re-acquaint yourself with those critical devices collectively called the *drive train* that begins at the back of your engine and ends at the drive wheels.

TRANSFER OF POWER

Some type of drive train was recognized as a necessity early in the development of the horseless carriage. After a few feeble attempts to connect the engine directly to the drive wheels, automobile designers realized that the internal-combustion engine needed torque multiplication to accelerate from a dead stop and on steep grades. At low rpm there wasn't enough power developed to put a car in motion, particluarly with their low-power "wheezers," much less launch it with the authority a street rodder expects. Once up to speed, torque multiplication was only needed to maintain speed. Then, there was the need to disengage the engine from the

drive wheels so the engine could idle with the vehicle at rest.

That task—harnessing the engine's power and propelling the car—is exactly what the drive train does. It accomplishes that by first temporarily releasing the engine from its grip so the latter might efficiently develop its power. Then it allows that power to gradually and controllably flow to the driving wheels.

The conventional manual-transmission drive train incorporates four major components: a clutch system, gear box with manually selected ratios, a drive shaft, and a differential/rear-axle assembly. The following paragraphs describe the basics of each.

FLYWHEEL & CLUTCH ASSEMBLY

Inertia—The purpose of the flywheel is simply to keep the crank turning at a constant speed while the engine is between power strokes. Consider a single-cylinder four-stroke (cycle) engine. Power is produced only 25% of the time—during the power stroke. Therefore, 75% of the time our single-cylinder engine absorbs power—expelling exhaust gases, drawing in a fresh air/fuel mixture, and compressing the charge. During these strokes, and laboring under frictional and inertia losses, the crank slows. But suddenly another power stroke comes along and accelerates the crank back to speed.

This uneven flow of power can be smoothed by increasing crankshaft rotating inertia—adding mass. Inertia resists any change in speed or direction of travel—the heavier the flywheel, the more resistant it is to changing speed.

Recalling the writings of Newton, which you no doubt diligently poured over in high school, a motionless object wants to remain at rest, but once it is set in motion, it resists attempts to speed it up . . . or slow it down . . . or change its direction. The flywheel, therefore, acting under the principle of inertia, resists the engine's tendency to speed up during the power stroke. It also resists slowing down during the exhaust, intake and compression strokes. In effect, the flywheel minimizes the effect of power impulses by absorbing some of the energy during the power stroke and releasing it during the remainder of the operating cycle.

This is exaggerated by a single-cylinder engine, but although the power impulses in a multi-cylinder engine overlap and produce a

Until about the mid'70s, Ford used Long style pressure plates (right). These feature three forged release levers and nine springs. Steel flywheel (left) is best for use with heavier cars. These are available from the aftermarket in several weights ranging from 20 to 50 pounds. As for the disc, use a sprung hub and organic facings (center).

For safety reasons, a street rod should not use a stock cast-iron flywheel. A forged-aluminum flywheel with a sintered-bronze heat shield is a good choice for use in a lightweight rod.

smoother power flow, additional leveling off is desirable, making a flywheel necessary. The flywheel performs other functions, as you'll soon read about. Before I broach that subject, however, let's look at the minimums for a street-rod flywheel.

Cast Iron—Stock cast-iron flywheels, by and large, are just fine for Uncle Mert, but you should not use one unless it's of the nodular cast-iron variety. Many are on Detroit muscle cars.

To determine what a flywheel is made of, hang it by a rope or wire and tap it lightly with a hammer. If it rings like a bell, it's nodular cast iron or steel. It's OK. However, if it's more like a thud, the flywheel is made of grey cast iron. Don't use it. They have a tendency to "blow up" at high rpm. Therefore, grey cast-iron flywheels should never lurk below your right foot.

Even ordinarily conservative street rodders have been known to over-rev mildly modified engines, and more than one cast-iron flywheel has been known to come apart with the fury of a hand grenade!

In general, a high-quality, 30—40-pound low-carbon, hot-rolled steel-billet flywheel is best for street rods weighing 2000 pounds or more. Aftermarket flywheels manufactured from stress-relieved low-carbon steel reduce the possibility of concentrated carbon deposits which, through usage, can be come harder than steel and ultimately prevent uniform surface wear. Uneven wear, of course, leads to poor clutch-disc life and erratic performance. Low-carbon steel also minimizes the danger of carbon embrittlement.

For street applications where a high degree of stored flywheel energy isn't necessary,

specifically in street rods weighing less than 2000 pounds, a high-quality aluminum flywheel may be just the ticket. Most Grade A aluminum flywheels are machined from forged aluminum alloy—6061-T6 or better—with a *heat shield,* or high-friction bronze insert—W-1247 or better.

OK, inertia—and a convenient place for the starter ring gear—aside, the flywheel also serves as a mounting and friction surface for the clutch assembly. In the case of a single-disc clutch, the pressure plate provides one friction surface; the flywheel the other.

Clutch Assembly—The primary purpose of the clutch assembly is to couple and uncouple the engine to or from the drive train. It is designed, however, to slip a little during engagement. Positive engagement at any engine speed above a slow idle and zero vehicle speed would result in a severe and, possibly, harmful impact to the drive-train components. Once coupling is achieved, the clutch must quickly stop slipping and maintain sufficient friction against the flywheel and pressure-plate friction surfaces to transfer full power to the transmission input shaft and, thus, driving wheels.

One of the two major clutch-assembly components is the friction disc. Most original equipment and high-performance street discs are of the unbacked facing type with cushioning. The friction material is riveted to a wavy thin steel disc called a *marcel.* Sandwiched thusly between the two pieces of friction lining, the marcel provides a degree of compressibility to smooth clutch engagement.

Another means of softening the shock of power transfer is a hub with coil springs positioned concentrically around it. These allow

slight torsional movement between the center of the disc—the hub—and the lining.

The second major clutch-assembly component is the pressure plate, a relatively complex unit manufactured in several different designs. In general, the pressure plate consists of a ductile steel or cast-iron face plate—*pressure ring*—a set of springs and a set of release levers or a one-piece slotted-steel stamping called a *diaphragm,* and a stamped-steel cover.

There are three basic pressure-plate designs. The type used in Ford cars for many years is known as the *Long style.* This pressure plate typically has nine coil springs. It is easily recognized by its hexagonal-shaped

Many General Motors cars use a *diaphram* pressure plate. At least one clutch manufacturer (McLeod) reports that it is the most carefree unit for street use. This type of pressure plate incorporates a single Belleville type spring that acts as the release levers and springs.

Borg & Beck style pressure plate is stock in some GM and most Chrysler V8-powered products. Its 12-springs and stamped-steel release levers make it easy to recognize. Note levers damaged from insufficient free play.

cover and the way its drop-forged release levers extend toward the center. There's a *CF* weight at the outer end of each lever.

CF weights—for *centrifugal force*—are reduced in size or eliminated for most high-performance applications. Unlike *static* plate load supplied by the springs, pressure-plate load from the CF weights increases with engine rpm. Thus, shifting at high rpm becomes increasingly difficult. The Long style pressure plate has gained favor among racers and street rodders alike because of its superior air circulation and resulting ability to dissipate heat.

The *Borg-and-Beck*-style pressure plate, original equipment on many pre-'80s GM, AMC and MoPar engines, is recognized by its more-or-less full-circle design, stamped-steel release levers, and 12 coil springs. They do not have CF weights on the release levers. Instead, centrifugal-assist rollers between the cover and pressure ring are used. The biggest high-performance drawback of this design is cover distortion during release at high rpm.

The *diaphragm* type of pressure plate—originally used by most GM built cars—does not use coil springs, but rather incorporates a one-piece, slotted, dish-shaped (Belleville) spring. This spring also incorporates the release levers. A diaphragm pressure plate is easily recognized by the many tab-like release fingers.

It has low pedal resistance, but, in stock form, has problems with high-rpm shifting. High-performance diaphragm pressure plates don't have this problem.

Clutch Operation—In the operation of a clutch—the mechanical coupling and uncoupling of the engine from the drive train—

the throwout (release) bearing becomes part of the clutch assembly even though it is not an actual part of the pressure plate. Instead, it's part of the clutch linkage. One of your primary considerations must be the operation of the clutch pedal and linkage needed to operate the throwout bearing. You must understand its operation in terms of pedal travel and effort.

When the clutch pedal is depressed, a pivoting lever, or fork, moves the throwout bearing forward. As the bearing moves, it operates the release levers, which moves the pressure ring away from the disc. Once unloaded, the disc moves back slightly from the flywheel on the splined transmission input shaft and disengages from the engine.

Releasing the clutch pedal, in turn, moves the throwout bearing away from the pressure-plate release levers, allowing the pressure plate to force the clutch disc against the flywheel. The clutch assembly and flywheel can once again revolve as a single unit, transmitting torque through the transmission and to the rear wheels.

If you've decided to go with a manual transmission, it's possible to use a stock flywheel and clutch, providing the engine will be close to stock. But street rodders as a group tend to be high-performance oriented. In my experience, even the most moderate street rodder occasionally winds up the engine in low gear. This can push a stock flywheel and clutch to its limit—possibly beyond.

I've already expressed my thoughts as to the marginal safety of the stock flywheel or clutch in a high-performance application. To restate my position, they have no place in a street rod.

Even though you may not intend to put your high-performance engine through its paces, recognize that the potential is there. So, install a high-quality safety bellhousing to protect your lower extremities just in case.

It's true, clutch-and-flywheel assemblies offered in "factory hot rods" are quite adequate. However, after comparing prices, you may be tempted to purchase a rebuilt unit from the local parts house. These are fine for Uncle Mert, but they simply cannot provide the kind of reliability and safety at high loads that street rodding often demands. Therefore, if you are planning on even a mild high-performance engine, use a top-quality SEMA approved high-performance street flywheel and clutch.

MANUAL TRANSMISSIONS

There was a time in street rodding when no self-respecting driver would be caught with anything but a manual transmission. And, since the commonly used column shift of the day—1940—1948 Ford—was anything but high-performance, the 1939 Ford floor-shift version was preferred by all save the "Kustom Krowd." In fact, the term *stick shift* at that time (1946—60) was reserved for the '39 gear box.

Soon after the introduction of the overhead-valve V8, the inherent weakness in the prewar Ford transmission soon became obvious. It was then that the Cadillac-LaSalle and Packard manual transmissions began to appear. These transmissions were first used on the drag strip, but to a lesser degree in full-time street rods driven by those who valued reliability above tradition.

Three-speed passenger-car transmissions in common use during the 1940s, '50s and early '60s were of the *selective* type with combination *sliding-gear* and *constant-mesh* features. *Selective* refers to the ability of the driver to choose (select) a gear without progressing through intermediate gears. This type of transmission has shift rails and a lever(s) that can be moved through a *gate* from one rail to another in an H-pattern. This allows the driver to select any one of the gear positions from a central (neutral) position.

The term *sliding gear* refers to gears that move fore and aft on internal splines and when the driver moves the gear-selector lever. The splined gear is moved along a shaft until its teeth *mesh* with the teeth of another gear.

If you are "fortunate" enough to have learned to drive with an early three-speed gear box, you may recall that you had to come to a complete stop before you could downshift into first gear. That's because first gear was the sliding type. If you tried to cheat and force the transmission into first before you were completely stopped, you were rewarded with a grinding gear clash . . . and an unhappy stare from your dad.

Constant mesh refers to gears that are *constantly* in mesh, remaining in a more-or-less fixed position. Engagement is accomplished by means of sliding sleeves (sliders) and *synchronizing* devices that match gear speeds before engagement occurs, thus preventing clash. Second and third gears in the old three-speeds used constant-mesh gears. Providing the synchronizing devices were in good condition, you could shift gears without worrying about raising the hackles on dad's neck.

All of this gear-box jargon may be confusing. So, let's get to how major transmission components work, and briefly look at the gear-shifting operation.

Input Shaft—The splined transmission shaft that pilots in the back of the crankshaft and slips into the clutch hub is called the *main drive gear* or *input shaft*. Some people call it the *pilot shaft*. The main drive gear is in constant mesh with the *countershaft gear*, commonly called the *cluster gear*; it has a number of gears *clustered* together in a solid assembly. The main drive gear and cluster gear rotate as soon as the clutch is engaged to a running engine whether or not the transmission is in neutral.

When the clutch is disengaged, the driver selects first one, then another forward speed in a modern four-speed transmission. He is not actually moving the gears—they are in constant mesh—he is moving sliders that are fitted with brass friction devices (synchronizers) that match the speed of the two gears so they can be engaged. Torque can then be transferred smoothly through the mainshaft and to the output shaft, then on to the differential and driving wheels.

If Three Speeds Are Good, Four Are Better—Does the typical street rod with an average of 300 cubic inches of engine displacement *need* a four-speed manual transmission? Of course not.

When I was young and foolish back in the mid '50s, I drove my 365-CID Cadillac powered '40 Ford coupe all over town using only second and high gears! That big Caddy—by contemporary standards—put out a bundle of torque. I was running a commonplace wide-ratio '39 Ford transmission and a super-low 4.44:1 gear with 28-inch tires. It wasn't a bad performer on the local drag strip and was fairly comfortable—again, by contemporary standards—on the city streets. But, it was far from being an efficient drive train by modern street-rod standards.

Most experienced street rodders are aware of the fact that even a big-displacement engine that develops a lot of torque is a better performer with a close-ratio four-speed. *Close-ratio,* of course, is the key as any truck driver with a "granny-geared" four-speed will tell you.

Close-ratio gears are those that have less of a ratio spread from one forward speed to an-

other. For instance, the 1965—73 Ford *top loader* four-speed was originally available in both a *close-* and *wide-ratio* version. The gear ratios in the close-ratio box are: first—2.32:1; second—1.69:1; third—1.29:1, and fourth—1.00:1. The ratio spread between first and second is 0.63; the spread between second and third is 0.40, and the spread between third and fourth is 0.29. The wide-ratio version, on the other hand is, respectively, 2.78:1, 1.93:1, 1.36:1 and 1.00:1, with spreads of 0.85, 0.57, and 0.36.

Correspondingly, in terms of performance differentials, there is less of a spread in engine rpm from first to second to third to fourth. And, because the whole idea of engine performance is to keep engine rpm up, there's less rpm drop or loss when a close-ratio box is delivering the horsepower goods. In other words, with the close-ratio four-speed, your engine will operate within a narrower rpm range when accelerating up through the gears.

If Four Is Good, Why Not Five?—Good question! And indeed, as we've seen with the current crop of modern five-speed—or four-speed with overdrive—transmissions, Detroit is certainly giving the street rodder more and more options.

Theoretically, a five-speed is much better choice over the four-speed in the same sense that the four-speed is a better choice over the three-speed. The price tag on these newer transmissions, unfortunately, is and will remain higher. For example, they sold in 1985 for three to four times what a good usable four-speed went for. The good news is the price difference will go down with time.

Back to the bad news, the ability of the modern aluminum-case high-tech five-speed transmission to withstand the punishment delivered by an older model, big-displacement, high-torque engine is in question. On the other hand, it appears that the old standby Muscle Car four-speeds are the best choice for the rod builder with an appetite for all the performance he can get.

WHAT'S AVAILABLE

By the late '50s, decent passenger-car four-speed transmissions were offered on selected Detroit models, but they were hard to find and expensive when one was found. Most street rodders either went to the automatic tranny or stuck with the fragile early Ford gear box. By the mid '60s, however, excellent passenger-car transmissions of more advanced design were appearing in the wrecking yards with regularity. And, although automatic transmissions had then captured the fancy of the majority of street-rod builders, a significant number still wanted to keep their left legs busy. It was the era of the domestic muscle-car four-speed.

The muscle-car four-speed transmissions built from the mid '60s through the late '70s are, like the V8s they were originally hooked to, still the manual transmissions of choice for today's street-rod builder. They remain plentiful and moderately priced. Beyond that, they are rugged and, although many are well worn, most rebuild parts are available. The four-speeds and current five-speeds are fully synchronized, constant-mesh transmissions.

Let's not go any deeper into the innards of the generic manual transmission. You've probably chosen your engine by this time, so let's take a look at what goes best with it.

Gran'Daddy Of 'Em All: The T-10—The hot rodder's enthusiasm for the heavy-duty, high-performance four-speed manual transmission dates back to the Borg-Warner T-10 transmission developed in 1956 and introduced in the 1957 Chevy Corvette. Actually, Chevrolet engineers came up with the original idea of using the older three-speed transmission with reverse in the tailhousing. The Warner Gear Division of the Borg Warner Corporation, however, produced it for GM. The design concept caught on and both Ford and Chrysler eventually followed suit. Within a few years, they were offering versions of the original T-10 in their own performance models.

Significantly upgraded versions in the form of the Super T-10 are still being produced today.

If you're wondering whether the transmission on the back of that Chevy block is a T-10 or an in-house Muncie, just count the side-cover bolts. If there are nine, the box is a T-10; Muncies have seven bolts. If the gear box is on an early Ford 221, 260 or 289, it's a T-10 if it merely has a *side* cover. Ford-design transmissions have a top cover.

T-10's are not created equal. You should be aware that there are two entirely different Borg Warner T-10 transmissions coupled with the varieties necessary to match GM, FoMoCo, MoPar or AMC clutch and engine hardware. The original T-10 was in production from 1957 through 1965. The new, improved Super T-10, or T-10P, was introduced on AMC muscle cars in 1965.

The 1957—59 T-10 transmission in GM applications had a cast-iron gear case and an aluminum tailhousing. For awhile, cases on later models—1960 Corvette and 1962—63 passenger cars—featured aluminum cases as well as aluminum housings. Eventually, cast-iron cases returned. Ford and MoPar T-10 cases and housings were always cast-iron. There are a variety of early T-10 transmissions, but for your purpose—the building of a modern street rod—don't use an early T-10. Not only are they too old, there are much better transmissions.

T-10/SUPER T-10 OUTPUT-SHAFT-SPLINE COUNT

1957—60 GM T-10: 16 splines
1963—65 GM T-10: 21 or 27 splines
1963 MoPar T-10: 23 splines
1960—65 FoMoCo T-10: 28 splines
1966 and later GM Super T-10: 32 splines

MUNCIE TRANSMISSION RATIOS

1st	2nd	3rd	4th	Description
2.20	1.64	1.27	1.00	Early Close-Ratio (1963—65)
2.56	1.91	1.49	1.00	Early Wide-Ratio (1963—65)
2.64	1.75	1.33	1.00	Super Muncie (1965—74)
2.52	1.62	1.24	1.00	Close-Ratio (1966—74)
2.52	1.88	1.46	1.00	Wide-Ratio (1966—74)

Chances are you'll buy your four-speed transmission at a swap meet. Use reasonable caution. Haggle for a good price, but assume that new synchros and seals are needed. This wise buyer is checking the Muncie's shifter.

The Super T-10 that came out in 1965 is one, and the "heavy-duty" Super T-10 that came out in 1972 is another. Even though introduced in the mid '60s, they are superior to their forebears. You can easily distinguish them from the early versions by counting the output-shaft splines.

The Muncie—The best General Motors four-speed transmission for street-rod use is the aluminum-cased Muncie produced from 1963 through 1974. This transmission was the first performance manual four-speed from the Big-Three. It is easily recognized by its seven-bolt side cover. There are three major versions: a heavy-duty close-ratio series known as the *rock crusher,* a high-performance close-ratio series, and a standard wide-ratio series.

Muncie four-speed transmissions manufactured from 1963 to 1965 are known as the *M20* and have a 7/8-in.-diameter countershaft seated in 80 needle bearings.

The Super Muncie, or *rock crusher*—so called because of its noisy, but strong *gearset*, or tooth angle—was introduced in 1965 as an option with the 396 big-block. It had a 1-in. countershaft. This transmission is more properly known as the *M22*.

In 1966, the factory increased the close-ratio high-performance and wide-ratio standard-transmission countershaft diameter to 1 in. and increased the number of needle bearings to 112. Close-ratio boxes of this period are coded M21; wide-ratio transmissions retain the M20 designation.

Responding to the need for greater torque capacity, GM increased spline count on the main drive gear from 10 to 26 in the 1971 models of the high-performance close-ratio and standard wide-ratio Muncie. The original 27-spline output shaft was also replaced with a 32-spline ouput shaft.

Ford "Top Loader"—In 1964, Ford introduced their fully-synchronized, constant-mesh, four-speed passenger-car transmission. The new model was so well accepted that less than a year later the company began phasing out the Borg-Warner T-10; it was first available in 1960. Both close- and wide-ratio gearing were available. In 1977, the transmission was factory converted to over-drive design and, in 1979, it was outfitted with an aluminum case.

The Ford transmission is different from other modern passenger-car four-speeds in that it is serviced through an access hole in the top of the case. The shifting forks are mounted in bosses cast into the side of case, one feature that makes this transmission stronger than those with removable side plates. This design feature is also responsible for the name *top loader,* which it has been known by since its introduction, much to the chagrin, I suspect, of the Ford engineers who designed it—Misters Thompson and Collins of FoMoCo's T&C Division.

SUPER T-10 TRANSMISSION RATIOS

1st	2nd	3rd	4th	Description
2.43	1.61	1.23	1.00	First Design, Special Close-Ratio (T-10s)
2.64	1.75	1.23	1.00	Special Competition (T-10X)
2.64	1.75	1.33	1.00	Special Wide-Ratio (T-10W)
2.88	1.75	1.33	1.00	Second Design, Extra-Low Ratio (T-10Y)
3.44	2.28	1.46	1.00	Second Design, Ultra-Low Ratio (T-10U)

Ford's top loader four-speed is a tough transmission. This one can handle all the torque your engine can dish out, and is available with streetable gear ratios. Note two sets of shifter-mounting bosses on tailhousing of transmission in foreground.

Forward speed changes are accomplished by means of synchronizer sleeves that allow quick, smooth shifts and permit downshifts into first while the car is in motion. The four-speed version of the top loader is the second in the modern Ford line of transmissions. Their three-speed was the first American manual shift transmission with a fully synchronized low gear.

Through the years many minor versions of the top loader appeared, as did other high-performance Ford products. The top loader has two different front bolt patterns and tail-shaft lengths—a long one and short one. Some tailshaft housings have two sets of linkage bosses, but most only have one set. The skilled transmission rebuilder, however, can switch most parts. And, all gear sets are interchangeable.

The 1964 through mid-1965 top loader three- and four-speed transmissions came with a 10-spline input shaft and 25-spline output shaft. In late 1965, output-shaft spline count was increased to 28 and, although for street performance this is a minor advantage, the 28 should be favored over the 25-spline output shaft.

For years, factory engineers have claimed that the top loader has a life expectancy of 100,000 service-free miles. That's a long drive, but I've never heard a street rodder dispute the claim. The 10-spline input-shaft version was designed for use with the small-block V8, so it is a natural for rod builders contemplating this source of power. As we shall see a bit later, however, the rather large external shift linkage will not fit without mod-

ification to the early Ford X-membered chassis.

Today, although it has been replaced with smaller, high-tech five-speed and four-speed-plus-overdrive transmissions, the super-tough T&C top loader muscle box is still the first choice for Ford-oriented street-rod builders who double as do-it-yourself shifters. In fact, there's almost universal agreement—the Ford design four-speed is probably the best low cost, high-performance manual-shift transmission available.

MoPar New Process— 1964 was a good year for "clutch-and-shift" buffs as the Chrysler Corporation, in addition to Ford, unveiled its heavy-duty, high-performance four-speed manual transmission. Through the years, the *New Process A-833* has met with such acceptance that it remains in production to this day. Since the mid '60s, however, it's been offered in a long tailshaft version for intermediate and full-size cars, a shorter version for smaller cars, and an overdrive version. In addition to these major variations, the company offers a large selection of gear ratios from which to pick and choose.

Except for a special racing case and the 1975—76 "Feather Duster" models, all other MoPar A-833 models have cast-iron cases. The more durable cast-iron unit is the one to use in a street rod. Two different input-shaft diameters have been in use since the A-833's inception: The common one has a 1-in. diameter with 23 splines. A super-duty version with a 1-3/16-in. shaft has 18 splines. The transmission with the 18-spline shaft was used behind the 426 Hemi. It remained in use

through the production years of the venerable 440 engines.

A number of different drive-pinion bearing retainers has been used. Consequently, mix-ups are common when inexperienced hands attempt to build a tranny from a box full of parts. So, avoid using anything but a complete transmission in as close to factory configuration as possible.

This wraps up my discussion of four-speed transmissions that are appropriate for the modern street rod. If you are sincerely interested in the specifics of their function and repair, there are scads of manuals available to you. What's more important is that, in the hands of a competent driver who knows how to use one effectively, the four-speed transmission is far and away the best means of bringing out the best from your street-rod engine.

Clutch activation can be either mechanical or hydraulic. However, a hydraulic line is much easier to install than a cable or pushrods and a bellcrank, particularly in tight quarters.

FORD T&C TOP-LOADER TRANSMISSION RATIOS

1st	2nd	3rd	4th	Description
2.78	1.93	1.36	1.00	Wide-Ratio (1964—73)
2.32	1.69	1.29	1.00	Close-Ratio (1964—73)
3.29	1.84	1.00	.81	Overdrive (1977—78)
3.07	1.72	1.00	.70	Overdrive (1979—86)

CHRYSLER A-833 TRANSMISSION RATIOS

1st	2nd	3rd	4th	Description
2.66	1.91	1.39	1.00	1964—70 (23-spline pilot shaft)
2.65	1.93	1.39	1.00	1964—70 (18-spline pilot shaft)
2.47	1.77	1.34	1.00	1971—74 (23-spline pilot shaft)
2.44	1.77	1.34	1.00	1971—74 (18-spline pilot shaft)
3.09	1.92	1.40	1.00	1974—75 (318 CID, 23-spline pilot shaft)
3.09	1.67	1.00	0.73	1975—80 overdrive (23-spline pilot shaft)
2.65	1.64	1.19	1.00	(18-spline pilot shaft, Red Racing-Stripe Version)

(All years of manufacture are approximate because factory interchanges were common.)

Stout bracketry at both master cylinder and slave cylinder (shown) is a must.

Install Engine 13

Engine installation requires checking and re-checking to be sure positioning is correct and clearances are adequate.

DESIGN & BUILD ENGINE MOUNTS

The mid '50s backyard builder could usually do early swaps. Even if his homemade engine mounts were somewhat crude, they were usually functional. Yet, because the variety was limited even then, some manufacturers saw the opportunity in mass producing mounts for installing the more popular engines in Ford chassis.

As for current engine-mount availability, if you decide to break away from the crowd and use an engine other than what's popular, particularly in a non-Ford chassis, you are right back where it all started . . . shade-tree engineering.

There's a price to pay for individualism, though, and that is the work that goes beyond merely welding or bolting-in commercial engine and transmission mounts. With the endless list of possible combinations, engine swapping truly becomes a do-it-yourself operation.

Do It On Paper First—If you are installing Brand X engine in Old Car Y, do your design work on paper before you reach for a cutting torch and wrenches. Carefully measure the engine hold and general underhood area from every direction and angle. Then, lay out your findings in three-view form on poster board—side, front and top, or plan views. Pay close attention to the configuration of the firewall and the exact location of the front crossmember and steering gear. Cross-sectional views are necessary if there are significant front-to-back changes such as an engine compartment that narrows from back to front. The point is, you should know the exact relationships that exist in the engine compartment.

Next, measure and sketch the engine and transmission you are going to install. Be sure the distributor, intake and exhaust manifolds, starter and alternator all are in place. That doesn't mean that some of these won't be modified or repositioned. You simply eliminate as many surprises as possible before you get committed.

This preliminary work might seem unneccessary, but don't be in a rush. An hour or two spent measuring and sketching can pay handsome dividends. It may also save you grief later on. If you do your homework, you should get a fair idea of where your engine swap problems lie . . . maybe even before you rush out and buy that "double-throw-down V12 rocket." Who knows, you might even decide that common-as-belly buttons small-block V8 isn't such a bad idea after all!

Place Engine—Regardless of how careful you are, you won't find every problem until you physically drop that engine into your engine compartment. There, suspended by a chain hoist and supported by a floor jack under the block, the engine and transmission can be moved up and down and back and forth until a suitable position is found. A carpenter's level on the intake manifold where the carburetor mounts will be a big help in determining the desirable attitude, but perfection isn't always attainable.

Once you have the engine where you want it, sit back and study the layout. Keep in mind when designing the engine mounts or any bracketry that the simplest design is usually the best. Note where the engine-mount bosses are cast into the block. If possible, use them for bolting on your custom mounts.

Anticipate what and where interference problems may occur. Consider accessibility for routine maintenance such as sparkplug removal, head-bolt torquing, oil-filter access and clearance to steering gear, exhaust manifolds, and transmission shift linkage.

Anything can be done in a dozen different ways, so review your options before you go too far. You should never weld or cut into a frame unless it is necessary. Review the situation from several angles and consider all methods of mount construction before you light the torch. Don't be over eager to cut away offending metal. Remember, even if *you* don't care if something is cut or crudely beaten into submission, a potential buyer somewhere in the distant future will care. So, don't trash the car and ruin a future sale by not doing things carefully and neatly. Do it right the first time.

Make Patterns—Steel is very difficult to work with. It's hard and it takes a lot of tiresome cutting with a saw or torch. Even grinding rough edges is time consuming. So, to speed the job, get some stiff poster board, a pair of scissors and a 12-in. rule. A straight edge, a roll of masking tape and a tape measure will round out your basic tools.

Following your preliminary design, cut out bits of poster board into various shapes and tape them in position. Cut and trim or add pieces on with masking tape until you achieve a perfect fit; don't be unwilling to change or modify the design. Poster board is cheap. It's easier, less costly and much quicker to use a pencil, paper and masking tape that it is to use a cutting torch.

Don't overdesign your engine mounts. But, keep in mind that your power package, which weighs more than 500 pounds, will try to jump right out of your car when you're on the power. The engine-and-transmission assembly must be supported in at least three places: left and right sides of the engine and somewhere under the transmission.

The carburetor base must be approximately level and the crankshaft must align with the drive shaft. Furthermore, engine mounts not only position the engine assembly and support it, they must also resist torque loads. Conversely, they must not transmit any deflection of the frame rails. In fact, the weakest feature of any mount is usually the method of securing it to the chassis, so design accordingly.

After you've finalized your engine-mount design, transfer the designs, full scale, to poster board and cut them out. Accurate bolt patterns can be obtained by holding a piece of poster board to the bosses on the block and tapping gently around the edges with a ball-peen hammer. To double-check the fit, tape the pattern pieces together and then tape the engine-mount mockups in place on both sides of the engine.

A good design may not develop first time around, but shouldn't take more than one additional attempt. Once you're satisfied with what you have, take the poster-board patterns to a sheet-metal shop that has a heavy-duty shear and have two sets or mounts cut from 1/8-in.-thick steel. This thickness is usually adequate unless you were too stingy with gussets. If you don't feel comfortable welding lighter-gage sheet metal, use 1/4-in. plate. It's bulkier, but certainly won't hurt anything.

When you return with your custom engine-mount kit, bolt the designated parts to the block and frame and fit in the connecting pieces. *Don't* weld the mount together on the bench; warpage and misalignment will result. The best method of assembly is to tack weld the pieces solidly together with the engine and frame acting as a holding fixture. Try not to burn the rubber-insulated supports.

After you have an assembly and are happy with the overall fit, finish the welding job on the bench. Run a weld bead on both sides of the joints whenever possible.

Store-Bought Engine Mounts—If you elect to install one of the mainstream engine-and-transmission combinations in an early Ford or Chevy frame, the design and fabrication has already been done for you by the street-rod-

components manufacturers. Prefabricated engine mounts can greatly simplify your engine and transmission installation and reduce overall cost. Not only that, you have a lot more time and energy to resolve the predictable, but often unique, swap-related problems for which there are no commercially available products.

In the mid-to-late '50s, a few manufacturers such as Hurst Performance and Trans-Dapt of California recognized the commercial possibilities in engine/transmission-swap hardware. They tooled up to bring adapters, mounts and full installation kits to market. Early engine mounts often were bolted to the very front of the engine in the fashion of the Ford flathead water pump/engine mount combination. Although this design was unquestioned, much room for improvement is equally unquestioned. The side-mount setup has long since become the standard Dearborn/Detroit method of engine support and has been adapted by most street-rod builders.

Today's commercial offerings are not significantly different from their forebears. Inasmuch as there is much less emphasis on dual-purpose drag-race/street-driven cars, and more emphasis on hardware show quality, engine mounts are lighter. And, they almost always incorporate factory rubber-insulated engine supports.

Whereas street rodders were once hell-bent on matching every conceivable engine to every conceivable transmission, today it is fashionable and often far more sensible to use the exact factory transmission and mating

hardware. Installation kits, therefore, reflect this trend and offer compatible engine and transmission mounts.

And, also, you should keep original old-car sheet metal intact. So, even though many prefer one or another of the stock exhaust manifolds for either quietness of operation or lower cost, using custom headers is more preferable than modifying vintage tin. Commercial kits are often designed with metal preservation in mind. Additionally, exhaust headers are sometimes available for popular engine/old-car combinations.

Indeed, if you are working with an ever-popular Chevy or Ford small-block V8 and the early Ford chassis, you will find that the world of commercial street-rod components is your oyster. You can pluck from it whatever variety of pearl you wish. Your choices are not limited to engine and transmission mounts, either. A wide array of related components such as radiators, alternator brackets, steering-box adapters, air-conditioning adapters, supercharger installation kits and so on and so forth, are available for the asking.

Even if you have only half the popular combination—a Chevy or Ford V8—you'll find enough universal engine and transmission adapters to fit your engine into most any old-car chassis. Commercial offerings typically include tubular-type crossmembers of longer-than-necessary length with end pieces. Some trimming will almost always get the job done.

Turn to page 194 for a listing of engine and transmission swap-kit suppliers.

Without the body in place on its '41 frame, it looks as if there's excess room around this small-block Ford. However, sheet-metal modifications in and around the firewall area will be required. But that's the price of using modern Dearborn power.

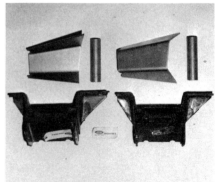

For mounting Ford small-block in my much-modified '40 chassis, I used rubber insulators designed for the engine and *unwelded* 1934 mounts on the frame side. Often, an item for one application will work in another. Most manufacturers will sell bits and pieces from kits for your particular needs.

Engine is suspended in place and angles checked with carpenter's level and Sears Inclinometer. Oil pan should have minimum clearance of 3/4 in. to crossmember. Room is also needed to remove oil filter and other crit l items.

Engine should be no more than 1/2 in. off-center in frame. Also, be certain engine is parallel to frame rails.

Once engine is positioned, tack-weld mounts so they will support engine block. Don't scorch rubber components.

Crew at Don McNeil's Specialized Auto Components tackled updating of this 1941 Ford chassis with relish. End result is a slick engine and transmission swap with a minimum of *frame* modification.

Don't complete welding until you're sure engine, now with its weight supported by the mount, is exactly where you want it. Re-measure in all directions to be sure.

SAC started with what was essentially a slightly longer '40 Ford tubular crossmember and ended up with a brand-new product that promises to meet the needs of any '40 owner who dreams of up-to-date Henry horsepower.

Some say 1946—48 Ford is on outer fringes of street rodding, but don't say that to anybody who built one. A newly rodded "late-model" Ford hits the bricks every day. And more and more street-rod-components manufacturers are taking notice.

Post-war engine compartments are a bit larger than earlier models in all directions. As in all other cases—without exception—the best all-around engine swap is the Chevy.

Small-block Chevy will easily install in bone-stock '39 Chevy coupe. Commercial mounts are readily available, but home-fabricated engine mounts utilizing stock rubber supports work equally well.

Not long ago, Don McNeil's Specialized Auto Components designed this engine swap kit for installing a 350 Chevy and Turbo 400 in a '48 rag top.

Engine mounts slip over factory-boxed frame rails and are secured by two long bolts.

SAC wishbone-splitting kit provided room needed for big GM tranny without need for significant sheet-metal modifications.

Chevy V8 in a stock 1937—40 Ford installation is 95% compromise-free with commercial mounts . . .

. . . except, in this case, for the need to split the wishbone for an automatic transmission and the utilization of an electric fuel pump.

Installation of Chevy small-block in 1939—41 pickup or panel truck is equally easy. Many of these models had a *deep-dish* crossmember to accommodate six-cylinder engine.

Several commercial kits offer high-quality engine mounts and other components to ease the pain of installing an engine.

Double-thickness C-channel frame members such as those for early Fords of the late '30s and early '40s, naturally lend themselves to more-or-less bolt-in engine mounts. Don McNeil demonstrates that many of his kits require only the enlargement of existing factory holes to install a tuck-in mount.

When your heart's desire is a V6, as it was for Brad Stone, it doesn't make too much difference what early car you chose to street rod—most every combination comes together like a dream. Brad's V6 Buick resides in a much-modified non-Ford body and chassis.

Ford small-block in 1937—40 Ford passenger car is a tight fit. Overall configuration of FoMoCo 221-351W clashes both at the firewall and crossmember.

Big installation help is the use of one of the late Ford oil pans with reduced front depths. These are available for both 289/302 (Bronco), 351W (van), and 351C (truck), engines.

Installation of Ford small-block in '40-type is a challenge. Even with a mid-sump oil pan, be aware that you must rework firewall in order to set engine behind stock crossmember.

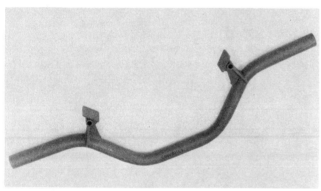

Progressive Automotive 6.5-in. dropped mount is made of heavy 0.120-in.-wall tubing. Assembly is jig-welded to ensure correct fit of Chevy V6 and V8 into any chassis. Most tubular mounts are designed to accommodate factory rubber mounts.

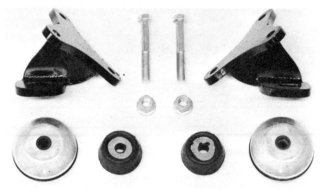

Pair of Chevy big- or small-block V8 side mounts permits installation of that engine in virtually any make of car. Mounts are manufactured by Bill Keifer's California Custom Roadsters.

Tubular engine and transmission mounts have long been street-rod favorites. They are relatively inexpensive, install easily in a variety of situations and look professional.

SAC's simple weld-on Chevy side mounts work well in boxed original 1932—34 Ford frame or their own handsome reproduction frame.

Before installing remainder of drive line, and particularly before modifying frame in any way, be sure engine and transmission are sitting at correct angle. Carburetor mounting surface should be level.

SHIFTERS & GEAR SELECTORS

Although many automatic transmissions in the wrecking yard will have their original floor shifters attached, many will not. So, you'll either have to pay extra for a stock shifter or purchase an aftermarket unit. Fortunately, the additional cost of a top-quality aftermarket automatic shifter is easily justified when compared with the original factory units. Not only do the aftermarket shifters better lend themselves to street-rod applications, they are designed for heavy-duty use. Simply, they are better for street-rod use. Many original floor shifters use cables and relatively weak linkages.

Better aftermarket kits, such as those offered by Hurst, incorporate positive latching and shift control. Once you are accustomed to using such a shifter, it's nearly impossible to miss a gear. What! Miss a gear with an automatic? Sure, ask the driver of any Ford-powered street rod with a C-4 or C-6 who has "gone through the gears." Or the poor street rodder who mistakenly *dumped* it in reverse.

A Touch Of Tradition—One of the slickest shifters to come down the road in recent years is Tom Phipps' *Gennie Shifter*. In true street-rodder fashion, Tom built the first one for

MAKE ROOM FOR THE AUTOMATIC

An automatic transmission for a V8 usually fits OK in the typical more-or-less original street-rod chassis. In cases where a reasonably small transmission is chosen—Powerglide, TH 350, C-4 or TorqueFlite 903—the primary problem is clearance in and about the area where chassis members converge at the center of the frame. Of course, all but the very early Chevy, Ford and MoPar frames have some type of K-member or X-member for strength, so some interference will occur in these installations.

Back in the days when little thought was given to neat and clean chassis modifications, the usual approach was to eliminate interferences with a cutting torch. Just get that engine and transmission bolted in. Afterwards, if the frame then seemed a little *too* flexy, channel-iron sections were welded in parallel to the transmission.

In actuality, the same thing is done today, only with much more finess. Instead of crawling under the chassis with torch in hand, you should do the job right and take your sweet time. In the case of vintage tin, the body should be off the frame. Regardless, transmission-to-chassis interferences should be carefully chalked out, then cuts should be made with a sabre saw or hacksaw. A cutting torch should only be used as a last resort.

As always, what was removed from the frame must be returned even though it may be in a different place. Parallel C-sections are still the most common approach but not just any old chunk of channel iron can be used. Several street-rod-components manufacturers offer bits and pieces for the more common installations. These time-savers are attractive replacements.

Where store-bought pieces are not available, take some careful measurements and either make a cardboard pattern or a sketch of what you need. Perfect-fit C-sections of the right gage and dimension are as close as the nearest sheet-metal shop. Prices are so reasonable you'd wonder why anybody would consider using a piece of channel iron.

Modifications to stock early Ford chassis are almost always required. Clearance for transmission shifter is being made. See also page 98.

Minor repair and modification of frame may be done without removing body. Specialized Auto Components fabricated replacement sections in same gage as original frame and welded them in.

Repro street-rod-chassis manufacturers provide for plenty of mid-section clearance for popular manual and automatic transmissions.

Bill Keifer's California Custom Roadsters offers this drop-out-type transmission mount. Made from 3/8-in. plate, mount bolts onto CCR T-bucket frame. Mount accepts all Chevy automatic transmissions.

Repro 1934 chassis built by Specialized Auto Components utilizes stout rectangular tubing in the center of frame with drop-out transmission mount.

Gennie Shifter has become a favorite for use on transplanted Turbo Hydra-matic. Shifter is most often found in the early to mid-'30s cars where original *stick-shift* look is cherished.

Sometimes, just sometimes, an automatic transmission will fit the confines of a stock firewall and floorboard. This lucky builder found this to be the case with a Turbo 350 in his '48 Ford.

himself with no commercial plans in mind . . . 'til someone saw it and wanted one like it. Basically, the Gennie has a look-alike early Ford shift handle with an attaching assembly that fits over and around the TH 350 and TH 400 transmission. It allows gear selection from the typical street rod's normal seated height. No bending over and twisting 'round to find a stubby gear selector down by your right heel. The shift handle comes up out of the floorboard in approximately the original position of the three-speed shifter.

The Gennie Shifter comes pre-assembled with full installation instructions. It is quickly and easily installed on the transmission. Depending on the location of the transmission,

floorboard modifications may or may not be required. Seldom are such modifications major, though. An added feature, and one well worth having, is the neutral safety switch included with each kit.

Column Shifts For Automatics—Not everybody wants a floor shifter, of course. Many family-oriented street rods, such as two- and four-door sedans, need all the passenger comfort and space they can get, particularly when there's no intention of doing any weekend racing.

There are two ways to eliminate the floor shifter—three if you count the old MoPar dashboard push-button shifter that incorporated solenoids. Unfortunately, the only available parts for these are in wrecking yards. They are getting along in years, and therefore are not reliable.

The two column shifts I recommend, however, are the adaptation of a later-model steering column with shifter, or the modification of the original column shift, if practical.

For a while during the '40s and early '50s, the competition-oriented 1939 Ford floor shifter lost its popularity among street-rod builders. And, many pre-'40 Ford based street rods were customized with 1940—48 side-shift transmissions, steering columns, steering wheels and column shifters.

Now, I certainly wouldn't tout the old side-shift transmission and its monkey-motion linkage. If you are old enough to remember when these were popular, you must also remember the need to replace shift-rod grommets frequently. They always seemed to break or fall out at night during an impromptu drag race!

The fact of the matter is, though, that thin, later-model columns install well and look at home in most pre-'40 Fords. They are also easy to modify for use as a column-mounted automatic-transmission shifter. To do so, you need only weld a tab on the shift tube down near the pillow block to attach either a rod or a cable running from it to the transmission. If a rod is used, get a 3-foot length of 3/8- or 7/16-in. aluminum rod and a pair of steel clevises. Avoid using a steel rod because its weight and resulting inertia may cause an involuntary downshift when you hit a severe bump.

Make a pattern for the shift rod from a piece of 3/32-in. welding rod . . . or simply an old coat hanger. Check clearances in the highest as well as the lowest shift-handle positions. Make sure that you can service that last spark plug, too.

Several brands of transmissions have one gear-selector lever for a console (floor) shift model and another for a column-shift model. Usually, the gear-selector assembly is easily exchanged. If your transmission has the opposite of what you need, drop by a transmission rebuild shop. They'll have scads of miscellaneous parts such as these.

The other method of changing gears by way of a column shifter is to use a housed, thick, but flexible cable. You can select one of the original-equipment units such as the Ford big-car type used from the late '60s through most of the '70s. It is a hefty, easily adaptable cable.

Another option is to go to a marine-supply house and have them make up a stainless-steel *Morse* type cable to the exact length required. Although a bit expensive, the Morse cable is classy and trouble free. Marine supply houses also have a good assortment of attaching

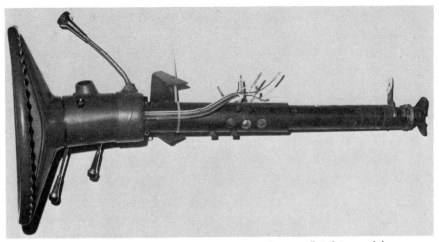

Tilt/telescoping steering columns from GM compact or intermediate late-model passenger cars such as '74 Olds Cutlass column offer modern convenience and safety. Also, their integral automatic-transmission gear selectors are easily adapted to early cars.

hardware that are the best pieces to use with a Morse cable.

Steering Columns—If you want the most modern of everything in your car, you may frown on the old-style steering column with its modified shifter. In this case, you may be a prime candidate for an energy-absorbing/tilt steering column such as found in passenger cars since the late '60s. These columns have been popular with luxury-prone street rodders for several years.

Energy-absorbing steering columns are designed to compress under impact during a collision to reduce injuries and save lives. The energy-absorbing feature is a particularly good idea when it comes to street rods because few owners have seen fit to install shoulder harnesses. This is strange when you consider the race-car heritage of street rodding; high-performance cars with low-performance passenger protection doesn't make sense. When was the last time you saw a race car without belt restraints?

The additional tilt and tilt/telescoping aspects of most energy-absorbing steering columns are perhaps even more desirable in a street rod than they were in the original car. Ford T and A models are notoriously difficult to get in and out of. I know of one middle-aged street rodder who claims the cockpit of his Model A shrunk!

Be that as it may, the modern tilt steering column has several different wheel-angle positions. It's a tilt-and-telescoping column, it also has an infinite number of distance settings between the driver's midsection and the steering wheel within a 2-in. range.

The telescoping feature is typically operated by a locking lever. The wheel is attached to an upper shaft that slides into the upper yoke. When the locking lever is re-

leased, pressure on the locking rod and wedge is reduced, allowing the shaft to move.

The steering wheel is adjusted by rotating the locking lever counterclockwise and then pulling or pushing the wheel into the desired position. When the lever is rotated clockwise, the wheel locks.

The most critical aspect of installing an energy absorbing/tilt/telescoping column in a street rod is not the actual installation; it's the removal of the unit from the donor car at the wrecking yard. If you purchase one that's been removed, inspect it carefully. If it looks OK, get a guarantee that it is not damaged. If you remove it yourself, you'll need a special wheel puller for that particular column. After you've removed the column, prevent anyone from leaning on the assembly or laying things across or on it. Of course, dropping an energy-absorbing column could shear or loosen the plastic fasteners that hold the shaft in place.

The column assembly may be disassembled and reassembled at home, but care must be taken not to confuse the screws, nuts and bolts that you remove. Be sure that no over-length bolts are used for re-assembly. There's no sense in going to all this trouble only to have something bind at that critical moment when you need it. All bolts must be re-tightened to the manufacturer's specified torque. Specifications and adjustments vary from manufacturer to manufacturer, so get the appropriate shop manual. If you can't get a manual, drop by the dealer some lazy Thursday afternoon when they're not too busy and ask the service writer or parts guy to photocopy the pages you need.

Although the installation of a modern tilt column is easiest when a late steering gear is used, the hook-up is no different from those

Tubular transmission mounts in earlier chassis that have been relieved of original K- and X-members solve many clearance problems and restore strength to frame.

Can't beat reproduction frame when it comes to room needed for transmission.

Installation of late-model manual transmission in early car frame usually requires as much room as does automatic . . . if not more. Picturered from top to bottom, modification to X-member for gear-selector clearance is almost always necessary. Specialized Auto Components offers this *chassis widener.* Installation is relatively simple, body on or body off. Offending tight spot on frame is carefully laid out and cut out slightly smaller than necessary. Widener is trial-fitted, frame is trimmed for a more precise fit, and widener is welded in. Ample room for four-speed is thereby provided with a minimum of surgery. In this instance stock clutch and brake pedals were used.

discussed in the chapter on steering systems, page 139.

MANUAL TRANSMISSIONS

Although I've said it before, you'll be better off using the transmission that belongs to the engine of your choice. If, however, you decide on using some other transmission—foreign both to engine and car—you must use an adapter plate or adapter bellhousing to bolt the two together.

'Way back before transmission adapter plates and bellhousings were commercially available, the hot rodder made his own. And, even today if you persist in mating an unusual power plant/drive train combination, you'd better have substantial metalworking skills and complete machine-shop resources.

Some adapter plates are no more than large, flat, steel or aluminum circles drilled to match the back of the engine bellhousing with separate threaded bolt holes laid out in a pattern that matches the transmission. The four-speed transmissions we suggested in the previous chapter, however, are built with smaller front case configurations than were earlier gear boxes. Therefore, the adapter needed is a more complicated cast-aluminum bellhousing that sandwiches between the engine and gear case.

A pilot-bearing adapter is also required. It locates the input shaft directly in the center of the crankshaft and, although it's a relatively simple bronze component, it must be precisely dimensioned.

Caution: Even though I touched on this earlier, I'll repeat: When installing a *hybrid* power package, pay special attention to the engine and transmission mounting points. The engine and transmission should always

be mounted at no less than three points. And, it is not good practice to use front mounts ala the flathead or, heaven forbid, a single mount even though Oldsmobile and a few other manufacturers have done so in the past. Powerplants supported at the front of the engine and at the rear are subjected to excess bending loads. This may cause damage to the transmission case, attaching bolts and the adapter. Aluminum housings and cases in this type of installation have fractured under high-performance use.

Installing a Four-Speed—Regardless of how neat you think it is to run through "real" gears, especially when that four-speed is behind a healthy V8, installing that fun-box between the frame members of an early car is rarely easy—if you want to do it neatly. What is often deceiving is the basic measurements. A transmission case is so many inches long and wide, and because most *are* small and slim, you may assume that manual transmissions install just as easily as an automatic. They don't!

It's true that a manual gear box usually doesn't take up any more space than its automatic brethren. In fact, it often has fewer bulges. And, year for year, the four-speed manual transmission frequently uses an identical spline count, the same length yoke and the same drive shaft as does the automatic. Automatics and four-speeds often share the same mount and crossmember.

The problem lies with packaging the shifting linkage. The Ford top loader shifter and linkage assembly, for instance, is about 27 in. to the rear of the flywheel and extends left of center about 6 in. You can guess where that's going to put it in the typical street-rod cockpit. Yep, almost under your right foot . . . or

Handsomely detailed Nash five-speed transmission installation with mechanical clutch linkage is excellent example of a well-excecuted driveline installation.

Hurst shifter is available in a wide variety of styles and applications. Often, changing shifter handle will solve a space dilemma.

worse, under your seat. Even bucket seats don't help much.

Because of that, and no matter how sacrosanct you may hold the original floorboard and frame members, there's simply no way of avoiding alterations. Frame and/or floorboard modifications can be performed without leaving irreparable damage, however.

Because most jobs will be done without prior knowledge of just what is required, you must put an access hole in the floorboard. Cut out a slightly larger-than-necessary section of the floorboard, but please use a sabre saw! And, save the cutout. Part of it can be welded back in after the frame work is completed. A big piece is a lot easier to modify and return than a too-conservative cut that may well require additional trimming . . . and leave you with a bunch of useless scraps.

Don't Forget the Clutch—Another thought-provoking problem is clutch activation. Fortunately, you have two ways to approach this problem: devise a one-off mechanical linkage or install an extra master cylinder and a hydraulic slave unit.

Mechanical Clutch Linkage—Designing a suitable mechanical linkage that fits in tight quarters and doesn't collapse or bind when you "lean into it" isn't easy. Notice that few modern cars have them.

But, that doesn't stop the aftermarket companies from offering suitable kits for the push-pull trade. McLeod Industries, well known for their huge inventory of street and competition clutches, has a universal kit for race cars. This mechanical clutch-linkage kit could easily be used in any street-rod frame as wide or wider than the 1935 Ford. The kit is based on the 1955 Chevy design, but lends itself well to modification as the need arises.

Hydraulic-Clutch Linkage—Because designing, building and mounting clevises, bell cranks and pushrods is often very difficult, many street-rod builders turned to hydraulic clutch linkages years ago. The major advantage with a hydraulic linkage is that you don't have to package all those bellcranks and pushrods, just a hose.

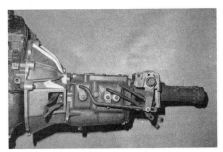

Hurst shifter gained its reputation on the drag strip, but remains one of the best for street-rod use.

Back in the mid '60s when the tough muscle-car four-speeds gained popularity, the hot tip was to use the 1958 Ford half-ton pickup slave cylinder for the custom installation of a "juice clutch." The unit worked well with any stock passenger-car brake master cylinder when the check valve was removed. A number of full-size Chevy and International pickup-truck models from the '60s and '70s use dual master cylinders and correctly sized slave cylinders that are easily adapted to the street rod.

There are also complete hydraulic clutch-and-brake-pedal assemblies offered by the aftermarket. Although they cater mainly to the racing trade, some companies are Neal Products, 7170 Ronson Rd., San Diego, CA 92111; Tilton Engineering, McMurray Rd. & Easy St., Buellton, CA 93427; Ja-Mar Off-Road Products, 293000 3rd St. San Rafael, CA 94903; and Speedway Motors, P.O. Box 81906, Lincoln, NE 68501.

SHIFTERS FOR MANUAL TRANSMISSIONS

A stock floor shifter will sometimes work in a street rod if the car is channelled. They are designed for modern cars that sit quite a bit lower than many street rods, particularly those based on 1935—48 models.

In the latter case, the driver must hunch over to reach the shift lever. Because he must

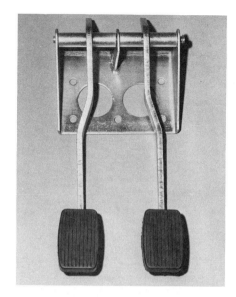

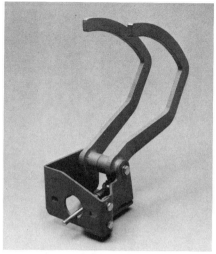

Clutch activation isn't always easily solved. Fortunately, however, components manufacturers offer several different types of replacement clutch and brake pedals. Frame-mount assembly is from the Deuce Factory and, although designed for repro 1932 frame, it can be used in a variety of applications.

Aftermarket hanging pedal assembly (top) has long been a favorite for street rods with cramped quarters, both in cockpit and frame. Designed to match GM dual master cylinder, they should be purchased as a unit to avoid mismatches. Substantial firewall bracing is required.

also depress the clutch at the same time, he can quickly grow weary. The *ergonomics*—mechanics of the body—just aren't there.

It is difficult to modify many stock shifters because the handle is often a tubular affair mounting finger levers with cables running through for reverse gear. In short, they are too complex.

The premier aftermarket shifter, of course, is the Hurst unit that dates back to the '50s. Not only does Hurst Performance manufacture a number of simple and extremely rugged shifters, they offer bolt-on, interchangeable shifter handles in a variety of shapes and lengths. Although they are designed primarily for late-model cars, the

likelihood of arriving at a workable combination is much greater than with stock parts.

Pedal Problems—The further you progress in the construction of your street rod, the more you'll become convinced that the task you so willingly accepted back in the beginning is more demanding than buying parts from catalogs and screwing them all together. Often it's an exercise in decision making and a test of one's problem-solving skills. In fact, devising a suitable clutch-and-brake pedal assembly can sometimes be one of those tasks that can tax your abilities to the limit.

Fortunately, you have a wide variety of domestic and import production car and light-truck assemblies from which to choose. The wrecking yards are full of 'em and a general survey of what's available is often the best place to start.

Rather quickly, however, you must make another one of those pesky little, but important decisions: Are you going to mount the pedal assembly in the frame below the floorboards like Henry and Louie did . . . or are you going to take what appears to be the easy way out and go for swing pedals mounted to the cockpit side of the firewall?

Of course, you must coordinate the approach to your pedal problems with the decision you make regarding the method of clutch activation . . . hydraulic or mechanical. Decisions, decisions.

Like so many other rod-building problems, however, I believe it is best to approach the

installation of pedal assemblies with pencil, paper and tape measure close at hand. The size and configuration of the frame at its mid-section, plus the width of the transmission, may be such that the firewall is the only practical place to mount a pedal assembly. An extreme example, but certainly not an unusual one, is the installation of a small-block Chevy V8 with a TH 400 transmission in a Fad T frame.

The largest of the GM transmissions in the smallest street-rod frame is a real challenge if floorboard pedals are desired because there's precious little space betwixt and between. Unfortunately, you must accept the fact that, as is, the stock firewall is usually too flimsy for pedal mounting. That means you have to design in extra beef if swing pedals are to be used.

Or, structural integrity and space considerations aside, perhaps you simply don't like the esthetics of firewall-mounted cylinders. In that case, you should look outside of the accepted street-rod parts resources at something akin to the polished aluminum mini-wonders that dune-buggy and off-road builders use.

Sometimes, when all is said and done, nothing will work "out of the box." Although there are literally hundreds of pedal assemblies to choose from, old-fashioned street-rod backyard engineering may still be required to achieve a sanitary installation that functions safely and properly. What that means, of course, is coming up with a unique design incorporating bits and pieces from stock and aftermarket assemblies. Street-rod building has always had that as its bottom line.

Regardless of which type of linkage you use and where you mount the pedals, pedal travel and load are two factors you must be concerned with. For instance, limit pedal travel to 6-1/2 in. and load to about 50 pounds—40 pounds if possible. This is done by calculating the various lever ratios and/or hydraulic-cylinder sizes you're considering for the clutch linkage.

Exactly how to design and choose mechanical or hydraulic clutch-linkage components is detailed in HPBooks' *Clutch & Flywheel Handbook*. It covers everything from the driver's leg, through the clutch linkage, pressure plate, and to the flywheel and bellhousing.

DRIVE SHAFT & U-JOINTS

Since the '30s, Ford cars were built with torque-tube drive lines. A universal joint was splined to a solid drive shaft, which was, in turn, attached to the differential pinion gear by means of a splined collar. The entire apparatus was enclosed in the torque tube.

Stout as this arrangement may appear, it was no trick to tear up a universal joint or shear the end off of a drive shaft with a mildly hopped-up flathead. Only a few purists and restorers were saddened by its departure.

The last hurdle in building the modern street-rod drive train, therefore, is fitting a tubular drive shaft—the so-called *open drive line*.

The drive shaft—technically known as the *propeller shaft*—is the connecting link between the transmission and differential. In order to transfer the rotary motion of the transmission output shaft to the differential, two facts of conventional front engine/rear-wheel-drive power-train design must be taken into consideration. First, the engine and transmission are more or less rigidly attached to the frame; and secondly, the rear-axle assembly is more or less flexibly attached to the frame by springs.

Now, this may seem like a simple mechanical challenge, but engine torque must be smoothly relayed to the rear-axle assembly while it is continually traveling up and down, twisting and tilting while going down the road. And as you can imagine, the geometry is far from simple. Drive torque, braking and road irregularities are constantly changing both the angle of drive to the axle assembly, and the distance between the transmission output shaft and differential.

Fortunately for us all, the English physicist, Robert Hooke, solved part of the problem about 300 years before the automobile was invented. Hooke's joint—two yokes on planes perpendicular to each other and pivotally connected by a cross-shaped piece—was the first successful means of transmitting rotary motion through two shafts that are at an angle to each other. Hence the modern universal joint or, simply, U-joint.

Two separate devices are necessary to compensate for the variation in angle and length in the modern automotive drive line, however. Universal joints are only used to compensate for variations in the angle of drive. Additionally, a *slip joint* is needed to allow fore and aft movement. Such slip joints usually have outside splines on one shaft and matching internal splines on a mating hollow shaft. This arrangement causes the two shafts to rotate together while also permitting the two to move endwise in relation to each other. Any change in the distance between the transmission and rear axle is thereby accommodated.

The slip joint is on the transmission end of the drive shaft and mates to the gear box's output shaft. And, although many different slip yokes are interchangeable—which theoretically means that you should be able to match any drive shaft to any transmission,

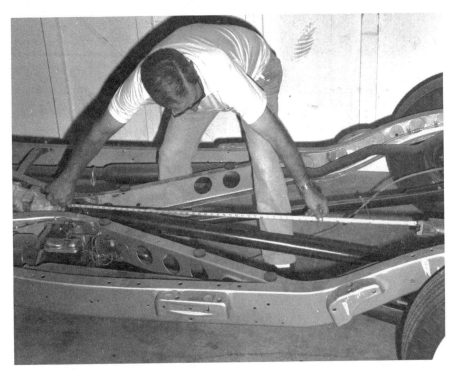

Measuring drive-shaft length is simple, but often not done correctly. Dan Dohan of Driveline Center in Mission Viejo, CA showed us how to do it the quick and easy way . . . slide yoke onto transmission ouput shaft until it bottoms. Measure space to be filled—from centerline of yoke U-joint to centerline of companion-flange U-joint—and subtract 2 in. That is the correct drive-shaft length, which incidentally, must be straight within a tolerance of 0.005 in., then balanced. *Always*.

even when you find one that fits—it will be too long. We'll deal with this problem in a moment, but first let's take a closer look at the basic U-joint and its limitations.

There are three different kinds of automotive universal joints, but two of them are rarely used in street rods. These include the *constant-velocity* joint, which consists of two U-joints linked by a ball and socket, and the *ball-and-trunnion* joint, which is a combination U-joint and slip joint,

U-Joint—The U-joint has the two-yoke combination with a journal cross supported by four needle-bearing cups that are in the *ears* of the yokes. These cups are held in place with retaining rings.

Universal-joint velocity fluctuates twice with every revolution of the drive line. The extent of this fluctuation depends on the angle between the driving and driven shafts. For instance, a relatively severe U-joint angle of 28° can develop a speed variation as high as 25%! Such a condition will lead to rapid U-joint wear.

In the typical front engine/rear-wheel-drive street rod with a wheelbase of 100—120 in., the irregularity in U-joint velocity can be eliminated. This is done by using one U-joint at each end of the drive shaft, providing the planes of the two joints are exactly aligned and the angle of the transmission output shaft and drive shaft is equal to the angle of the drive shaft and the differential pinion yoke. Nevertheless, it is important to plan your drive train installation so the U-joint angles are as small as possible—perhaps 5° or 6° when the car is at rest with a maximum of 18—20° when the suspension is in full rebound.

Getting In Phase—Installation geometry, however, is only part of your concern. All components must mate with precision. Usually engine/transmission/differential matings from the same family are easily accomplished after the drive shaft has been shortened. But not always. There are enough variations within every manufacturer's product line to ensure a mismatch once in awhile, not to mention the hybrid drive line—Ford transmission and Jag IRS, etc., etc.

Of course, there's no insurmountable problem regardless of what transmission and differential are destined to work as a team. You, however, need the skills of a competent and knowledgeable machine shop, preferably one versed in drive-line service. There, you can either have your mismatched parts modified or a completely new drive shaft tailored to your car's unique requirements.

Prior to that, you should be certain that the engine, transmission and rear-axle assembly are correctly located in the frame and in *phase*—the transmission output shaft is parallel with the axis of the pinion gear.

As long as the engine, transmission and rear axle are squarely installed in a frame that is perfectly square, the drive line will be in phase in the horizontal plane. This can be verified in your shop with nothing more than a tape measure. To check the rear-axle installation, measure the distance from the left rear axle centerline to some fixed point on the left frame rail, such as a factory rivet or hole. Find the same point on the right rail and measure from there to the right axle centerline. Both measurements should be within 1/16 in. of each other.

To verify that the engine is square in the frame, measure from the center of the crankshaft snout to both sides of the frame. Then, measure from the center of the transmission output shaft to both sides of the frame. If the center of the crank nose is closer to the passenger side frame rail than it is to the driver side by 1/2 in. (for instance), that's OK . . . *if* the transmission output shaft center is equally as close to the same rail. If it isn't, now is the time to correct the problem.

You can verify the angles of your drive line to be sure it is in vertical phase with an inexpensive Sears Craftsman "Inclinometer." These handy little gadgets, sometimes called *angle finders,* pay for themselves time and again. With the frame positioned level, determine the angle of the pinion shaft, by placing the inclinometer on the flat side of the pinion yoke.

Install a slip yoke on the transmission output shaft to determine its angle because the output shaft is too far inside the housing to support the inclinometer. If these two components are in phase, the sum of the *positive*—pointing down—angle of the transmission and the *negative*—pointing up—angle of the pinion shaft will equal 180°. If they don't . . . well, like the old song says, "There'll be some changes made." Or, at least, there should be.

After all of the foregoing has been squared away, the determination of the length of the drive shaft is a simple matter. Assuming the engine, transmission and rear-axle assembly are solidly bolted down, slide the slip-yoke onto the transmission output shaft. Push it all of the way on until it bottoms, then measure from the center of the yoke ear back to the bearing cup hole in the pinion flange. A helping hand will ensure accuracy. Subtract 2 in. from your measurement. This distance is the length of the drive shaft you'll need. You can either start looking for one of that exact length—good luck!—or one a few inches longer to cut down. Better yet, you can have one custom made.

Measuring U-Joints—Chances are a longer drive shaft will be easier to find. But hold on. Before you leave for the machine shop, measure what you have in the way of universal joints so you'll know what you still need.

The way to measure a universal joint depends upon the type of bearing retention it uses. Street-rod builders typically use American passenger-car rear axles manufactured since 1957 without constant-velocity or ball-and-trunnion U-joints. In those cases, the most common methods of bearing retention are either inside or outside retaining rings, with either U-bolts or straps binding the bearings and cross at the differential yoke.

An exception to the above is the Jaguar independent rear suspension. It uses a drive shaft incorporating a flange yoke. But, even there, the U-joint is locked within the flange by means of outside retaining rings.

Remember, though, that there are about three-dozen different universal joints that could conceivably be used in a street rod. Getting the correct fit could be a real hassle if it weren't for the fact that about six U-joint conversion kits are made. You'll likely find a compatible pairing for your drive line regardless of its origin. Any good parts-house counterman can give you exactly what you need if you can tell him exactly what you started with, or the transmission and third member you'll use.

Select Suspension 15

Negotiating through bales is a safe and enjoyable way of finding out how well your street-rod chassis performs.

Shortly after you've sought out and found a suitable body and frame, and selected and installed an engine and transmission, you must come to terms with planning and designing the rest of the car. And, nowhere will your ingenuity, inventiveness and building skills be put to a more-demanding test than when doing the suspension system.

Technically, an automobile's suspension is comprised of the springs, shock absorbers and bushings, rods, arms and other locating linkages that connect the wheels to the car's frame, body, engine and drive train. An examination of two of the major components—springs and shocks—should prove worthwhile.

SPRINGS

The springs, as mundane as they may appear, are those critical, elastic components that flex under load, but return to their original shape when the load is removed. They allow the vehicle to travel more comfortably over the road by allowing the wheels to comply with the irregularities in the road. Sometimes the springs also provide full or partial wheel location.

There are three basic types of springs: leaves, coils and torsion bars.

Leaf Springs—Until recently, the most common spring in general use was the leaf-spring *bundle*—a combination of two or more leaves. Leaf springs come in a variety of shapes: the traditional transverse buggy style, semi-elliptical, quarter-elliptical, and cantilever. There is also the GM-resurrected fiberglass-reinforced-plastic *monoleaf* spring used on '84-and-up Corvettes. Barring the latter, however, the steel leaf spring is a manufacturer's delight—it's cheap to produce and works reasonably well. Not great, mind you, but reasonably well.

The reason for this so-so rating is that automotive springs are technically judged and compared in terms of energy stored per unit of weight—the typical steel leaf spring only stores 300 inch-pounds of energy per pound. This measure is one of efficiency and not to be confused with *spring rate*—load per unit deflection.

Spring rate refers to the force in pounds required to compress a spring 1 in. A spring

Early Ford suspension—transverse leaf spring and I-beam axle—has been with us since the dawn of street rodding . . . and will remain for as long as the sport exists.

Coil springs, whether installed over a shock absorber as are the ones on these coil-over shock absorbers, or simply located in upper and lower pads, are relatively light and friction-free.

Torsion bars, the *most* efficient of all springs, have been installed in street rods since the late '60s.

Lowly shock absorber, often installed without much thought beyond support bracketry, is critical to good handling.

with a 200 pound per inch (lb/in.) rate requires 200 pounds to compress it 1 in., 400 pounds to compress it 2 in. and so forth.

Spring rate should be relative to the weight of the car; the lighter the car, the lower the rate and vice versa. It's wheel *deflection*—how much the wheel travels from full rebound to normal ride height—that's important. It governs ride quality.

Coil Springs—Coil springs are more efficient than leaf springs. They store approximately 700 inch-pounds of energy per pound of spring weight. Therefore, a friction-free coil spring weighing less than half that of a leaf-spring bundle will do the same amount of suspension *work*. That's the good news. The bad news is that much of this weight advantage is lost when you consider that leaf springs do double duty. Unlike a coil spring, a leaf spring also helps locate the suspension. On the other hand, the advantage of a coil spring is its relatively small size and ease with which it accommodates an independent suspension.

Ten to 12 feet of *wire* is used to wind the typical automotive coil spring. When the coil is compressed, the wire twists—just like a torsion bar. This is how the energy generated by the movement of the suspension is stored.

Torsion Bars—The most efficient type of conventional springing used in suspension systems is the *torsion bar*. Careful quality control and the finest spring steels must be used in their manufacture. These factors drive up their production costs. Functionally, they can be thought of as nothing more than an unwound coil spring, yet few suspension systems offer the elegance of those that utilize torsion bars. As such, they are close to ideal for use in a street rod.

Torsion bars can store 1000 inch-pounds of energy, more than three times that of the leaf

spring. They are not without drawbacks, however. Carefully engineered space allocation is a must, as is the avoidance of nicks or surface scratches. Surface irregularities create *stress risers* that will lead to cracks and eventual failure.

Unlike most other types of suspensions, torsion-bar suspensions usually have built-in methods for adjusting ride height without altering spring rate. Subtleties such as this make a torsion-bar suspension the experienced rod-builder's first choice when the design of the car permits it and the cost is not prohibitive.

There are other suspension springs in use today—air bags, gas-filled cylinders, hydraulic cylinders and rubber cushions—but their application to street rods is so limited as to render them interesting only to the devotee of automotive exotica. So, let's move right along to a discussion of the second major component in the suspension system.

SHOCK ABSORBERS

As critical as springs are, adequate ride cannot be achieved with them alone. At rest, the weight of the car compresses the spring a given amount. This is called *static deflection*. As the car moves over road irregularities, the springs compress and extend. Once past a bump, the spring tries to extend from its compressed position. In doing this, the springs go past their original position and thrust the chassis upward.

Without shock absorbers, a vicious oscillation is set in motion. When this oscillation becomes too severe, the wheel may leave the road surface or the frame may drop . . . or both. Even if he has the saddle stamina of Teddy Roosevelt, the driver will soon grow weary. Worse, he may lose control of his car.

The solution is the shock absorber, that component in the suspension system that restricts and damps suspension movement. Although some operate on friction or compressed air, the conventional *telescoping* hydraulic shock is what you should choose for your car.

Standard direct-action, *double-tube* shocks are velocity-sensitive damping mechanisms containing hydraulic fluid that is forced through a multi-stage system of restricting valves and orifices during suspension movement. The inside tube is considered the *working* tube because the shock piston moves in it. Surrounding this tube is an outer tube that contains fluid in reserve, thus the name *reserve chamber*. The resistance to fluid movement is what retards spring (suspension) motion and oscillation. The energy generated (heat) is dissipated into the shock body, fluid in the reserve chamber, then to the surrounding air.

The high-pressure gas shock is movement sensitive—it begins damping the instant the suspension moves, rather than depending on suspension movement. Therefore, it's ahead of the game and superior to the conventional *double-tube* shock described above.

A high-pressure shock absorber—invented by Dr. DeCarbon—has a single tube in which the piston moves; there's no reserve chamber. A floating piston in the tube is backed up on the side opposite the working fluid by gas under high pressure. Consequently, there's no need for the conventional reserve chamber to compensate for displaced fluid during shock-piston movement.

The work cycle of a shock—single or double tube—is divided into two phases: *compression,* where the piston is thrust down in the cylinder displacing fluid through the valves into the opposite chamber; and *extension,* where the piston is pulled up, forcing the fluid back into the original chamber. Changes in pressure and fluid movement are controlled by piston movement, the displacement of the piston rod, the area of the valves, and the amount of restriction to fluid movement through the valve or orifice system.

STEERING

With the overview of springs and shocks fresh in your mind, let's take a look at steering. Making the front wheels turn left and right is not a matter of major consequence as long as the car utilizes the traditional rigid-beam axle, a steering arm attached to each spindle, a tie rod with flexible ends to connect them, and some kind of triangulated linkage connecting one wheel to a steering mechanism.

The steering mechanism need not be a big deal. In its most basic form it is nothing more

Recirculating ball-and-nut steering gear is found in most medium and heavy American production cars. It has also assumed an equal distribution in the majority of modern street rods.

than a system of reduction gears between the steering wheel and the steered wheels. Reduction gears, by the way, are needed to give the driver enough *mechanical advantage* (leverage) to generate the force necessary to steer the car. You may wonder if gears of any kind were in that rusted pre-WWII hulk you muscled into your garage.

Back in the '20s and '30s when the straight-axled, buggy-sprung cars were under 3000 pounds, and tires were tall and skinny, their plain-Jane manual steering, crude as it may appear today, was considered adequate.

Design-wise, things took a turn for the worse when independent front suspensions were first introduced. The conventional tie rod simply couldn't handle the job when each front wheel went its own way. Early attempts to coordinate two independently sprung wheels and a single steering box resulted in a morass of bearings, ball joints, long arms, short arms, idlers and dampers, all moving in arcs that would baffle a geometry professor.

In time, of course, a host of engineers worked the bugs out of the independent front suspension. Improved bushings were developed and low-friction bearing materials, such as nylon, were introduced. Steering gears also made great strides. Today's heavier cars, regardless of their origin, will have a *recirculating ball-and-nut* or *rack-and-pinion* steering gears.

The recirculating ball-and-nut gear came from General Motors' Saginaw Steering Gear Division. Although it was conceived for the 1940 Cadillac, it hasn't changed much since. Internally, a long worm gear positioned at the end of the steering shaft is fitted with a large coarse-threaded nut. The grooves in the worm and inside the nut are machined to accept a number of loose ball bearings that perform the function of conventional threads, but with

much less friction and a better ability to absorb steering gear loads. As the car is steered to the right or left, the ball bearings circulate around the worm, changing direction when the steering wheel changes direction.

In modern lightweight cars, however, the recirculating ball-and-nut steering gear has all but disappeared. The steering gear of choice is now the *rack-and-pinion*. It is simple in construction and light, and it takes up very little room.

With the rack-and-pinion gear, turning motion at the steering wheel is transmitted through a steering shaft to a *pinion gear*. The pinion is meshed with a straight gear—the *rack*. Rotation of the pinion is converted into lateral sliding motion by the rack. With the rack positioned laterally between the front wheels, short tie rods attached between each end of the rack and wheel transmits right and left movement to steer the front wheels.

The ratio between steering wheel turns and the full left to right sweep of the front wheels is low, resulting in quick steering action. Furthermore, the driver gets more "feel" than he would with the conventional gear.

Rack-and-pinion steering has its drawbacks, however. For one, more effort is required to steer at slow speeds, such as when parking. The driver also gets more *feed back*—harshness or kickback through the steering wheel—because of lower friction in this type of steering gear.

Now that you've read about the two types of steering gears you can incorporate into your street rod, let's look at the suspension system proper.

EARLY FORD FRONT SUSPENSION

In the more primitive front suspensions, particularly those that are under early Fords, there's a more-or-less full-width axle—typically a curved I-beam or oval tube. Instead of modern ball joints, kingpins are used at each end of the axle to mount and pivot the spindle for steering. The kingpin leans inward at the top and outward at the bottom. I'll not try to explain this, but this king-pin angle reduces steering-wheel kickback and increases down-the-road stability. It also causes the body and frame to rise slightly as the wheels are turned in either direction, thus creating an increase in steering effort.

The spindle assembly is a combination *steering knuckle* and *stub axle*—spindle. It accepts and supports the wheel hub and bearings and has an arm to which the tie rod is connected. The function of the tie rod is uncomplicated. It transfers steering motion from one steering arm to the opposite one. In the old Ford tradition, a *drag link* runs from

the *Pitman arm* on the steering-gear shaft to one spindle.

Speaking of the steering gear, the old Fords use the "ancient" *worm-and-roller* Gemmer design.

Wheel Alignment—To get on down the road without ruining the tires requires a practical application of geometry to the art of front-wheel alignment. The wheels on a car may not look as if they are sitting at 90° to the ground because they usually aren't. They are leaning either inward or outward a slight amount—*negative* or *positive camber,* respectively. If the wheels are sitting straight up, camber is zero, or 90° to the ground. Although slight, most passenger-car front suspensions have some positive camber specified.

They do, however, have a fair amount of *toe-in*—front of the tires are closer together than the rear. Initial toe-in is intended to compensate *toe-out* caused by slight deflections in the steering linkage caused by drag on the tires as the car moves down the road. Don't confuse this toe with toe-out during turning—*Ackerman steer*—gained with steering-linkage geometry. This is done to turn the inside wheel more because it turns around a "shorter" radius that the outside wheel. Toe-out increases and the turning radius tightens, or gets smaller.

Then there is *caster,* the angle of the king-pin as viewed from the side. It is *negative* when it leans toward the front of the car at the top; positive when leaning to the rear. Positive caster forces the front tires to point straight ahead as the car travels down the road, forcing the car to travel in a straight line with little effort on the part of the driver.

Solid Axles—The brief discussion of I-beam axles and camber, caster and toe, along with the earlier review of leaf springs and shock absorbers, covers the basic components and operation of the typical front suspension found in most American cars through the mid '30s and Ford products into the late '40s.

There were significant differences between makes and models through the years. Some manufacturers favored parallel leaf springs over buggy springs. Some used tubular shocks where others used lever-action shocks. Nevertheless, the solid front axle, regardless of construction, springing or damping, was and is still a relatively poor design. But, it is inexpensive and durable. Regardless, it still has a major shortcoming. When one wheel is deflected by road irregularities, the opposite wheel is affected—not as much as the first wheel, but enough to cause a perceptible difference in handling. Worse, if steering components are the least bit worn, severe front-wheel wobble can result. So bad, in fact, that the car must be

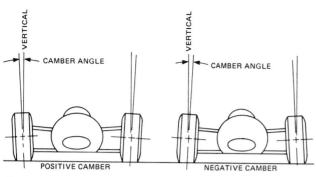

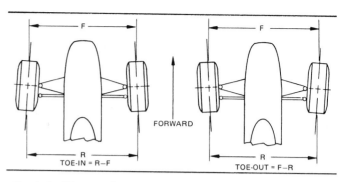

Caster, camber and toe-in are the three basic suspension settings. Camber is zero when tire sits perfectly square to road surface, positive when it leans out at top, and negative when it leans in.

Toe-in is difference between measurements from centers of tire treads at front and at rear. If front measurement is less than rear, tires are toed in; vice versa if the front measurement is greater.

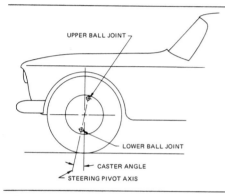

Caster angle is determined by steering pivot axis, or line drawn through kingpin or upper and lower ball joints. As viewed from side, if axis leans back at top from vertical, caster is positive; negative if vice versa.

brought to a complete stop to stop the wobble.

With the above thoughts in mind, the only reason for using a beam front axle in a modern street rod is, plain and simple, *tradition*. No excuses need be made, nor is an elaborate justification for running an archaic suspension necessary. The I-beam axle looks "right" under a street rod. That's why street rods have always used them, and that's why they will be used until the last man hangs up his rock 'n' roll shoes. To him and his comrades, the engineering deficiencies are not important.

INDEPENDENT FRONT SUSPENSION

If, however, you were to take a look under the front sheet metal of a modern passenger car or light truck, you would find something quite different from the beam axle and leaf spring. Instead you would find some sort of independent front suspension (IFS) with ball joint and either coil springs or torsion bars. An *independent* front suspension allows each wheel to move up and down . . . well . . .

independently. Gone are the solid I-beam axles and kingpins. In their place is a variety of linkages and ball joints.

Independent front suspensions were originally designed with a pair of suspension-locating links in the shape of the letter A for each of the front wheels. The bottom *A-arm* was longer than the upper A-arm and the two were non-parallel. The legs of the A-arms were attached to the frame, and rubber bushed; the wheel spindles were attached to the points of the A with pins and bushings and were, thus, able to move up and down freely.

Significant design variations appeared regularly through the early years of the development of the independent front suspension. First, the legs of the A-arms were spread farther apart for improved load distribution and improved durability. In late designs, a straight control arm combined with a compression or tension strut are used instead of a bottom A-arm. This strut, which is attached to the control arm near the spindle, runs forward or rearward to a mounting bracket.

Done correctly, rack-and-pinion steering, independent front suspension and premium tires improve ride and handling of any street rod.

Variations on this latter design are used in most American passenger-car front suspensions. Several European designs are similar in concept, except more delicate appearing forged-steel is used instead of stamped-steel control arms.

There are other types of independent front suspensions, of course. No doubt you've heard of the MacPherson strut. After all, it *is* the most popular front suspension in the world. And it may well be on your very own "grocery getter," particularly if it's small, is a sports car, or has front-wheel drive. If so, you may have considered it for a street rod project. The sliding strut/coil spring/shock absorber unit to which the wheel and rake assembly is connected will work in theory on a lightweight street rod. Practicality is another story because of the high mounting position of the strut. To my knowledge, however, no one has ever made a serious attempt to mate one to an early car. And it's just as well.

The same holds true for Ford's highly touted Twin I-beam truck front suspension. It actually consists of two straight axles, each pivoted at the opposite side of the chassis from the wheel it supports. It is as massive as the MacPherson strut is delicate. But it, too, fails to find a home under the early chassis. As a matter of curiosity, Terry Berzenye of Specialized Auto and I took some preliminary measurements of the down-sized Twin I-beam IFS used under the front of a Ford Ranger. Forget it. The basic stamped-steel control arms with their coil springs nestled between the upper and lower arms, or the more sophisticated forged-steel A-arms with either coil springs or torsion bars, are best for street-rod use.

REAR SUSPENSION
Solid Axle—Although there's a 99% probability of finding an independent suspension under the front of any post-1949 American

Mustang II independent front suspension may not be as traditional as modern versions of buggy spring/I-beam are in street rodding, but Model A builders interested in improved ride and handling are not tradition-bound.

Soon after installing engine, next step is installing rear suspension. Solid axle with coil springs is a good choice, but additional hardware is in order.

passenger car, there's less than a 10% chance of finding an independent suspension at the rear. There is a much better probability—perhaps as high as 35%—if we confine ourselves to imported sports and touring cars. These account for an ever-increasing number of new car sales. However, increasing numbers of domestic cars are turning to independent rear suspension.

After you do some comparison shopping, you'll probably decide to go with a domestic rear-axle assembly. Until recently, the most popular American rear suspension was far and away some version of the *Hotchkiss* type—with parallel *semi-elliptical* leaf springs. Loosely speaking, the springs take the shape of 1/2 of an ellipse. This suspension is a workhorse with a conventional, strong, one-piece axle housing and gear carrier.

The typical *semi-floating* live axles—axle shafts drive and support the wheels—are durable and easily removed. *Live axles* have shafts that revolve with the wheel. They may be driven, as in the case of the conventional rear, or simply along for the ride as ye olde stage coach. Beam axles or *dead* axles have non-rotating shafts. Typically, the Hotchkiss type rear suspension is both located and sprung by its pair of semi-elliptical leaf springs.

Although the Hotchkiss rear suspension is popular with cost-conscious manufacturers, it has shortcomings in performance applications. It is bulky and heavy, resulting in a high *unsprung weight*—weight is on the road side of the springs and shocks. Also, the springs wrap under acceleration and braking loads. As drag racers learned a long time ago, wheel

hop is a problem that was corrected by some type of traction-assisting device.

There are several versions of rear suspensions that incorporate live rear axles. Many use coil springs instead of leaf springs. Coil-spring rear suspensions use control arms and/or some type of links to locate the rear axle. Late '40s Buicks even used a torque-tube rear axle.

Linkages used include the *Panhard rod,* sometimes called a *track bar.* It is a long, transversely mounted link that goes between the frame and axle to control lateral axle movement. The *Watts linkage,* similar in function to the Panhard rod, is a more complicated, straight-line mechanism. The Panhard rod describes an arc when it goes up and down. The Watts link has an idler at the axle with two links, one going to each side of the frame or body.

In recent years, and particularly with the advent of lightweight front wheel drive economy cars, several different types of non-independent rear suspensions have appeared. Among these are the rigid axle with trailing arms, and versions of the old de Dion mix of the link-type, solid-axle rear suspension. Few, if any, of these offer significant advantages over other solid-axle rear suspensions.

Independent Rear Suspension—Just as with an independent front suspension, the wheels of an independent rear suspension move independently—they aren't tied together with a solid axle. In rear-wheel-drive cars with this type of suspension, the differential carrier is mounted to the chassis—to reduce unsprung weight—and the wheels are driven by shafts that move with the wheels

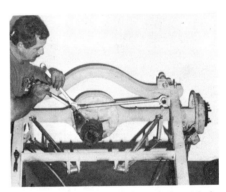

Sturdy radius rods and Panhard rod help control axle movement. In most cases these are required on solid-axle rear suspensions.

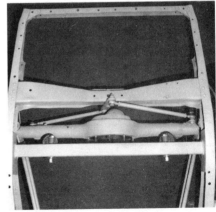

As with Panhard rod, Watts link controls lateral axle movement. Setup has seen limited use in street-rod chassis.

Corvette independent rear suspension is relatively easy to install at home . . . and well worth the effort.

and are pivoted at the differential carrier.

There aren't many independent rear suspensions in production for one very good reason—cost. Regardless, there are several varieties to choose from. Most are not practical for street-rod applications, but some are naturals. Of course, they command the highest prices.

If you've been eyeballing some fairly old sports cars in the local boneyard, you probably noticed independent rears under some. Chances are they are the *swing-axle* type. Popular in the '50s and '60s, this is one to avoid like the plague. Used under early VWs, Corvairs and Sprites, the swing axle consists of a pair of axles in housings with the wheel and brake assemblies fixed at the outboard ends. The axles are free to pivot up and down at the inboard end, or at the third-member housing. Each half axle is as long as practical in order to minimize camber change, which can be extreme at times. This can cause rapid tire wear. Worse, swing axle rear suspensions have a high *roll center*—point about which the wheels swing. This creates a tendency of the car to jack up while cornering, causing severe oversteer—sending the back end sliding out of control.

Swing axles are outdated and not in use any longer, but they are relatively inexpensive and therefore might be appealing if money is tight. However, if you have been thinking about adapting one into a rod with a narrow chassis such as a T-bucket or Model A, forget it.

Another IRS design that you may come across is the sliding strut/coil-spring/shock absorber used in the older Datsun Z cars. It is sometimes called the *Chapman strut* after the racing genius, Colin Chapman, who first used a modified MacPherson strut in his classic Lotus Elite. Although not a great IRS design, it is better than some of the less expensive designs that have since replaced it. That's

immaterial, though; it does not readily lend itself to street-rod adaptation for the same reason the MacPherson strut doesn't at the front—packaging.

If you assumed that the finest sports cars on the road today—Corvettes, Jaguars and Porsche 928s—would have the finest independent rear suspensions, I believe you'd be right. These and a few other not-so-exotic imports use a version of the double A-arm rear suspension.

The pivot axis for each wheel is near 90° to the car's center line. In these layouts, the roll centers are low and camber change is much less severe than the swing axle. Most use coil spring/shock combinations, but the Corvette uses one transverse leaf spring. Control rods and lateral linkages tie the wheel assemblies to the chassis.

This system is costly to manufacture, but it is the best handling rear suspension so far devised. The double A-arm rear suspension is also one of the best looking. You'll know this if you've ever looked under the rear of a street rod with a Jag IRS. But that's not the only reason the Jag unit was one of the very first street-rod IRS adaptations.

It and the Corvette are the two most frequently adapted independent rear suspensions because their design configurations and dimensions are just about perfectly matched to the early Ford's frame—matched, that is, after a few modifications and one of the several installation kits on the market. But more about that later. For now, if you are willing to spend the extra time and money, your efforts will be well rewarded should you choose either a Jag or a late Corvette IRS for your street rod.

Anti-Roll Bars, frequently used on both front and rear suspensions, resist roll by transferring load from an inside wheel to the outside during turning maneuvers. The anti-roll bar is confusing, not because of what it does, but for what hot rodders have called it through the years: *sway bars, anti-sway bars, roll bars, stabilizer bars* and who knows what else. Well, the most accurate term is *anti-roll bar.*

In resisting body roll and resulting weight transfer, the anti-roll bar makes the outside wheel *work harder,* thus decreasing its cornering ability. If on the rear suspension, "too much" anti-roll bar can cause *oversteer*—tendency of the vehicle to spin while turning; on the front, it creates *understeer,* or *push.* This is the tendency of the vehicle to go straight ahead while turning.

VEHICLE DYNAMICS

That's what the engineers call it, and it's a neat sounding phrase. It refers to the science of what makes a car handle. But, what does

that mean to you? Well, the old hot-rod action movies of the '50s portrayed *inadequate* vehicle dynamics dramatically—a pair of fenderless roadsters winding through the rugged Southern California mountains at high speed, burning rubber on the straights and fishtailing in the curves, until finally one driver miscalculates, loses control of his car and goes sailing over the cliff to his death.

Old movies often incorporated a gloomy object lesson. In "Hot Rods To Hell" and others of its kind, the message seemed to be that hot rodders were brainless adolescents who drove flashy little cars that were unsafe in the final analysis. The fruits of their labors were bitter, indeed.

Yet, as corny as many of the old movies were, they weren't too far off base when they dealt with the handling characteristics of more than a few '50s street rods. Unfortunately, some modern street rods are still being built as if they will only be driven in a straight line.

If the job is to be done well, you must be acquainted with the basic concepts of vehicle dynamics. You should know and understand all there is to know and understand about the kind of hardware you expect to put between yourself and the highway. I don't recommend racing on the public roads, but you must work toward achieving the best handling possible for your car. Trouble is, unless you are an engineer, as soon as you start doing your research, which for the most part consists of bull sessions with your buddies, you'll be surrounded by concepts and terminology that sounds both scientific and mystifying.

So, although you may not end up being able to compete with a 928 on its stomping grounds, you can build a car that will corner as well as it will accelerate!

Vehicle dynamics is the science of what makes a car handle. Handle? Yes, that's a difficult concept to define. Some say it's simply when your car does what you want it to do. At any rate, you know when you have it . . . and you know when you don't.

It is commonly accepted that in a two-wheel-drive vehicle, rear-wheel drive is best for ultimate handling on hard pavement. Fortunately, that's the way most street rods are built.

Weight Distribution—Another commonly accepted axiom of automotive design is that any car with rear-wheel drive will handle best with a rearward weight-bias. Sports-car manufacturers have generally achieved this fundamental advantage by placing the engine and drive train behind the passenger compartment, something that's more difficult to tackle. It's weight distribution that counts, however, not necessarily the location of the hardware. It is simply practical for the manufacturer to put his engine in the rear to obtain the rear weight-bias if it fits within other design requirements.

With this in mind, it behooves you to keep the front end of your car as light as practical, and to shift whatever you can to or toward the rear. Although not many American cars have been built this way, several models of the Corvette and some station wagons have nearly as much weight on the rear axle as on the front. This was done on the Corvette through engine and passenger-compartment location. On wagons, it was accomplished with additional weight in glass, sheet metal and structure over the rear wheels. The first option is best: moving heavy components toward the rear.

Dynamics—If you will recall your introduction to high school physics, Issac Newton declared that any mass—such as an automobile—once in motion, must be acted upon by some external force in order to change direction or velocity. He also said that for every action there must be an equal and opposite reaction.

With regard to cars, the forces of reaction are applied primarily by the ground and, to a lesser extent, the atmosphere. Furthermore, the ground forces are generated through and limited by the friction of the tires. In fact, although inertia forces—acceleration, deceleration and centrifugal—act on the mass of the car, and are spread out according to the distribution of the car's weight, a significant percentage of vehicle dynamics is in some way or another related to the tires.

Picture in your mind our "Hot Rods To Hell" roadster going around a curve. Centrifugal force is applied at the car's center of gravity, but the roadster's tires are providing a reactive force by virtue of their friction with the road. As long as these two forces are equal, the roadster will maintain its equilibrium. Ah, but should centrifugal force get the upper hand, that is, should it overcome the force of the tires, it's a quick trip off the road.

As important as the equality of the sum of the forces is to our understanding of handling, that isn't all of it. The sum of the *moments* must also be equal—force applied at a distance. If those turning moments are not equal, the roadster will spin out—either around its center of gravity, or either axle. But don't trouble yourself about these sophistications. There are simpler things to worry about.

Tires—Although automotive dynamics are primarily based on the above considerations, there is that crucial variable—the aforementioned tires. To further your understanding of the auto in motion, let's take a look at the characteristics of said tires.

First, let's assume that frictional forces are the same in all directions. If two or more

One suspension device that was slow in coming to early Ford front suspension was the anti-roll bar. It first appeared on '40 models, but will adapt back to the 1937 production models.

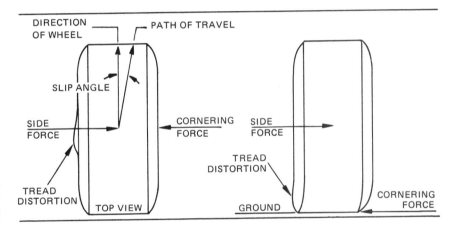

Drawing from HPBooks' *How to Make Your Car Handle* illustrates what happens "when the tire meets the road." Tire distorts during cornering and must be turned sharper than path it travels. Difference between turning angle and tire path is *slip angle.*

external forces are acting on a body, the net or equivalent single force cannot be greater than the limit of friction—fancy wording in explanation of why a sliding tire is incapable of steering a car or even of maintaining a desired course. In short, the tire must be rolling—not sliding—in order to maintain directional stability.

While rolling, tires must provide driving or tractive forces, cornering or sideways forces and braking forces. Together or separately, they cannot be greater than the tire's limit of friction. This limit of friction we keep talking about, sometimes called the *coefficient of friction,* is defined as the sliding force applied to a vehicle, divided by the vehicle's weight. More accurately, this is called *grip* when applied to tires. Now, although friction is never

zero when two surfaces are in contact, it is common practice to simplify problems in mechanics by assuming it to be zero. Likewise, for tires on any ordinary paved surface, grip is close to 1.0, a number that is close enough to be held true.

Therefore, a wheel and tire that is capable of supporting 1000 pounds will develop a side force of 1000 pounds before it slides. What all this means is that from the standpoint of friction, weight distribution alone has no effect upon the *balance* of a car while cornering. So, the next time a buddy tells you that the heavy end of a car will break loose first—a common misconception—look down your nose at him and tell him he's wrong.

Slip Angle—From there, we come to one of the least understood factors influencing

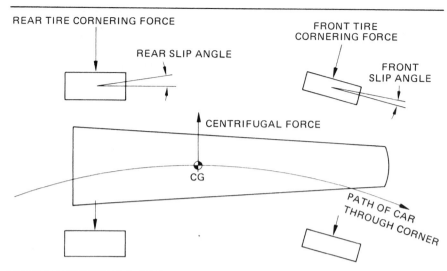

Drawing shows car rounding right-hand corner. Slip angle of rear tires are greater than fronts, causing oversteer condition. Only outside slip angles are shown because outside tires do majority of cornering work.

Both cars are following same line, but one at front is oversteering; rear car is understeering. A car with slight understeer is generally best for street use. Drawing courtesy _Road & Track Magazine_.

handling—the all-important _slip angle_. Slip angle is the difference, measured in degrees, between the direction the wheel is traveling, and the direction in which the wheel is aimed. If the slip angle is greatest at the front, the car understeers (pushes). If it's greatest at the rear, the vehicle oversteers—is loose.

Understand that slip angle is not created by the tire sliding or slipping; it is _changing shape_. An inflated tire is an elastic body, and when it is subjected to a strong side force, it deflects. If it is rolling and cornering on a flat road surface while it is in its deflected or

out-of-shape condition, it will diverge from the path that it would have otherwise taken— the path that the driver steered into. In other words, the roadster pilot of the old hot-rod movies cranked the wheels to the right, but the rod understeered straight ahead and sailed over the cliff!

Don't draw too many conclusions. If the rear tires experienced excessive slip angle from excessive deflection, the car would've gone backward over the cliff. The result would've been the same. If the tires deflected the same—neutral steer—the roadster would have negotiated the corner, assuming all four tires maintained traction. In other words, slip angles, centrifugal forces and the intended path are all interrelated and form the basis for vehicle dynamics.

Although centrifugal forces and the angle of the steered wheels are major causes of slip angles, they are not the only causes. Wind gusts can easily affect slip angles as can irregularities in the road surface. And, too, there are the changes in the attitude of the tires to the road surface because of suspension deflection and or geometry, particularly camber. Then there are changes in vertical force or pitch—the fore and aft rocking motion which alternately compresses the front springs while extending the rear springs, all of which are caused by acceleration, deceleration and resulting weight transfer.

Rearward weight bias is accepted almost without question. If the rules allow, all world-championship racing cars are rear-engine, rear drive with about 60% or more of their

weight on the rear wheels. Should you then build your car in the conventional manner, then weigh it and calculate how much lead will be needed at the rear to make it handle? Although this is exactly what my racing partners and I did a few years ago with our Bonneville Salt Flats blown gas roadster, the situation is not the same here. We were after traction, not cornering ability. Although it was just a straight-line runner, under full boost, that extra 900 pounds of lead in the rear helped it handle pretty well at over 200 mph! Beware: Weight alone can hurt handling.

Weight distribution by itself is immaterial with regard to good or bad handling. If you'll remember from the discussion on anti-roll bars, if a tire is made to work harder, its slip angle increases. The same occurs by adding weight-induced load to a tire rather than doing it "artificially" with an anti-roll bar. Excess weight, just as too much bar at the rear, will cause oversteer. The same holds true at the front when understeer is created. This is a good-news/bad-news situation.

You can compensate for weight-induced steer at either end of a vehicle by adding or increasing anti-roll-bar size at the opposite end of the vehicle. Or, generally speaking, you can increase tire size at the end that has excess slip angle. For the basic street roadser or coupe, however, rearward weight-bias usually improves handling simply because of the extreme forward weight bias.

Acceleration—Let's take a look at some other advantages of rearward weight bias— acceleration, for instance. It is true that the rear tires are given an extra "bite" in a rearward weight-biased car. Look what the move to rear-engine dragsters did for their times. In the same vein, traction is further enhanced by the weight transfer from front to rear.

How about braking or sudden deceleration? Well, there's certainly an advantage here. Any vehicle, particularly a street rod with an equal or even a slight forward weight-bias, must do most of its braking at the front. Very little braking is done by the rear wheels. The front brakes quickly heat up while the rears remain cool, but almost useless. The situation improves with a rear weight-biased car. Weight transfer is somewhat offset and braking is more equally distributed to both the front and rear wheels.

What about those pesky slip angles we discussed earlier? If you're building your street rod from scratch, you can begin to compensate for the differences that occur between front and rear slip angles in three ways—tire design, suspension design and vehicle proportions.

Tire Selection—Of these, tire design and selection is paramount. Although I already mentioned tire size, a tire's basic structure—radial, bias ply, tread configuration and "rubber" compound—can also be used to balance front-to-rear slip angles. Just putting tires with slightly better cornering characteristics, coupled with higher pressures and wider rims—at the heavy end of the car can significantly improve handling. Unfortunately, if you put bigger tires on the front than on the rear, the drive-in crowd will look at you as if you were crazy. Just one more reason for figuring out how to get a rearward weight-bias.

Roll-Couple Distribution—As already alluded to, one way of balancing slip-angle differences between front and rear wheels is to deal directly with the distribution of *lateral dynamic forces*. These occur in cornering as the vertical forces from the inside wheels transfer to the outside wheels. The vehicle *rolls* on its suspension due to lateral (centrifugal) forces. The rate of force transfer at the front or rear is expressed as a percentage of the total. This is called *roll-couple distribution*.

Just as anti-roll bars can be used to tailor roll-couple distribution, spring rates can also be used. This includes using stiffer springs at the front of a rearward weight-biased car or a stiffer bar at the front. The latter is preferable. The anti-roll bar twists in roll, but does not twist when both wheels hit a bump at the same time. "Better" tires at the rear can also help in reducing oversteer.

Conclusion—Although I touched briefly on chassis dynamics, I hope you've gotten more from the discussion than merely confusion. It's a deep and difficult subject. However, I've pointed out a few of the more important points and I hope I've left you with a little practical knowledge. This knowledge will prove helpful when you begin to wade through the suspension-kit catalogs and the maze of components that make up a street-rod suspension system.

If you want a complete understanding of suspension systems and vehicle dynamics, get the best book on the subject—HPBooks' *How To Make Your Car Handle*. This book covers everything you'll need to know about suspension systems, components and their effects on handling.

16 Traditional Rear Suspension

Out of sight, but not out of mind. Rod-builder's thoughts turn to updated rear-axle assemblies soon after engine swap.

With the exception of engine swaps, more time is spent swapping the original drive train than anything else in street rodding. Even in the flathead days, one could live with an old-fashioned front suspension, but once horse-power was increased, failures to the rear of the flywheel could be expected.

The worst offenders in early Ford drive lines were the axle keys, the axles proper and the drive shaft. It didn't take much torque to break something. Surprisingly, original Ford transmissions and U-joints were reliable.

Today, only a few die-hard street rodders chance using early Ford rear ends. Even owners of the most original cars have long since relegated their torque-tube rear axle to a corner of the garage so it can wait for some restorer to ask for it.

The same is true of the rod builder who goes the repro route. He certainly shouldn't build questionable reliability into his new car just to regain the traditional mystique. If you're in this category, use modern drive-train components.

Reliability alone is not the only reason you should swap rear ends. Comfort, style and handling rank high on the list.

Although you may pride youself on being able to do most of what needs to be done on your project car, not everyone can be a "renaissance man"––design engineer, machinist and prototype fabricator. You should draw on the skills of your acquaintances and street-rod component manufacturers.

The universal problem of safely installing a late-model rear axle assembly demonstrates this. The manufacturers, almost from the very beginning of street rodding, have met the need with well-designed and economical rear-suspension products. If you wanted to tag a date on this, my money would go to February 11, 1959, when Gene Scott, originator of Hot Rod Hardware, opened the doors of Performance Specialties, Inc., better known as *PSI*.

Until that time, non-professional rod build-ers toiled over the design of a locating and anchoring device as well as spring and shock mounts. Material for fabrication was done too many times from rusty salvage steel plate. It was great fun, though. That's why some of us stayed around the sport for so long. Many times, the end product of those labors wasn't the best appearing piece of hardware. Gene Scott's PSI not only changed that, he almost single-handedly launched the entire street-rod-components industry.

REAR AXLE

The installation of a late-model rear end begins with the selection of one you'll find in most metropolitan-area wrecking yards. A brief stroll through the better of those vast parts wonderlands will quickly overwhelm you with the variety of sizes and designs. Some, such as the exotic Corvette and Jaguar independent rear suspensions, will impress you with their price tag as well as their engineering. Others, not quite so sophisti-cated, either in basic design or difficulty of installation, will make almost as good a choice for most street rods even though you may concede that an IRS is the ultimate.

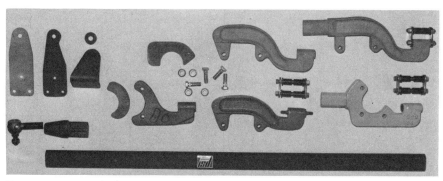

Transverse spring, just the way Henry turned 'em out, still holds the minds and hearts of many a street rodder. And this is the Gran'daddy of all late rear-suspension hardware. Gene Scott's PSI kits have been in production since the late '50s.

Every rod builder is a natural-born parts accumulator. Among the miscellaneous parts is a 9-in. Ford rear axle, unquestionably the most-popular rear axle used in modern street rodding.

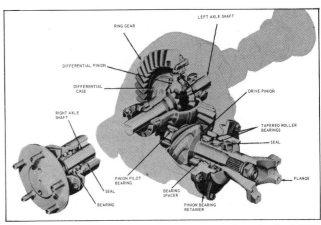

Ford axle assembly has removable center section. An 8-, 8-3/4-, 9- or 9-3/8-in.-diameter ring gear is turned by a pinion that's mounted low relative to centerline of ring gear; 9-in. gear is best.

Inside the Differential—In order to make a wise choice, however, you should be familiar with the workings of an automotive differential.

The differential incorporates a matched pair of bevel gears to accomplish its torque-multiplication function. The driving gear, called the *drive pinion,* is linked directly to the engine by means of the flywheel, clutch or torque converter, transmission and drive shaft. The pinion meshes with a driven gear called the *ring.* It is fitted to the axles through a set of *side gears,* or *differential gears.*

If a vehicle didn't have to turn, it could do without rear-axle differential gears. But, when negotiating turns, the inside wheel covers less ground than the outside wheel. Consequently, if you made a turn without differential gears, the inside tire would spin, wearing off rubber in the process. The solution is the addition of the differential gears—two to four smaller *pinion gears.* The technically correct name for these is *differential side gears,* commonly called *spider gears.*

Driven by the ring gear, the differential gears mesh with bevel gears at the ends of the axle shafts. They transmit the power flow to either axle, but not always with the same torque or speed. For instance, if one axle offers less resistance, it gets more torque. If resistance is equal, torque is transmitted equally. This torque-splitting feature can be a problem, as you may well know if you've ever been stuck in sand, snow or mud. But, there's a solution.

The limited-slip differential has an added feature internally. It contains a complex assembly of clutches and springs or ratcheting-type gears that interact to provide some torque to each axle, regardless of how little traction a wheel may be getting. Unfortunately, limited-slip differentials are much more costly than a run-of-the-mill conventional rear end.

Ring-&-Pinion Support—The conventional rear axle has seen wide service in American passenger cars since the '30s. It is easily identified by its one-piece axle housing that rigidly connects the right and left wheels.

There are two major variations of the conventional rear axle: one employs a removable gear carrier; the other an integral gear carrier. For street-rod use, the former is usually more desirable.

Removable-Carrier Axle—The removable carrier, sometimes called the *third member* or a *drop out,* contains the drive shaft yoke, drive pinion, ring gear, two to four differential side gears, and supporting bearings. The splined end of each axle splines into a side gear.

Within the gear carrier, the drive pinion is mounted in two tapered roller bearings. It is *overhung* at the gear end, as opposed to being straddle mounted, as is the case with the integral carrier-type of axle. The drive pinion is preloaded by a spacer and precisely located by a shim between it and the rear pinion bearing. The front bearing is held in place by a washer and locking nut. Ring-and-pinion backlash is regulated by the adjustment of two threaded sleeves.

The entire differential assembly is supported in the carrier by two more tapered roller bearings. Any adjustment or modification to the carrier assembly, particularly the replacement of the drive pinion or ring gear set—always replaced as a set—requires the skill and tools that only a professional mechanic will have. Consequently, you should farm out such work to a competent specialist.

Drive Shaft—Conventional rear axles are almost always used in conjunction with an open drive shaft. This consists of a stout tubular member with a U-jointed slip yoke at the transmission end, and a U-joint and companion flange at the differential end. In this configuration, it is readily adaptable to almost any American transmission or rear-axle assembly manufactured since the '50s.

Axles with removable carriers have been used in most Ford products from 1957 to date, many 1955—64 GM passenger cars, and several 1957—70 Chrysler passenger cars. The Ford axle, however, is the only serious contender for use in a street rod, unless an independent rear suspension is used.

An open drive shaft with the modern Ford type rear-axle assembly—substantial unitized axle housing with its massive gears and thick, non-tapered axles—is so far superior in strength to its early Ford counterparts as to render any comparison absurd. It is the most reliable axle you'll find in a wrecking yard. By contrast, the traditional 1932—48 Ford drive train with its solid drive shaft housed in a torque tube, its delicate drive pinion mounted in a *banjo* and its small-diameter axle tapered down to a pencil point and bolted into a relatively weak ring and spider-gear assembly, was hardly a match for the unbridled stocker, much less a modern V8.

Putting reliably aside for the moment, the beauty of a removable third member is the ease with which gear sets can be changed. With the exception of a true quick-change rear axle, no other design permits easy gear-ratio changes. As noted above, *setting up* a ring and pinion is a job for the professional. But once done, these assemblies have been known to live for 100,000 miles with nary a peep out of 'em! As to their versatility, some street rodders gather two or three gear ratios: one for high-performance acceleration, another for around-the-town cruising, and a third one for open-road hauling.

GM 10- and 12-bolt rear axle uses a straddle-mounted gear carrier as opposed to the Ford overhung setup. Gear swaps and maintenance—this one needs it—are jobs for a pro.

Integral Gear-Carrier Axle—The other type of conventional rear-axle assembly—integral-carrier design—has not gained as much acceptance by street rodders. The most common versions are GM's 10- and 12-bolt Salisbury, and Chrysler's Spicer 60 series axle, which is manufactured by the Dana Corporation. Both use a similar appearing cast iron, non-removable gear carrier with pressed-in steel axle tubes.

Generally speaking, they are strong, rugged differentials on their home turf. But they don't adapt to street-rod uses as well as the Ford axle with its removable carrier. Each and every gear ratio change must be farmed out. Worst of all, the welding of radius rod adaptation brackets will easily warp the thin steel axle housing, often causing axle bearing failures. Also, the brackets have been known to rip right off during hard acceleration when traction is good.

More Than One Ford—With all things being equal, the *Ford* axle with its removable gear carrier is your best choice, assuming you are going to a solid-axle rear suspension. But not all Ford rears are created equal. If you plan on running a modified V8, some are more better than others.

Within the Dearborn line-up, there are three different ring-and-pinion assemblies: an 8-3/4-in. ring-gear variety with a two-pinion—side gear—differential; a stronger 9-in. ring gear with a two-pinion differential; a beefier one yet with a four-pinion differential; and the toughest of them all, the 9-3/8-in. ring gear, four-pinion differential, encased in a nodular-iron housing. The last one can be identified by a bold N cast on the front. All 8-3/4—commonly, but erroneously, called an *8-in.* gear—and most 9-in. rears have 28-spline axles. The 9-3/8-in. heavy-duty units have 31-spline axles. Needless to say they are not interchangeable as is.

The 8-3/4-in. rear is intended for intermediate-weight cars with six-cylinder or small two-barrel V8 power. Consequently, it should only be used in like situations. On the other hand, the standard five-lug, 28-spline, 9-in., four-pinion axle assembly that was used in 1967—72 Cougars, Falcons, Fairlanes, Mustangs, Montegos and Torinos and many others from the late '50s until well into the '70s, is more than able to handle all of the torque of any healthy V8. That's why the majority of street-rod components are designed to adapt to the Ford rear axle.

If you need the toughest rear axle you can get because it's behind a blown or "mega-inch" engine, then by all means use the heavy-duty, super high-performance 31-spline, 9-3/8-in. Ford with the nodular-iron gear carrier.

Limited Slip—Another question: What about the limited slip varieties? There are the Ford design Equi-Lok and Traction-Lok units, and the Detroit Locker that wasn't manufactured by Ford, but used in Shelbys and other exotics. Of these, the torque-sensitive Traction-Lok, which uses a multiple-disc clutch to control differential action, is the best for general high-performance street use. But again, it is costly, and sometimes noisy and temperamental. You must be the judge because you must live with the axle.

So much for the rear axle itself. It's easy to pick one; it's not quite so easy to mount one.

SUSPENDING THE REAR AXLE

The Transverse Spring—The conventional rear axle in an intermediate-weight stocker is typically suspended by two semi-elliptic leaf springs. However, larger cars use coil springs with a variety of control arms, struts, rods and/or torque arms to locate the axle and to provide ride isolation and handling stability.

The best of these approaches have been duplicated by the street-rod-component manufacturers in function, if not in form.

Back in the early '60s when Gene Scott was getting PSI in operation, the most popular rear-axle-mounting kits were those that emulated the early Fords. Therein lies one of the great perversities in street-rod rear suspensions. For, as weak and unreliable as the early Ford axles and drive shaft are, the method of mounting the rear-end assembly in the early Ford—enclosed universal joint, massive torque tube and its substantial triangulated radius rods with forged-steel ends—is darn near bulletproof.

Conversely, the super-strong components of the modern axle are mounted and located in the flimsiest manner imaginable—U-bolted to a pair of parallel leaf springs. It is only logical to try to capture the best of both worlds. Not surprisingly, one of the first PSI

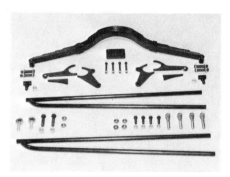

Transverse spring, albeit least efficient of spring designs, has proved adequate in countless numbers of street rods. The secret, aside from a proper installation, is to use a new spring with plastic interleaving.

Bill Keifer's California Custom Roadsters Fad T transverse-spring kit includes radius rods and all mounting bracketry and hardware.

Specialized Auto Components offers their version of do-it-yourself transverse-spring suspension for 1937—41 Ford.

kits featured heavy-duty ductile-steel spring hangers that looked exactly like those in the back of a '36 Ford.

It was popular in the early days of drag racing to hack the spring hangers off an old Ford axle and graft them to a big fat Olds or Pontiac rear. Scott simply used an old idea and took it one better.

Substantial radius rods that mount far forward in chassis are important to reduce loads and minimize suspension-geometry changes with wheel travel of any type of conventionally suspended rear axle.

Specialized Auto Components rear-suspension installation: One shock mounts ahead of axle and the other behind, which is out of view.

Starting from third photo above, Specialized rear-axle installation includes Panhard rod, radius rods and mounting brackets, and cross-tube shock mount.

The PSI kit may be cumbersome by today's standards, but this standard design has been refined only slightly and forms the basis of all current commercial transverse-spring mounts and radius rods.

I've mentioned radius rods several times without defining them. Most everyone is basically familiar with the type used on the early Ford torque tube. Street-rod versions are made of steel tubing. Technically, however, radius rods are suspension locating links. With regard to the rear-axle assembly, they attach to the frame and the axle housing so that they prevent fore and aft movement, but allow vertical movement. They also serve as traction devices during hard acceleration; consequently, they are subjected to considerable forces.

A correctly designed *hairpin-type* radius rod should be fabricated out of at least 7/8-in.-OD X 9/16-in.-ID cold-drawn seamless steel tubing with at least one cross-tie between the two bars. The longer the bars, the more cross-ties. Although graceful curves in the fore end of radius rods have been popular for many years, they should be avoided if you anticipate any high-performance driving or occasional drag racing.

The mounting of radius rods and the Ford buggy spring on a late-model rear axle should be well within your capability, assuming you've mastered the art of electric welding. The first order of business, however, is to clean it. Drain the gear lube and scrape all the grease and crud off the housing. Pull the axles and gears if you wish. After the housing has been cleaned, replace the gear carrier and axles. It is best to do all or most of this work with the gears and axles in place to minimize warpage. Although the assembly is heavier, it keeps it about as rigid as can be without a holding fixture.

The removal of semi-elliptical spring-mounting pads is not difficult, but the job must be handled with care. Careless torch-work can do irreparable damage to the stoutest of axle housings. Depending on the design of the spring pad, cut about half away then switch to the other side and do the same. The idea is to keep heat build-up to a minimum and balance out any warpage. After the cutting has been completed and the housing has air cooled, smooth the rough edges with a body grinder.

There may be two or four pieces to weld to the housing, depending on the spring and radius-rod-kit manufacturer. Some brackets do double-duty, so you may only have to weld on one per side. As for length, you may need to shorten the housing to make it fit under a full-fendered car, or just to make it look right.

Late Ford housings with their long and short axles make shortening the long side fairly simple, providing the welder has access to a lathe. See the photo sequence, page 116.

Most fendered street rods are best fitted with an axle housing just over 50 in., flange-to-flange, with about 53 in. being maximum. Fender shapes and sizes as well as brake drum/disc bulk, and wheel and tire widths and diameters vary so greatly that there's no set rule. You must, of course, anticipate and allow for tire clearance and suspension travel when calculating the width of your rear axle.

Before any bracket welding can begin, their exact locations on the housing must be established. If instructions are not provided by the kit manufacturer, mock up the entire rear suspension. To do so, bolt the loose spring in the crossmember, position the wheeled axle assembly where you want it under the car—or frame—on jack stands, and wire or tie pinion yoke approximately 5—6° up from level. The center of the axle should be directly under the rubber axle snubbers in an early Ford frame. Mock up the radius rods as best you can with locking pliers and C-clamps. Now, determine where the spring hangers and radius-rods brackets should be.

Once you're satisfied with the measurements, design and fabricate some kind of holding fixture to which you can clamp the brackets. Fit the brackets level against the axle housing, measure again and tack-weld them on. Check the locations and symmetry

Machine-shop charges are high for narrowing Ford rear axle. If you have access to a lathe and quality welding, you can easily do it for less. Start by carefully removing stock spring pads.

Two approaches can be used when narrowing Ford axle: Match modified half of the axle housing to a shorter existing axle, or modify housing and have axle shortened to match. First method costs less as axle won't have to be machined.

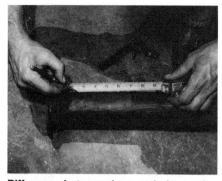

Difference between long and short axles determines how much long housing can be shortened to place gear carrier in apparent center. In example, it was 2-3/4 in.

Large tubing cutter is used to cut off flange and excess housing material. Tube ID is then deburred.

Flange is chucked in lathe and excess piece of axle housing cut away to expose sleeve.

Flange is tucked into shortened housing, realigned and welded. Long threaded rod and a plate at each end makes a simple, but effective clamp. After welding, housing should be checked for straightness and trued.

of the brackets before finish welding. Weld completely around one side of each bracket; then, while it's hot, check and tap it back into square if need be. Repetitive verification of bracket-to-frame squareness is critical because some warpage is almost impossible to prevent without securing the axle housing and brackets in a full-length holding fixture. Switching from side to side during welding process will minimize heat build-up and warpage.

Installing Parallel Leaf Springs—Hanging a modern rear axle from a buggy spring is about the simplest suspension-installation job you can do. The parallel leaf springs are typically U-bolted to pads on the axle housings a foot or so inboard from the brake assemblies. Each end of the spring is mounted in hangers riveted to the frame rail or to a gusseted section of the floor pan of a unitized body.

Problems only appear when the driver "stands on the gas." With high horsepower and under hard acceleration, a Hotchkiss type rear suspension becomes a victim of *spring wrap-up*, which causes *wheel hop*—wheels jump up and down. Torque reaction on the axle twists the springs into an S-shape. The springs cause the axle to snap back, resulting in wheel hop causing loss of traction, but sometimes control as well.

Hot rodders figured out what was missing from the rear suspension a long time ago. Short, stout traction devices were used to link the springs to the frame in order to, combine the qualities of flexible open-shaft drive and the sturdiness of torque-tube drive. These traction devices first began to appear in 1953. They translated to somewhat longer and smaller-diameter early Ford type radius rods in street rods when the builders took an inter-

Parallel leaf springs were Detroit's answer to giving a soft ride with low cost. Street rodders have also found them quite satisfactory.

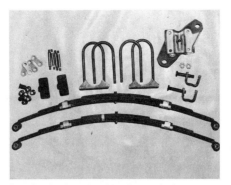

Parallel leaf-spring kits for early frame are offered by many street-rod-components companies. Kits are not only great time savers, you'll avoid potential installation problems.

Springs and their mounting pads must be directly below frame rails or spring hangers. And rear axle must be centered transversely in chassis. Find center of housing by measuring from backing plate to backing plate.

Before welding spring pads in place, set pinion angle—approximately 5—6° up at front—while pads are sitting level. Tack-weld pads to underside of axle housing.

Turn over axle housing and weld spring pads in place. Leave gear carrier and both axles in place while welding to minimize warpage.

Leaf-spring hangers are easily fabricated from steel plate and pirated hardware.

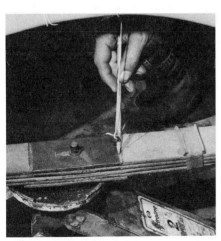

Correct location of spring-pad locating bolt is easily found by dropping plumb bob from center of original axle snubber.

After careful verification of all reference points, note where new spring-bolt holes should be.

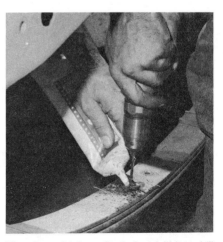

Use sharp, high-quality industrial bit to drill springs. Go slow and use lots of lubricant. Pilot hole is drilled with springs in place. Remove them and enlarge holes to final size on drill press.

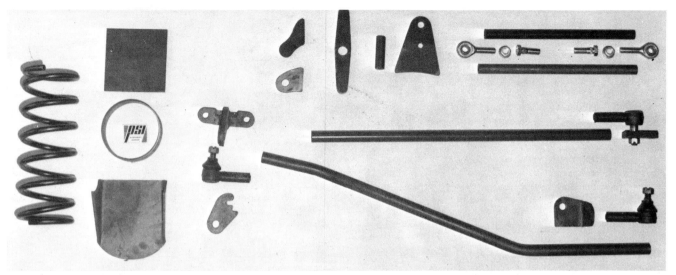

Coil-spring suspension, although a good setup and easily installed, has lost some of its appeal with advent of coil-over shocks. Many in Fad T contingent still take this route, however. Kits such as PSI's are available from several manufacturers. All you need to mount springs is a pad for each at the axle and one at the frame.

est in Hotchkiss rear ends. The added benefit of the softer ride offered by parallel leaf springs was the icing on the cake.

Early installations frequently required overhead welding, an art mastered by few street rodders. And few welding shops had a hoist or any way to get a car high enough to do a good job. As a consequence, parallel leaf spring suspensions have somewhat languished. Today, however, Chassis Engineering of West Branch, Iowa, offers a completely bolt-in, parallel leaf-spring suspension kit that doesn't require any welding on either the frame or the recommended Ford Maverick rear end. Of course, rear radius rods are highly desirable even if you don't think you'll get that occasional urge, so mounting brackets would be necessary and installed in the same manner as they are when a transverse spring is used.

Installing a Coil-Spring Rear Suspension—If you choose to forsake both the buggy spring and parallel leaf springs for coils, you'll find several manufacturers with the needed hardware. Builders have fancied coil-spring suspensions since the days of the Fad T.

More work is required than with the simple transverse spring, but a well-designed coil-spring suspension has its advantages, too. First and foremost, coil springs have no interleaf friction. Secondly, they can be mounted in an otherwise restrictive location. Also, they are easier to change when "tuning" for a different ride or handling.

Coil Springs—To review, rate is the measure of a spring's softness. Rate is determined by the weight required to compress it a given amount, which is usually pounds per inch (lb-in.). And, if we trust Hooke's Law, spring rate will remain constant. For example, if 600 pounds compresses a spring 3 in., 1200 pounds will compress it 6 in. Spring rate is 600 pounds ÷ 3 in. = 200 lb/in.

Free height—unloaded height—of a coil spring corresponds to the *free arch* in a leaf spring. If a suspension spring that has a free height of 15 in. and a rate of 300 lb/in. is loaded with 600 pounds, it will compress 2 in., or to a height of 13 in. A spring with a 17-in. free height and a 100-lb/in. free height will compress 6 in., or to an 11-in. height under the same 600-pound load.

When the load is removed, each spring will return to its free height. The stiffer spring—15-in. free height—extends 2 in., whereas the 17-in. spring extends 6 in. It's obvious that the 17-in. spring is "softer," thus will give a smoother ride.

Selecting a coil spring with the appropriate free height and rate is a problem that must be solved before mounting is ever a consideration. You'll need to know the actual or anticipated rear-wheel weight of your car, and the rear-wheel weights of as many late-model passenger cars with coil-spring suspensions that you can come up with.

If you are thinking that it would be better to match gross sprung weights, you're absolutely right. Unfortunately, sprung weights are

close to impossible to get, even for your own car. So, you must rely on another of those convenient generalities and assume that the unsprung weights of your car and donor car are close.

When you arrive at a pairing of weights that is reasonably close, chances are you'll have a set of coil springs that won't be too far from what should go at the rear of your street rod. And, unless they are unusually short or long, height is not a significant factor because that can be compensated for at the spring mounts.

Spring Seats—The installation of coil springs alone is straightforward. If you want to make your own hardware, start by fabricating upper and lower spring *cups* (seats). Two install on the frame and two on the rear-axle housing. Cups are easily fabricated from steel tubing large enough to fit over the spring, but with a snug fit. The tubing should be about 1-1/2-in. long, or enough to contain the spring's *pigtail*—free end—and at least one coil. One end of each cup must be capped to provide a seat for the spring.

Most builders run the shock absorbers inside the coil springs, so provisions for them must also be incorporated into the cups. This will be either in the form of a hole for the shock to pass through or a mounting.

There are many ways to bring coil springs, a modern rear axle and an early frame together. In general, though, the springs should be positioned as close to the wheel as practical and equally spaced on both sides. If you are using a stock frame, you may be able to incorporate the upper cups into the stock rear crossmember. A straight, heavy-wall rectangular tube usually works well in a repro frame if it doesn't have an existing crossmember.

The lower cup and its bracketry is welded to the axle housing. Its position is determined by the free height and rate of the spring and the location of the upper cup.

Coil-Over Shocks—If you want to eliminate the need for spring cups, go directly to coil-over shocks. This way, you only have to mount the shocks, one end at the axle and the other at the frame. Mounting must be strong enough to support the vehicle. Components manufactures can help you with shocks and their mountings. Springs are easier to come by because they can be purchased from component manufacturers.

As with conventional coil springs, position the coil-overs as far outboard as possible.

For more about coil-over shock absorbers, turn to page 120.

Panhard Rod—Once the spring cups are in place, turn your attention to how the axle will be located. A fairly uncomplicated approach to anchoring a coil-spring suspended rear end is a combination of radius rods and a Panhard rod. A Panhard rod is surprisingly effective under ordinary driving conditions. Its biggest disadvantage is that if it isn't long enough—at least 3 feet—and close to horizontal, roll-center height will change with wheel travel. But, this is true with most conventional suspensions. Regardless, it can be a problem in a stock-bodied, top-heavy coupe or sedan such as those from the late '30s and early '40s. Another problem arises when the springs are too soft and there's excess lateral movement. In such a case, the car will wander, particularly on undulating roads at high speeds.

Watts Link—A better, but slightly more complicated lateral locator is a Watts link.

If you'll recall, a Watts link consists of two equal-length horizontal bars connected by a pivoting vertical bar—*idler*—at the center in a Z-configuration. The preferable way of arranging a Watts link involves mounting the vertical pivot bar at the center of the axle housing and the horizontal bars at brackets on each side of the frame; another involves dropping a bracket down from the frame to a point in space that is to the rear and in line with the center of the axle housing. The pivot bar is then mounted to it and the horizontal bars are mounted to the axle housing at opposite ends. The advantage of the first method is that the roll center does not change with wheel travel; it does with the second method.

Either way, the movement of the axle assembly is restricted to the vertical plane, but the preferred method for street-rod use is to fix the center pivot to the chassis and not the axle housing. A street-rod suspension, which combines coil springs, integral shock absorbers, Watts linkage and radius rods, is a hard number to beat.

Radius Rods/Control Arms—Because Panhard rods or Watts links only do lateral locating, they must be located longitudinally—fore and aft. This is the preferred method with a *three-* or *four-bar link-type* setup.

With both three- and four-bar setups, two radius rods are used under the axle, spaced as wide apart as possible. Placed in line with the center of the vehicle, the bottom radius rods pivot at the front in brackets at the frame, and at the rear in brackets that extend down from the axle. They can be positioned parallel to each other or be slightly closer together at their front pivots. Also, they should be parallel to the ground or slightly—no more than 1-in.—higher at the front. Speaking in practical terms, the longer the radius rods, the better.

As for the top radius rod(s), one is used for the three-bar setup and two for the four-bar. Although it can be done differently, the single radius rod of the three-bar setup should be pivoted in a bracket atop the axle housing at the center. It doesn't have to be exactly in the center, but the rod should be parallel to the center line of the vehicle. At the front, the bracket is mounted to the frame.

In the four-bar setup, it's best to have the radius rods parallel to each other. They don't have to be spaced as wide apart as the lowers, but they should be more than 12-in. apart. Otherwise, you might as well go to a three-bar setup.

The length of the upper radius rod(s) should be about 75% of the lowers. For example, if the bottom radius rods are 36-in. long, the top one(s) should be about 27 in. This will give the pinion-angle change needed to maintain the correct drive-shaft U-joint angle. The front pivot point can also be lower by about 1 in. This will accomplish the same thing and give a slight amount of *anti-squat*—geometry that resists rear-end squat under acceleration.

Anti-squat *increases* when the front pivot(s) of the top rod(s) are *lowered*, or the fronts of the bottom rods are raised. Be careful here. Although it's nice to have anti-squat, too much can result in wheel hop under hard acceleration.

Let's take a look at where you can go to purchase much of the suspension hardware I've been talking about. You'll find a listing of the suppliers at the back of the book, page 203.

17 *Coil-Overs & IRS*

Jaguar IRS has been used under street-rod rears since the late '60s. Complete assemblies are getting harder to find—and are always expensive. When correctly installed, though, the Jag works better than most anything else.

COIL-OVER SHOCK ABSORBERS

Like anything mechanical, the simplest way to build a street rod is usually the best way. Rear suspensions are no exception. Keeping them simple gets the car out of the garage and on the road where it belongs, not propped up in super-sophisticated, but non-functioning, splendor.

This approach, however, doesn't mean that you have to compromise anything to keep the rear-suspension simple. There's an alternative to traditional transverse, or parallel-leaf or coil-spring suspensions that approaches the same simplicity, but functions better; the coil-over-shock suspension unit.

There's not much doubt, at least in my mind, that coil-over shocks owe their immense street-rod popularity to the Jaguar independent rear suspension's fame. Coil-overs first appeared on European road-racing and grand-touring sports cars in the late '50s and early '60s. Soon thereafter, they found their way to American circle-track and road-race cars of every description. By the mid '70s, they were used with great frequency on street rods. Today, they challenge all comers on equal footing for the title of the street-rod builder's favorite way to spring and shock a suspension.

Coil-overs incorporate two normally separate suspension components in one handsome, efficient package. It's greatest single advantage, of course, is the small, but stable, coil spring wrapped around the tubular shock. The coil spring is virtually friction-free because it has no sliding or rotating surfaces. Also, unsprung weight is minimized in coil-overs because one set of mountings is needed rather than separate ones; a set for the springs and a set for the shocks. And, ride height can be changed by merely turning the lower spring seat on the threaded shock body with a spanner-type wrench.

There are several manufacturers of coil-over units, both in the United States and abroad, and they offer a wide assortment of springs. Although experimentation can get expensive, most rod builders who anticipate a varied lifestyle could easily afford several sets of springs for different applications. These, along with several sets of ring-and-pinion gears, lend a new dimension to "quick-change versatility."

The greatest advantage however, is the fact that coil-overs are easy to mount under *any* street rod. Add this to the fact that spring and shocks are available with complete installation kits for all popular early Fords.

Most of the kits use an upper mount fabricated from 0.120-in.-wall mild rectangular steel tubing. It is typically welded and gusseted in place a few inches fore or aft of the

Triangulated four-bar, coil-over-shock rear suspension dominates repro-kit street-rod scene. When used with popular Ford 9-in. rear, it works well.

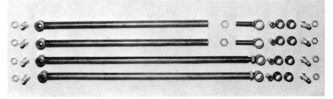

Basic four-bar-link kit offered by with Specialized Auto Components consists of the links and attaching hardware.

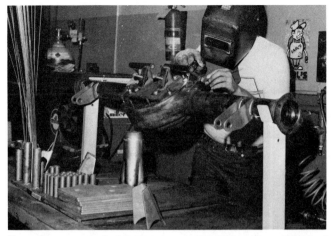

To weld on rear-axle bracketry, you should be an experienced welder and have a holding fixture. Otherwise, take advantage of Specialized's axle-bracket installation deal to make sure the job is done right.

Installing Specialized Auto reproduction 1933—34 frame and rear coil-over kit is a snap. Modified housing is supported under frame according to instructions.

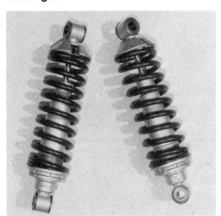

Coil-over shocks and springs are supplied with Specialized Auto Components four-bar-link kit. Springs come in varying rates, depending on vehicle weight.

Lower links are installed first. Specialized kit includes aircraft-quality bolts and urethane bushings.

Upper links are then installed. Triangulated upper links control axle laterally. Angle of brackets at frame and axle housing must be same as links.

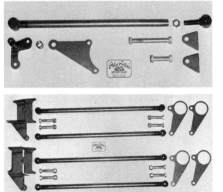

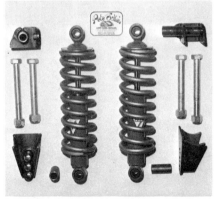

Installation of coil-over units is no more complicated than that of ordinary shocks. Specialized's lower bracketry allows for ride-height adjustment.

Pete and Jake Panhard rod (top) can be used for coil-spring or coil-over rear suspension. Bracket bolts to Ford center section at axle end. Four-bar radius-rod assembly kit (bottom) is designed for all early Fords.

Pete and Jake coil-shock kit includes upper shock mounts that also serve as brackets for stock Model A bumper irons. Lower mounts fit 3-in. axle tubes.

Installing coil-over rear suspension in a relatively large early Ford isn't easy. First raise the hind quarters so you can perform the work. Once that's accomplished, rear crossmember is removed.

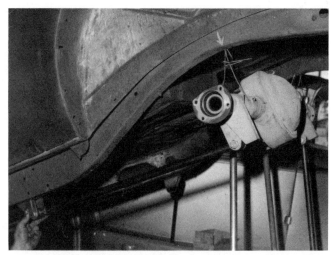

With axle hung in position with wire, Kelly Stoehr positions lower radius-rod brackets, then temporarily attaches them to frame with sheet-metal screws.

After crossbar is welded in place, sections of tubing in place of coil-over units support axle housing. Forward radius-rod brackets are now welded to frame.

Additional gusseting was used in several areas because coupe will be used for severe duty. Job would've been much easier with body off. Considerable overhead welding was required.

rear axle. The exact location of the support member is determined by the body and chassis configuration, clearance requirements of the suspension unit, and type of rear-axle locating device—Watts linkage, Panhard rod or triangulated struts.

Heavy-duty lower mounts are welded to the axle housing in a manner similar to standard shock-absorber mounts. They are more substantial, though, because the coil/shock assembly supports the weight of the car.

Coil-over suspension units should be mounted as low and as far apart as practical, with a 37-in. spread considered minimum. The shocks should not be inclined more than about 20° from vertical.

As previously discussed, locating devices must be used with a conventional axle if coil springs or coil-overs are used. A Watts link or Panhard rod can be used for lateral axle locating; radius rod for longitudinal and torsional locating. The radius rod brackets on the axle housing must not interfere with the lower shock mounts, or with other components in general.

In recent years there has been a move away from Panhard rods and Watts links in favor of the triangulated strut for rear-axle locating, particularly those with coil-over shocks. Many of the designs owe their origins to the GM coil-spring/link-type rigid-axle suspension. Such suspensions use upper control

arms that are angled in the *plan view*—view from above. Going back from their pivots on the frame, the control arms go inboard to separate pivots on the axle at about a 45° angle. Two parallel lower control arms are used.

Triangulated street-rod versions are really a combination of triangulated and longitudinal control arms. Other versions, such as the Deuce Factory's three-bar-link kit, are a combination of lateral and longitudinal control arms. The rod builder has, therefore, quite a few designs from which to choose. I'm not prepared to say one is "the best," but most work well. Which way you go depends on your car and personal preferences.

Independent Rear Suspension

The class act in street-rod rear suspensions is, without a doubt, the independent. For most rodders, that is spelled J-A-G-U-A-R. The Jag unit isn't the only suitable IRS, but it's one that frequently finds a home under the street rod.

Installing an IRS is not as simple as installing a suspension that incorporates a conventional axle. That's one of the reasons why only two IRS assemblies—the Jag and Corvette—have ever made the street-rod builder's Top Ten list of preferred rear ends. Let's take a closer look at the Jag unit first.

JAG IRS

Without a doubt the Jaguar E-type IRS is the most common street-rod IRS, independent or otherwise. It first gained popularity in the mid '60s in roadsters, but the larger Jag sedan independent rears have been used in larger street rods. In fact, they've been mounted in every conceivable kind of custom car from lightweight Fad Ts to 4000-pound Ford F-100 pickups—but not always correctly. Too many times, the ride and handling characteristics of the original suspension have been ruined by incorrect radius-rod geometry. Or, unsuitable mountings were used to replace the steel cross beam—known by street rodders as the *cage*—which was removed from the differential assembly.

Cross Beam—In the stock Jaguar, the entire rear-suspension unit is enclosed in and supported by the cross beam. The cross beam is mounted to the body through four rubber blocks. The fore and aft position of the suspension unit is maintained by two radius arms mounted in rubber bushings on each side of the car between the lower control link and unitized body structure.

Most rod builders, however, think that the cross beam hides the beauty of the Jag IRS. Maybe they are right. Who can deny that the rotating axle shafts and action of the springs and shocks is a handsome sight? The practice of uncaging the Jag began with the first street-rod installations. It seems that it's here to stay.

Third Member—The differential assembly in the typical Jag rear end is the Salisbury design with an integral gear carrier. A Thornton "Power-Lok" limited-slip unit is usually used. In lieu of conventional axles, short drive shafts—sometimes called *half shafts*—with universal joints at each end. The inboard ends are mated to axle output shafts. The output shafts also provide a mounting for the inboard disc brakes. The rotor in the early E-types is approximately 10 inches in dia-

As already mentioned, Jaguar IRS is the best rear suspension in common street-rod use.

meter. Although the brake-pad area is on the smallish side, it still has enough capacity for most street rods. Some of the later sedans use larger calipers on the rears than on the fronts.

Each wheel of the Jag rear is supported by two coil-over shocks. The coil-overs install between the frame and lower control arm. As noted earlier, this installation set the pattern for most *non-independent* rear coil-over-shock suspensions, although only one coil-over is normally used per wheel.

The rear wheels are located laterally by two control arms. The half shafts double as the upper arms. In technical terms, this is called a *stressed half shaft*. The inside end of each lower control arm is attached to the differential carrier; the outside end pivots in an aluminum housing, or *suspension upright*. The upright supports the rotating spindle (stub shaft), bearings and wheel. As the wheel and control arms move up and down, the coil-over-shock units compress and extend.

An anti-roll bar connects the right and left lower control arms. At the center, the bar is mounted to the chassis at the center. The anti-roll bar provides additional roll control.

Cross-Beam Removal—The desire for maximum visibility and subsequent removal of the cross beam has gotten many street-rod builders in trouble. For the cross beam does more than simply secure the rear-suspension assembly to the body. It ties everything together.

For one, the cross beam provides inner pivot points for the lower control arms and upper mounts for the shocks. It also houses the cable operated scissors-type parking-brake assembly and mounts much of the brake plumbing.

If you remove the rear-axle assembly from the cross beam, you must provide new bracketry that faithfully reproduces all original mounting points. This new bracketry must

also be strong enough to compensate for the loss of the original structure. Fortunately, making this substitution is not that difficult. Because of the Jag's popularity, the street-rod-components manufacturers have come to the rescue. Installation kits are available. They are the best and easiest way of successfully installing the complicated Jaguar IRS.

The stock rear tread of early E-type coupes and roadsters is 50 in.; the rear tread of V12 models is closer to 54 in. Sedans with comparable rear ends vary from 52 to 58 in. Earlier cars used knock-off hubs, which must be modified for conventional stud/lug-nut wheels. Later cars use studs and a 5-hole 4-3/4-in.-diameter (Chevy) bolt pattern.

Jag IRS Kits—Virtually all commercial Jag IRS installation kits are designed for the Model T through early '40s Ford frames. These rear ends, however, have been installed in at least one of everything. The formula for success in the non-Ford street rod is your ability to adapt all or part of the Ford-oriented hardware to your particular vehicle. The main thing is you start with correct third-member, suspension and brake mounting points.

Therefore, assuming you start with an adequate supply of crossmembers, radius rods, straps, struts, brackets and miscellaneous hardware—which you should have with a Jag IRS-to-Ford kit—the following general outline should get the installation job done. Before you get started, it's best to have the body off the frame.

Install Jag IRS—Start by establishing the centerline of the original rear axle. Mark the location on the frame. Many frames have rubber *jounce bumpers*—sometimes called *snubbers*—to cushion suspension bottoming. These are located directly above the axle centerline. The bolt hole for the snubber is an ideal reference point. It should be directly over the original axle.

Next, position the Jag assembly under the frame. Keep it caged if possible. But, if the cross beam had been removed, it won't create a significant problem. Depending on the chassis in question, stock rear frame sections or crossmembers may or may not have to be removed. If in doubt, leave everything alone until you're certain.

The Jag differential is typically mounted to a thick steel plate approximately 7-in. square, which is, in turn, welded to a length of square or rectangular tubing of at least 1/8-in. wall. Although this can be fabricated in its entirety, it's often possible—and better—to modify an existing kit piece. Either way, the Jag rear needs to be spaced 1-in. down from the bottom of the crossmember in order to clear the parking-brake calipers. Jag bracketry must be beefy enough to secure the differential and

Specialized's instructions put installation of Jag IRS well within the average rod-builder's capability.

Corvette IRS is another suspension that captured the fancy of street-rod builders in the late '60s.

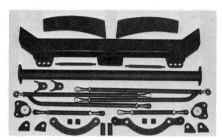

Don McNeil's Specialized Auto Components was first to offer a Jag IRS kit for 1937—40 Ford frame.

prevent it from winding up under torque loads.

The frame, crossmember and Jag rear should then be set in position to check fits and clearances. Match the Jag rear and crossmember to the original axle reference points on the chassis. If all is OK, tack-weld the crossmember in place.

If knock-off hubs were used and you have not changed over to studs and lug nuts, now's the time to get it done. Several street-rod suppliers such as Kugel Komponents in Whittier, California, are equipped to handle the necessary machine work.

Once the correct wheels are mounted, the suspension assembly can be uncaged and the *dog bones* installed. These are the fabricated links between the lower suspension arms. They provide the inner pivot points for the lower suspension-arm pivots that were lost when the cage was removed. They are available from any street-rod shop that handles IRS kits.

Now, measurements for radius rods and strut rods can be made. Again, they can be either fabricated or pirated from a Ford installation kit. They should be long enough to clear the stock rear anti-roll bar, and strong

enough to handle acceleration and braking forces. With regard to the latter, remember that rear end wrap-up occurs under acceleration *and* braking. When the inboard disc brakes are applied, torque loads are transferred to the third-member housing and its mountings. Also, fore and aft loads must be taken at the wheel. This is done with radius rods or struts that run from the frame to the suspension upright.

Thirty-inch-long radius rods seem to be a good compromise in most installations. Strut rods, which often mount to the forward dog bone, will be about 35-in. long.

There are many chances to mess up the Jag's rear-suspension geometry. The most frequent one is the angle of the coil-over shocks. A major deviation from the original angle will cause problems. So, if you're fabricating a crossmember from scratch, duplicate the original upper shock mounts using the original cross-beam mounting points as reference.

Alignment—This completes the high points of installing a Jag IRS. But, you're not finished. Once installed, you must align the wheels. Unlike a solid axle, an IRS must be aligned in the same manner as a front suspension. Otherwise, handling will be unpredictable and excess tire wear may result.

Typically, the wheels of some independent rear suspensions toe-in under acceleration and toe-out under braking. As for the Jag setup, approximately 1/8-in. toe-out is built in to ensure that toe will be zero while under power. If you replaced the cross beam with your own structure, chances are that this built-in toe setting changed. This isn't a problem because you can compensate for the change by adjusting the radius rods. Although you can get close on your shop floor, final adjustment should be done on an alignment machine.

CORVETTE INDEPENDENT REAR SUSPENSION

Equally as popular as the Jaguar IRS is the Corvette IRS, particularly the 1965—79 models, and to a lesser extent the 1980—82 models. The initial cash outlay for a Corvette rear is more or less comparable to the Jag, but many rod builders have preferred to "stay home" with their selection of suspension components for secondary economic reasons as much or more than patriotic ones. Corvette rebuild bits and pieces are typically less costly than those for the Jag.

In addition to economics, there are mechanical advantages to the 'Vette rear. For instance, brake-pad area is more than twice that of the Jag's. And many more gear ratios are available. Another big plus is the wide assortment of aftermarket suspension hardware available for Corvettes that transfers to street-rod applications.

The early three-link Corvette IRS uses a single trailing arm to locate the rear wheels fore and aft. As with the Jag, a stressed half shaft is used also as the upper control arm and there's a separate lower control arm. The stock lower arms are rather large, bulky affairs and are almost always modified or replaced when used in a street rod.

The Corvette single transverse rear leaf spring is unique. It mounts to the underside of the differential-carrier assembly. Early models use seven, nine or ten leaves.

Although the 1963—64 Corvette rears are essentially the same as the 1965—79 rears, they are less desirable. This is because drum brakes are used and the Eaton-design Positraction limited-slip differentials are not quite as strong as the Dana units first used in 1965.

When given the opportunity to choose from any of the older 'Vette IRS units, most knowledgeable high-performance rodders

Although not used as often as Jag, 'Vette IRS lends itself well to either homebuilt (pictured) or commercial conversion.

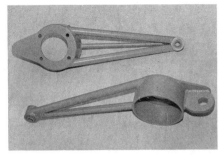

Progressive Automotive has tubular trailing arms for Corvette installation utilizing their kits.

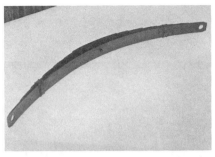

Progressive also offers a new spring for Corvette/street-rod applications called the *Pro-Slip.*

Not for the faint of heart: Tom McMullen's '32 High Body incorporates custom-built IRS with quick-change center section and inboard disc brakes. Torsion-bar springing is used with height adjustment immediately above exhaust outlet. Photo by Tom Monroe.

favor the 1975—79 models that have beefier half-shafts and strut-rod ends, and a 10-leaf spring. Next choice is the 1969 issue, which has a stronger third-member case and other components than previous models.

I would be remiss if I didn't mention the sophisticated 1983—factory calls it an '84—and later Corvette five-link IRS with its numerous aluminum components, fiberglass-reinforced transverse single-leaf spring, Bilstein gas shocks and other high-tech innovations. This setup is light years better than previous 'Vette IRS setups. Even when compared to the Jag IRS, it is destined to become the preferred IRS. This will take time, though. Regardless, not only are the numbers better, the sophistication of design and aesthetics are also greater.

Unlike its predecessor, the five-link setup doesn't exhibit severe *bump steer*—toes in or out during wheel travel. Ever follow a 'Vette with a three-link IRS down a bumpy road? Next time notice how the rear darts from side to side as it goes over the bumps. The five-link IRS in '83 and up 'Vettes doesn't do this. And, it's more-softly sprung.

Due to the high initial cost and lack of street-rod-installation kits for the five-link setup, however, it hasn't found the general acceptance the older models have. Just give it time, though. Back to the three-link 'Vette rear:

In its natural habitat, the Corvette gear carrier is bolted to a rubber-mounted crossmember. It hasn't often found such a cushy home in street-rod installations. Furthermore, street-rod builders of 10 or 15 years ago weren't fortunate enough to have the variety of commercial installation kits now available.

Early builders did realize, however, that the lower control arms and half shafts could be shortened—just like conventional drive shafts—for improved fender clearance. Ex-

perienced builders were also able to modify the original control arms and design appropriate bracketry for early Ford under-chassis mountings. Some even elected to dispense with the transverse spring in favor of Jag-type coil-over-shock suspension units.

If you wish to forego a commercial installation kit with its attendant instructions, you'll find no less of a challenge designing your own Corvette hardware than you would with the Jaguar. The installation is similar except for the indelicate control arms.

In some early Ford installations, a *tuck-in* mounting plate for the Corvette differential carrier can be incorporated into the stock rear crossmember. If, however, an entirely new crossmember is fabricated, it should be made from at least 2 X 2-in. heavy-wall steel tubing. Either way, an additional crossmember serving as a carrier front support must be fabricated. One-inch-minimum diameter round or square heavy-wall tubing must be used. This crossmember can also function as the top mount for the shock absorbers.

If you wish to design your own control arms, pay close attention to the configurtion of the stock units. They must be at least as

strong. A bracket fabricated from 3/8-in. steel plate with a bolt pattern to match the holes in the Corvette bearing carrier can be designed to mount both the replacement radius rods and spring. High-quality spherical rod ends or some of the top-notch aftermarket hardware should be used at the front pivot of each radius rod so there's free suspension movement.

All in all, the readily available Corvette rear suspension assembly is well worth the installation effort. This, of course, depends on whether you're prepared to face up to the engineering demands of doing the job right.

If you have doubts, however, review the wares offered by the manufacturers. With the sophistication and potential problems that come with modifying an IRS, you've got to be right-on when installing a Corvette or Jag rear. On the other hand, if you're sharp, you can come up with a number of installation innovations. But, professional builders, by virtue of their day-in, day-out exposure to all of the possible problems—and fixes—are far more likely to come up with a more efficient approach to the installation of a complicated independent rear suspension.

For a listing of suppliers, turn to page 203.

125

18 Early Ford Front Suspension

Early Ford front suspension was outdated when street rodding began in '30s, but its classic good looks keep new builders returning to it year after year.

In previous chapters, I dealt with a variety of rear-suspension components and their desirability as applied to the modern street rod. The majority of early Ford street-rod builders, however, are simply going to put all that nice theoretical stuff on a mind shelf and stay with the traditional I-beam axle and transverse spring suspension on the front end. And who can blame them? This combination has served countless thousands of street rodders for half a century.

EARLY FORD FRONT SUSPENSION

The front suspension used by Fords from the Model T days up to and through the 1948 passenger car consisted of a transverse leaf spring, a solid I-beam axle, and triangulated radius rods. The radius rods, commonly called the *wishbone,* are securely bolted to the axle at the front and pivoted in a single ball joint at the rear, forming a V. The axle is nothing more than a dished solid steel I-beam incorporating steering knuckles with yokes—called *spindles*—that are fitted over

the ends. The wheel assemblies are mounted with bearings on the spindles and supported at the axle with kingpins.

The vehicle is supported on the axle on a transverse leaf spring that's securely U-bolted to the frame's front crossmember. Shackles link the ends of the spring to perches at the axle. The spring-shackle studs were the rubber type up to 1932; later models used studs with a lubricant-impregnated fabric.

Springs are mounted above the axle on pre-'35 models and ahead of it on later models. A reduced spring rate for a smoother ride was achieved by lengthening the spring when it was moved ahead of the axle. Other minor design changes were made through the years, one of which was the slight widening of the *spring base*—mounting points at the axle—in 1940. A torsion-bar stabilizer was also added to control side-sway.

Nevertheless, as faithfully as the transverse-spring suspension has served, it has a major fault shared by all solid axles. And that is steering shimmy caused by

gyroscopic procession when one wheel travels over a bump and its angular deflection is transmitted through the axle to the other wheel. A spinning wheel reacts like a gyroscope. If it is tilted, it tries to resist the tilting force, hence causing the shimmy with which every street-rod driver is all too aware.

This gyroscopic action causes axle *tramp*—the axle *dances* like a teeter totter. When one wheel bounces, it causes the opposite wheel to bounce. This sets up a self-generating back-and-forth motion that can only be stopped by stabbing the brakes or slowing the vehicle, sometimes bringing it to a complete halt if conditions are severe.

Other faults commonly attributed to this suspension include the erratic movement of the axle assembly from braking and cornering forces. These movements usually come from excessive wear and/or inappropriate modifications to the radius rods. The street-rod-components industry has new products that help with reducing wear, roll-center changes, and variations in steering geometry.

Consequently, even here, we find that "traditional" is more often a state of mind rather than any hard and fast rules requiring genuine early Ford parts. Therefore, I'll try to bring you up to date on the latest hardware as well as introduce you to the techniques that are successfully used to modify the Ford buggy-spring and I-beam axle.

DROPPED AXLE

Beauty is in the eyes of the beholder. For more than four decades, street rodders have seen greater beauty in a car that's lower in the front than one sitting on an even keel. In less-complicated days when few rodders considered anything other than a Ford based front suspension, the choice was between a stock axle and one with a greater-than-stock arch. The so called *dropped axle* was designed to lower the front ride height of the car 2—3 in. Smaller tires account for another 1 in. or so. The lowered front end is still very much with us; so is the demand for dropped axles.

You may have the problem of not knowing exactly what to look for as you wander up and down swap-meet aisles, or ponder over aftermarket catalogs. This is understandable because there can be more than one name for the same product, or worse, more than one product with the same name. As a result, many an

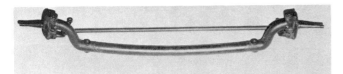

Major street-rod modification to early Ford front suspension is dropped axle. *Stretched* Deuce I-beam is compared to stock axle.

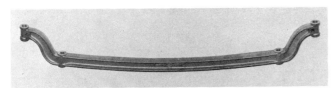

Hot tip in updated traditional street-rod front suspension is Super Bell tubular dropped axle . . .

. . . and newer Super Bell dropped I-beam.

Bill Keifer's California Custom Roadsters' Fad T front-suspension assembly with four-bend, 4-in. dropped tubular axle. Tight bend allows use of longer spring for a smoother ride. Axle is also equipped with special spring hangers to extend wheel base.

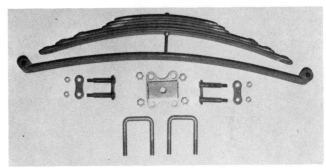

Specialized Auto Components' early '30s Ford transverse-spring kit features reversed eyes on main leaf for additional front-end drop.

unwary buyer has purchased an axle that did not quite fit as planned.

It's no wonder. There were five major varieties of Ford passenger-car beam axles manufactured in Dearborn between 1928 and 1948. In addition, a number of aftermarket axles were reworked during the early commercial years of hot rodding. Add to this the several different axles being scratch-built today, and it is easy to see why there's so much confusion.

Stock Ford axles, because of their uniformity of manufacture and clear-cut model designation, are relatively easy to categorize. See the nearby table. The varieties of early aftermarket dropped axles, unfortunately, are not so easy. It isn't that there were so many, just that most early manufacturers were obscure even then.

One thing for sure: We know that the original concept of a dropped axle—ends that have been reshaped to raise the spindles (lower the car)—is the brainchild of Abe Kobeck in San Diego back in the late '30s. The dropped axle gained its fame, however, through the aggressive marketing efforts of Ed "Axle" Stewart, also of San Diego, in the '40s and '50s. The so-called "Dago axle"—evolving from *Diego*—became so popular that virtual-

FORD MOTOR COMPANY AXLES: 1928—48

1928—31: A relatively straight axle with only a 2-3/4-in. arch; 51-7/8-in. long with radius-rod centers 36-1/4 in. apart. Radius-rod bosses are 2-1/4-in. thick.

***

1932: A prominently curved design with a 4-1/2-in. arch; 51-3/4-in. long with radius-rod centers 36-9/16-in. apart. Radius-rod bosses are 2-in. thick.

***

1933—36: Slightly thinner I-beam than 1932 axle, but dimensionally the same.

***

1937 Tubular: Lightweight tubular axle used only in the 1937 Model Fords powered by 60 horsepower, 136-CID V8. Has a 4-1/2-in. arch and is 50-in. long with radius-rod centers 38-1/2-in. apart. Radius-rod bosses are 2-1/4-in. thick. (Only non I-beam

passenger-car axle produced by Ford during the buggy-spring era.)

***

1937—41: Standard I-beam axle with a 4-3/8-in. arch; 49-7/8-in. long with radius-rod centers 38-1/2-in. apart. Radius-rod bosses are 2-1/4-in. thick.

***

1942—47: The most prominently curved of the Ford I-beams with a 5-3/8-in. arch; 52-in.-long with radius-rod centers 40-3/4-in. apart. Radius-rod bosses are 2-1/4-in. thick.

***

1948: Dimensionally the same as 1942—47 models, but with an extra hole in the I-beam web between the kingpin boss and radius-rod boss to accommodate mounting of tubular shock absorbers.

Installation of stock early Ford spindles on dropped axle requires recontouring steering arms so tie rod and drag link will clear radius rods.

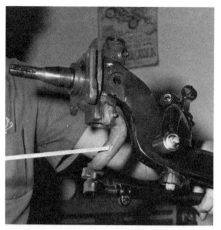

Heating and bending is primarily confined to this area of each steering arm. This is a hot job, so wear protective clothing and safety goggles.

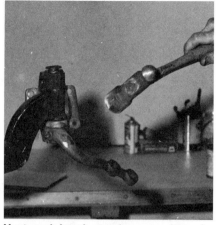

Heat and bend steering arm down by hammering. Caution: Do not overheat arm. Stay within the *cherry-red* range.

Pipe wrench isn't used often in street-rod building, but one is in this situation. While arm is hot, bend arm down and back.

Final bending brings tie rod and drag link bosses back to level. Once opposite spindle is recontoured and matched to this one, steering links will clear radius rods.

Early Ford spindles are best honed—rather than reamed—prior to rebushing. Precision fitting of kingpin to honed bushing will triple service life of front end.

ly all street rods were built with them until the Corvair independent front suspension gained a minor following in the mid '60s.

For many years, dropped axles were actually re-manufactured stockers. The first of these were the *stretched jobs,* which can be identified by the slight narrowing in the middle of the *S-curve*—short section between each wishbone boss and kingpin boss. Next came the forged, dropped axle, where the S-curve is a constant width. Ultimately, the most popular axles were *filled*—open section between the I-beam flanges was boxed, creating a square cross section. The height of street-rod fashion during much of the '50s was chromed, filled axles, with the open I-beam between the wishbone bosses neatly painted red.

Before the end of that decade, though, the "Bell" axle had achieved top-of-the-line sta-

tus. The Bell axle wasn't a dropped axle at all. Rather, it was a replacement axle manufactured by the Bell Auto Parts Company headquartered in Bell, California. The original Bell axle is not seen as often as reworked stockers because it was a relatively expensive item back then. Consequently, there aren't as many around.

Today, several different types of reproduction dropped axles are manufactured. One of the original dropped axle companies, Mor-Drop, which was started in 1955, is still going strong. A complete listing of currently available axle suppliers is at the end of this book.

RAKING EARLY FORD FRONT ENDS

Let's get down to the nuts and bolts of actually installing a traditional street-rod front suspension. A front-end drop of 2—4

in. is the most desirable, but some brave souls have gone as far as 6 in. However, if you plan to do a lot of driving on less than glass-smooth roads, it's best to err on the side of moderation. Stay within the 2—4-in. range.

Other Things Change—When a front end is lowered, the entire frame and body is raked (tilted) forwarded. Naturally, any suspension components secured to the frame will also be angled forward. For example, front-wheel caster angle will be decreased, headlight beams shortened, fuel level in the carburetor-float bowl will be affected, and the gas-gauge reading may be upset.

Moderate changes won't cause major problems but, if compensating changes aren't made, too much rake will affect driveability and excessive tire wear. Putting it mildly, changing the rake of that old car *the right way* will take a lot of work.

128

In more or less stock form, early Fords tend to oversteer—rear-tire slip angle is greater than the front when cornering. This condition is worsened when the front end is lowered.

The 1940-type front anti-roll bar helps, as do smaller front tires and larger rear ones. On the unsophisticated side, you can run lower tire pressure at the front and higher pressure at the rear. Further down the sophistication scales, you can compensate for poor handling by learning how to drive a lowered Ford. Pay close attention to "seat-of-the-pants" cues that tell you when you are on the edge. Many race cars oversteer. It merely behooves the driver to know the particular characteristics of his car and to drive accordingly.

Camber is not significantly changed with a dropped front end, but caster and toe-in are. So, no matter how slight the rake, have the front end realigned. Re-aim the headlights, too. The change in carb angle shouldn't be a problem, but you'll have to familiarize yourself with changes in gas-gage readings.

Installing a dropped front axle with a stock Ford radius-rod assembly is a "simple, but difficult" job. Original matings aren't easily changed. I'll get to that in a moment, but the tricky problem is to regain full rotation of the spindle once it has been installed on the dropped axle. The steering arm will not adequately clear the bend of a dropped axle. Although some additional muscle will be needed, you should be able to make this change.

You'll need a large vise, an oxyacetylene outfit with a #5 tip, a large pipe wrench, and two straight edges. A length of steel tubing or heavy pipe can be used to lever steering arms. It's possible to reshape the steering arms with the dropped axle and spring assembly mounted in the frame, but it's easier to do it on the bench.

The process of heating, bending and reshaping early Ford steering arms is essentially the same for all models, but the 1937—1948 spindles are more difficult. Before you bend the steering arms, study the accompanying photos.

REBUSHING SPINDLES

The next step in updating an early Ford front end is to rebush the spindles and replace the kingpins. If you've ever driven an old Ford with a "bad front end," you know what "shimmy and shake" means. This condition and the tendency of a solid axle to cause wheel tramp can be most often attributed to worn kingpins and bushings. When the kingpins start to wallow around in the spindles, all semblance of driveability disappears.

Fortunately, spindle reconditioning is relatively easy, requiring no more than two or so hours of work and a trip to an automotive machine shop for a hone job. Yes, a *hone job*.

Granted, the traditional way to rebuild spindles has been to ream the new bushings. Mail-order hand reamers have been available for a couple of bucks since my coupe was new.

Unfortunately, hand reaming can't give the precision needed for reconditioning a street-rod front. Anything less that a precise fit and you'll have to redo the job after 10,000 miles. However, if you still insist on using a hand reamer, here's how to do it.

First, a hand reamer is a tool-steel shaft with spiral cutting edges. The reaming operation begins with inserting the reamer in the bushing bore. Rotate the reamer slowly with a wrench. The far end of the reamer is held "more or less" straight and steady by the bushing opposite the one being reamed. To fit the pin, you may have to account for a variance in bore accuracy and smoothness by installing it in the super-snug bore with a hammer. If you over-did the ream job, the kingpins will fall in.

Fortunately, there's a much better way to *re-bush* a Ford front end. The few extra dollars it takes won't be missed. Every automotive machine shop has a honing machine. These are used primarily for fitting piston pins and reconditioning connecting rods. They simultaneously hone both spindle bores in line to ensure perfect alignment and full pin-to-bushing contact. Again, the photo tells the story better than words.

THE BUGGY SPRING

If you're going the traditional route, sooner or later you must deal with the transverse leaf spring. These springs are available from antique-car-parts houses in six varieties: 1928—31 (A-5310), 1932—34 (40-5310), 1935—39 (78-5310), 1940 (01A-5310), 1941 (llA-5310), 1942—48 (51A-5310).

Manufacturers of street-rod components aren't such sticklers for detail. They usually lump 1928—34 models together and 1935—40 passenger-car models together. There's no harm done. Only a purist would find fault—and purists don't build street rods.

Although it is certainly possible to recondition an original spring bundle by breaking it down, thoroughly cleaning it, and then reassembling it, don't do it unless you need the exercise. Old springs are just that . . . old. There's no sense in trying to make do, considering that a new spring assembly is reasonably priced and, when assembled with polypropylene liners, ride improvement is significant.

Reworking 1923—34 Ford Radius Rods—

You can purchase parts from a handful of street-rod-parts catalogs to complete your front suspension. Everything you need is as close as your mailbox. It's a far cry from the early days of rod building where you used

scrap steel and miscellaneous suspension parts pirated from a variety of cars, old and new. Once again, we must thank the pioneers of the street-rod-parts industry for the change.

Two who have been in the business for many years are Pete Chapouris and Jim "Jitney Jake" Jacobs of, you guessed it, Pete & Jake fame. They, and the cars so long associated with them, first came to glory in the old *Rod & Custom Magazine* and "California Kid" movie days. But, their long-lived claim to fame is the trend-setting "4-Bar Suspension," their registered trademark for the parallel radius-rod kits manufactured and sold by the Temple City, California, street-rod-parts emporium.

Pete & Jake didn't actually invent the parallel radius-rod suspension. It showed up on track roadsters built right after WWII. But, P&J did "re-invent" it, because it wasn't seen on many street rods until they came along!

The parallel radius-rod suspension is deceptively simple. It eliminates some of the suspension problems encountered when an early Ford front-suspension assembly is modified. For instance, it has long been common practice to cut off the ball joint at the rear of the stock triangular-shaped radius rods, then spread apart the rods. The chassis side rails are then mounted on the frame side rails. This gives plenty of room to work on the bottom end of the engine, or to install a larger engine and transmission. To repeat, this operation in practice is known as *splitting the wishbone*.

Ah, but now the axle must pivot from *two* separate points rather than one. What this does is make the axle a huge anti-roll bar, causing severe understeer. It also introduces high loads at the radius-rod mounts, in the axle, frame and the radius rods themselves.

On rough and irregular roads, unilateral wheel movement induces a twisting and binding, along with small, but unequal caster-angle changes. The least you can expect is poor ride and handling; the worst is metal fatigue and failure.

The four-link setup, with its parallel radius rods, basically eliminates binding and caster-angle changes. The ends of the axle can move up and down independently, if installed correctly, with virtually no twisting or binding. Ride and handling are improved considerably over the more-traditional modification of splitting the wishbone.

The installation of the Pete & Jake 4-Bar Suspension is simplicity itself. The frame brackets are positioned on the side rails using factory holes as reference points. Once located, they are welded in place. The remainder of the components are bolted together.

One final feature of the Pete & Jake four-bar kit is the *Microflex* bushings they have used since 1979. They originally installed

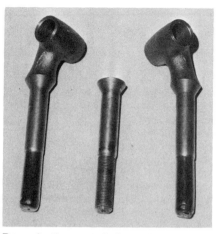

Wishbone-splitting kits are available from many components manufacturers.

They spread stock Ford radius rods to X-member just far enough to accommodate a modern transmission.

Reproduction parts industry has outdone itself when it comes to front-suspension hardware. Super Bell spring perches are as good as the originals.

Don McNeil demonstrates how easy modern street-rod front suspension is installed. Radius-rod *bat wings* are pinned to Super Bell axle by the spring perch. Lower shock perch is on floor.

Spring is attached to perches with shackles fitted with urethane bushings. Gone forever are those blasted rubber-bushed shackle studs.

Almost always, the installation of a later-model engine and transmission will require some modification to the radius-rod assembly. If, however, you are working on an original chassis and you plan on reinstalling a flathead V8 or other power plant and drive train that will not interfere with the stock radius rods or their mounting, by all means leave things alone. When you've rebuilt the buggy spring and installed new shackle bushings and good shock absorbers, the stock assembly will work reasonably well. In short, *don't fix what ain't broke!*

However, if you're going to install a big engine and/or transmission, particularly an automatic, adequate clearance will be lacking. Although the clearance may be minimal, the need to perodically service an automatic transmission makes a modified radius-rod assembly mighty appealing. This, of course, requires splitting the wishbone.

Not only that, the center member of a more or less original car will probably have been modified. So, there simply won't be any

GM-type rubber and steel sleeve bushings in each end of the four radius rods. Although the rubber bushing worked very well, when urethane bushings showed further improvement, they incorporated them into their suspension kits. Soon, everybody did.

Reworking the 1935—48 Ford Radius Rod—If you're building a 1935—48 Ford based street rod, it's not as easy to get front-suspension parts as it is for the earlier 1909—34 Ford based street rod. For instance, only a few companies offer parallel radius-rod kits for 1935—40 Fords. Chassis Engineering of West Branch, Iowa was one of the first, however.

There are many components available though, for rebuilding and updating the stock 1935—48 suspension. But, for the most part, you must either start with or acquire a fairly decent original radius-rod assembly before

you can mount your dropped axle and reworked spindle assembly. Your only compensation is that this installation will be closer to being traditional than any other.

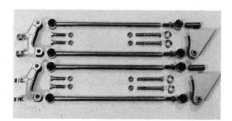

Four-link radius-rod kits are more-or-less standard front-end equipment for 1928—34 Ford street rods. Pioneered by Pete & Jake's, second-generation versions are available such as this Deuce Factory assembly made primarily of stainless steel.

Precise installation and high-quality welding of four-link frame brackets is critical. Complete instructions usually come with each kit.

place to mount a stock wishbone—even if one exists. What is usually found is a split and bent radius-rod assembly with welded-in tie-rod ends, bolted directly to the frame, or crude hangers that are attached to the side of each frame rail. This has often seemed to be the easiest thing to do. But, again, the problem with this modification is front-suspension binding, resulting in poor handling and overloaded mountings.

The key to splitting the wishbones and minimal binding is to mount the split radius-rod ends as close together as possible. The logical place to do this is on the bottom side of the forward legs of the X-member. This closely retains the stock suspension geometry and provides ample clearance for many automatic transmissions.

In earlier years, the favorite split-wishbone pivot was the tie-rod end. Another solution is the spherical rod-end bearing. This useful piece of hardware is compliments of the aircraft industry. Caution must be taken, however, to use high-quality rod-end bearings. There are cheap versions that don't have the durability and load capacity needed. So, get the best spherical bearing: Teflon-lined stainless steel.

Disassembly—But before we get too far into the modification of the radius-rod assembly, I'll acquaint you with the really tough part—disassembly. Few components of an old car are as difficult to break down as the early Ford front suspension. In fact, it may be *the* most ornery of all.

The first order of business—after removal of the suspension from the car—is to disconnect the spring and knock the shackle bolts out of their bosses. Old timers used to drill a 3/8-in. hole in a piece of 3/4-in.-diameter soft iron rod to drive out the shackle bolts without swelling or distorting them. Even though you shouldn't reuse the shackle bolts, don't wedge them in tighter than they are. The original bolt often separates, leaving a thin sleeve in the shackle boss. If this happens, put on a pair of safety glasses and carefully chisel it out.

Now that you're finished with the easy part, removing the stock axle from the wishbone is what separates the men from the boys. To save the axle bolts, carefully heat them to break the scale and rust that binds the nut in the concave boss. If all goes according to plan—don't count on it—the radius-rod bolts can be driven out with ease.

Approach the job with optimism, though. Flip the assembly upside down and squirt a liberal dose of Liquid Wrench or similar product around the bolt shanks. Let the assembly marinate overnight. Next day, replace the original nuts with cheap standard nuts, but don't run them down all the way. (Lubricate

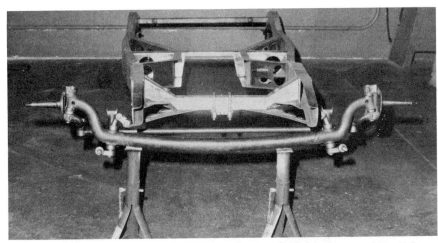
Modernized early Ford style axle assembly tucks up into crossmember as did its forbear.

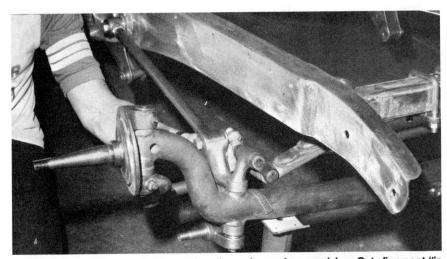
Installation and adjustment of four-link radius rods requires precision. Get alignment "in ball park," then take completed car to front-end alignment shop for final alignment.

the threads, first.) Now, drive out the bolts with a 10-pound hammer. Or, at least try to.

If they won't come out in 15 minutes or so, stop. Take the radius rod assembly to a machine shop that has a 20-ton hydraulic press, no less. If this doesn't work, go back to your torch. Preheat the area around the radius-rod bolt until it's bright cherry red. At that point, make diagonal burns across the breadth of the axle to free the bolt shank.

When two pieces of steel are rust-fused together for many years, it takes a delicate hand with a cutting torch to free them. Just remember, the part that is being cut—in this case the axle—will absorb the greater percentage of applied heat. Work very carefully to protect the part, or parts, you wish to save.

Once the radius rod assembly is free of the axle, cut off the wishbone ball close to where

the forging was originally welded to the tapered arms. Don't cut the radius rods any shorter than necessary.

If you were able to save the old radius rod bolts, great. Replacement bolts for 1935—40 cars are not always available. The same goes for the axle, even if you don't personally need it for an exchange. Chances are one of your street-rod buddies will need it.

KITS FOR EVERYTHING

Several street-rod components manufacturers offer "Wishbone Splitting Kits" for 1935—40 Fords. Among these are Specialized Auto Components, Chassis Engineering and Pete and Jake. Specialized and Chassis Engineering use tie-rod ends; Pete and Jake use urethane-bushed adjusters. Installation is similar in all cases.

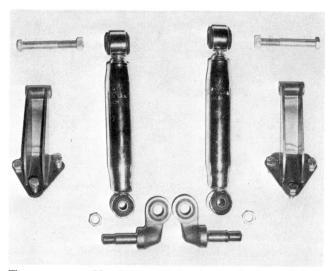

There are several front shock kits for street rods. Shown is Specialized Auto Components' bolt-on 1933—34 Ford kit which incorporates Super Bell lower shock mounts.

Specialized Auto's well-detailed, all repro components, 1933—34 Ford chassis reflects many hours of labor. This allows you to maintain the traditional approach, but with as much modernization as possible. The labor is free . . . you and your buddies provide it.

Chrome shocks offered by Specialized Auto Components have been selected for 1933—34 Fords with small-block Chevy or Ford power.

First, a threaded spud for the adjustable fitting is welded into the end of each radius rod. Both rods are then assembled on the dropped axle. It's best to use new or replacement radius-rod bolts, but used ones in good condition still have a lot of service left. The kit brackets are then installed on the chassis. In some cases, new bolt holes will have to be drilled; in other applications, existing bolt or rivet holes are used. Either way, they must be positioned in a location compatible with the length of the radius rods. Some of the brackets are small; all are substantial. Others that do double-duty, such as a rear transmission-support plate, are fairly large.

Install Front-End Assembly—Install the new radius rod/dropped axle assembly under the frame. Bolt the adjustable ends in the brackets and center the axle so it aligns with the spring-shackle bushings. When the wishbone is split and the radius rods are moved outward, the shackle bushing-to-axle angle changes. To correct this, heat the arm and twist the boss back out to its original 90° relationship.

Although this can be approximated before the axle assembly is moved under the car, final adjustments must be made with the assembly bolted in the frame, front and rear. Now the re-conditioned spring and new shackle bushings can be installed.

For a list of early Ford front-suspension-component suppliers, turn to page 203.

Independent front suspension equipped with coil-over shocks provides superior ride and handling. Custom-fabricated setup uses urethane bushings at the frame pivots and conventional ball joints at the spindles. Photo by Tom Monroe.

If you think that putting an independent front suspension under an early Ford was something dreamed up during rodding's rebirth in the late '60s, think again. In the spring of 1947, Ak Miller happened to notice that the coil-spring independent front suspension on a 1941 Chevy could be unbolted and, with a bit of modification, fitted under his Deuce High Boy roadster. No sooner said than done, he welded it in place and boxed the frame, added in some well-guarded tricks to add torsional rigidity to the frame and went to the Lakes. In a test run on El Mirage in July, 1947, Ak clocked 106.25 mph with no problem. Later, he fondly recalls, he could "thread a needle with that thing at 120 mph! No more Ford dead axles for me."

Ak Miller, a dedicated hot-rod racer and president of the Southern California Timing Association at the time, could never be called a traditionalist . . . his nonconformist power plant in the same roadster was a straight-8 Buick.

It's true, though, that the general popularity of the independent front suspension didn't catch on until 20 years later when the attractive Jaguar IFS began to appear under show roadsters. Half-hearted attempts to popularize the more mundane Corvair IFS in the early '60s excited few fenderless car owners and only slightly more full-fendered rod builders.

WHY THE INDEPENDENT FRONT SUSPENSION?

There are several good reasons for using an independent front suspension under a street rod. It is better than any solid axle could ever hope to be in terms of both ride quality and handling superiority. Also, if the installation is properly done, it will enhance the market value of the street rod should a parting of the ways ever come.

Unfortunately, even though most rodders admit an IFS is superior, most of them are—in a word—UGLY. The ego trip that owning a street rod provides leaves no room for anything that doesn't look good.

If you elect to install the expensive Jaguar front suspension, you'll get the best of both worlds—engineering *and* aesthetics. But, as the supply of available Jaguar suspensions dwindles and price skyrockets, new products are appearing—fabricated independent front suspensions incorporating a mix of aftermarket components and inexpensive wrecking-yard parts. But, let's not get ahead of ourselves.

There's a growing contingent of full-fendered rod builders who recognize the

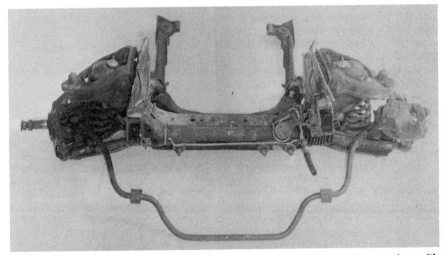

1974—78 Mustang II—and 1974—80 Pinto and Bobcat front suspension complete with disc brakes and rack-and-pinion steering: Not pretty, but inexpensive and readily available. Suspension assembly is well suited to out-of-sight installation in 1935—40 Fords.

Progressive Automotive was first company I know of to offer installation kit for Mustang II IFS. Custom crossmember is welded in frame, then suspension components are bolted on. Kit shown is for 1933—34 Ford.

Wrecking yards usually do a quick cut-and-chop when removing Mustang II front suspension. Carefully cut remaining body sheet metal from crossmember.

Stripped Mustang II crossmember should look like this.

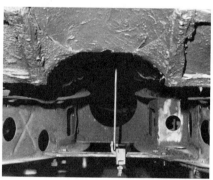

Installation begins with removal of stock early Ford crossmember. Drill out rivets, then "muscle" out stubborn crossmember.

Front of stripped chassis is fitted with spreader bar—to hold frame rails in position—and boxing plates. Plates are needed to restore frame strength lost with removal of original sheet metal. Specialized Auto Repair's Terry Berzenye recommends thick material be used—at least a 1/4-in.

Center of frame was determined and marked with pointer. Equidistant measurements were then found at forward end of rails.

engineering superiority of inexpensive modern IFS units that come straight out of Dearborn and Detroit. They know, too, that with a little planning, several of these suspensions can be neatly tucked away out of sight under the vast expanse of sheet metal that covers the front ends of most 1935 to 1948 cars. If only the driver knows the low-buck, high-performing IFS is there, they reason, why not go for the better ride and handling qualities?

CHOOSING AN IFS

Cost and aesthetics aside, there are three major factors you must consider when selecting any particular independent suspension for a given street rod—frame width, vehicle weight and suspension adaptability. Although an IFS works like a charm in one vehicle, it may be totally inappropriate for your street rod.

Minor variations in frame width can be compensated for in the design of the replace-

ment crossmember. A hundred pounds either way in load capacity can be accommodated with rewound springs or interchanges from another, heavier, model.

Awkward configurations and mountings can often be dealt with by installing a fabricated crossmember that accepts the new suspension components and fits the street rod. Another approach is a judicious re-engineering of the original suspension hardware. That's part and parcel of street rodding. But, you must start from a logical point. The front suspension being considered should be close in terms of width, beef and overall adaptability.

Fortunately, there's an independent front suspension that is close to ideal for installing in a mid '30s—'40s-based street rod. It's the 1974—78 Mustang II and its slightly smaller clones that use many of the same components. These include the 1974—80 Ford Pinto and Mercury Bobcat.

MUSTANG II IFS

In its natural setting, the Mustang II front suspension with its stabilizer bar and compression-type struts mounts in a sub frame. The coil springs are on the lower control arms with the shock absorbers mounted in the center. The Mustang II front tread is 55.6 inches—a fraction narrower than its rear tread. The variable-ratio rack-and-pinion steering is available in both manual and power versions, but the power version is the better choice.

The Mustang II's 9.3-in. disc-brake rotors are an excellent plus, making this suspension even more desirable. Best of all, the 1978 Mustang II with the V8 option had a curb weight of about 2750 pounds—close to the typical full-fendered coupe, sedan and pickup street rod.

The Mustang II has conventional short upper and long lower control arms. The control arms are isolated from the body structure by

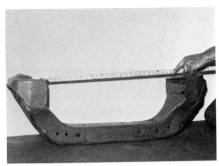

Important consideration is distance between inside edges of Mustang II shock towers; 27 in. must be maintained. Crossmember must be slipped under, up and around early Ford frame.

Width of shock tower determines width of notch in frame.

Measure from centerline across to each frame rail and determine location of notches in rails so that 27-in. spread between shock towers is maintained.

Saw cut in the center of the crossmember allows it to be opened up a bit to fit it to '40 frame. This minimizes material removal of stock frame.

To pinpoint shock tower notches in frame, use original rubber snubber to determine centerline of original axle on frame . . .

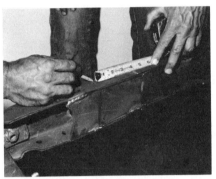

. . . and extend it up and over rail. This will locate exact center of frame notch for the shock tower.

large rubber bushings. Because the coil springs are mounted on the lower arms, the spring towers are low. The compression struts, which extend from the lower control arms to an anchoring bracket on the frame, are also mounted in rubber. This feature allows the front wheel to deflect slightly to lessen road shock.

The Mustang II front suspension was engineered to minimize toe change from wheel travel and turning to improve handling and minimize tire wear. Finally, the control arms are angled—as are all modern front suspensions—to minimize *nose-dive* during braking.

About the only drawback to the Mustang II front suspension is the installation. Although the control arms and excellent power rack-and-pinion steering packages easily under a variety of 1930s and '40s street-rod-able cars, the mere thought of such a complicated installation could bring a shudder to even an experienced rod builder . . . at least, without some help from the experts.

The Progressive Approach—Experts in installing the Mustang II front suspension are Tom Artusi and Frank Shetrone, co-owners of *Progressive Automotive*. Progressive is located in the rolling hills of south-central Ohio, but these fellows have spread their fame wherever street rodders congregate.

Artusi and Shetrone use their own custom crossmember when installing the Mustang II suspension. This beefy crossmember serves several purposes: it contains the top spring pockets, and lower control-arm and steering-gear mounts. The crossmember is fabricated of 7-gage (0.1793-in. thick) steel, which is thicker than the steel used in early car frames. Such a critical component cannot tolerate any short cuts, and the Progressive crossmember is no cost-conscious weak sister.

For most street-rod installations, the Progressive Automotive IFS kit requires some, but not a great deal of modification to the stock sheet metal. The kit includes the main crossmember, a pair of strut-rod brackets, a pair of new, longer-than-stock tie-rod ends and, of course, complete instructions.

The Specialized Approach—Terry Berzenye's *Specialized Auto Repair* in Anaheim, California, zeros in on the installation of the Mustang front suspension in early cars and trucks from a slightly different perspective. They retain the original Mustang II crossmember after trimming off a few nonessentials. This is a practical approach, first,

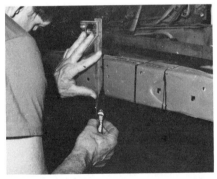

Carefully scribe cut lines on top and sides of frame rails.

because the Mustang front end and many early-car front ends have similar tread widths. Also, the strong Mustang crossmember is more-or-less removable.

As for modifications to the street rod's frame, the original crossmember must be removed, as well as a few healthy chunks of side rail. And, as with all re-engineering projects such as this, the one doing the fabricating

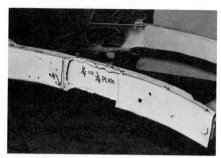

Make frame cuts using marks as reference. Frame looks sad, but all will be healed when Mustang II crossmember is installed.

Note tight crossmember fit and how frame tucks under shock towers. Patient trimming and fitting will result in good fit.

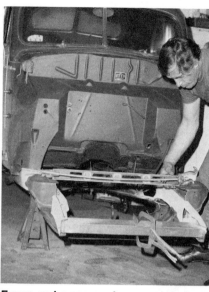

Frame and crossmember are periodically checked to be sure both are level.

To avoid cutting away *too* much frame, notch Mustang II crossmember. Frame can then drop closer to ground for the popular "California tilt."

Crossmember is re-checked to be certain it is centered in frame and tilt of crossmember relative to the frame is correct. If 2—3-in. body rake is desired, positive 6—7° front-end caster is built in. Otherwise, crossmember is kept at about 3°.

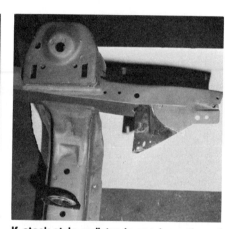

If stock-style radiator is used, section of frame that supports it can be reinstalled.

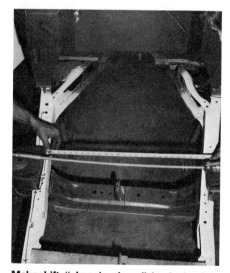

Makeshift "chassis clamp" is devised to draw crossmember back to previously determined width. Precise measurements are a must to ensure correct front-end alignment

must be expert at handling a torch and welder. Solid welding skills are a must.

E-TYPE JAG IFS

All of a sudden, E-Type Jag front suspensions started showing up under some mighty nice roadsters in the late '60s. Why they were immediately accepted is no mystery. They fit well under many early street rods . . . and they *look good*. Only a stranger to this sport underestimates the street rodder's penchant for beauty and grace in things me-

chanical. Such things in other folks' cars are usually covered with road grime and grease.

The early '60s E-type Jaguar coupe and roadster with wheelbases and front/rear treads of 96 and 50 in., respectively, had overall dimensions not unlike early Ford coupes and roadsters. True, they weighed several hundred pounds more than the typical Deuce High Boy, but the weight was in the body and engine where it could do the street rodders no harm, not in the fully independent suspension.

Once crossmember is welded to frame, lower strut rod must be heated and bent in under frame. Mounting brackets can then be welded into place.

Rack-and-pinion steering is bolted to crossmember and suspension partially assembled for one last check prior to smoothing welds and detailing frame.

The E-type Jag IFS is not that different from the Mustang II's in basic design. It consists of a pair of unequal-length control arms, spindle attached to the outer ends of each pair of control arms and tubular shock absorbers. Instead of coil springs, torsion bars are used. The torsion bars are attached at their forward end to the lower control arm and at their rears to brackets on the frame. The top of each shock is mounted to a frame bracket; the bottom to the lower control arm.

Unlike the Mustang II's stamped-steel upper control arm, the Jag's upper arm is a one-piece forging. It is pivoted on a shaft which is, in turn, mounted on a pair of rubber and steel sleeve bushings. The lower arm is a two-piece assembly, with the inner ends mounted at another shaft on bushings. Ball joints are used at the outer ends of the control arms to mount the steering knuckle (spindle). An anti-roll bar is fitted between the lower control arm and attached to the chassis front member by rubber-insulated brackets.

The stock Jag wheels that are secured by knockoffs are not suitable for street-rod use. Consequently, the wheel hubs must be modified to accept studs and lug nuts. Each front brake consists of a hub-mounted disc and a caliper that is rigidly attached to the spindle. The original Dunlop bridge-type calipers and 11-in. disc can be replaced by more modern brake components.

E-Type Jag IFS to the Deuce—One of the oldest hands at installing an E-Type Jag front suspension in an early Ford is Jerry Kugel. Kugel started building installation kits in 1969 for '32 Fords. Jerry has improved and expanded his line continuously. His one-piece jig-welded front crossmember adapts the Jag IFS—less rack-and-pinion steering gear—to the '32 Ford-based street rod with relative ease. His unique adaptation of the Vega cross steering to the Jag IFS is an in-

teresting blend of components that has proved roadworthy over the years.

Jag IFS to the '40s—In seasons past, the *fat-fendered* Fords of 1937—40 were rarely treated to more than a dropped axle. But, today they command premium prices. When the general value of a specific model year goes up, rod builders are more apt to install exotic—and expensive—components.

Don McNeil's *Specialized Auto Components* (SAC) of Anaheim, California, is the only manufacturer of a kit to install the E-Type Jag IFS in the 1937—40 Ford. The SAC kit includes a beefy crossmember and adjustable rear torsion-bar mounts.

T-Bones, Too—Not to be outdone by the West Coast contingent, *Total Performance, Incorporated* (TPI), located in Wallingford, Connecticut, offers their own E-Jag IFS installation kit for the Model T, A, Deuce and 1933—34 Ford. The TPI kit includes front shocks and mounting brackets of their design, which necessitates modifications to the spindles. TPI provides the instructions or will perform the machining and welding operation in-house for you. Total Performance also has a kit to mount either the Saab rack-and-pinion or Vega cross steering in place of the Jag gear.

HOMEGROWN IFS

I'm sure there's no immediate threat of a shortage of Mustang II, Pinto and Bobcat front suspensions, but the supply of available E-Type Jag front suspensions is growing smaller each year. So, because of the increasing demand and smaller supply, several enterprising street-rod shops are marketing a hybrid blend of stock Detroit front-suspension hardware and aftermarket components that look and function similar to that of the Jag. It would appear that they are beginning to excite the fancy of more than a few rod builders.

The Kugel IFS—In the forefront of this "new wave" is, once again, Mr. Kugel. The heart of Jerry's "Kugel Komponents Stainless Steel Independent Front Suspension" is a one-piece spindle and upright, and a bolt-on steering arm. Both the upright—on which the spindle has been relocated vertically for a lower ride height—and the steering arm have been investment cast of 17-4 stainless steel. Stainless-steel caliper adapters, JFZ aluminum calipers and Chevy disc-brake rotors, bearings and ball joints round off the wheel assemblies. Kugel's upper and lower A-arms are fabricated of 7/8-in. X 0.156-in.-wall 304 stainless-steel tubing. The lower arms are made of 1-in. X 0.188-in.-wall 304 stainless.

The Kugel IFS breaks with the Jag influence with regard to steering and springs. Coil-over shocks and Vega cross steering is used, an idea, Jerry reports, that is borrowed from Porsche.

All in all, the Kugel IFS is a tidy, carefully engineered package that I predict will soon be found under many so-called *high-tech* street rods.

Meyer IFS uses Opel control arms and spindles, and Honda rack-and-pinion steering. Custom crossmember fits all Fords through 1934, and most Chevrolet frames through 1936.

Tom Ayers spent a lot of time mentally building his 1940 Chevrolet coupe. He then chose the 1975—80 AMC Pacer IFS for his Stovebolt. As you can see, it was a good choice.

Power rack-and-pinion nestles nicely into hybrid frame. Pacer anti-roll bar fits in as well, a major plus not achieved in many IFS/street-rod swaps.

Tom fabricated chassis mounts and support structures, then welded them to the Pacer crossmember. Modified crossmember was bolted to slightly altered frame. If you are a Ford builder, you'll be pleased to know that Chassis Engineering offers a kit for adapting the Pacer suspension.

Small-block Chevy installs easily after front-end work is completed. Engine swap is about as compact and sanitary as they come. Modifying surrounding sheet metal in any significant way was unnecessary.

Interesting feature of Pacer suspension-to-Chevy swap is how suspension components package below inner fender panel.

The Meyer IFS—There's a street-rod shop tucked way up in the Pacific Northwest, run by a fellow named Jim Meyer. Jim markets what he feels is one of the finest custom independent front-suspension kits available.

The kit contains a cross member with mounts for the lower control arms and a Honda rack-and-pinion steering. Tubular control arms are fitted with urethane bushings at the inner pivots; Koni adjustable coil-over shocks are supplied with brackets, pivot shafts and tubular tie rods. The installation features adjustable ride height, adjustable caster, camber and toe-in, and adjustable bump steer. All of Jim's shop-manufactured components are TIG-welded in precision fixtures. The standard width of Meyer's IFS is 56.5 in., flange to flange, but special widths are available.

In addition to the Honda rack-and-pinion steering, Jim's kit incorporates 1967 Nova upper ball joints, 1972 Chevelle lower ball joints, and 1964—72 Chevelle/Camaro spindles, rotors, calipers and steering arms. This is readily available hardware.

Street-rod builders have come a long way since Ak Miller first peaked under that '41 Chevy.

Turn to page 203 for a listing of suppliers of independent front suspension kits and components.

Steering and suspension components are put to test on unforgiving railroad tracks. If your car has a steering or suspension problem, you'll find it when driving over rough surfaces, particularly at high speed.

If you chose the now-traditional early Ford/parallel radius-rod front suspension, your steering-gear selection is more or less predetermined by the kit manufacturer. Their predominant choice—the late-'60s Mustang or Cougar recirculating ball unit—has been well tested and not found wanting in any way. If you're using a Jag or Mustang II independent front suspension, the factory steering gear is usually the logical choice. There are, however, a few options offered by some kit manufacturers. But, if you have chosen to go it alone, your options are as many as there are different steering systems in the salvage yards.

A wide variety of different steering setups have been used by street-rod builders through the years. These range all the way from rebuilt Model A gears to the latest power rack-and-pinion plucked from an expensive import. Nevertheless, the vast majority of builders still rely on fewer than six manual and power-assist recirculating ball-and-nut steering gears and two or three rack-and-pinion selections. The best steering, however, is one that is compatible with the type of front suspension you've selected. Additionally, it should come from a car that's in the same weight range as your street rod.

In the early days of street rodding, before and just after World War II, the most popular steering-gear swap, believe it or not, was the 1934 Ford *Gemmer*. Compared to its predecessors, it had a very fast steering ratio. It slipped neatly down along side the flathead V8 in a Model A or Deuce frame. Guys who drove later-model Fords rarely changed the factory steering *boxes* (gears) unless they were completely dry of grease. Parts were available, most rods were light and easy on their feet, and few builders felt the need to look any further.

By the mid '50s, however, the ravages of old age were beginning to be felt. The 1940—48 Ford Gemmer-3 gear and its cross-steering drag-link arrangement began to show up in 1935—36 Fords, even though 1940-type spindles had to be used.

The parallel drag-link-steering school of thought elected to use the then-new steering gears from 1954 and later Ford and Chevy pickups. The Ford F-100 gear was preferred, but the Chevy gear was easier to install. The Chevy unit only required minor frame trimming to fit; the F-100 gear required reworking or replacing the Pitman arm and fabrication of a bracket. Regardless, all of those possibilities are behind us now.

NEW STEERING SYSTEM

Instead of using a traditional steering gear, use the best. In doing this, keep a few critical considerations in mind when choosing and installing steering components. Otherwise, you risk upsetting the already disturbed sleep of old Rudolph Ackermann, the father of modern steering geometry.

Steering geometry is not a catch-all phrase. It refers to the arrangement of the steering-system components in relation to the suspension components. For instance, it determines how much effort and turns of the steering wheel are required to make a turn. Steering geometry also determines how much each front wheel turns to negotiate a corner and how much road feedback is transmitted through to the steering wheel.

Rudolph Ackermann devised the basic method of geometrically "correct" steering over 160 years ago. When doing this, though, he was working with low-speed vehicles. A horse-drawn wagon was considered to be a high-speed vehicle. And, *slip angle* was unheard of. Let's look more closely at Ackermann steering.

Ackermann steering is based on the premise that, during a turning manuever—right or left—the inside front wheel of a front-steer vehicle must turn sharper than the outside one. Some people refer to this as *toe-out* in a turn. This is because the inside front wheel must turn on a shorter radius than the outside wheel—they turn around the same point, which is on a line that's a projection of the rear-axle center line. As the turn tightens—turning radius decreases—the turn-angle difference between the front wheels must increase.

This steering arrangement reduces *tire scrub* which would occur if both wheels turn at angles different from that of a perfect Ackermann geometry. However, because Ackermann didn't take into account slip angles—which moves the center about which the vehicle turns forward—perfect Ackermann is incorrect, but close enough.

What determines Ackermann? It's the relative locations of the inner and outer tie-rod pivots to themselves and the steering arms, and the angle of the steering arms. For instance, angle the steering arms in on a front-steer setup and Ackermann *increases*—steering angle between inside and outside

Many suppliers offer adapter brackets. Because of high loads at steering-gear mount, use correct fasteners; long enough and aircraft quality or Grade 8. Nuts should be castellated type with cotter keys.

wheels. On rear-steer setups, the reverse is true. Similar changes can be made to inner and outer tie-rod points. It gets pretty involved. So, if you want to know more about steering, get a copy of HPBooks' *How to Make Your Car Handle*. It's all there, including the following on *bump steer*.

Bump steer is more important that Ackerman because it affects down-the-road handling. Bump steer at the front occurs when steering angle changes from nothing more than vertical wheel travel, such as from going over a bump or negotiating a turn. If steering-wheel angle doesn't change, the vehicle is said to have *neutral steer*. Toe-out from bump steer promotes understeer; toe-in causes oversteer. It's oversteer that can be dangerous. However, an excessive amount of understeer is undesirable.

To reduce oversteer in a *front-steer* vehicle—steering linkage is ahead of the front-wheel center line—raise the inner tie-rod points. For a *rear-steer* vehicle, lower the inner tie-rod points. Do the opposite at the outer tie-rod ends to achieve the same effect.

Choosing a Steering Setup—If your street rod has parallel drag-link steering, and you don't want one of the commercial cross steering kits, keep out of trouble and stay with your current setup. Changing to cross steering on your own can get you in trouble quickly. In fact, there's no pressing reason to use a cross-steering setup on a transverse-spring, early Ford type front end. Most builders only use cross steering for cosmetic reasons—they don't want the steering to show.

One of the prime considerations in choosing a steering gear, or any other factory component for a street rod, is that a *steering system designed for lightweight stockers should only be used in lightweight street rods*. I don't

know why this is often overlooked. Don't even consider a component—from steering to drive line—if the donor car weighs less than 90% of your street rod. And, if you have to guess, for safety's sake guess on the heavier side.

Steering Modifications—Unless you are a certified welder, *don't think about welding Pitman arms or other steering components*. Restrict steering modifications to machining whenever possible. If this can't be done, look for alternatives. Proceed with caution even if you are a certified welder. Have *every* welded component Magnafluxed at a USAC, FAA or similarly approved inspection station. These are usually found in the vicinity of municipal airports. Automotive machine shops are *not* the place to have critical suspension and steering components inspected. Go where the flyboys go.

If you are planning on using a steering gear more than 10 years old, have it checked. A good front-end-alignment shop can do this. It'll never be cheaper or easier to do than right now.

Most street rods with a curb weight of 2500 pounds or less don't need power steering. But, as you get closer to 3000 pounds, you'll appreciate a helping hand. If you have the room and want faster steering—power units are usually about 25% faster than their manual counterparts—go with the power gear. The pump and other components can be dressed up with chrome and stainless-braided lines.

Before making your final decision, check out the street-rod-component manufacturers, page 194. Many installation kits are available for the popular steering gears. So, it simply doesn't make sense to skimp where safety is involved. Professionals have already done the engineering—and found the problems you can expect if you re-invent a steering setup. You are buying safety when you go with one of them.

CONVENTIONAL STEERING GEARS

The first of the modern conventional steering gears used in street rods was the early '60s Corvair, particularly the aluminum-cased version. It is a steering gear that has remained popular with the builders of lightweight street rods such as the T-bucket. When polished and detailed, the aluminum Corvair gear is probably the best looking steering gear around.

At about the same time the Corvair steering was being accepted in street-rod applications, along came the Ford Econoline and Dodge van parallel drag-link steering. These appear on occasion, but not nearly so frequently as they once did.

It wasn't until the mid '60s that street rodders got a manual steering gear that met most

Corvair steering box, cast-iron or aluminum case, has been popular with Fad T builders since the first was used in the early '60s. Corvair box is often mounted on top of frame, but to do so, input shaft must be reversed in housing.

of their needs and has stood the test of time. This is the FoMoCo recirculating ball-and-nut gear used in the first Mustangs. It was the first reliable manual steering gear for a 2500—2700-pound street rod. Adaptation required nothing more than simple bracketry.

Later, the 1971—77 Chevrolet Vega steering was discovered to be very adaptable in lightweight street rods. Controversy originally surrounded its use in cars weighing more than the Vega's curb weight of 2310 pounds.

The real star in the GM line-up, however, is the large Saginaw gear in both manual and power-assist versions. Pete and Jake helped popularize it when they offered an adapter plate for the manual version pirated from the 1964—65 Chevelle. This steering gear has a Pitman arm that can be re-tapered for Ford tie-rod ends. The power-assist Saginaw gear is larger than the manual, but not much. It has gained favor with builders of larger, heavier street rods, particularly later sedans.

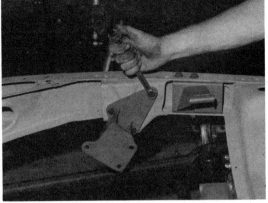

Topside mounting aims Pitman arm down where it operates drag link in traditional early Ford fashion. Several street-rod suppliers offer installation kits.

Nowhere is late Mustang steering more popular than in 1937—40 Ford passenger cars and 1940—41 pickups and panels. Hefty bolt-on adapter bracket is available from Specialized Auto Components and several other street-rod suppliers.

VW Microbus steering gear works well in tight areas. Florida Rod Shop offers a complete box with a shortened Pitman arm for Model T installations.

Specialized Auto offeres bracket that mounts 1979—81 El Camino Saginaw steering in 1946—48 Ford frame.

Chevy exhaust-manifold clearance is adequate with Specialized mounting in post-war Ford frame.

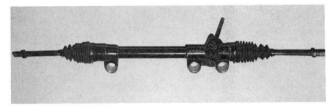

Early Pinto/Mustang II non-power rack-and-pinion works well on car weighing 2500 pounds or less. Rubber mounts reduce shock loads and road noise. Steering ratio is 24:1, with four turns lock-to-lock.

For larger and heavier street rods such as 1937—40 Fords, power-assist Mustang II gear is best.

With exception of a few rack-and-pinion designs, the foreign-car contingent offers little beyond the VW Minibus and Toyota four-wheel drive—which has more adherents among the F-100 contingent than street rodders. The VW bus steering, however, has several devoted followers. At least one manufacturer offers a swap-in kit for this gear.

These, then, are the *popular* conventional steering gears. This is not to infer that some other gear(s) is not as good or better for your installation. The wrecking yard is full of possibilities. Just don't forget, experimentation with steering gears can get tricky in a hurry. Use good common sense and prudence when looking over the wrecking-yard crop.

RACK-&-PINION STEERING GEARS

In discussing steering systems, just as with everything else, there are differences of opinion. Some builders prefer the plain and reliable engineering of the conventional recirculating ball-and-nut steering gear; others lean toward the sophistication of rack-and-pinion gears.

141

The German BMW first perfected rack-and-pinion steering in the mid '30s. The 1951 MG was the first rack-and-pinion-equipped car to be sold in the United States. The first American car with rack-and-pinion steering, the Ford Pinto, didn't hit the road until 20 years later.

If you'll recall, turning the steering wheel transmits turning motion through a series of jointed shafts to a pinion gear in the rack-and-pinion steering gear. Pinion rotation is transformed into lateral sliding motion at the rack. Tie rods attached to each end of the rack transmit this lateral movement to the front wheels. Drag links or Pitman arms are not required as in conventional steering.

The ratio between turns of the steering wheel and of the front wheels is low. The result is quick, responsive steering. This quick ratio coupled with fewer parts between the steering wheel and the front wheels transmits more "feel" of the road than does conventional steering. All in all, it shouldn't be difficult to see why many builders think rack-and-pinion steering belongs in a street rod. It occupies little room in cars that most often are already crammed full of V8 engine. In fact, of all the possible steering setups, the average rack-and-pinion gear interferes least with the engine and exhaust.

Unfortunately, the worst street-rod-steering installations I've encountered over the years have been poor rack-and-pinion swaps. Many of the problems involve a rack-and-pinion gear that is simply not designed for the suspension it is mated to or the loads foisted upon it. Consequently, it has often been unjustly maligned in favor of conventional steering systems. And that's too bad. Rack-and-pinion steering is the best choice in many instances.

There's one that doesn't make any sense. The installation of a rack-and-pinion gear with a solid-axle front suspension is possible, but not practical simply because a single tie rod must *tie* both front wheels together. And, the tie rod must move with the axle. Consequently, to achieve correct steering geometry, the gear assembly would have to be mounted on the axle. This, of course, increases unsprung weight. And, because the axle moves, splined, flexible couplings must be incorporated into the steering shaft. Rube Goldberg would be proud. So, if your car has a solid front axle, stick with conventional steering.

The reverse holds true for street rods with independent front suspensions. In this case, the steering linkage is divided into at least three separate components: two tie rods about as long as the suspension control arms and pivot in similar arcs, and an idler arm to a relay rod—center link—across the width of

the frame to an idler arm if a conventional steering gear is used. Attempts to reproduce this hodge-podge of hardware in a street rod almost always wind up with the builder pulling out his hair before he gets everything right. This is where the rack-and-pinion has the advantage. It's relatively easy to install. Just remember that the tolerable margin of error is very small with a rack-and-pinion installation.

The rack-and-pinion gear is normally bolted to brackets on the front-suspension crossmember of the donor car. When installed in a street rod, the gear must be mounted on brackets that are equally flat and parallel. Anything less will warp the housing when it's bolted down, causing it to bind.

Furthermore, bump steer will occur when the steering geometry is not absolutely correct. This can result if the length of the tie rod is not equal to the length of the suspension control arms, if the tie rod angle and the angle of the control arms are not equal, or if the centerline of the frame mounting is not in line with the tie rod pivot. "Good road feel" can suddenly become very annoying when the front wheel vibrations work their way back up to the steering wheel.

If that's not enough to scare you off, an improperly matched rack-and-pinion gear will make the car hard to park. It's because of that low steering ratio I spoke of. Mechanical advantage is also low, and if the wrong rack-and-pinion is installed, the effort required to steer the car at low speeds—or to park—is considerable.

It is common knowledge that the effective ratio of a conventional steering gear can be modified by shortening or lengthening the Pitman arm, but other than actually changing the size of the pinion gear in a rack-and-pinion assembly—which is hardly recommended—is the only way to change the overall ratio is to shorten or lengthen the steering arms on the spindles themselves. This, of course, is possible, but it would be a touchy operation.

Finally, the location of the rack-and-pinion assembly is critical. The tie rods should generally be placed near and parallel to the lower control arms. Likewise, the inner tie-rod pivots should be in line with the lower control-arm inner pivots. Obviously, some compromise may be required in a custom installation, but not much. You can only compromise on steering geometry a little bit.

In no way is the foregoing meant to scare you away from a rack-and-pinion steering system. On the contrary. Rack-and-pinion steering, in conjunction with an independent front suspension, is far and away the best steering system for a modern street rod. On the other hand, it's risky to design your own

Some types of steering-gear-adapter brackets are designed to be welded to fully boxed frame.

steering geometry without an in-depth knowledge of automotive engineering. Consequently, a rack-and-pinion installation kit offered by such shops as Kugel Komponents, Progressive Automotive, Specialized Auto Components and others is the best route for most rod builders.

Rack-&-Pinion Gears To Consider—The best recent rack-and-pinion steering gears include the late-model T-Bird/Cougar and Jaguar sedan power gear for 3500-pound street rods, and the '70s Audi sedan gear for rods weighing 2600—2800 pounds. Of course, this doesn't exhaust the possibilities; there's a whole new crop available every Fall. Just remember what I said about the weight of the donor car relative to that of the intended recipient.

THE MISSING LINK

The connection between a steering gear and steering column is of major importance. I am passing on to you the cardinal safety rules impressed on me by the SCTA inspectors many years ago: 1) All welding on steering components should be performed by a government certified welder, not a novice with a $300 arc welder. 2) All welding on steering components must be subjected to appropriate non-destructive testing methods by a USAC or FAA certified-testing station. Test stations can be found listed in the Yellow Pages under TESTING.

Now, let's get on with the missing link. I hope you had the foresight to get all the hardware bolted to the steering gear when you purchased it from the wrecking yard. If you did, chances are you already have most of what you'll need to connect the steering gear to the steering wheel. If you didn't, you must buy a few odds and ends.

If your steering gear included the common flexible coupling—sometimes called a *rag joint*—it should be used. It is a safe and

Once again, steering-gear loads on frame are high. If in doubt about your welding skills, tack bracket in place, then have a certified welder complete job.

Installing steering gear of your choice is one thing; connecting it to steering column is another. Fortunately, a variety of couplers are available, allowing a simple and neat link-up such as Tom Ayers' AMC Pacer-to-'40 Chevy.

Only use steering components from donor cars that weigh at least as much as your street rod. Audi U-joint was used at steering-gear pinion; Jaguar U-joint at column.

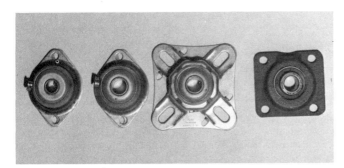

Aircraft surplus stores and industrial suppliers have a large variety of couplers and pillow blocks that you may find useful. Do not use any component in a steering application that's not adequate. Consequences of a failed steering component are not good.

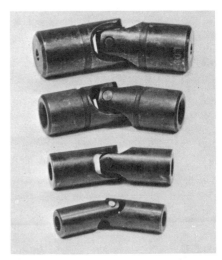

Bill Keifer's California Custom Roadsters offers selection of high-strength universal joints. Several are adequate for steering applications.

suitable piece of hardware, even if it isn't very attractive. You'll also need a *pillow block bearing*, which has a housing that can be mounted on a flat surface, and a small aircraft-quality universal joint.

The amount of work that will be required to make the installation depends largely on what steering column you are using. In the case of the Ford coupe shown in the photo sequence, the original column and steering shaft unit was shortened several inches and installed in its original location, but at a slightly different angle. This was done to facilitate the hook-up. A careful analysis of the photos and captions should be sufficient for you to evaluate your own situation.

21 Brakes

Brakes should have sufficient capacity to stop vehicle without fading or undue effort, and in a straight line.

The hot setup for brakes on early street rods were *juice stoppers*—hydraulic brakes— pirated from a 1940 Ford. The hydraulic brakes from a '39 Ford model worked equally well, but most rodders considered the hubs and wheels to be far too ugly to hang on a fenderless roadster or coupe. The better looking '40 Ford wheels were fitted to earlier spindles with the help of an adapter kit. This kit consisted of two bearing spacers and two rings for locating the backing plate. These kits were probably the earliest brake-conversion components manufactured and sold to rod builders. The hydraulics sure worked better than the original mechanical brakes.

In the late '40s, Ansen Automotive Engineering began manufacturing a complete hydraulic-brake conversion kit for 1928—38 Fords. It incorporated the "new" 1948 Ford backing plates, wheel cylinders and shoes, Ford master cylinder, and all the brackets, fittings, flexible hose and *copper* tubing needed for the installation. Today, of course, copper tubing is definitely forbidden. Nothing but special hydraulic tubing such as the tin-plated soft-steel double-wall (Bundy-Flex) tubing manufactured by Bendix should even be considered.

The best aftermarket brakes in those post-war days, however, was the fabled Kinmont

Safe-Stop disc brakes. In 1950, Roy Richter, of the fabled Bell Auto Parts, bought the manufacturing rights to the Kinmonts. He offered them to the racing and hot-rod market, but their relatively high cost—about what a basket-case roadster sold for—kept them in the wish-book category. Those old '40 Ford brakes, mean as they were to adjust, had to do for the vast majority of street rodders.

In the mid '50s, however, some unknown street rodder got totally fed up with how much effort was required to stop his '34 with those old-fashioned Ford passenger-car brakes. This was all the incentive he needed to start scouting around. He noticed that the F-100 pickup-truck backing-plate bolt pattern was similar to that of his converted coupe. Not only that, the F-100 brakes were *self energizing*. The rotation of the brake drum against the shoes helps apply the brakes, reducing pedal effort considerably. For the next 10 years or so, F-100 brakes were installed on many street rods, although the 1940—48 systems continued to be more popular.

Kinmonts were still available, but out of production—and more expensive than ever. A few others such as the early Lincolns, with their massive lining area, and pretty finned aluminum drums from late-model Buicks vied for the street rodder's attention. But,

only when the stock rear end was replaced with a late-model axle and some sort of self-energizing brakes were swapped up front, did any significant improvement in street-rod stopability occur.

All that changed in the early '70s when disc brakes, plundered from a wide variety of foreign and domestic cars, began to appear on street rods. As often as not, the adaptation was by means of relatively crude brackets. A few enterprising machine shops—usually owned and operated by street-rod enthusiasts—began offering the first of many professional conversion kits. Today, it's a rare home-garage street rod that isn't equipped with front-wheel discs. Before we get too far along, let's examine the basic brake system before we talk about bolting this to that.

THE HYDRAULIC-BRAKE SYSTEM

A hydraulic-brake system consists of two basic components: the foot-pedal-operated master cylinder and the individual cylinders located at each wheel. In between each is the hydraulic system, in which fluid is contained. When the driver steps on the foot pedal, the force from his foot is transmitted from the pedal into a pushrod, which forces a piston in the master cylinder against fluid, pressurizing the contained fluid in the brake's hydraulic system. The pressurized fluid is then converted to a force on the pistons in each wheel cylinder and, thus, the brake pads and/or shoes against the rotors and/or drums, respectively. Forces on the pistons are in direct relation to their sizes—the bigger the piston, the bigger the force and vice versa. The force of the friction material against the rotors and/or drums is converted to a stopping torque at the wheel.

This operation, the force exerted by the brake pads and/or shoes from hydraulic pressure in the system, is a practical application of Pascal's principle. It states that, "Pressure applied to an enclosed fluid is transmitted throughout the body of the fluid equally in all directions without loss."

In essence, that's about all there is to it. Beyond the basics, however, the most important consideration in the design of a brake system is component compatibility. The system is, after all, going to be assembled from parts gathered from a variety of sources. All these parts—master cylinder, power booster,

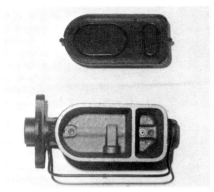

Mustang dual master cylinder is a favorite among street rodders. Several suppliers offer pedal assemblies for its installation in a variety of early frames.

Bill Keifer's California Custom Roadsters offers this master cylinder and pedal assembly for Fad T use. It bolts directly to side of frame and takes up little space.

So-called *fruit jar* FoMoCo single-reservoir master cylinder is also popular. Most modern master cylinders are available either for disc-brake or non disc-brake applications.

proportioning valve, front- and rear-wheel cylinders, shoes and/or pads, hydraulic lines and, even the fluid—must work together. That means they must be matched, or sized, one component to the other. More brake-system shortcomings have arisen from trying to marry a hodge-podge of unrelated parts than from any other single factor.

MASTER CYLINDER

As soon as the first major brake component is installed, the general parameters of the rest of the system are established. Although the master cylinder is rarely installed first, let's start with it because it is the principle unit in the basic hydraulic system.

The job of the master cylinder is to pressurize fluid in the brake's hydraulic system. A larger master-cylinder piston gives a lower system pressure and vice versa, simply because the force from the brake pedal is distributed over a larger or smaller area, respectively. This pressure is then converted to a force at the wheel cylinders.

The master cylinder also corrects for temperature changes and fluid seepage by maintaining the required volume of fluid in the *closed* hydraulic system. That's why master-cylinder fluid level may be low, but the system still functions. Finally, the master cylinder charges the system with fluid upon each release of the brakes.

Let's take a look inside the basic master cylinder. In its released position, the master-cylinder piston rests against a stop. A compensating or bypass port opens in this position and—if the master cylinder is designed for disc brakes—a residual-pressure check valve is closed. The open port connects the cylinder with the fluid-supply reservoir and *compensates* the system for changes in volume caused by expansion or contraction of the fluid, friction material, rotors and/or drums.

The closed check valve holds approximately 6—18 pounds per square inch (psi) *residual* pressure in the lines so the disc-brake pads don't retract from the rotor surface. If this were to happen, *take-up* pedal travel would be excessive.

Force applied to the brake pedal is multiplied several times at the piston by the pedal's *mechanical advantage*—leverage. As the pedal is pressed, moving the piston off of its stop, the compensating port is closed by the piston and the residual check valve is overcome. Hydraulic pressure now develops and fluid moves from the reservoir into the rest of the system. A 100-pound force on the pedal with a 7.5:1 lever ratio will result in a force of 100 lb X 7.5 = 750 pounds at the master-cylinder piston.

When the pedal is released, spring tension on the pedal arm pulls the piston pushrod away and an internal master-cylinder spring retracts the piston. At the same time, the wheel cylinders retract and fluid flows into the master cylinder as the residual check valve is forced off its seat.

The returning fluid cannot flow as fast as the spring-loaded piston returns, however, and this develops a vacuum in the cylinder. The vacuum causes reserve fluid to enter through an intake port. This extra fluid flows through ports in the face of the piston, collapses the primary cup lip, and continues on around it to reduce low pressure and re-charge the system. Surplus fluid returns to the master-cylinder reservoir through the open bypass port.

The residual check valve also maintains a slight pressure in the system when the brakes are released, not only to prevent excess wheel-cylinder retraction, but also to lessen the possibility of air leaking into the system during bleeding.

There are dozens of master cylinders available at any parts house. But, because you must maintain system compatibility, let's put the discussion of the master cylinder on hold. For now, let's take a closer look at disc-brake rotors, drums and wheel cylinders, and their mountings.

Note: Because of the limited space in this all-encompassing book, there's not enough room to cover the subject of brakes in-depth. Therefore, I strongly suggest that you get a copy of HPBooks' *Brake Handbook*. It covers everything from basic brake theory, to designing your own brake system, and Formula 1 and Indy Car brakes that you can pattern yours after.

FRONT-WHEEL BRAKES

Under hard braking, where 70% of the stopping is done by the front brakes in the conventional front engine/rear drive car, the rod builder has several options. Although the Fad T brotherhood has a No-Front-Brakes contingent, I won't comment on that approach simply because it is street rodding at its worst. *A real street rod must have front brakes.*

The *sensible* rod builder has five alternatives for front brakes. These include the stock hydraulic brakes, bigger and better drum brakes, professionally welded hybrid spindles that will mount disc brakes, homemade disc-brake-adapter plates, and commercial disc-brake-adapter kits.

First, I have absolutely no qualms in advising you to scrap the stock brakes on a car built prior to 1949. In fact, almost nothing built prior to 1953 is worthy of consideration. Some builders have beefed up early brakes with top-quality lining, and other hardware, but the basic engineering isn't good enough. This is particularly true with regard to early Fords. Passenger-car drum brakes got better during the '50s. Even then, few conversions

Conventional expanding-shoe drum brake continues to be standard at the rear of most street rods.

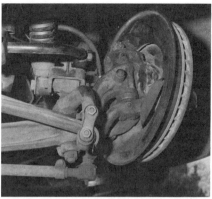

I used this machine-shop adaptation of '69 Ford Fairlane/Torino disc brakes-to-'40 Ford spindles for 15 years with absolutely no problem. Welded components were Magnafluxed and certified before installation.

are worth the effort except for the 1953—56 Ford F-100 pickup swap.

There's simply no question that disc brakes have been the first choice for several years now. And with good reason. They offer three distinct advantages over the best drum brakes. First, discs are more effective even after repeated high-speed stops and during normal driving. This is because, unlike the interior of a brake drum, the rotor surface is exposed directly to the outside air. Consequently, heat buildup is easily dissipated, although the disc brake operates at a higher temperature.

Disc brakes are also relatively immune to the effects of water because the rotor sheds the water. The third advantage of discs over drums is uniform braking, giving straight-line stops.

Although there are many varieties within a car-manufacturer's product line, only three basic disc-brake designs have evolved over the years. These are fixed calipers, introduced on many 1965 models; floating calipers, first used in 1968; and sliding calipers, introduced in 1972. Popular modern domestic variations are listed in the table, page 148.

Mechanical variations aside, the most important thing to you is how easily a caliper can be mounted on early spindles. Barring the installation of a complete late-model front suspension such as the Mustang II, you can either design and fabricate a one-off adaptation or go to a professional machine shop or street-rod components company for help.

In my opinion, it is best to include home-made disc-brake adaptations in the "fergit it" category. Certainly not because I am against the do-it-yourself approach. It's because I've seen far too many rather crude and, what's worse, dangerous, home-made conversions. When you are talking brakes, you are talking

safety and reliability first and foremost. If you are not a professional who fully understands brakes assemblies, do yourself—and everyone else on the road—a big favor and take a less-risky approach. Save a few bucks somewhere else.

When a machine-shop disc-brake adaptation is competently performed, safety and reliability is assured. For instance, *Henry's Machine Shop,* a favorite of Southern California hot rodders for many years, combined my original '40 Ford spindles and a pair of 1969 Fairlane/Torino spindles back in the early '70s.

This setup saw approximately 25,000 miles of service per year until the entire early Ford front suspension was retired in 1985. Oh yes, I had "Henry's" work independently tested by a USAC-certified Magnaflux station before they went on, so I had full confidence in the setup before I left home on the maiden voyage . . . and I wouldn't recommend anything less to you.

Finding a first-class shop can be a chore, waiting for the work to be done often tries one's patience, and the cost of their services is always on the high side. But, the bottom line is that you cannot afford to compromise on the quality of your brake system.

Kelsey-Hayes Fixed-Caliper, Opposed-Piston Disc Brake—If you are interested in building a hybrid early spindle/late spindle disc-brake system through machining and welding, one of the most adaptable assemblies are from the Ford line. The Kelsey-Hayes disc brake, used on the 1965—67 Mustang, uses a fixed, four-piston—two on each side of the rotor—caliper on a ventilated rotor. The caliper assembly consists of two housings bolted together. Each half contains two cylinder pistons fitted with a seal and molded-rubber boot to prevent dust contamination.

Kelsey-Hayes Floating-Caliper Disc Brake—Another good choice is the one I used on my '40 Ford: Kelsey-Hayes' single-piston, dual-pin floating caliper found on late '60s/early '70s Mustangs, Cougars and other intermediate and full-size FoMoCo models.

This assembly is made up of a floating caliper mounted on an anchor plate. The anchor plate is bolted to the spindle upright. The caliper is attached to the anchor plate on pins with spring-steel stabilizers. The caliper slides back and forth on the two guide pins, which are also attached to the stabilizer. Instead of two pistons as in earlier models, only one large piston is used to force the pads against the rotor.

Bolt-On & Almost Bolt-On Disc Brakes—There's one term in the street-rodder's lexicon that's overworked: it's *bolt-on.* Most bolt-on components aren't bolt-on. Many come close to being bolt-on items without the need for fitting or modifying. Few can honestly lay claim to the title.

Fortunately, there are some honest-to-goodness bolt-on disc brake assemblies that won't send you scurrying to the machine shop or certified welder. The best known of these is the *Super Bell Axle Company's* Mustang kit. This kit is the logical outgrowth of a company involved in building axles and spindles, and is designed for the heavier street rod in the 3000-pound class. It adapts rotors and calipers from the 1968—69 Mustang and Cougar to 1939—1948 Ford passenger-car spindles. The Super Bell kit will also mount other Kelsey-Hayes floating-caliper disc brakes used by Ford intermediate cars during that period.

The Super Bell Kit, and those from other manufacturers listed at the end of this book represent Grade A professional street-rod engineering where it's needed most—in the safety department. If you are building a car with an early front suspension, give serious consideration to the bolt-on approach.

GM Disc Brakes—Of course, not everybody is building a car with early Ford spindles, and not everybody wants Mustang brakes. *Butch's Rod Shop* in Ohio, *Engineered Components* and *Total Performance* in Connecticut, *Linken Manufacturing* in Canada, *Magoo's* in Southern California, *Jim Meyer* in Oregon, and *Gene Reese* in Texas all have top-notch disc-brake conversions.

Many of these use Type 1 Delco-Moraine single-piston disc brakes with two mounting bolts. This is a sliding-caliper design and incorporates a one-piece housing. The inboard side of the housing contains the piston.

When the brakes are applied, fluid pressure forces the piston against the inboard pad, which is then forced against the inboard side of the disc. This action causes the caliper assembly to slide on the mounting bolts and force the outboard lining into contact with the rotor. Both linings are then forced against the rotor in direct proportion to hydraulic pressure.

Delco-Moraine Opposed-Piston Disc Brake—Four-wheel discs have been used on Corvettes since the early '60s, and Delco-Moraine opposed-piston disc brakes through the '82 models.

Most rod builders who install the Corvette IRS favor the compatible front discs even if they are a bit more expensive. The caliper assembly has four pistons, two on each side of the rotor. The rotor is riveted to the hub flange at the front wheel and to the spindle flange at the rear wheel. It rotates through the caliper assembly, which is bolted to a support attached to the steering knuckle at the front wheel and upright at the rear wheel.

The parking-brake system consists of a miniature set of brake shoes mounted on a flange plate and shield assembly attached to the rear-wheel upright.

As you may realize, not everything lends itself to a true bolt-on procedure, no matter how badly you'd like it to. But that doesn't mean you must give up or use something you don't want. There are kits for just about every disc-brake assembly that could possibly work on a street rod. And, although some of the kits for less popular, but equally reliable conversions require extra machine work, don't let that deter you.

REAR-WHEEL BRAKES

As we have seen, the most popular street-rod rear end is built around the conventional live axle . . . and most of them are equipped with drum brakes. That's OK because they are simple, inexpensive, and more than adequate. If you'll recall, most of the work is done by the front brakes.

There are two types of drum brakes: *non-servo* and *servo*. Non-servo brake shoes are individually anchored to the backing plate. With a double-ended wheel cylinder—two pistons—acting on the upper ends of the shoes, the front shoe *self-energizes*. That is, the forward rotation of the drum increases the force of the shoe against the inside of the drum. The front wheel-cylinder piston acts against the *leading* end of the shoe. The reverse acting shoe is *de-energized* because drum rotation against it unloads the shoe. The rear wheel-cylinder piston acts against the *trailing* end of the shoe.

Some non-servo brake systems use two separate, single-piston wheel cylinders—one at the top and one at the bottom. Each acts against the leading ends of one shoe.

Both Bendix and Delco-Moraine have manufactured non-servo brakes with automatic adjusters for various GM and MoPar applications. Chrysler Corporation has also favored a unique non-servo brake called the *center plane* or *total contact* design. In this layout, both shoes are mounted within a saddle formed by two support plates. This localizes most stress on the plane of the shoe webs rather than on the backing plate, the latter acts more as a dust shield.

Because of the vast popularity of late Ford rear axles, and to a lesser extent, the GM 10- and 12-bolt axles, the majority of rear drum brakes that rod builders use are of the *servo* or *compound-action* type manufactured by Bendix, Delco-Moraine and Wagner. In this design, the brake shoes are linked together in a single operating unit. The combined action of the primary and secondary shoes compounds the braking effect in a wedging action similar to the leading shoe just explained.

Servo-type brakes are easily recognized by the single shoe anchor attached to the backing plate directly above the wheel cylinder between the ends of the shoes. The bottom ends are linked together by a spring-loaded assembly that includes a star-wheel adjuster.

When the brakes are applied, the rotation of the drum assists the wheel-cylinder piston in moving the forward facing shoe out against the drum. At the same time, the shoe is forced against the floating link. The link, which is also attached to the secondary shoe, forces the leading end of that shoe into contact with the drum. The braking force is, thereby, compounded; thus the *servo*, or *self-energizing*, action. The secondary shoe actually performs most of the work in forward movement. That's why it usually has more lining.

Wheel Cylinders—The conventional wheel-cylinder assembly has a straight-bore, double-end cast-iron housing with two tiny aluminum pistons. A short link is typically used between each piston and the end of one shoe. The most important design characteristic or specification of the rear brakes you must keep in mind is cylinder-bore diameter. Knowing the piston area and bolt-pattern dimensions of the cylinders is important. Piston area, which determines fluid displacement of the wheel cylinders—as we shall shortly see—is critical to the overall efficiency of the brake system. Piston area in square inches = bore diameter in inches squared X 0.7854.

Although there is considerable interchangeability within every manufacturer's brake components, it isn't necessary for you to go overboard with regard to using the biggest possible brakes at the rear. In terms of drum size, lining area and wheel-cylinder size, the rear brakes of intermediate cars such as the Mustang or Camaro are suitable for all but the very largest of street rods. And, isn't it just dandy that Mustangs or similar rear axles are used by most rod builders? So, if you're using one of these, measure—and record—the diameter of the wheel cylinders.

All rear axles don't use drum brakes. And, you may prefer disc brakes on the rear. In this case, you may be interested in the Z28 Camaro rear end with disc brakes. Or, there's the narrowed Thunderbird, Lincoln or Cadillac rears with discs. You may go for a chromey street rod with either a disc-braked Corvette or Jaguar independent rear suspension.

If you choose a rear-axle assembly with disc brakes, there's no real difference in the design of the brake system. But, the other components in the system must be compatible. The master cylinder and brake booster, etc., must be selected accordingly. For now, measure the diameter of the disc brake-cylinder-caliper bore and count the number of pistons on *one side*. Record this data in your spec book.

DISCS TO THE REAR

If you've decided to use a conventional rear axle, you don't have to forego the use of four-wheel discs. Both GM and Ford have produced solid rear axles with disc brakes that are suitable for street-rod use.

Delco-Moraine Rear Disc Brake—This is the design used on all GM four-wheel disc-brake systems, except Corvettes. When the brakes are applied, an internal cone and piston move out as one part. When lining wear occurs during service, the cone and piston do not return to their original position, but rather leave a small gap equal to the lining wear between an adjusting nut and the cone. An adjusting spring rotates the nut on the high lead screw to close the gap, thereby adjusting the caliper.

When the parking brake is applied, a lever on the inboard side of each caliper turns the

If you want rear discs, adapt a big-car disc-braked rear axle. FoMoCo axle could be shortened and trimmed of at least 50 pounds.

screw and adjusting nut to move down the screw, which clamps the lining. Upon release of the parking brake, the cone rotates on the clutch interface and re-adjusts the caliper. The clutch prevents the cone from turning when the parking brake is applied.

Ford Rear-Wheel Disc Brake—A hydraulically powered brake booster (Hydroboost) provides the power assist for the Ford-design four-wheel disc-brake system. Except for the parking-brake mechanism and a larger inner brake shoe anti-rattle spring, the rear-wheel caliper is basically the same as the larger front-wheel caliper. The parking-brake lever, located at the rear of the caliper, is actuated by a cable system similar to that used on rear drum-brake applications.

Upon application of the parking brake, the cable rotates the lever and operating shaft. Three steel balls, located in pockets between the opposing heads of the operating shaft and thrust screw, roll up ramps formed in the pockets, forcing a thrust screw away from the operating shaft. This, in turn, forces the caliper piston-and-brake shoe assembly against the rotor. An automatic adjuster in the assembly compensates for lining wear. It also maintains correct clearance in the parking-brake mechanism.

Rotor cooling is improved by cooling passages created by curved vanes that join the inner and outer rotor surfaces. Unlike most disc-brake assemblies, the Ford rear-wheel rotors are not interchangeable because of the directional nature of the curved rotor vanes. They are identified by a RIGHT or LEFT cast inside the hat section of each rotor. The rotor is secured to the axle flange much the same as a brake drum. A splash shield, bolted to an adapter, protects the inboard rotor surface.

There is one drawback to rear axles that incorporate disc brakes. They are usually heavier simply because the axle may have come from a heavy car. And that, of course, means higher unsprung weight. If your car is big and heavy, you probably won't notice the difference. But if you are running a lightweight 'glasser, you should do some weighing and thinking before you run out and buy a Cad or Lincoln rear axle.

MASTER CYLINDER

As I said earlier, there are many appropriate master cylinders for a street-rod brake system. The late-model Ford dual-master cylinder, however, seems to have gained acceptance by a great many rod builders. Generally, it is two conventional master cylinders combined in a single cast-iron housing. One portion actuates the front brakes and the other the rears.

A failure of either system does not impair the operation of the other. On factory installations with disc brakes at the front and drums at the rear, the dual-master cylinder has the outlet port for the rear brake systems on the bottom of the master-cylinder body. A bleeder screw is on the outboard side of the casting. The front-brake system outlet port is also on the outboard side. This type of master cylinder also contains a pressure-differential valve assembly and a switch that activates a warning light located on the instrument panel of the donor car.

Earlier, I was emphatic with regard to system compatibility. This means that you must use a master cylinder that is compatible with the wheel brakes. Taking this further, you should use one that matches the *front-wheel* brakes. For instance, if you installed a late-model disc-brake-conversion kit, the disc-brake master cylinder of the type used in the donor car will work best. Fortunately, it is rare that the disc-brake master cylinder and front disc brakes for which it was designed won't be compatible with almost *any* drum-brake rear.

Although there isn't that much difference in modern rear drum brakes, there is a procedure for determining the fluid requirements of the complete system to ensure the compatibility of the master cylinders and all wheel cylinders. Apply the following procedure to be absolutely sure you're maintaining system compatibility.

A Few Calculations—Keep two things in mind when using miscellaneous brake-system components: The master cylinder must have the capacity to displace as much fluid as required by the combined wheel units plus 30% for a margin of safety. Any master cylinder used with disc brakes is designed for use with disc brakes. Otherwise, the residual-pressure check valve must be removed.

For illustrative purposes, let's see what master cylinder you need for a typical street rod with 1968 Mustang front discs and a 1969 Fairlane rear with drums. Starting with the rears, a direct measurement of the piston diameter finds it is 15/16 in. This converts to 0.9375 in.

Now, calculate the area of the top by using the formula mentioned earlier, or 0.7854 X diameter in inches squared = piston area in square inches (in.^{2}). Plugging in the numbers, 0.7854 X (0.9375 in.)^2 = 0.6899 in.^{2}

Rounding off, we have 0.69 in.^{2} of piston area. And by simply multiplying that area by a convenient constant used for all drum brake strokes, or 0.2 in., we get 0.69 in.^{2} X 0.2 in. = 0.138 cubic inches (cu in.), or 0.14 cu in. rounded off. But wait! There are *two* wheel cylinders on a Fairlane rear end, right? So, total fluid volume demand of the rear drum brakes is 2 X 0.14 cu in. = 0.28 cu in. Don't forget that number.

Going to the front, check the disc-brake pistons. The '68 Mustang has one piston per caliper. It measures 1.625 in. Plugging into the formula, we come up with 0.7854 X (1.625 in.)^2 = 2.07 cu in. rounded off. Multiply that area by the constant for all disc-brake strokes, or 0.07 in., and get the following: 0.07 in. X 2.07 cu in. = 0.14 cu in. fluid displacement.

Although disc brakes are usually designed with one, two or four pistons per rotor, we only need to concern ourselves with how many are on one side of the rotor to calculate the fluid demand per caliper, but because there are two calipers, double the figure to obtain 0.28 cu in. total fluid displacement for the front disc brakes.

Combined fluid requirement will require a master cylinder that can adequately displace the 0.29 cu in. front discs plus the 0.28 cu in. rear drums for a subtotal of 0.57 cu in. Add that 30% safety margin I mentioned earlier, or 0.17 cu in., for a grand total of 0.74 cu in. That's the minimum volume requirement of the master cylinder. Any less will lead to inadequate operation. A master cylinder displacing *more* than that won't be a problem.

If you are building a brake system on your own without the help of street-rod suppliers, the easiest way to determine the capacity of any given master cylinder is to ask the parts-house counterman to look up the bore of the master cylinder that is designed for your front brakes. His catalog will list that figure, but they seldom list strokes. It's a good idea, therefore to bring along a depth gage so you can measure stroke directly. Once you have that, apply the formula: piston area squared X 0.7854 X by stroke = fluid displacement. If you luck out and find that the master cylinder contains at least 30% more than your wheel units need, you're on your way.

Actually, unless you have some outlandish rear-wheel cylinders, chances are good that the master cylinder designed for your front discs will be OK for the rears. Not always, but usually. Nevertheless, measuring and calculating your brake system demands is necessary to prevent problems later on.

POPULAR AMERICAN DISC- & DRUM-BRAKE SPECIFICATIONS

Manufacturer Brake Design	Brake Design, No. of Pistons per Caliper	Bore Dia. (in.)	Cylinder Volume (cu in.)	Rear-Drum Brake Cyl.-Bore Dia. (in.)	Rear-Cyl. Vol. (cu in.)
AMC Javelin/AMX (1968-70)	Bendix, 4	2	0.22	7/8	0.24
(1971-73)	Kelsey, 1	2.75	0.41	7/8, 15/16	0.24, 0.28
FoMoCo Ford, Merc (1965-67)	Kelsey, 4	1.94	0.21	15/16	0.28
(1968-71)	Kelsey, 1	2.75	0.41	15/16, 31/31	0.28, 0.29
Mustang, Comet, Cougar, Fairlane, Falcon (1965-67)	Kelsey, 4	1.63	0.14	13/16, 7/8, 29/32	0.21, 0.24, 0.25
Cougar, Mustang (1968-73	Kelsey, 1	2.34	0.32	13, 7/8	0.21, 0.24
Montego, Torino (1968-71)	Kelsey, 1	2.34	0.32	29/32,31/32	0.25, 0.29
Fairlane, Falcon, Comet (1968-70)	Kelsey, 1	2.34	0.32	15/16	0.28
Pinto (1971-73)	Bendix, 1	2.125	0.25	23/32, 7/8	0.16, 0.24
GM Camaro, Chevelle (1967-68)	Delco, 4	1.88	0.19	7/8	0.28
	Delco, 1	2.63	0.38	15/16	0.28
Chevy II, Nova (1969-70)	Delco, 1	2.94	0.47	7/8	0.24
Chevy II, Chevelle, Nova, Camaro, Monte Carlo (1969-70	Delco, 1	2.94	0.47	7/8	0.24
Corvette (1965)	Delco, 4	1.88	0.19	1	0.40
Corvette (1966-82)					
Camaro Z28 (1968-69)	Delco, 4	1.88	0.19	1.38	0.10 (Rear Disc)

Compact Midland Ross power booster was originally designed for small Dodge-based motorhome. It can be installed anywhere between master cylinder and wheel cylinders. Specialized Auto Component installation is shown.

POWER BRAKES

Power brakes have been around since the mid '50s. So, even if you don't have disc brakes, consider a power booster. If, however, you have disc brakes, chances are you'll need a power booster. Disc brakes simply need higher line pressure for proper operation. In fact, the pressures required for drum brakes are seldom above 1000 psi. Disc brakes can reach as high as 14,000 psi. Therefore, unless you are using something like the Mico dual-piston master cylinder, you'll have to choose—and find a place for—a conventional power booster.

The modern passenger-car power-assist unit is either a conventional *vacuum-suspended* type (VSPB) that operates off engine vacuum or is hydraulic assisted, drawing its supply of pressurized fluid from the power-steering pump. The power unit of both systems is usually bolted directly to the back of the master cylinder. And they are big, ugly things.

If at all possible, try to package all the hardware under the floorboard. It is usually best to fit it after you've installed the engine and transmission, but before the exhaust system is built. Installing the master cylinder below the floorboard is worthwhile for more than just cosmetic reasons; it is structurally desirable. Adequately beefing up a firewall can be difficult. Adding support to the chassis is relatively easy.

An alternative to the conventional power-boost unit is the remote unit manufactured by Bendix and others. The Bendix HydroVac has been around for years. It is a derivative of the conventional vacuum-suspended booster. The significant advantage of the HydroVac and its cousins is that it can be mounted in the brake line wherever convenient.

Although the unit is fairly large—about as big as a volley ball—and must be mounted with access to the air-bleeder valve, after you place it, basic plumbing is relatively simple. It is installed in the line after the master cylinder, but before the tee-off to the wheel cylinders. There's one catch: By the very nature of their design, most remote power boosters can not be used in conjunction with a functioning dual master cylinder.

METERING & PROPORTIONING VALVES

Two of the most misunderstood components in the brake system are metering and proportioning valves. Some combination of metering and proportioning valves, however, is a must when a combination disc/drum brake system is used.

A metering valve prevents the disc brakes from being applied under light braking—low line pressure. The discs function when line pressure reaches about 135 psi. This allows pressure at the drum-brake wheel cylinders to overcome tension on the brake-shoe return springs so the shoes contact the drums at the same time the disc-brake pads contact with the rotor.

Installed in the line to the rear brakes, a proportioning valve, on the other hand, is designed to reduce pressure at the drum brakes when a pre-set line pressure is reached. This helps prevent rear-wheel lock-up during heavy braking. Weight is transferred from the rear to the front wheels, reducing in proportion, the braking requirement at the rear and increasing it at the front.

Beginning with most early '70s models, American cars equipped with front discs and rear drums, with the metering valve and proportioning valve, were combined into one

unit. As you can imagine, this is better from a manufacturer's standpoint than using two separate valves.

Although several different types of metering, proportioning and combination valves are available, the unit(s) the factory installed, along with the master cylinder you select, should work in your car if the weight distribution and center-of-gravity (c.g.) height are similar to that of the donor car. So, it is best to avoid master cylinders and valve combinations originally designed for big or heavy cars.

Early Mustangs and mid-'60s T-Birds used adjustable proportioning valves manufactured by Kelsey-Hayes. For a while, they were out of production. However, the demand for these valves from the racers has resulted in their being available through Ford, Chevrolet and Chrysler high-performance catalogs. Additionally, Tilton Engineering, McMurray Road & Easy St., P.O. Box 1787, Buellton, CA 93427, offers a lever-operated *prop valve*.

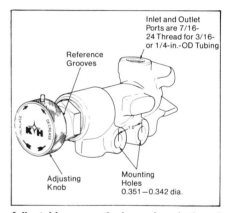

Adjustable proportioning valve designed for race-car use is offered by Kelsey-Hayes and some domestic auto manufacturers through their performance-parts catalogs. Drawing courtesy Kelsey-Hayes.

Bendix non-adjustable, push-type metering valve may be useful in street-rod applications using intermediate GM disc-brake conversions. Valve is available from brake and street-rod suppliers.

METERING & PROPORTIONING VALVES SUITABLE FOR STREET RODS

Make & Model	Year	Metering	Proportioning	Combination
American Motors				
AMX, Javelin, Hornet	1969-70		Yes	
All	1971-up			Yes
Chrysler Corporation				
Barracuda, Dart & Valiant	1965-69		Yes	
Dart & Valiant	1970-up		Yes	
Barracuda	1970-71	Yes	Yes	
	1972-up			Yes
Ford Motor Company				
Mustang, Fairlane, Falcon & Comet	1964-71		Yes	
Ranchero & Cougar	1967-71		Yes	
Torino & Montego	1968-71		Yes	
Mustang, Cougar, Montego, Torino	1972-up			Yes
Pinto, Maverick & Comet	1974-up			
General Motors				
Camaro	1967-70	Yes	Yes	
Camaro, Chevelle, Nova, Monte Carlo	1971-up			Yes
Corvette	1965-82		Yes	

Note: See also aftermarket brake-component suppliers.

THE REST OF THE SYSTEM

In addtion to the major components, there are a few more brake-system components you must deal with. They are the brake lines, fluid and pedal assembly. If you decided to install a manual transmission, chances are you have already tackled the problem of pedals. If not, and your project car is based on a 1927—34 Ford or replica, you'll find ample reproduction floor-mounted pedal assemblies in the catalogs of most street-rod parts manufacturers and dealers.

If you are building a later Ford or a non-Ford based rod and there are no reproduction pedal assemblies available, I hope you still have the originals. If so, adapt the modern master cylinder to the stock pedals. There are some adapter plates on the market, but if these won't do, a simple 3/8-in. piece of aluminum usually gets you started. Once again, try to avoid fire wall-mounted pedals wherever you can unless you build in a significant structural reinforcement.

With regard to brake lines, the best advice is to buy a number of commercial double-flared short, medium and long lengths and a fistful of connector fittings. Often, you can get return privileges if you don't bend, cut or scratch the tubing. Use them as is when you can; shorten only one end when necessary. There are several inexpensive brake-line-bending tools available. You'll need a good flaring tool and tubing cutter with a sharp blade.

As for fluid, about every major brand is Department of Transportation (DOT) approved. Many rod builders, however, prefer silicone fluid. It is expensive, but it isn't something you use by the gallons. One or two quarts should supply the needs of one street rod for several years.

Finally, use the best parts in your brake system. Brakes are not the place to skimp. Always buy *new,* not rebuilt master cylinders. And, be absolutely sure wrecking-yard rotors, calipers and drums are in top condition. It's a good idea to have all wrecking-yard supplied components checked at a USAC-certified Magnaflux station before rebuilding and installing them. After all, cars in wrecking yards have been wrecked!

Put your best effort into your brake system the first time around . . . you may not get a second shot.

Super Bell, a top name in disc-brake kits, offers several to choose from. Super Stopper kit is designed to be installed with no machining of stock steering components or spindles.

Super Stopper adapts brake hardware from Airheart or Volkswagen Type III and IV.

Disc-brake kit is from Strange Engineering.

Super Bell's Mustang/Cougar disc-brake kit is for cars weighing over 3000 pounds. Ron Adams demonstrates how easy installation is. Precision-cast caliper bracket simply bolts to stock 1939—48 Ford spindle.

Special hub center bolts to late-'60s/early '70s Mustang/Cougar rotor.

After rotor/hub assembly is slipped over spindle, Ron installs kit-supplied outer bearing and seal.

Mustang calipers, brakes pads and caliper mounting bolts are assembled just as easily as was stock installation.

Ron installs braided stainless-steel brake hose to give that custom touch.

Not only is Super Bell Mustang kit a heavy-duty stopping package, it is truly *bolt-on.*

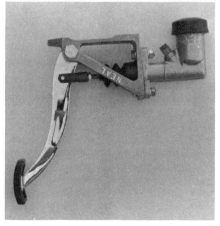

Pedal, bracket and master-cylinder assembly from Neal Products can be mounted on floor or suspended.

Owner: Roy Fjastad, Jr.

The repro parts industry will ensure the survival of street rodding. And nowhere is that more apparent than in the car that belongs to the scion of one of that industry's giants—The Deuce Factory's Roy Fjastad. About the only thing that is *not* reproduction on the car is the basic small-block Chevy! And that's probably the only piece of original equipment that is not threatened with extinction.

The chassis is Deuce Factory all the way, fully boxed and with Pop's four-link radius-rod/coil-spring front suspension. At the back is a 9-inch Ford with a coil-over suspension from you know who. Front and rear brakes are from Strange Engineering.

Perched atop that frame is one of the best fiberglass bodies in the country—the Wescott Deuce—sprayed Henna Red and hand-rubbed to absolute perfection. The custom top was built by Bud Matthews of Huntington Beach, CA and trimmed by Mark Stevens.

Speaking of trim, those "seat covers," are made from nothing but the best, fine leather and wool—no plastic! The work was handcrafted by Vic Kitchens (Vic's Place) of Fullerton, CA. VDO gages sit in a Deuce Factory dash and those cute-as-buttons foot pedals are right out of the Deuce Factory catalog.

Since street rodding began, one thing, and one thing alone, has never failed to turn on the street rodder; horsepower. The Magnacharger M220 blower setup with twin Holley carbs takes care of that department quite nicely, thank you. In fact, that small-block will quite literally sweat oil when Roy, Jr. puts his foot in it. You have seen the future. Don't you want a piece of it?

'31 Ford Closed Cab Pickup

Owner: Bruce Geisler

Bruce, a long-time 200 MPH Club Bonneville racer, simply can't bear to be without a blown Chevy in everything he drives, on or off the Salt. His strictly street pickup sports a 6-71 blown 1964 Chevy 283 with a 0.030-inch overbore, '57 2-bbl heads with polished and matched ports, 8:1 TRW pistons, stock rods with Rocket bolts and nuts, an Isky cam kit inclusive of anti-pump-up lifters, a pair of 625-cfm Carter AFB carbs, Isky blower drive, Stinger ignition, and Doug Thorley headers. A Walker radiator is used.

Geisler's drivetrain includes a Ford top-loader four-speed transmission and Hurst shifter, McLeod clutch and scatter shield, a Halibrand quick-change rear end with late Ford axles, and a coil-over-shock suspension from the Deuce Factory.

The front suspension incorporates '79 Firebird discs on a Super Bell I-beam axle with a TCI spring and four-bar setup. T/A radials are mounted on custom wheels built by Hoppy at American Racing Wheel Company. The wheels have powder-painted centers and chrome outers. A Vega steering box handles the steering chores in this 2450-pound car. Pressure to the brakes is supplied by a Mustang "fruit-jar" master cylinder with a Midland-Ross booster.

The 1931 frame is boxed, with custom crossmembers by Bud Matthews of Huntington Beach, CA. The body features a 4-inch chopped top by Bud, who also installed a '57 Chevy pickup sliding rear window and a '32 cowl vent. The original body and bed is supplemented by Anderson Industries 'glass fenders all around, and is painted '64 Corvette Riverside Red catalyzed acrylic enamel with gold leaf and pin striping by Mitch Kim of Portland, Oregon. The sheet metal and 'glass combo is protected by '32 bumpers. A Gennie light bar handsomely supports King Bee headlights.

The interior is attractively done in tan Naugahyde by Tony's of Whittier, CA. The seats are from a Fiat Spider. The dash is from a '32 three-window coupe with a full complement of Stewart-Warner gages. A Bell Auto Parts steering wheel operates a Pontiac GTO non-tilt steering column. A Ron Francis wiring kit is used with with Bruce's trademark—Harley-Davidson turn signals and an International air horn!

Bruce is a member of the Rod Riders Racing Team (Bonneville and El Mirage), and the Slo-Pokes Street Rod Club of Vancouver, Washington.

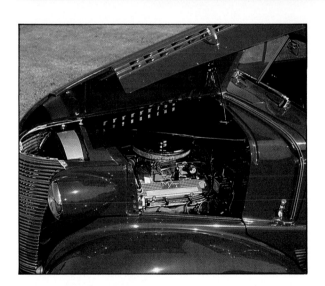

Owner: Bob Sands

Bob Sands is best described as a man with a mission, not to go to Mars or anything as simple as that. No, he really took on a tough assignment—he's out to build the World's Nicest 1938 Chevy coupe. Admittedly, Bob doesn't have much competition; '38 Chevy coupes are not exactly "belly-button" cars. But the few who own one cherish it as a prized possession and resto-rod it accordingly. So Bob wasn't "Sandsbagging" when he jumped in feet first.

This was a body-off project from the git-go. The stock chassis was endowed with a '72 Jag independent front suspension inclusive of the Cat rack-and-pinion. The hindquarters were similarly suspended: '72 Jag IRS with a 3.31:1 gear. Bob added a Bendix HydroVac power boost to a brand new '38 Chevy master cylinder.

With that kind of running gear, and naturally under a Chevy bonnet, does anyone think that a Hudson engine was used for power? Hardly. The motivation is a 327-CID small-block in essentially stock configuration, except for TRW pistons and a Holley manifold, Carter Super Quad carb and Mallory igniter. Bob installed the popular Turbo 350 automatic transmission behind the engine. A Gennie Shifter is used.

Bob can only credit himself for the custom-mixed light maroon catalyzed-acrylic enamel deftly sprayed over impeccable sheet metal. After all, he runs an auto-restoration center in Costa Mesa.

About the only thing Bob farmed out was the upholstery. A wise decision that was. Radillo Coach Works in Costa Mesa made their Singer sing as it was fed a steady diet of the finest vinyl.

Is Bob's Chevy the best? Don't know, but it must be close. For example, it was The Pick Of The Show when it made its debut at The Western Nationals in Merced, CA in 1985.

'40 Ford Deluxe Tudor Sedan

Owner:
Mike Denney

On paper it sounds almost mundane . . . a '40 Tudor with a small-block Chevy power. But once you've seen Mike Denney's sky blue fat-fendered sedan, you'll never forget it. It exudes class. Mike came by his '40 the easy way. His grandfather bought it new in Joplin, Missouri; his dad acquired it in 1955 for a go-to-work beater; and Mike came into possession of it in 1961 when he turned 14. And you can bet that he'll never turn it loose. Well, Mike may have had his Tudor all through high school, but it's only since 1981 that he got serious about completely refurbishing it. Many "big ones" turned a plain-jane '40 into this low-key show piece.

The 1970 Chevy 350-CID powerplant sports a factory performance cam and an Edelbrock manifold with a Carter quad. In order to install the small-block and Turbo 350 transmission, the wishbone was split. That done, a late '60s Ford rear axle was slipped in place and the whole drive train buttoned up.

Mike kept the suspension basically "updated stock"—a 2-1/2-inch dropped axle, '56 pickup drum brakes, reversed-eye transverse spring at the front, and parallel leaf springs at the rear. Steering is a rebuilt stocker. Monroe shocks are used all 'round.

Mike painted the car himself at home with a 1982 Volvo blue. The body is all steel except for fiberglass rear fenders.

The interior of this sedan can be described in only one word; plush. Taylor's Trim Shop in Costa Mesa, CA used copious

amounts of '74 Lincoln deep blue fabric and carpet. The steering wheel and '56 Ford steering column were painted to match. Is it any wonder that Mike's '40 won the coveted "State Of The Art Forty" award at the recent All Ford Picnic?

Owner: Dick Torres

There are some cars that are outstanding, even in grungy grey primer. It's all a question of the flow of the lines. Such a car is the 1934 Ford Sedan Delivery. It'll turn heads no matter what condition it's in. What happens when you pound the metal into absolute perfection . . . and then spray it Candy Apple red? And just for laughs, add a little gold-leaf flash? You guessed it—eye-poppin', heart poundin', splendor. At least if your tastes run to street rodding. You know I'm not exaggerating just by glancing at these photos of Dick Torres' magnificent delivery.

The engine is the ubiquitous small-block Chevy, all 350 cubes of which are fed by an Isky cammed, Weiand manifolded, Holley carbed, Stinger ignited, Hedman exhausted, Specialized Auto Repair high-performance rebuild, and backed up with a Terry Berzenye-massaged Turbo 350. No hype here, friends. This cars runs every bit as good as it looks.

Let's talk about chassis and suspension. This car has the best: fully chromed Jaguar front and rear independent in a boxed '34 original with the X-member *removed, reversed and replaced!* Pretty slick, huh? Can't say any more than that, can I? Except, thanks again to Terry and Specialized Auto in Anaheim, CA.

The interior was all done in saddle tan Naugahyde with camel corduroy by Specialized's house trimmer. Much polished stainless steel was used throughout. There is so much attention to detail and creature comfort that it is difficult to know where to begin . . . or stop: cruise control, air conditioning, tilt steering column, roll-up rear window, power seats, Stage III Stewart-Warner gages, CB, lots of NOS goodies, and on and on. Torres' Specialized Delivery doth bring home the gold every time Dick can tear himself away from it long enough to enter it in a show. Can you blame him?

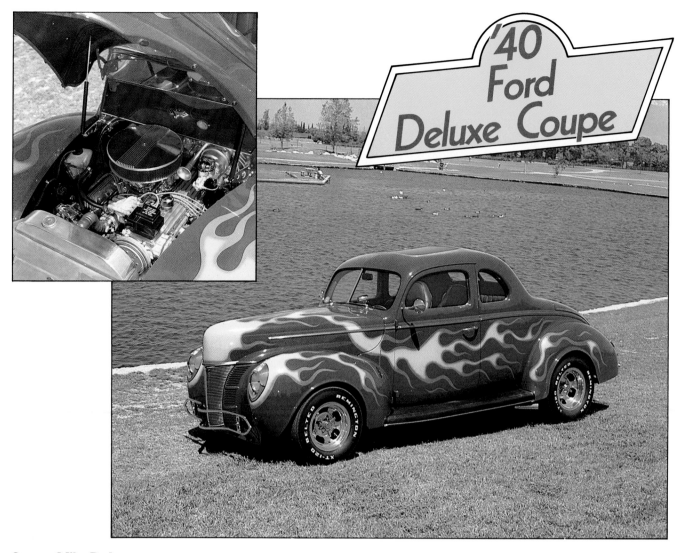

'40 Ford Deluxe Coupe

Owner: Mike Rodgers

If all it took was money to build a really nice street rod, only the rich would have them. But, of course, it takes much more; it takes time and talent. Don't know 'bout Mike Rodgers' pocketbook, but he told me he spent four years on his Project '40 . . . and I could see for myself that he sure wasn't short-changed in the talent department: he built, painted and upholstered his '40 in his own garage! Mike started out with a stock coupe body and frame that he paid a "whopping" $65 for in 1980! It didn't stay stock for long.

Mike completely reworked the chassis from stem to stern. The front was the recipient of a 1973 Dodge Demon torsion-bar independent front suspension inclusive of the manual steering. A '57 Ford rear with coil-over shocks was grafted under the backside. Because I've ridden in this car, I say with authority that it rides well.

Mike then replaced the body, did the basic metalwork, and for a tour-de-force, welded the fenders to the body and molded everything in. Sounds simple? It isn't. Normally this is not a long-lived custom touch because the filler usually cracks or otherwise shows fatigue. Mike's doesn't, even though the car has been on the road for several years. The owner-applied paint is '76 Opel Crimson Red with tangerine and yellow flames.

Mike installed a small-block Ford 289 with a Sig Erson RV grind, Edelbrock high-rise intake manifold and a big Holley carb. He built his own headers and topped off the engine with a Mallory ignition system.

Rodgers then turned his attention to the interior. Although he had little or no previous experience, he did an outstanding upholstery job in vinyl. Those Monte Carlo swivel bucket seats have nearly 270° turning radius! And, if these were moving pictures, he could show you that the side windows, even the quarters, are power operated! After all of this, little things such as a sun roof, custom fiberglass dash, air conditioning, cruise control, and nerf bars seem inconsequential!

'33 Dodge Four-Door Sedan

Owner: Diane Geisler

Diane's sedan is typical of the almost stone-stock early car that undergoes a mild street-rodding update. The powerplant is a stock 273-CID Dodge V8 backed up to a Torqueflite transmission.

The body with Anderson Industries fiberglass fenders is painted '74 Cad Black Watch Green.

The stock chassis is outfitted with a 4-inch dropped axle and Mustang 8-inch rear, power Volvo disc brakes, Mustang steering, VW bus air shocks, and shortened '57 Chevy parallel leaf springs at the back.

'33/34 Ford Tudor

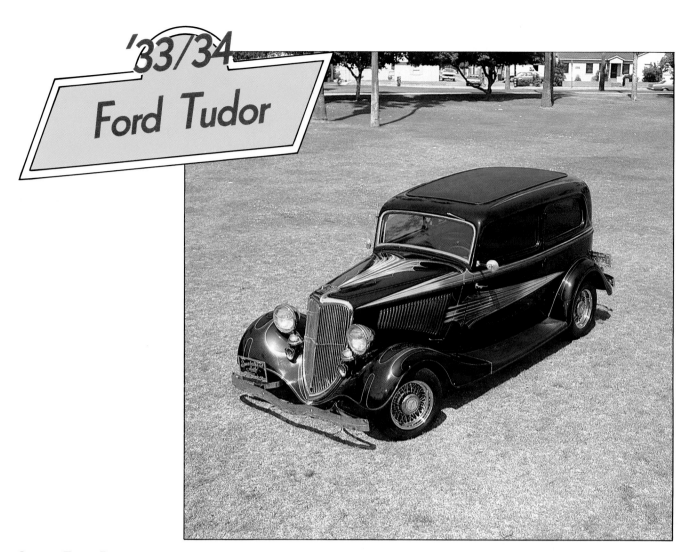

Owner: Terry Berzenye

What do you drive when you own a street-rod-building shop? Something flashy, that's for sure. Well, nobody every accused Terry Berzenye, owner of Specialized Auto Repair in Anaheim of being a shrinking violet, even if his Model 40 double-door is painted a color something along those lines. Its inclusion here is not just to showcase it, but rather to point out just how eye-catching modern street-rod graphics can be. The acrylic lacquer was mixed by that "Rembrandt of hue," the Master himself, Stan Betz (Betz Speed and Color, Orange, CA). Stan calls it *Candy Brandy;* I call it *beautiful.* I won't even begin to try to describe the rainbow effect, but then I don't have to. You can see it for yourself.

The rest of the car is not exactly ho-hum, either. It has a front and rear Jag independent suspension, a full-house Chevy 350 and one of Terry's very special Turbo 350 trannies, and yes, purple . . . no, errr . . . violet . . . errr . . . no! Candy Brandy upholstery!

Engine Cooling & Exhaust Systems

The trouble is, temperatures can actually reach as high as 4500F in the combustion chambers. Much of this heat is passed out the exhaust system, but a significant percentage is absorbed by the heads, cylinder walls and pistons. In order to keep the engine in the narrow, but efficient, temperature band, the cooling system must remove about 35% of the remaining heat.

WATER PUMP & RADIATOR

The conventional street rod uses a liquid-cooling system with coolant, a copper/brass or aluminum radiator and a belt-driven mechanical water pump on the engine. The water pump is typically a cast-iron or die-cast-aluminum housing with an inlet and out-let. The pump contains an impeller with curved vanes or blades. As the impeller rotates, vanes force coolant through the outlet and into the engine, where it is circulated through galleys and jackets. The jackets are voids cast into the block and heads that encircle the cylinders, combustion chambers, and valve seats and ports.

Street rods are faced with cooling and exhaust-system problems. Healthy engine such as SOHC Ford 427, needs a larger-than-average radiator and an equally healthy exhaust system.

Cooling System

The automotive cooling system must maintain an efficient operating temperature regardless of driving conditions and road speed. If too little heat is removed, cylinder-to-bore clearances go away, causing metal-to-metal contact as the pistons attempt to expand larger than their bores. This is quickly followed by disastrous results such as pistons seizing and galling. If the engine runs too cool, thermal efficiency—the relationship between power output and the latent fuel energy—drops off. Excess bore wear also results. Efficient operating temperature is precariously balanced somewhere between too hot and too cool. If you haven't already guessed, few street rodders have ever had to worry about an engine running too cool.

Since the days of the flathead V8, and probably before, street-rod builders have had

to deal with overheating. Even the best-built cars suffered from this malady. Part of the problem is that most street rods are equipped with modified engines that tend to run hotter than their stock brethren. Along this line, the engine is usually bigger than the original, leaving less room in the engine compartment for air to flow.

Another part of the problem arises from external modifications to the radiator, shrouds, ducting, fan location, and so on, which further reduces airflow.

Finally, street rods built from vintage tin are all too often equipped with worn-out or inadequate radiators. Overheating is the price you pay.

Automotive lubricating oils have been improved with the advent of emission-control regulations and the introduction of unleaded fuels. Nevertheless, the lubricating properties of most grades rapidly break down when engine temperatures climb past 600F.

Latest addition from Walker Radiator Works is for 1937—38 and 1939 *Standard Ford*. It has an integral condenser for cars equipped with air conditioners. Photo courtesy Joe Mayall.

Deuce Factory's stainless-steel coolant-recovery tank is available in four different lengths—13, 15, 17 and 19 in.—and fits any radiator with flanged side mounts.

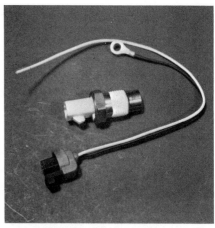

Walker's street-rod radiators feature built-in automatic-transmission fluid cooler and all necessary connections.

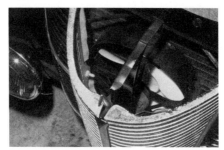

To ensure cooling at all times, use an electric-driven fan rather than power-robbing engine-driven fan. If possible, mount assembly behind radiator. A *draw-through* fan is more efficient.

Thermostat switch from Lobeck's Hot Rod Parts which installs in Chevy small-block cylinder head, turns on fan when engine coolant reaches 200F. It shuts off at 195F.

As coolant is routed through the engine, it absorbs rejected heat and carries it to the radiator where it is transferred to the air. The coolant is then recirculated to the engine.

The radiator most often used in street rods has a top and bottom tank, and a core in the center. During its cycle, heat-bearing coolant is delivered to the top tank; it cools as it flows down through the core to the bottom tank, then the coolant is drawn into the pump from the radiator through a hose in the bottom tank. The radiator is designed to move a large volume of air through a large volume of coolant, both through the core, thereby transferring heat from the coolant to the air.

The radiator core has two separate components—tubes and fins. The two types of core designs in standard use are the *tube and corrugated fin*, and the *tube and plate fin*. Both have a series of flat tubes extending from the top tank to the lower tank. Air passing between the rows of tubes absorbs some of the heat.

The fins aren't there just for decoration; they improve heat transfer. Cores manufactured with 7—20 fins per inch are standard. Higher counts are considered heavy-duty and are usually more expensive.

The number of tubes determines the cooling capacity of an automotive radiator. The standard tube is approximately 7/16 X 3/32 in.; heavy-duty tubes are closer to 1/2 X 1/8 in. Although special radiators can be built with as many as six rows of tubes—Ford flathead radiators had four—cooling efficiency falls off somewhat as the core increases in overall thickness due to reduced airflow.

Pressurized System—Radiators do not cool by virtue of tubes and fins alone. The efficiency of the cooling system can be dramatically improved by increasing coolant pressure and preventing evaporation and surge losses. Atmospheric pressure is nearly 15 psi at sea level and, at that pressure, pure water boils at 212F.

By merely installing a pressure cap on the radiator, cooling-system pressure is increased. For each additional psi, the boiling point of pure water is increased 3-1/4F. Coolant, therefore, can operate at a higher temperature. The payoff is this: Because the difference between the coolant temperature and the temperature of the air surrounding the radiator is greater, coolant-temperature drop is higher.

Radiator Cap & Hoses—The radiator pressure cap is more complex than you may realize, containing two separate safety devices. One is a blow-off valve, which is held against its seat by a calibrated spring. The valve lifts when system pressure exceeds a specified pressure.

The other safety device is a *vacuum-release* valve. This is needed to compensate for the partial vacuum that develops when an operating engine has been shut off and begins to cool. When vacuum reaches the danger point, the valve opens and admits air into the system.

Therefore, neither excessive pressure nor vacuum increase, both of which are potentially dangerous, can develop.

Caution: A modern high-pressure cap cannot be used on a leaky, vintage-tin original radiator. Older tanks can't withstand the 12—18-lb pressure created with these caps. This may be academic because the radiator-neck flange is different. Old radiators were only built to handle 4 psi or so and their flanges accept only low-pressure caps.

Another expendable item is the radiator hose. Once you find the hoses that match the radiator and water pump, record the part numbers in your spec book. Change the hoses at least every two or so years, particularly the bottom one. It's more likely to fail first because coolant is *sucked* through it.

The best hoses for street rods with engine swaps are the flexible spiral-wound types with wire reinforcement. The wire helps maintain a full diameter even when sharply bent. This is particularly important for the bottom hose that operates under low pressure. And it's a rare engine swap that doesn't have at least one or two sharp bends somewhere betwixt and between.

Mechanical & Electric Fans—A fan draws air through the radiator to improve coolant-to-air heat transfer. Unfortunately, some rod builders give the fan the old heave-ho. Don't do it. It is true that the fan is of relatively little value once the car is moving more than 30 mph, and a fan does use horsepower if it is driven by the engine. There are alternatives.

One way to keep an engine cool without sacrificing horsepower is to install an automatic or clutch-type fan. Most have a bimetallic-spring thermostat. The spring senses air temperature and regulates a control valve. When the valve opens, a silicone-base oil is released into the drive-plate housing and the fan speeds up. As air from the radiator cools, the fan idles and horsepower drain is reduced.

Another option is the flexible fiberglass or thin stainless-steel-blade fan. These lightweight designs typically have variable-pitch blades—a kind of self-adjusting action. Blade pitch is at a high angle during low-rpm operation, causing the fan to draw in plenty of air. The blades deflect and flatten out at higher rpm, resulting in less power loss at higher speeds.

One of my favorites, however, is the heavy-duty electrical fan built specially for street rods. They are adaptable to different radiator sizes and are relatively easy to install. Some have a built-in, adjustable thermostat, which cycles them on and off. Others are simply controlled by a manual switch under the dash and a watchful eye on the temperature gauge.

An electric fan/radiator combination that works very well is the pre-'83 Corvette radiator fitted with the Chevrolet Celebrity fan/motor/shroud assembly. The fan-and-motor assembly is mounted to the shroud. Mount the shroud to the back of the radiator and you're in business.

Fan Shrouds—When a fan is mounted on the engine side of the radiator, it should pull air through the radiator core. If, however, the fan is more than an inch or so away from the radiator, or a little off-center, efficiency is lost. The solution is to install a fan shroud. The shroud ensures that all air pulled by the fan is drawn through the radiator.

Various fiberglass fan shrouds are available from new-car dealers, but finding the right one can be difficult. The shroud should be about 1-in. larger than the fan diameter. When installed, the fan should be about half the way into the shroud at the blade tips.

One way to find a shroud is to sample a variety at the local wrecking yard. These, though, are frequently in damaged front-end wrecks, and tend to crack in ordinary service. New shrouds are reasonably priced, and once you know what size and shape you need, buy a new one.

Thermostat—The thermostat, like the radiator fan, is another cooling-system component that's often misused, abused or not used at all. Leaving it out, in fact, is the most common mistake made with the cooling system.

A functioning thermostat is absolutely necessary for coolant-temperature control at all times. Its job is to close off the water passages between the engine and the top of the radiator to ensure quicker engine-warmup time and that the coolant operates at a minimum temperature. A thermostat that's in good operation condition does not cause an engine to operate at an excessive temperature.

Otherwise excellent radiator setup has one thing missing—a fan shroud. Shroud that's sealed to radiator will improve maximum cooling dramatically. Fan should extend about half way into shroud and have minimal tip-to-shroud clearance.

The thermostat is nothing more than a spring and a valve. When the spring is cold, it holds the valve closed. As engine temperature increases, the spring expands, opening the valve, allowing coolant to circulate through the radiator and engine.

Thermostats are designed to operate within specific temperature ranges. The popular 160F unit starts to open between 157F and 163F and is fully open at 183F. "Hotter" thermostats rated at 180F and 192F are popular in northern climates. Many late-model cars, however, use 225F thermostats for more efficient engine operation, resulting in lower emissions. Fortunately, engine-oil improvements have kept pace with higher operating temperatures.

Coolant—Most any major brand of ethylene glycol antifreeze/antiboil concentrate is adequate. Water is not the best coolant you could fill a radiator with. It won't lubricate the water-pump seal or control corrosion and electrolysis. Also, pure water boils at a lower temperature than a mixture of water and antifreeze/antiboil.

I use a 50/50 mix of distilled water and antifreeze/antiboil. I live in an area with notoriously *hard* tap water, which is full of numerous minerals. The extra expense of bottled pure water is insignificant.

Temperature Gauge—The final cooling-system component to consider is the temperature gauge. It alerts the driver to abnormally high engine temperature. Two types of temperature gauges are available: electrical and mechanical.

An electrical gauge consists of a pair of coils and an armature to which a needle is attached. As engine temperature rises, resist-

ance of the sending unit drops and additional current is passed through the coils. The greater magnetic field attracts the armature, and the needle moves correspondingly. Unfortunately, I have found many electrical gauges that are off by several degrees. So, at best, the run-of-the-mill, uncalibrated electrical gauge is useful merely as a point of reference.

I have found top-quality mechanical gauges to be much more accurate. The fact that they are more expensive than electrical units doesn't bother me a bit. The conventional mechanical or vapor-pressure gauge uses a sensing bulb containing a liquid that evaporates at low temperatures. The sensing bulb—sending unit—is inserted into the water jacket in the intake manifold or cylinder head where it comes in direct contact with engine coolant.

The bulb is linked to the gauge by means of a transmission line. The gauge contains a small curved *Bourdon tube,* which, in turn, is linked to the indicator needle. The liquid in the bulb reacts to a rise in temperature by evaporating and creating a pressure that is relayed through the transmission line to the gauge. As pressure increases, the Bourdon tube changes shape and the needle indicates the temperature rise. As a rule, coolant temperature in the engine is about 10F hotter than in the radiator.

Although they are admittedly more unwieldy and somewhat difficult to install, I prefer mechanical temperature gauges.

Paying the Price—Regardless of how well individual components work, and how they interrelate, sooner or later you must make some hard economic choices. My experience tells me to choose new water pumps over rebuilt ones, electric fans over belt-driven fans, and mechanical temperature gauges over electrical gauges. And when it comes to the most important component of them all, the radiator, I believe in the best.

For example, if you're building a repro rod, don't get an original radiator for your, say, 1934 'glass roadster, then send it out for a "flush-and-patch" job. Radiators can wear out just sitting there.

Before there was a reproduction-radiator industry, rod builders roamed through wrecking yards for a late-model radiator that was close enough to fit their early car, and whose tank and outlets accommodated the late-model engine they were swapping in.

Finding a radiator that fit usually wasn't that difficult. Practical choices were noted and passed on from rodder to rodder. That was how I learned that a 1964 Ford radiator neatly tucked behind a 1940 DeLuxe Ford grille shell when my original finally quit. That was 15 years ago.

Today I wouldn't dream of sending a rodder to a wrecking yard for a street-rod radiator; not with the products that are currently on the market.

If you are truly fortunate enough to have a top-quality set of original tanks and side brackets, find a radiator shop that is willing to work with you to build their own version of a repro. The correct cores are available and sometimes, too, the parts necessary to fabricate new tanks or repair marginal ones.

The bottom line is that most any radiator shop can also turn an old-timey 4-psi design into a modern 12—18-psi radiator. If your 40-odd-year-old radiator is like most, and looks every bit of its age, cast it aside without a second thought and consider the offerings of companies such as The Walker Radiator Works. You'll never buy another *dead* radiator out of the wrecking yard again.

Exhaust System

What goes in must come out. That's what you eventually must deal with your car's exhaust system. Of course, there is the cheapskate approach. If the stock exhaust manifolds do not interfere with the steering gear or any other major component, just tow that turkey over to the nearest muffler shop and have the man weld up a pair of header pipes. Also have him install two mufflers, bend up a pair of exhaust pipes—no longer, larger diameter or more complicated than they absolutely have to be—top them off with a pair of chrome tips, and you're done.

But if you want the best bargain in the high-performance field, consider a proper exhaust system. Nowhere else in all of street rodding can you get a picture-perfect engine swap, an honest increase in net horsepower and a *simultaneous* increase in fuel economy. It will cost more, but a first-class plumbing system is guaranteed to please.

I briefly discuss the engine swap first, because that's where the story begins. Installing a V8 in any early car is, in most cases, surprisingly easy. If it wasn't, there wouldn't be so many cars with engine swaps running around. With few exceptions, however, the most difficult part of the swap is finding appropriate exhaust manifolds. Aside from providing good exhaust flow, the manifolds must be able to bolt up flush to the cylinder heads, not exit right into the steering gear, new engine mounts, chassis or firewall. They must also allow you to change sparkplugs with ease.

There are a few engine swaps that meet all three of the nuts-and-bolts criteria. The first to come to mind is the blessed Chevy V8 and its ram's horn manifolds. Rare indeed is the early Ford—and to a lesser extent early Chevy—that this combo can't accommodate. The Ford small-block with the standard passenger-car right-hand manifold and the high-performance left-hand manifold also fits popular street-rod choices fairly well once all other headaches are taken care of.

There are two more choices. But, when you're talking V8, and particularly any V8 that isn't a size and configuration twin of the engine it replaces, such as the unique small-block Chevy/Ford flathead trade-off, you've got potential problems in the exhaust department.

Ins & Outs Of Headers—The only reasonable solution is the custom or semi-custom exhaust header backed up with a compatible muffler and exhaust-pipe package. Custom headers go wherever to circumvent steering gears, engine mounts and the like. And, the best part is, no matter how circuitous they become, they are usually more efficient than the finest cast-iron manifold ever built.

That's the *upside*. The *downside* is that custom headers are noisy, tend to leak, and rarely fit properly. Fit is often a problem because headers are difficult to build, even for the professional. "U-Fab Kits" are available, however, and rod builders who can weld light-gage sheet metal and fabrication could build headers without a lot of waste and frustration. Some decent headers have been built by non-professionals who had the patience and took the trial-and-error, do-and-redo, approach.

Maybe you need a little more convincing that the cost of a custom-header system is justified.

The honest horsepower any normally aspirated internal-combustion engine is capable of producing depends largely on the quantity of air/fuel mixture drawn into its cylinders and the evacuation of the burned gases after combustion. Most production-car engines fall short of their potential volumetric efficiency in the high-rpm ranges. That's why hot rodding was invented in the first place.

The most significant aspect of the exhaust problem is back pressure—the resistance to exhaust flow through the stock manifolds. Oh sure, Motown took a giant step forward in reducing back pressure when dual exhausts

John Athan's '29, built in 1939, demonstrates that early street rodders were aware of need for low-restriction exhaust. Amazing because many modern street-rod builders use restrictive cast-iron exhaust manifolds.

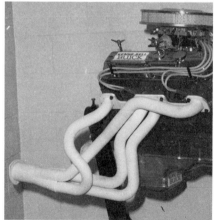

High-performance exhaust system such as used on Kenne-Bell built Buick has equal-length primaries. It's not always possible to package the perfect exhaust system in a street-rod chassis.

Sanderson stainless-steel Chevy small-block headers may not be fully appreciated . . . unless you realize they were mail ordered . . . and they fit with no modifications!

Only cast-iron headers I accept on a street rod is the modern reproduction Fentons for a flathead. Headers fit in almost any early Ford chassis from 1937 to 1952 with steering gear in stock location. Photo courtesy Speedway Motors, Inc.

Collector on high-performance header is critical. If you are having a custom exhaust built, pay attention to this often over-looked item. Photo courtesy Speedway Motors, Inc.

were first installed on Cadillacs in the '50s. But, with rare exception, that's about where they stopped. Detroit has seldom strayed far from the practice of installing cast-iron log-type exhaust manifolds until recently. Ford, for example, is using tubular stainless-steel headers on the 302 in some installations. However, cast-iron manifolds have some redeeming qualities, at least for a production passenger car. They are cheap, quiet, easily installed and last nearly forever. What more could the masses ask for?

But when it comes to volumetric efficiency, conventional exhaust manifolds aren't the answer. And excessive back pressure isn't the whole story.

On a normally aspirated engine, outfitted with typical log-type manifolds, when one exhaust valve opens, high exhaust pressures from that cylinder force burned gases into the adjacent low-pressure cylinder as the second cylinder's exhaust valve is about to close. This mixing of hot exhaust gas with the fresh, cool, incoming fuel/air mixture is known as *charge dilution*. It tends to increase with camshaft overlap, too. Charge dilution and the fact that some exhaust gases remain in the combustion chamber after the piston reaches top dead center (TDC), downgrade performance.

There's another problem, indirectly related to exhaust-gas flow, that cast-iron manifolds exaggerate—excessive underhood temperatures. Manifolds not only retain a lot of heat, they store it right up alongside the cylinder head. Think about it. We've just finished discussing the best way to get rid of some of that heat, and yet with stock manifolds, a lot of heat is stored where the cooling system can't do it much good beyond what air flows through the engine compartment. Tubular headers, on the other hand, dissipate heat rapidly.

Tubular headers do not make up the entire exhaust system. All of the plumbing from the exhaust valve to the chrome tip must provide a reasonably straightforward exit for the gases. True, there is a helping hand in the form of combustion pressures. For, unlike the fuel/air mixture, which enters the combustion chamber more or less under atmospheric pressure in a normally aspirated engine, exhaust gases are hurried along by high combustion pressures.

As soon as the exhaust valve unseats, the work of the exhaust system begins. The burned gases rush past the valve into the port, where they immediately collide with the air that fills the port and its extension. This sets off a pressure wave that travels down the header and exhaust pipe faster than the actual speed of the gases. When the pressure wave reaches the end of the tailpipe, it expands and sends a negative pressure wave back up the pipe to the still-unseated exhaust valve. This assists in extracting the exhaust gases from that exhaust port.

Many long hours have been spent designing and developing the extractor effect in racing engines. But for ordinary street-rod purposes, we need not go into any exotic design formulas. The most basic set of headers with primary pipes—those that are welded to the flange and bolted to the cylinder head—of equal length is good enough for the boulevard cruiser.

The high-performance street-rod header design in common use today is the four-into-one system. In this layout, primary pipes are separate until, after a reasonable approximation of equal length, they are conveniently joined together at a collector. This is a practical design for both the commercial manufacturer with a full-run production line and the small shop that builds one-off custom headers for the street-rod and street-machine market.

Although some low-end torque is lost, the headers install "easily" and are attractive. In fact, even with its shortcomings, the design is so far superior to cast-iron exhaust manifolds that no one seriously compares the two. Also, it has been universally accepted by all high-performance buffs with the exception of the hard-core racer.

Custom Exhaust System—There are still several tubing artisans set up where there is enough race-car business to sustain them. In general, custom-header building is fast becoming a lost art. Nevertheless, if you decide to go this route, here's why the price tag is so high.

The biggest problem the custom-header builder must contend with is preserving the car's sheet metal or fiberglass. He is well aware that the owner will be upset if he takes a ball-peen hammer to the firewall or burns a hole in a fenderwell. The second biggest headache is achieving equal lengths for all primary pipes. That Chevy small-block street-rod engine will generally require longer primary pipe lengths than a racing engine because it should develop peak *usable* horsepower at a much lower rpm.

Equal-length primary pipes are important to performance. The ideal is no more than 1/2-in. variation. A 1-in. variation is no problem for general street use, but plus or minus more than 2 in. will reduce performance. Be forgiving of the header builder in tight situations, for achieving equal-length primaries is much easier said than done.

Determining the correct primary-pipe diameter is simple. It should equal the inner diameter of the exhaust-valve seat. If it is a little larger, no problem, but it should not be much smaller. Also, the inside diameter of the pipe should not exceed the diameter of the exhaust port, if at all possible.

One of the more-critical aspects of header design is collector length. It is there to gradually reduce the pressure of the exhaust-pulse shock wave before it reaches the atmosphere. By doing so, it improves mid-range performance, perhaps the only performance band that counts for most street rods. The rule of thumb states that the collector should be approximately twice the volume of one cylinder, and at least 5-1/2-in. long. Some commercially available headers fall short here. If you have a pair that fits otherwise, you can retrieve some mid-range performance by taking the headers to a muffler shop and asking them to lengthen the collector until it equals the volume of two cylinders.

Semi-Custom Header—Header sets have been offered for years by companies catering to the Fad T-bucket trade and have gained general acceptance. More recently, however, several non-Fad T street-rod-parts man-

External exhaust system is only practical on Fad T or fenderless street rod. Care must be taken to protect passengers from hot pipes and exhaust gases.

manifold exhaust system. Sanderson has a surprisingly large variety of headers for just about every popular combination. Some are even fabricated from stainless steel.

After the Headers, What?—If at all possible, you should have a *balance tube* installed in your exhaust system. This is a short connecting tube running perpendicular between the header pipes. It should be at least 2-1/4-in. OD. A balance tube reduces back pressure even more, and also enhances the resonance and tone of straight-through mufflers. In effect, it doubles the volume of the exhaust system.

With regard to the exhaust pipe, it, too, should be at least 2-1/4-in. OD for best performance. If you want to build the best system, and you are willing to go to the added expense, install a 2-1/2-in. "Y-bend" behind each collector, and run two exhaust pipes per bank toward the rear bumper. Then, trim them in enough to install a pair of Corvair "turbo" mufflers or MoPar *reverse-flow* mufflers *per side*. Four mufflers can be costly, but you'll get it back in usable performance.

I dislike quoting figures that can't be verified, but if you discard the stock cast-iron manifolds and install a set of custom or semi-custom headers and only two good high-performance mufflers on any strong Chevy or Ford small-block, you'll recoup 10—20 HP that would otherwise be lost to back pressure. In short, you'll never spend a better performance dollar than what you spend on a first-class exhaust system.

Turn to the supplier index, page 203, for suppliers of cooling- and exhaust-system components.

ufacturers have begun offering header sets matched to their own products. One of the earliest has been Specialized Auto Components of Anaheim, California. Their repro 1933—34 chassis, engine mount and steering swap became so popular that they designed headers to bolt right up to the Chevy that was installed. It wasn't long after that they began offering headers for their "Chevy In A Forty" kit. Judging from the response, such *semi-*

custom headers are here to stay. I suspect that eventually every company that makes engine mounts and steering-swap kits will also offer matching headers.

Of course you don't have to wait if you want headers for any of the really popular street-rod engine choices. Sanderson Headers Company from South San Francisco, California, has a catalog that you should see before you get too far along with a cast-iron-

Before mail-ordering headers, carefully measure and photograph several critical areas, particularly around steering gear. Pass information on to supplier to help him make a reasonable judgement as to whether or not there will be an exhaust-clearance problem.

This chapter will attempt to simplify the technical complexities as much as possible. I can't trace the installation of every possible gadget or accessory or include a detailed schematic for every possible ignition and charging circuit, not with the ever-expanding popularity of so many import powerplants. If you decide to go beyond the domestic "Big Three," you simply must have the appropriate service manuals, not only for the wiring diagrams, but everything else you will sooner or later need to know. Also, wouldn't you know it! HPBooks has a book on the subject: *Automobile Electrical Handbook*. Get it before you wire your car yourself.

AUTOMOTIVE ELECTRICAL CIRCUITS

In most cases, the street-rod electrical system and its wiring is no different from standard American production cars in the simpler days before the on-board computer and confusing array of pollution controls. The only possible exception is the wooded-fiberglass reproduction body. Even that doesn't significantly alter the wiring.

An understanding of the basic automotive-electrical system begins with the electrical circuit—a closed path through which electric current can flow. Most automotive circuits consist of low-resistance wiring that conducts current to electric appliances and accessories with minimal voltage drop.

Smaller cockpits make it difficult to route wires and place components. Terry Berzenye places most electrical-system junction blocks and components under seat cushion in Model A 1/2-ton pickup.

Few tasks come with as much uneasiness as laying out the wiring circuits and the electrical system. There are more complex assignments, such as rebuilding the automatic transmission, but you know that such a job shouldn't be attempted without a great deal of experience, so there is no ego involvement or anxiety. When it comes to the electrical system, however, you've probably read numerous magazine articles that say wiring a street rod is relatively easy. Yet, chances are you're not at ease looking at all those mysterious tabs and terminals sticking out of the alternator, starter, distributor and the backs of all those gauges.

Of course, you've probably installed an extra light, accessory gage or cassette player. And, although a fuse or two might have bitten the dust before everything was "kosher," that doesn't qualify you to do an entire car. Or does it?

Wiring the entire car is done one component at a time, just as with a tachometer. And, just as you wouldn't have tried to complete high school in one sitting, neither should you try to wire an entire car in one night. Even

if you got everything to work, chances are it would look chaotic. In street-rod building, the wiring not only must be correct, it should be neat and attractive.

Pete and Jake offer tidy under-body battery box for Model A and other early car frames.

Recreational-vehicle shops have plastic terminal blocks suitable for battery cables.

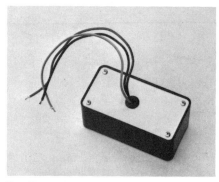

Ron Francis' "voltage reducer" drops input of 12 volts to exactly 6 volts. It is designed to reduce the voltage to up to 3 gauges through electronically controlled circuit.

Auto-parts stores have a variety of voltage-drop devices if you want to retain an original 6-volt accessory.

Here are but of a few of many different terminal blocks available.

Try to achieve neat and *accessible* fuse panel when wiring your street rod.

12-VOLT FUSE DATA	
Circuit	Amps
Turn Signals	10
Cigar Lighter	15
Radio, Stereo, CB	15
Heater, A/C Controls	10
Headlights	15
Brake Lights	10
Taillights	10
Parking Lights	10
Electric Fan	15
Fuel Pump	10
Horn	10
Electric Wipers	10

Each appliance or accessory should have enough resistance to make the electromotive force drop 12 volts (in a 12-volt system) when the required amperage is passed through the circuit. If it doesn't, there will be overheating.

Viva La Difference!—Almost all automotive circuits are of the *one-wire (common-ground)* type, so called because the body or chassis completes the circuit. The battery, the source of electromotive force in the car, is grounded to the engine block through a heavy woven-copper strap or insulated cable. Its live, or *hot,* post completes the current path through a heavy, insulated copper cable to the starter solenoid.

If the hot lead or conductor touches any other part of the car, resistance is insufficient for circuit balance, and a *short circuit* occurs, followed by arcing, burning or similar fireworks. Another, not-so-easily detected but more-benign source of trouble, arises from improper grounding. Electricity will always

seek the path of least resistance to ground. If the normal path is blocked or has high resistance, current will seek an alternate route. For example, if a sparkplug lead is broken internally, the 40,000-volt current will arc to the engine block, exhaust manifold or any other convenient metal object that provides the best ground. Or, if the engine is improperly grounded, current may travel down the throttle linkage, shift linkage or driveshaft. Depending on the amperage involved, this can cause the linkage to be arc-welded in position or cause metal transfer from the driveshaft to output bearing or vice versa. If the ground is insufficient, it may also show up as dim or flickering headlights, or no lights at all.

AUXILIARY CIRCUITS

Sometimes it's necessary for automotive components to have auxiliary circuits. For instance, it takes relatively high current to operate the headlamps, far too much to be handled by a simple, low-capacity instrument-panel switch. The options are to replace the low-capacity switch with a high-capacity one and heavy-gage wiring, or bring the cur-

rent directly to a relay near the headlamps. This allows you to use the low-capacity instrument-panel switch to operate the circuit to the relay, which in turn kicks on the headlights. An auxiliary circuit that controls another circuit by means of auxiliary switches is known as a *relay circuit.*

Fuses & Breakers—All circuits should be protected against current overloads caused by an unwanted ground or excessive voltage. The conventional way of providing this protection is with fuses and circuit breakers. These should be in readily accessible areas. Fuses, it seems, tend to burn out at night, and if you can't find the fuse panel or see the burned fuse in the panel, you are only going to add to your frustration. Of course, merely replacing the fuse or resetting the circuit breaker doesn't solve the problem. The blown fuse or tripped breaker is only a symptom of the problem. Find the cause and correct it. And never install a higher-capacity fuse as a temporary fix. This may overload the circuit and cause more serious problems at another weak link somewhere else.

Starting Circuit—The starting circuit consists of the battery, cranking motor, starter switch, and the cables and wires. Although it is fairly straightforward in its basic wiring, this circuit has the all-important task of spinning the flywheel and crankshaft so the engine can operate under its own power. Electrical load is high and these components draw the most current.

Ignition Circuit—The ignition circuit consists of the key switch, coil, distributor, sparkplugs, low-tension wiring, high-tension wiring and battery. In reality, however, there are two separate circuits. The primary, or low-tension, circuit is one. It includes the ignition switch, coil primary winding, distributor breaker points and condenser, and the battery. The frame or body serves as the conductor to complete the primary current path

Lever-activated switches are useful for operating brake lights, back-up lights and many other mechanical on/off functions.

Alternator is installed on differential housing—great for a clean engine compartment, but unsprung weight goes up and alternator is in hostile enviroment.

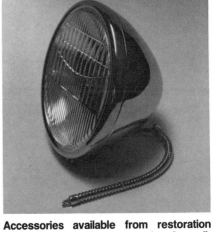

Accessories available from restoration market are more than appropriate for well-dressed street rod. Vintique, Inc. stainless-steel headlamp is for 1928—34 Ford.

from the battery, through the components and wiring in the circuit, then back to the battery.

Most 12-volt ignition systems also incorporate a *ballast resistor*—a special circuit to bypass it—within the primary circuit. The ballast resistor reduces total voltage going to the distributor once the engine starts. The bypass circuit allows full battery voltage to flow to the starter when cranking power is needed.

The other main ignition circuit is the secondary or high-tension circuit. It includes the secondary coil winding, distributor cap and rotor, sparkplugs and their wires, and the grounded portion of the entire circuit.

Charging Circuit—The charging circuit is the complete generating and energy-storage system. It furnishes electric current for engine cranking, ignition, lights and all accessories. It consists of a generator or alternator, voltage regulator, the wiring, appropriate gauges or lights to indicate state of charge or voltage and, of course, the battery.

When the engine is in operation, the generating circuit—exclusive of the battery—supplies current for the electrical load, and keeps the battery charged. The amount of current diverted to the battery depends upon battery condition and the electrical load.

Alternators & Regulators—The modern automotive generator, of course, is the alternating-current (a-c) generator or *alternator* that supplies rectified alternating—direct—current to the system. The alternator became standard equipment on production cars in the early '60s because it provides substantial current at idle speed as well as increased maximum output. It is also more durable than the old-fashioned three-brush, direct-current (d-c) generator. Alternators come in a wide variety of sizes and shapes, and there are just as many internal differences.

Although alternators do not require current limiters as did the old-style d-c generator,

they still need some kind of controlling device. These are popularly called *voltage regulators,* typically consisting of a magnetic switch with adjustable contact points, resistors and voltage windings. Since the early-to-mid-'70s, most regulators are of the solid-state design and cannot be adjusted. One of the best to use with all types of alternators is the late Chrysler unit. Many rod builders, however, are switching over to integral-regulator alternators, such as the GM Delcotron, which incorporate voltage controls in the alternator body.

Lighting Circuit—The automotive lighting system includes—besides the battery, frame and wiring—all lights and the various switches that control their use. There is a number of individual circuits, each having one or more lights, switches and the required conductors. In each separate circuit, the lights are connected in *parallel*—components are connected from one side of the circuit to the other. Each light has its own hot lead and ground to the chassis. The switches, though, are connected in *series* between the battery and the group of lamps they control. In series circuits, current flows from one unit to the next, and resistance is added together to determine total circuit resistance.

Usually, one switch is used to control the individual circuit, regardless of how many units are on that circuit. An example is the parking-light circuit, where one switch controls at least four lamps that are connected in parallel. In some cases, though, one switch controls the connection to the battery, while a selector switch determines which circuit will be placed in operation. The high-beam and low-beam headlight circuits are a good example of this. Yet another variation is the

panel-lighting circuit in which the main lighting switch controls the connection to the battery; a panel-light rheostat controls the brightness of the panel lamps.

As already mentioned, relays are often used in circuits with a high current requirement. Besides reducing voltage loss, headlight-circuit relays are also used to increase the normal brilliance of the light. Those used in the lighting circuit are designed for continuous duty.

Horn Circuit—There are two ways of laying out the horn circuit: One is in series with the battery, with the horn button going to ground. Another way is to insert a relay between the battery and horn. This latter method is better. When a relay is used in the circuit, the horn button acts only as a grounding switch and handles the relay-control current alone, resulting in less current through the switch.

By the way, the relay used in the horn circuit is not intended for heavy-duty use. It is designed for short, intermittent service and will overheat if used continuously. Several variations in horn/relay circuits are possible depending upon the components used. I've included a general schematic suitable for most street rods. Some aftermarket horn kits include a specific diagram and indicate the appropriate relay.

Accessories & Gauge Circuits—All other electrical items fall into this general category. Typically, the circuits are traced from the battery to the switch(es) where they may divide and go to the individual accessory. Each accessory must be grounded to the body—if steel—or the frame. It is usually best to actually use a ground wire rather than rely on the metal-to-metal contact of the component to the body or metal instrument panel.

Finding place for fuel filter and electric pump was solved in this case by mounting both to mid-section frame-rail boxing plate.

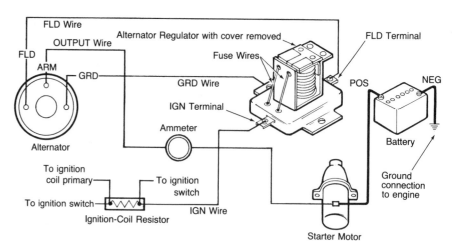

Easiest voltage regulator to install is late-'70s Chrysler unit. Don't try to *polarize* alternator, be certain negative post of battery and regulator are well grounded, and take care not to ground field circuit between alternator and regulator.

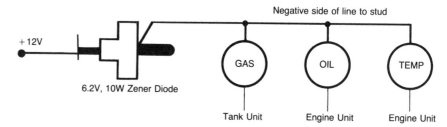

One way of partially converting 6-volt to 12-volt system is to connect 6.2-volt, 10-watt silicone zener diode in series with 12-volt battery line to 6-volt gauges or accessories. Attach diode to aluminum bracket, then secure to piece of 1/4-in. epoxy board.

Occasionally, rod builders use a two-wire system with a ground wire going all the way to the battery rather than coming through the frame, but normally this isn't necessary. This is called a *floating ground*. Most accessories require a fuse, and many incorporate it within the hot lead. One or two fuses discreetly hidden out of sight—but always readily available—are OK, but too many of them bundled together is unsightly. Nothing beats a neat fuse panel.

WIRING DIAGRAMS

The typical modern automotive wiring diagram appears as a puzzling criss-crossing of lines. All too often, every light bulb, appliance and accessory in the car is represented symbolically in a single, bewildering nightmare of circuitry. Therefore, to get the novice rod builder started, and to help him develop the self-confidence necessary to take on the job, I've dropped these confusing electrical or electronic symbols in my major diagrams whenever possible.

Instead, I use pictorial representations of the starting-, charging- and ignition-system components. In addition to this, I've separated as many of the circuits as possible, all in the interest of clarity. However, if you are installing new electronic gadgets, it's best to use the wiring diagram supplied by the manufacturer.

FIRST STEP IN WIRING A STREET ROD

Before you jump into wiring your car, list all of the electrical components you plan to install, including the gauges and switches. Then, after studying the schematics, draw your own individual schematic. Try to lay out the system to scale, so you have some idea of how much wire you'll need. You can also get

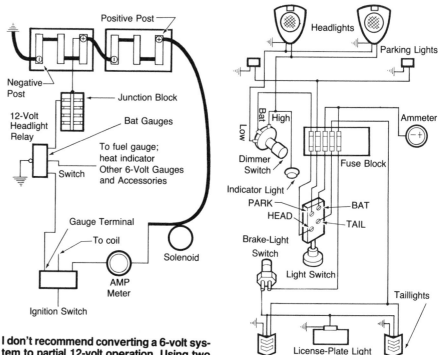

I don't recommend converting a 6-volt system to partial 12-volt operation. Using two 6-volt batteries is traditional way of doing it.

Lighting Circuit

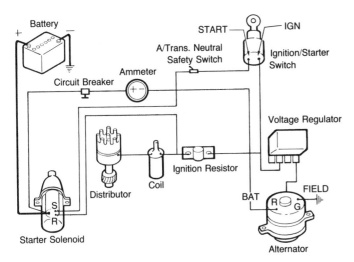

GM Ignition and Charging Circuit

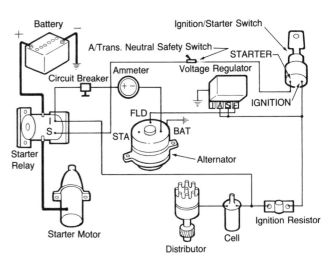

FoMoCo Ignition and Charging Circuit

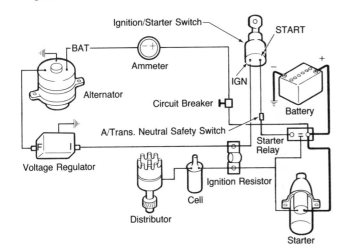

Chrysler Products Ignition and Charging Circuit

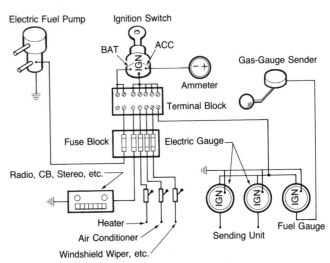

Accessory and Gauge Circuit

some idea of which wires will group together neatly.

The cost of the wire alone may be substantial, but don't cut corners. Be generous in estimating lengths. The fewer splices you make, the better.

Color-coding your system will aid any subsequent troubleshooting efforts. Also, you may want to add or change something later on and color-coding helps. Although all yellow wiring may look neat against a glossy-black-lacquered firewall, some day you'll pull your hair out—or maybe the wiring—trying to determine which wire goes to what.

Although most parts outlets carry five or six different wire colors, it's best to have a different color for every component. That could easily mean dozens of different color schemes. To obtain these, try a distributor that services professional wiring shops, or a new-car dealer.

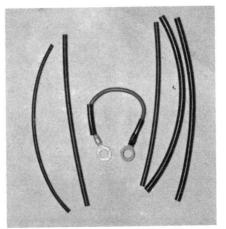

Heat-shrink plastic tubing, available in several diameters, makes wiring task relatively easy. Don't use adhesive-backed electrical tape.

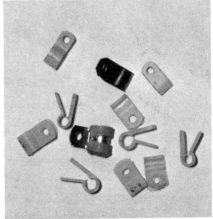

Adel clamps offer quick and attractive way to bundle and secure wire looms.

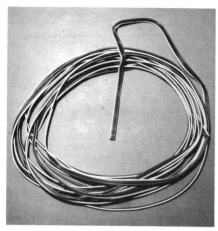

Wire is available in a variety of gages and color codings. One of my favorites is multi-lead truck-and-trailer harness that is sold by the foot in both 16 and 14 gage, and with up to 12-strand widths, each a different color.

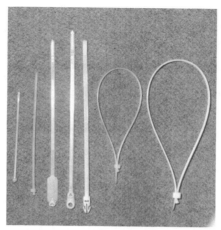

Plastic tie wraps are used throughout when wiring a street rod, but don't overuse them. One about every 6 in. is plenty.

Get the best crimping tools you can afford. You'll use them over and over.

12-VOLT WIRE SIZES

Gage	Safe Amperage
20-22	3 amps
18-19	5 amps
16-17	7 amps
14-15	15 amps
12-13	20 amps
10-11	25 amps

Gage	Service
16	Headlights
16	Taillights
16	Parking Lights
16	Turn Signals
16	Electric Fan
16	Heater
16	A/C Switches
16	Electric Fuel Pump
16	Dash Instruments
16	Radio/Stereo/CB
16	Ignition
14	Alternator Field
10	Alternator "Bat"
10	Ammeter
10	Starter

Even though you may use solderless terminals, don't throw your faithful soldering iron away. You may need it somewhere else while building your street rod.

As you actually begin wiring, record everything you do right away. Later, you can draw a clean, permanent, coded diagram of the entire electrical system and carry it in your spec book. Take this precaution now and you'll never be out on an limb when minor problems arise.

Keep It Neat—I have to admit that visually impressive wiring jobs require a certain artistic flare. Of course, that doesn't mean that planning and patience won't be rewarded. Aside from the fact that those qualities are indispensable to correctness, they are exactly what will convert mundane terminals and wire of an electrical system into something that you can take pride in.

Beyond that, much of the attractiveness of automotive wiring is largely due to the varied and relatively inexpensive hardware available in most RV/trailer-supply houses. There are scads of bits and pieces that, with a little ingenuity, can be turned into shining examples of street-rod detailing.

Tools—You don't need much in the way of tools and equipment to get on with the wiring; a pair of crimping and stripping pliers, a test light, a drill motor, and a couple of screwdrivers are essential. But, there are some really slick professional tools that you may wish to get. The best place to buy these tools is, in most cases, electronics-parts houses and military-surplus stores. These have a wide selection of quality tools. Too many auto-parts stores carry imported cheapo tools that are a waste of money.

Organizing the Electrical System—The best way to organize the wires is to run those for each system as an independent *harness*. For instance, all wiring for the driving-light circuit should be in one harness, the wiring for the taillights in another, and so on. And although wiring is obviously a permanent part of the car, harnesses should be designed with junction blocks and quick disconnects to allow removal of electrical *and* mechanical units without the need to cut or significantly uproot more than 1-foot or so of wire.

Ready access in front of the firewall is of particular importance. You should always allow the removal of the front sheet metal, engine and transmission. Rear placement of disconnects is a good idea, too; back fenders and decklids may have to be taken off.

In the interest of neatness and safety, pull the wires taut and smooth out any kinks. The harness should be kept as straight as possible, and when bends are required, they should be graceful. Keep the harness away from sharp edges, places where it could be pinched, and by all means, the exhaust system. A fire in my street rod was caused by the installation of a new exhaust pipe too close to the electric fuel-pump wiring.

There are two schools of thought with regard to routing wiring—those who prefer to hide the wires so they can suddenly appear out of nowhere and shoot up to the component, and those who prefer neat, but visible wires. Of the two, my preference is the latter. Murphy's Law will get you if you hide too much wiring; ease of maintenance is a factor to consider. All you have to do to make the wiring blend into the background is to follow body and panel lines. Keep the harness off

Nothing works quite as well as clothes pins when mocking up wire looms in a street-rod chassis.

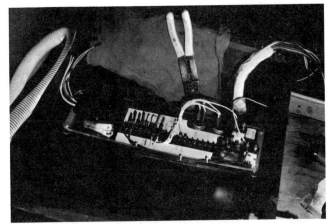

Whether bulk of electrical-system components are behind the dash or under seat cushion, be aware of potential fire hazards. Make sure you'll have troubleshooting and maintenance access.

Want to get turned on? Check with any auto, marine, electronic or RV parts house. They may have a switch you will like.

Ron Francis' Wire Works offers this stainless-steel component panel. Terminal-strip covers are labeled as is fuse holder. Photo courtesy Joe Mayall Associates.

Solderless terminals have all but replaced those requiring solder for automotive use. Can't find what you want in this selection? This is a small sampling of what is available.

broad expanses of sheet metal where it stands out like a sore thumb.

The alternator and voltage regulator should be mounted on the starter side of the car whenever practical. This allows you to keep the charging- and ignition-circuit wiring on one side of the engine.

Use the smallest tie wraps and clamps you can find to bundle your wiring, and don't try to get away with too few; or go ape with too many. Space the ties out about every 6 in., and the clamps every 8 in. or so. Sheet-metal screws often look crude. My preference is for 8/32-in. machine screws. They are neater looking and more easily removed and replaced. Most early-car sheet metal is thick enough for 8/32-in. threads.

If you really want to be neat, use *loom* tape—*not* electrical tape—to wrap the wires. The stuff sticks to itself without adhesive! Consequently, it's easy to unwrap.

Wiring Kits & Other Goodies—Just as in every other aspects of street-rod building,

manufacturers have dreamed up a number of items that range from handy to indispensable. The most significant one is the complete wiring kit. Ron Francis of Chester, Pennsylvania, was one of the first, if not *the* first to offer a complete kit. Since late 1974, his catalog has been a must on the workbench when it comes time to *fish* the wires from one end of the car to the other.

Other electrical-system goodies are more mechanical in nature. Items such as alternator brackets that many manufacturers offer, do, indeed, take some of the perplexity out of that final task. Others, like billet aluminum pulleys, are purely cosmetic.

If it's your first time, the task of wiring an entire car *is* a challenge. But the complexity of that task doesn't justify the negative reputation all too often associated with it. Planning and patience will net you all the desired results.

For electrical-component sources for your street rod, turn to page 194.

For electrical-component sources for your street rod, turn to page 194.

Some Basic Electrical Measurement Terms

Ampere—Amount or quantity of electric current that flows in a circuit having a resistance of one ohm with an electromotive force of one volt.

Electrical Pressure—Quality of electricity that causes current to flow.

Electrical Potential—Pressure difference between two terminals of a battery or generator, also referred to as Electromotive Force (EMF) and measured in volts.

Ohm—Amount of resistance in a conductor through which the current of one ampere will flow with an electromotive force of one volt. Resistance in a circuit keeps the current flow down to a safe value. Resistance should be in the appliance or accessory, not in the conductor.

Volt—Unit of electrical pressure or electromotive force.

24 Restoring Vintage Tin

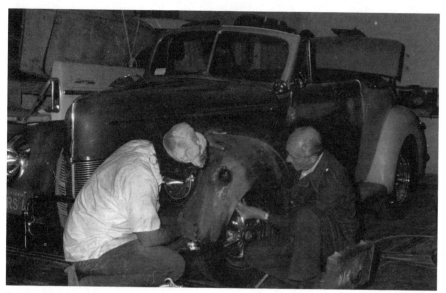

Basic metalworking is a developed skill. As Ron Fournier, author of HPBooks' *Metal Fabricator's Handbook,* says, "By choosing your tools well and developing your skills, you'll find projects go easier."

It shouldn't surprise you that available vintage tin for new street rods is scarce. The quality of what is left is often so marginal it is discouraging. Yet, unless you are determined to own a genuine 1932 Ford phaeton or some other rarity, metal-bodied cars can still be found. On the other hand, you can't deny that the *newest* of the models commonly accepted as the authentic basis of a street rod, the 1948 production run, approached retirement age in the mid '80s.

Even with the best of luck, automobiles surviving four or five decades haven't done so without suffering battle scars, metal fatigue and a lot of *rust*. And those are the good ones. The bad ones sometimes defy description, but committed rod builders will restore them.

Repairing and restoring a metal-bodied old car isn't the same as repairing a modern automobile body. The primary difference is the amount of rust that must be removed before any bodywork can be done.

BUST THAT RUST

The traditional tools for removing rust, in order of their effectiveness, include wire brushes, disc grinders, muriatic acid (hydrochloric acid) and the sandblaster. Wire brushing is usually minimally effective. Disc grinding is hazardous to sheet-metal gage and texture. Muriatic acid, even when diluted, is an extremely dangerous product requiring great care when handling. Use sandblasting only as a last resort, because it's so destructive to tender vintage tin. Think of it as the Dirty Harry of rust removal: All too often it blows everything away.

Rust can now be removed through alkaline electrolytic immersion. The Redi-Strip company, exclusive owners of this process, was founded in Southern California in the '50s. They were primarily concerned with chemically removing paint. During their research and development, they discovered an alkaline method of eradicating rust.

Their process was known to a few local street rodders in the early '60s. But because Southern California cars were blessed with less rust than those in most other areas of the country, it didn't gather a significant following.

Today, when *every* old car is a potential street rod, safe rust removal has the highest priority. Fortunately, this outstanding service is available to rod builders throughout the United States (and parts of Canada, too) because Redi-Strip has franchised branches in nearly 24 metropolitan areas.

Their process is often confused with acid bathing. Racers dip stock bodies into a mild hydrochloric acid to thin the metal and save weight. As far as street-rod bodies are concerned, removing good metal is unacceptable. We want every fraction of an inch intact.

Dipping car metal in hydrochloric acid also causes *hydrogen embrittlement*. This is a condition in which free hydrogen molecules work their way into the metal's core and eventually cause brittleness, which causes cracks. Old car metal has its share of fatigue to start with.

Redi-Strip only removes rust and non-metallic coatings such as paint or rubberized undercoatings; no metal. When your pride and joy is lifted from Redi-Strip's bubbling caldrons, it is as close to new metal as it can be.

Derusting at Redi-Strip takes place as follows: The chemical solution in the dipping tanks is charged with direct current. The part being derusted is the *cathode* or negative electrode. Rust molecules are released from its surface and every crack and crevice in the body or component. Rust and paint settle to the tank's bottom; lighter coatings disperse and float about the solution.

There are two Redi-Strip processes: one for removing paint and similar coatings, and another that strips surface oxidation. So, a part can be derusted without damaging desired surface coatings. Or, one that isn't rusty need not be subjected to the derusting process if removing paint is all that's necessary.

The combined process will remove just about anything that is brushed, glued, splattered, sprayed, forming or growing on metal except chrome plating. It will remove: acrylics, asphalt, chromate, enamel, epoxy, lacquer, latex, plastic body filler, resins, synthetic rubberized compounds, shellac, tar, urethane, varnish and even zinc!

Redi-Strip's first step for derusting an automobile body is usually paint stripping. Although the body need not be completely disassembled, efficiency is improved if doors, fenders and so forth are removed. The window glass should be removed, not only to protect it, but to ensure that the stripping solution can get down into all those little pockets. The paint stripper is chemically similar to hot-tank caustics, so be careful what you leave on the car. Some of the wood supports will swell and plywood glues will dissolve.

Complete stripping of tough original paint and all interior undercoating used on old Ford bodies takes from two to three days. Fenders and smaller components require less time. When the body or part is removed from the stripping tanks, it is brought over to a large concrete pad. Here, the soft paint goop still clinging is hosed off with high-pressure hot water. After this cleaning, the rusty, but paint-free body, is ready for the second step.

Some precautions are required before the body or component goes into the derusting tanks. Because the rust removal solution is compounded to remove oxidation from steel, it adversely affects most die-cast soft-metal alloys, aluminum, brass, copper and lead. When practical, all components made of these materials should be removed from the body, or they will be damaged. In fact, some die-cast pot metals will completely dissolve. No need to worry about stainless steel, though. You are responsible for detaching these parts before taking the body to Redi-Strip.

I have seen the results of Redi-Strip's operation dozens of times, and never cease to be impressed. The rod builder unfamiliar with or skeptical of this method should submit a sample to evaluate their capabilities. I suggest that you, too, will be amazed. Every square inch of metal is "in the white"—totally bare—showing only the die-forming marks of when the piece was originally stamped in the 1930s or '40s.

One more step in derusting is worth its cost. After the body is removed from the

Before vintage-tin restoration can begin, remove every spec of paint and rust. Rust, by far, is the most difficult to remove. That's where the services of Redi-Strip come in handy.

Body and frame of seasoned '34 was quickly immersed in paint-stripping tank, first of two separate Redi-Strip processes.

From paint tank, body and frame went to rust-removal tank. A relatively small body such as this only requires two or three days in each tank. My '40 coupe took a week in each.

A week or so later, body and frame were completely stripped of paint, thoroughly derusted, phosphated, and ready for mucho metalwork, particularly the frame.

Dark spots are areas that never rusted. Lighter spots are those that were substantially rusted, meaning the metal is thinner there.

It was once customary to "lead-in" the cowl vent; a truly despicable act. A good lead job, however, is not significantly affected by Redi-Strip.

Coupe body after *phosphating*—dipped in mild phosphate solution to prepare it for primer-sealer. This should be applied soon after body is brought home.

What's that you say, you don't want to do metalwork? If you have a 1929—32 Chevy, you can obtain new rear fenders from Bow Tie Reproductions. How's that for a major time saver?

tanks and is drying, a white residue forms on its surface. This is a solution byproduct that is a preservative. It is water soluble, however. If wetted or washed off, the metal begins to oxidize. In fact, faster than ever because there is no paint or other protective coating. As long as the metal is kept dry, no rust will form. When it's time to paint, meticulously scrub off the white coating. Otherwise, nothing will stick.

I recommend that Redi-Strip *phosphate* the body or component right after derusting. Phosphating is similar to metal-prep solutions painters use before they apply primer. Next, spray the part with a quality primer/sealer as soon as you get it home. It can be tucked away in dry storage until the bodywork begins in earnest.

SHOULD YOU ATTEMPT METALWORK?

If you're not a professional metal fabricator—or at least have the skills—don't take the chance of ruining a costly fender by doing your own metalwork. My purpose isn't to stop your do-it-yourself desires, but I'm not going mislead you about metalworking skills that take time to master.

It's unrealistic to expect a single chapter here to explain all phases of metalworking auto bodies. For thorough explanations of professional techniques and how to apply them, see HPBooks': *Metal Fabricator's Handbook* and *Paint & Body Handbook*.

Basic auto metalworking tools and techniques are the same for both early and late model cars, stockers and custom jobs. Still, there are specific considerations to remember about converting an early automobile into a street rod. We'll concentrate on those next.

Metalworking Fundamentals—The sheet metal used in manufacturing pre-WWII auto bodies was low-carbon steel typically in the 20-gage range. This relatively soft low-carbon steel lends itself to factory stamping. It's also easier to repair than the tougher steels used today.

Some metals are more *elastic* than others. They return to original size and shape when deforming external forces are removed. Although a metal is elastic for a range of stress or force, if that limit is exceeded, the metal becomes *plastic*—it permanently deforms. When the force is removed, it doesn't return to its original shape.

Plasticity is what makes the manufacture of sheet-metal products possible. Plastic deformation without heat occurs when flat sheet metal is turned into a body panel, hood or fender in a giant metal-stamping press. Plasticity allows you to reshape it, or *cold form* it—shaped without applying significant heat—without breaking or cracking. Large machines do this at the factory. But, repair shops and you have to use heat for some metal reshaping. That's why recognizing heat ranges by color is so important when working sheet metal.

When steel is heated beyond 400F (205C) its color goes from pale to dark yellow, then brown, purple, and into shades of blue. It grows darker until the temperature reaches 600F (315C). After that, the dark blue fades to gray or green. It begins turning red at about 900F (483C), and stays dull red until 1550F (844C), when the brightness increases to

SHEET STEEL GAGE

Manufacturers Standard Gage Number:	Inch Equivalent For Steel Sheet Thickness
10	0.1345
11	0.1196
12	0.1046
13	0.0897
14	0.0747
15	0.0673
16	0.0598
17	0.0538
18	0.0478
19	0.0418
20	0.0359
21	0.0329
22	0.0299
23	0.0269
24	0.0239
25	0.0209
26	0.0179
27	0.0164
28	0.0149
29	0.0135
30	0.0120

what is commonly called *cherry red*. As the temperature rises, the color changes to orange, then yellow and finally white. At that point, approximately 2600F (1428C), most of the common alloys begin to melt.

Heat causes several reactions in auto sheet metal, including *scale* that forms on the backside of body panels when a heated area is exposed to oxygen. Other reactions are changes in grain structure and expansion, which affect hardness and cause warping, respectively.

Basic Metalworking Handtools—You can't do metalworking without the proper tools. Gas welders or disc sanders can be used for many shop applications. But, bodyworking tools, such as hammers, dollies, spoons and vixen files, are relatively useless except for metalworking.

Hammers—Body hammers are the most basic of all fender-bending tools. There are a variety of styles and weights. Most are two-headed combination hammers. One head typically has a large, flat face designed to distribute the force of the blow over a panel's surface. The head has a flat spot in its center which blends into a slightly curved edge. This shape is designed to avoid putting sharp edges in the panel. The combination hammer's other head is usually pointed and is called the *picking* end. It is designed to raise small low spots in the panel.

Dolly—Hammers are seldom used by themselves to work metal. They are often used with a companion tool called the *dolly block* that backs up the metal. Dollies have variety too. There are general-purpose dollies for deep-skirted fenders and shrinking. *Heel* dollies are used for sharp corners and wide radii. *Toe* dollies are for dinging flat surfaces. *Loaf* dollies are suitable for roughing out metal. *Fender* dollies are for working angles, creases and curves in body panels and fenders.

A dolly is not merely an anvil; its working face is used to raise a panel whether it's struck directly by the hammer or hit nearby. Dollies usually weigh several times as much as hammers, and are sometimes used as hammers, too.

Spoons—Similiar to dollies, but not quite so basic to an amateur's needs are various bodyworking spoons. They look something like thick, bent butter knives with one relatively flat end. Spoons are used for hammering, slapping and surface metal finishing when it's necessary to spread a blow's force over a larger area. They are also used as pry bars in tight places.

Shears—You sometimes can't proceed with repairing an old car body without trimming out badly damaged or rusty sections of sheet metal. A welding torch's cutting attachment is one way of doing so, but special body-panel cutters do a neater and better job. These shears leave clean-cut edges required when replacement patch panels are butted against older sections.

Other metal-cutting shears will be needed sooner or later if you pursue auto bodywork. At least three types are required: straight cut, right cut and left cut. Beyond these, tinner's snips and other small metal snips will be useful.

Files—Some of the most important metal-working tools are a selection of flexible body files. The file holder has a large handle and turnbuckle for a range of concave and convex adjustments. A permanently attached strap accepts 14-in. blades of various shapes and cutting grades.

Files only cut in one direction, and they should be moved in the direction of the flattest section of the panel being straightened. This way, the teeth's cutting edge will rake across the high spots and untouched low spots can be easily seen. It is good practice during filing to turn the file a little to one side to get the maximum cut with its curved teeth. High and low spots that show up during filing can be reworked or filled in.

Disc Sander/Grinder—This tool is useful for removing paint and rust, and shaping lead and plastic filler. Although air-drive sanders are fine in many light-duty applications, electric disc sander/grinders are best for medium and heavy-duty jobs. These are available in ranges from 3/8 to 1-1/2 HP.

The disc pad usually has a 6-, 7- or 9-in. diameter and plenty of flexible sanding discs are available. Discs have a stiff fiberboard backing with aluminum oxide or another abrasive coating. Grit coarseness is indexed numerically and by *open-coat* and *closed-coat*.

Open-coated discs are used for removing paint and other soft materials—to reduce clogging—and closed-coat discs are used for most steel cutting.

Gas-Welding Torch—A basic gas-welding set is essential for bodywork. It should have:

- Oxygen regulator with low- and high-pressure gauges.
- Acetylene regulator with low- and high-pressure gauges.
- 20 feet of hose.
- Torch and cutting attachment with selection of tips.
- Lighter, goggles, tip cleaners, leather welding gloves, soapstone for marking metal.
- Selection of welding rod and flux-coated brazing rod.

High-pressure gauges indicate supply pressure in the cylinders; low-pressure gauges indicate delivery pressure at the torch.

Pressure-reduction regulators are delicate devices designed to reduce the pressurized gas in the bottles to working-line pressures.

There are two types of regulators. The *single-stage* regulator will compensate for slight delivery pressure changes. *Two-stage* regulators are best for most bodywork and other rod-building tasks requiring a constant delivery pressure over *varying* inlet pressures.

For safety, all oxygen and compressed air hoses are green and right-hand threaded. All fuel—acetylene or hydrogen—hoses are red and left-hand threaded.

An equal-pressure welding torch allows oxygen and fuel to flow together in equal amounts. Oxygen flows through an inner tube in the torch handle and is directed through the center hole at the tip. Acetylene flows through orifices that surround the oxygen port, but exits at the center hole in the tip. Knobs attached to the handle adjust oxygen and fuel mixture. Welding tips are selected according to the gage of the metal being welded. Smaller tips are used for bodywork and most other rod-building tasks.

Although not normally used in bodywork, the cutting attachment is invaluable around a shop. Besides oxygen- and fuel-adjustment valves, it has a third valve that releases a jet of high-pressure oxygen through the tip. The tip has an orifice in its center for oxygen flow and several others surrounding it for the pre-heat flame.

You'll need welding gas *bottles* (cylinders). Many welding supply houses will work out an arrangement where you can keep a pair of bottles for as long as you need them. You exchange the empties for a fresh pair when you run out, with no delay. Unless you lack the space, get the biggest bottles you can afford.

You'll always run out of oxygen before acetylene. Its consumption rate is 1.1 times that of acetylene when a neutral flame is used. Chain both gas cylinders upright to something stable: a sturdy cart, workbench or a stout wall hook. If a high-pressure oxygen bottle falls over and the valve breaks, it will blast off like a misguided missile, probably through the garage wall and who knows what!

Goggles are a must. Working with gloves on may take some practice, but you only have to burn the hair off your fingers once to know how useful they are.

Basic Metalwork Technique—Hammers and dollies are used at the start of bodywork for *bumping*—bringing the panel into rough shape. It may seem more an art than a science, but it's within your capability if you practice. Begin practicing on a fender—not a good one. Don't saddle yourself with the stress of making a practice job perfect.

Buy an extra fender for your car. It needs to be reasonably solid and bolted to the car. Few professionals would chase a loose fender around with a hammer, so why should you? Consider the fender's price an investment in developing your metalworking skills. Besides, you can always sell it to a novice after you've mastered the skill!

The basic technique of hammer-and-dolly work is learning to swing the hammer accurately and with just the right amount of force so it bounces back after the blow. During the blow, the dolly must *not* bounce away from the panel. It should remain in contact with it as much as possible.

Hammer-On—In this hammer-and-dolly work, the hammer strikes the high spot of the damaged area and the dolly backs up the blow. The usual sequence is to start in the middle, but to move quickly to and concentrate around, the circumference of the damaged area.

Hammer-Off—This is another bodyworking method. The dolly is not exactly opposite the hammer blow, but rather off to one side and under the low spot. The hammer blow pushes the high spot down while the dolly forces the low spot up. Yes, plenty of practice is necessary before you can do this well. But an old fender and an in-depth discussion of the correct technique—see HPBooks' *Paint & Body Handbook*—will be invaluable.

Hole Filling With Solder—Holes and punctures up to 1/8-in. diameter can be filled with solder. Holes bigger than that will usually require a metal patch. Pieces cut from a food tin are ideal because they are lightweight and don't require too much heat for solid bonding.

Of course, such imperfections can be welded, brazed or leaded-in. Simple soldering has this advantage over conventional metalworking: The repaired panel isn't heated excessively and distortion can be minimized. The melting point of most lead-tin solders is 361—437F (183—225C), which is far less than the heat required for the other approaches.

Soldering is straightforward. First, thoroughly clean and *tin* the surface to get the solder to adhere. When filling a hole with solder alone, bevel the edge of the metal slightly with a small rat-tail file for a better bond. *Acid-core solder* melted onto the pre-heated work area works quite well for tinning. The soldering-gun tip must be tinned, too, so oxidation won't interfere with the bond during soldering.

After tinning, the work area will be bright and shiny. Then, more solder can be melted in to fill the hole. *Flux* is necessary when soldering to chemically clean and remove any oil or oxides that might accumulate. A *rosin-core solder* will do this.

Deuce roadster body after Redi-Strip and sealing, a perfect example of valuable sheet metal that can be more quickly put back in street service with the addition of a reproduction *patch panel.*

One item in long list of patch panels available from the V-8 Shop is stamped-steel, perfectly contoured 1933—34 Ford wheel well with all stiffening ribs. Photo courtesy Joe Mayall.

In soldering, only enough heat is applied to keep the solder plastic. The broad tip of the soldering iron or gun is used to spread the solder. Work slowly around the hole's edge to fill it in.

A thin metal patch is necessary for 1/4-in. or larger holes. Outline the hole on a piece of scrap, then slightly taper and tin the hole's edges. Bond and blend in the patch with solder. Spread more solder over the patch's face after the joint has cooled.

After soldering is complete and cooled, clean off excess resin with lacquer thinner. The filled patch can then be ground down with a #36 or finer open-coat disc.

Patch Panels—My '40 Ford coupe was rear-ended. Although far from totaled, the damage was severe enough to buckle the frame and tear the engine and transmission off their mounts. The deck lid was badly dented and warped, and the panel below it was mangled. This repair was going to be expensive.

Fortunately, I had the room and cooperative neighbors to stash a couple of spare coupe bodies in my backyard. One of them had a fairly decent deck lid, and the other a salvageable deck panel. Out came the torch for the sections I needed.

Howell's Sheetmetal Company offers repro '32 Ford five-window and roadster trunk floor pan in case you must deal with rust-out in this vulnerable area.

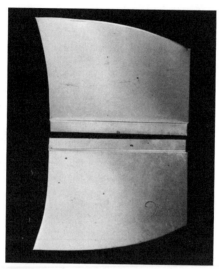

If you have a "reel steel" '29, you may need one of these bolt-on cowl panels from Howell's Sheetmetal Company.

The result of my vintage-tin hording was a well-repaired rear end at a moderate price. Today, both parts cars and moderate repair bills are memories. Your best resource now is the first-class reproduction sheet metal industry.

This industry isn't a newcomer. It's been active since the '50s. Much of the early pieces were manufactured in Argentina and primarily aimed at the Model T and A restorer. Even though the panels weren't perfect replacements, they were better than none at all. In the mid-'70s, the quality of sheet metal replacement panels improved. Nowadays, a dozen catalogs specify nearly everything you might need for the early Ford and other models.

Installing Patch Panels—Discretion is the better part of economic valor when it comes to major metalwork on a valuable vintage body. Don't learn a skilled trade on a $5000 early-Ford coupe. Nevertheless, if you've done gas-welding on light-gage sheet metal, and know how body metal responds to heat, in-

As I mentioned earlier, floorboards of *every* old car are likely to have met with ravages of time or acts of short-sighted '50s rod builders. Dennis Carpenter to the rescue if you have a 1939 or 1940 Ford.

stalling a reproduction panel is within your skills.

Veteran body repairers often speak of *crowns,* a term that refers to a panel's curvature. There are four classifications of crowns in automotive sheet metal panels: low curvature, high curvature, a combination of both, and reverse curvature.

Panels with *low crown* have very little curvature, and very little load-carrying ability. The full metal roof first used on the mid-1930s Fords is an example of a low-crown panel. A *high-crown* panel curves rapidly in all directions. Think of a 1940 Ford front fender; that's a high-crown panel. It is strong and resists deformation.

Combination high- and low-crown panels are used in several places on early cars, most notably in the doors. These, too, are quite strong and require little reinforcement. *Reverse crowns* are rare in the simple designs of 1930—'40s cars. They are found in '50s and later cars. An example is the flaring out of a fender's section to accept a taillight assembly. Duplicating this effect is called *Frenching* among customizers.

Most flat patch panels are large enough to replace more than the rusted-out area. For example, the expected rust-out in a 1934 lower cowl panel is perhaps 2 X 6 in. The replacement panel will be 6 X 12 in. You'll have to judge how much of it is necessary for the repair. It's usually better to keep weld beads—and heat—to a minimum, so the smaller the patch, the better.

Mark the area to be removed with a heavy black line. Then trim the patch panel to fit. *Don't cut out any body section* until you've carefully matched the patch to the pattern.

Don't end up with a patch that is 1/8-in. smaller than the cut-out it's filling.

Cut out the section of original metal with "cold tools," a rotary pneumatic or electric cutter, or appropriate metal snips. Avoid using heat. Don't cause any more warpage than absolutely necessary, and remember there are structures behind the panel that must be preserved.

Damage behind a rusted panel can be more extensive than you assumed. If so, internal repair will be needed. Rusted-out sheet metal should be cut away and new pieces welded in. An interior, out-of-sight repair doesn't require the same cosmetic attention as an exterior one, but don't be sloppy, either.

Next, hold the patch panel to the body with C-clamps and tack it in using low heat and mild-steel rod. Readjust and fit it as required as you proceed. Once it absorbs heat, the panel will seem to have a mind of its own. Place the tacks 2—3 in. apart and let each cool a bit before starting the next. Bodyworkers differ in their approach, but many recommend tacking one full-length seam at a time. If the panel seems to absorb too much heat, apply a damp rag to help cool it.

The tedious part of this job is the final welding. A bead must be run all the way around the patch with precision and patience or the panel will warp.

After the replacement panel is fully welded, grind off the excess bead. The seam need not be any thicker than the gage for strength. A disc sander/grinder is the best tool for this job, but a small air-driven sander and drill motor are adequate as long as the proper grit disc is used. Avoid grinding with too much pressure or you'll gouge the surrounding metal. Carelessness here could spoil an otherwise good job.

Hammer-Welding—I've assumed that if you use the previous method of installing a panel, you'll use lead or plastic filler to cover the weld. The next step up in quality is *hammer-welding* and *metal shrinking*. They require more experience and skill than simply welding sheet metal.

Hammer-welding involves working a hot weld with hammer and dolly. The bead is worked into the base metal and only a thin, discolored line reveals the touching edges of original metal and patch panel.

The first step in hammer-welding is to precisely fit the patch panel to the cut-out in the body or fender. If there is much of a gap, the job simply won't turn out well. The patch is tack-welded in as before, with a tack every 2—3 in. Work quickly and carefully to minimize heat distortion.

Once the panel is tacked in place, select a broad, flat-faced body hammer and a dolly that matches the contour of the work area.

Pete, expert metalman at Fast Johnny's Speed Shop, points out poor repair job to lower deck panel. Problem was quickly repaired with fresh patch panel.

Old panel was cut out with an air chisel. Note that cut was made well inside original mating lines to preserve them.

Pete then cut out a little more of original panel with rotary cutter, but still inside mating line.

Final cuts are made after checking fit of patch panel.

Hammer-welding requires alternating torch heat with hammer-and-dolly work. Switch from torch to hammer and dolly every few minutes, and prepare a safe, handy place to store each when using the other.

The technique works best when short sections of the seam—2 in. at the most—are welded in and then followed by hammer-and-dolly work while the joint is still hot. To work the weld bead down into the surrounding metal, move rapidly from torch to hammer before cooling sets in.

Add a minimum of filler rod. It's that much more metal to be worked. The key to successful hammer-welding is in the ability to weld and follow up with hammer work before the weld cools. But admittedly, that's easier said than done.

Metal Shrinking—Depending upon how well you master patch-panel installation and hammer-welding, there will be some lumpiness in the end product. The artful way of smoothing it out is by metal shrinking.

Metal shrinking is just what its name implies: reducing raised or stretched places in

worked sheet metal by heating, gentle hammering and rapid cooling. Depressed areas are *leveled* similarly.

It is a painstaking process. Small sections of panel are worked a little at a time. Hammer force is concentrated on the heated area and, as the metal cools, it draws slowly inward. With lots of practice, the desired shrinking can be achieved with minimal hammer-and-dolly work. Overworking the metal with a hammer and dolly can cause excess shrinking when it cools, which adds to the overall distortion. Shrinkage can be controlled by using a wet cloth to speed cooling.

A dolly can be used as a hammer from the underside to raise the metal. Then, shrinking is used to flatten and reform the metal to the desired shape. Different metals require different amounts of heat. Learning how much to apply for how long requires practice.

One indicator of a metal's temperature is the size of the blue ring that develops on it around the torch flame. The metal is soft inside this ring: It's the area that can be worked with effectiveness.

Less ambitious patch-panel installation is flat, single-thickness Model A cowl panel. As above, damaged area is carefully noted and trimmed out.

Patch is then clamped in place and tack-welded. Use mild-steel rod and low heat to minimize warpage. Wear goggles!

When satisfied with fit, panel can be fully welded. Remember: Keep heat as low as possible . . . and wear goggles.

When weld has cooled, edges are re-formed with hammer and dolly. Basic body hammer can be used for this and a thousand other repair jobs.

Take care when grinding welds on sheet metal. Too much force and heat will gouge and distort entire patch. Seam must be smooth, however.

Small holes and other minor imperfections don't need aid of welding torch. Piece of metal trimmed from a tin can, some solder and a soldering iron can be used to fill hole in hood panel . . . or a hundred holes in firewall!

Like so much metalworking, panel shrinking is one that requires considerable practice before perfection can be achieved. If you aspire to a satisfactory level of work, you can look forward to long hours on a practice fender. But that's better than ruining a good fender.

Filler—This is the material used to smooth a repaired section after welding, hammering and shrinking. There are two types of body filler: lead and what is commonly called *plastic*. Lead was used exclusively for many years, and is generally preferred over plastic by many traditional rod builders. Often, I think, just because it is traditional.

I don't want to rekindle the debate about which is best. Either material properly used will result in a satisfactory job. It is true, however, that more experience and skill are required in lead work. It has developed a certain mystique and desirability over the years.

Leading—It is tempting to think of lead work as a lost art, but it isn't. Like hammer-welding and metal shrinking, it is just not economical for the body shop geared for maximum profit in the least time. If you want professional lead work, you must find some-

one with ability and time to do a correct job. This service will not come cheap.

Lead is the time-honored metal filler. In general, the better the metalworking job, the less the filler. Even so, it's not practical to pound and grind away at a panel until it's smooth enough to paint.

Lead must be applied with heat. Its melting point is low enough to keep body-metal distortion to a minimum. And its expansion rate is closer than plastic's to that of 20-gage sheet metal used in early car bodies. If a lead job is done well, it will not crack or peel away from a repaired surface. All in all, lead actually makes the repair job easier, but it does require more talent and time.

Lead typically used in quality metalwork is a mixture of about 70% lead and 30% tin. The major tool required is an oxyacetylene-welding outfit with a *leading tip* that fits over the conventional tip and passes only acetylene.

Holes in the leading tip draw in air to support the acetylene combustion and produce a flared, gentle flame for melting the lead without warping the sheet metal.

You'll need a flat, stubby hardwood paddle to move the soft metal around, and a tray of

beeswax to coat the paddle so that hot lead doesn't stick to it. Get some tinning compound specifically designed for body leading, and coarse steel wool to apply it.

These tools are for applying the lead. Some of it will have to be removed. For that, use a flat and a curved *vixen file*. These files have well-spaced, curved cutting edges that won't load up while the lead is being planed. A sanding block and a supply of #80-grit sandpaper are needed for finishing work.

Before beginning the lead work, grind all paint, primer and old lead off the panel. The area to be leaded must be exceptionally clean or the lead won't adhere. If a panel that was once leaded is being refinished, check for pits or holes that may leach old tinning residue. These show up as small dark spots in the metal. If not worked out, the residue can prevent the new lead from sticking.

Once the work area is clean, heat it and brush on the tinning compound with steel wool held in a pair of rusty pliers. The acid-based tinning compound cleans the work surface. The small amount of lead in the compound remains as a thin coating of lead on the sheet metal. This helps to bond the body lead to the surface.

Filler must be used in virtually every metal-repair job, be it done by professional Phil King, or a street rodder like you and me. *Bondo*, first and foremost plastic filler, must be mixed on a clean surface.

Filler is applied to roughed repair area with commercial plastic paddle. After drying—not rock hard—"cheese grater" is used to shave off excess material.

Block sand, first with relative coarse paper, then #220 grit, and finally #400 grit—wet or dry. Don't sand too hard. Following sanding, prime panel.

Spreading the tinning compound over a larger area of the sheet metal than needed will ensure an adequately clean and prepared work surface. Let the area cool after it is tinned. Then wash the surface with tap water to rinse away remaining acid.

Next, apply lead to the area. Best results are achieved with a thin coating. Don't build up more than a 1/4-in. If more lead is needed to fill the low spot, more hammer-and-dolly work is probably needed.

The key to successfully applying lead is mastering the paddle. Heat the beeswax until it starts to melt and forms a slick surface on the paddle's bottom. Then melt enough lead onto the tinned surface to complete the job. The molten lead shouldn't stick to the waxed paddle.

First, practice leading on a horizontal panel. Practice leading a vertical panel after you've better mastered the technique.

Avoid overheating the metal when melting and flowing the lead. As soon as there is sufficient lead melted on the work area, start shaping it to the desired contour with the waxed paddle. Keep the torch moving all the time.

Work the lead as smooth as possible to reduce the filing and shaping yet to come. Excess lead can be spread onto the untinned metal and discarded, it will not stick to metal that hasn't been tinned.

When the lead has cooled, it can be shaped with vixen files, then finished with #80 sandpaper on a sanding block. If any depressed areas are noted during filing, a pecking hammer can be used to raise them from the back. Then file the high spot smooth.

Plastic Body Fillers—A new word entered the street rodder's vocabulary during the mid-'50s: *Bondo*. This is another registered trademark that has become a generic term. Dynatron/Bondo Corporation's product, Bondo Plastic Filler, *Bondo*, for short, has become synonymous with plastic fillers.

Bondo, and most of the plastic fillers that

followed it, are compounded from a putty-like resin base and a syrupy hardener. As long as the two remain separate, they stay pliable. Once some hardener is mixed into the resin, the compound hardens in a few minutes.

Plastic fillers, in their characteristic pink, green, gray or black, were looked down upon by most custom and street-rod builders when they first appeared—and for some time afterward. Their quality has improved since the '50s. Today's plastic filler will easily last as long as lead.

When properly applied, high-quality modern plastic filler will produce a hard finish. It will not crack, shrink or lift off the base metal even under extreme operating conditions and temperatures.

Avoid "economy" fillers. Major companies have paid their dues over the years, so take advantage of this and use their superior products even though the price may be higher.

Also, avoid the many economy fiberglass repair kits. Although major brand names are of good quality, they are primarily designed to repair damage in fiberglass bodies. They will work reasonably well on metal bodies for repairing a small rust spot. But, there usually isn't enough material for the type of repair job we're discussing.

Plastic fillers won't last if they are used in body areas subjected to stress and flexing. We can't overlook that the bolt-together body of the '30s and '40s is, under the best of circumstances, a "flexy flier." Those billowy fenders flop around in the wind! Don't use plastic fillers in an exposed edge because they will chip away. Repair edges with lead.

Applying Plastic Filler—As in all bodywork, the surface of the repair area must be clean and dry. All paint and rust must be removed, and the surface cleaned with lacquer thinner.

Plastic filler won't adhere to a super-smooth surface as well as it will to one with a bit of roughness. So, scuff it with a sander/grinder using a #24-grit open-coat disc.

Next, follow the manufacturer's directions for mixing resin and hardener. Usually a few drops of hardener are mixed into a golf-ball-sized wad of resin. The mixture takes about 30 minutes to harden at room temperature. The resin and hardener can be mixed on plastic palettes and applied with plastic applicators. Both are available at auto paint supply stores. But bodyworkers have used everything from cardboard to coffee can lids for applicators.

Apply the filler as soon as the hardener is worked in. Use an applicator flexible enough to follow the contours of the fender or panel. Remember, you must work within the drying time limit of the filler.

Don't apply more than a 1/4-in.-thick coating of filler during any one application. Apply it in the shallowest part of the repair area first. Work out any bubbles. Small applications are best, with adequate drying time between coats. Take care that no filler gets on surrounding painted areas. Aside from being a sloppy job, the filler won't adhere properly and will start to lift from the panel.

The most popular tool used for shaping plastic filler, called the *Surform cheese grater*, is manufactured by Stanley Tool Company. There are several styles of blade holders. They use replaceable steel blades with a non-clogging design that passes the shavings through the teeth openings. Flat, half-round, and round blades are available.

It's not necessary or even desirable for the completed filling to be rock hard before beginning to shape it. Work can start as soon as it is firm, and long shavings will pass through the teeth of the cheese grater. Use a light touch with a fresh blade when shaping with a cheese grater.

When shaping is almost completed, let the filler harden completely. Finishing touches are made with a regular body file, then #180 and progressively finer grits of sandpaper.

Turn to the Supplier Index for a listing of reproduction sheet-metal components.

25 'Glasswork

Fully reinforced 'glass body is no featherweight. You'll need some helping hands to set body on frame.

Inspect the New Arrival—The day that freight truck pulls up to your house with a crated fiberglass repro body will be a memorable one if you're a first-time street-rod builder. Let's hope it will be a happy one, too. The joy of taking delivery of your brand new 'glass body fuels the fire of resolve to build a street rod. But sometimes not if shipping damage is discovered.

I dislike beginning this chapter on a negative note, but having been on the receiving end of damaged goods once or twice, I have found that the time to inspect a new shipment is right now; the time to complain is immediately after damage is found.

Fiberglass bodies are big and unwieldy, and occasionally they get smacked about a bit. Not always, but enough to warrant a careful inspection of every square inch of exterior 'glass. If, indeed, damage is found, immediately photograph it and contact the manufacturer. He will advise you of the steps to take. These words to the wise should be sufficient to cover the bases insofar as shipping problems go.

Now, let's jump right into the main thrust of this chapter—getting the 'glass body ready for its more-or-less permanent installation on a rolling chassis.

Supplemental Work on the New 'Glass Body—For our purposes, supplemental work is that work necessary to ready a fiberglass body for permanent installation, both inside and out. This work excludes paint prep, which is covered in the next chapter.

The amount of supplemental 'glasswork required on even the least costly bodies currently available is well within the skill range of the average hot rodder, so you should be able to handle this work. Even if you make mistakes, you can just as easily correct them. That alone makes the 'glass-repro street-rod body an awfully attractive alternative to high-dollar vintage tin.

There are several grades of fiberglass bodies and, in most cases, they are easily categorized by their prices. The most expensive grades require the least *supplemental work* prior to painting, and the least expensive grades require the most. Those that are in the

mid-price range usually require a middling amount of work.

Supplemental work primarily includes reinforcing wood or metal and the installation of a plywood floorboard and firewall. It also includes fitting the body to the frame, hanging of doors and deck lids, fitting fenders, grille and hood, and installing dashboards, seat risers, insulation and accessories such as windshield frames. But before any of that can begin, you must be absolutely certain your repro body is bolted to the frame and aligned to it.

Initial Body Bolt-Up—The builder of a vintage-tin street rod is—or should be—aware that once the body and frame are separated, things like door jambs and deck lid openings are likely to distort. The problem is far worse in open cars than in coupes. But steel car bodies bolt back in place to their original frames fairly easily. To be sure, there will be some shimming here and there, and the doors and deck lid may have to be adjusted slightly to re-align them, but that's a straightforward operation.

Ah, but what about those repro bodies that were not stamped out on precision presses and securely welded together in the days before craftsmanship became a foreign word? Bodies that are . . . well, poured out of a can, so to speak, and then set to rest on a reproduction frame that also may or may not be an absolute mirror image of an original? We owe all street-rodding's hopes to the reproduction

Thorough inspection of newly received fiberglass body is first order of business. Damage incurred from shipping is common.

Uncrate new body and set it on frame. Installation doesn't have to be permanent, but should approximate final bolt-up.

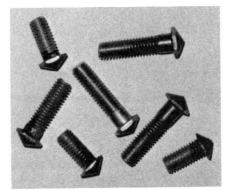

Most new 'glass bodies don't have mounting-bolt holes. Bolts with their heads ground to a point make fine marking tools. Install them in frame, then set on body.

Plan on using body shims to bring 'glass body into alignment. Shims may have to be relocated as work progresses.

body and frame industry. But no one I know is bold enough to claim perfect interchangeability between the products of a dozen different body manufacturers on one hand and an equal number of chassis builders on the other. And close doesn't count in today's street-rod building.

In short, it will take time to properly fit a 'glass repro body to a repro frame even if you have done your part to keep things on the straight and narrow.

All but the most economically priced basic fiberglass body shells are now routinely available with floorboards glassed in at the factory. And, unless you have plans for a channeled car, your best bet is to order a body with an integral firewall and floorboard, as well as latched and hinged doors and deck lid. The additional cost of this is relative to the time and effort you have to expend.

For a long time now, I have frequently recommended in print that the rod builder defer his purchase of a fiberglass body until

his chassis is at least on wheels. Even top-quality 'glass bodies that are well cured will eventually warp if they aren't supported in perfect alignment for very long. They simply must have the all-points support of a frame. In short, the day that delivery truck delivers your repro body is the day the body should be bolted to the frame. Of course, it may have to be removed a half dozen times or more, but that's alright. The point is, even a temporary shoring up is better than none at all.

Trim off any excess material along the lower edge and floorboard area. Lightly sand all edges with #220-grit paper. Even the best bodies will occasionally have a few sharp edges and burrs.

Most fiberglass bodies with integral floorboards aren't pre-drilled at the frame mounting points. Instead, these are marked by indentations. Naturally, the 'glass manufacturer has designed his body to fit on a stock frame, so most reproduction frames have the body mounting holes in the same location as

stock—more or less. Nevertheless, your first major task is to precisely position the body on the frame.

In some cases, that is fairly easy. Sometimes the contours of both body and frame are such that you can't get the body exactly in position without fanfare. However, a miss is as good as a mile. Just pinpoint the mounting holes with as much precision as you can muster. One of the best ways of doing this is the method Don McNeil of Specialized Auto Components demonstrates in the accompanying photos.

Bolts, ground to a point, are installed point up in the frame mounting holes. The body is then gingerly placed on the frame and carefully shifted into position. A gentle tap at each mounting point marks the exact center of the frame mounting points. The body is then lifted from the frame and turned upside down or placed on saw horses to expose the "center-punch" marks. All that's left to do is drill 'em out. Nothing to it.

Once this is done, the body can be securely bolted to the frame until such time as you wish to resume work on the project. In the meantime the body can sit and cure during the supplemental work. A fresh fiberglass body requires from four to six weeks to completely cure, depending upon temperatures and weather conditions. However, inasmuch as you can't know for sure when the body you have was originally laid up, it's best to begin the supplemental work as soon as possible.

Check Alignment—To check the alignment of your body, you'll need some simple tools: 25 feet of good nylon cord, two or three lightweight plumb bobs made out of big washers, and a 25-foot tape measure.

Door fit in 'glass body indicates basic alignment and compatibility to frame. Belt line at top of door should match that of cowl and deck.

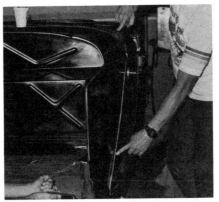

Doors should open and close with no binding or stiffness . . . and there should be absolutely no misalignment. If there is, rearrange shims until all is right.

Fiberglass bodies that sit unsupported for long can easily distort. Simple plumb bob and strings are used to check alignment.

Unfortunately, problems are not easily corrected. To re-align a 'glass body, jack it into shape and apply heat lamps.

Start by establishing a basic point of reference; your *baseline*. Assuming the frame is straight and true, its centerline will be that point. The longitudinal centerline of the frame is easily determined with a tape measure if the engine and transmission are not in place. The frame should be squarely supported on four jack stands so it's level. If the suspension has been installed, the wheels should be off the ground.

With the body well secured with bolts, find its longitudinal centerline along the floorboard using a tape measure. It should exactly correspond with the longitudinal centerline of the frame.

It's a little more difficult to find the centerline of the body on its topside. Use the decklid opening to find the centerline at the rear. The mid-point of the cowl vent is a good starting point at the front end. Drop your lightweight plumb bob straight down to find the centerline of the floorboard at the rear, and to the frame somewhere around the transmission access port at the front. Anything more than 1/4-in. or so off center could be the first indication of trouble.

In the worse case—significant cowl tilt, which will result in extremely poor door alignment—straightening the cowl section may have to be done with a body jack. Walker's Body-Jak is frequently found in rental yards that cater to automotive hobbiests. It can be placed in the cowl section with one end in the lower passenger-side corner, and the other end in the upper driver's side corner, or vice versa. With the application of heat lamps and very gradual pressure over a long time period—10—12 hours—and using your plumb bobs as well as the fit of the doors for indexing, a cowl can be brought back into alignment.

Maintaining the re-alignment, particularly in an open car body, can be a task more easily

discussed than accomplished, however. One of the best ways is to build and install a mini-roll bar. When bolted to the frame, such a structure serves two purposes: It maintains the alignment of the cowl and, at the same time, provides a strong and convenient perch for the steering column and, possibly, the pedals.

WOODING THE 'GLASS BODY

Most low- and middle-priced fiberglass bodies will require at least some additional reinforcing material. Although steel or aluminum tubing is probably more desirable than wood, the latter is better if you're short on equipment and experience.

Your tool collection should include all that's needed to add wood reinforcement to a fiberglass body—drills, saws, chisels, scissors, razor blades, putty knives and old paint brushes. The fiberglass supplies required are inexpensive and readily available at paint or hardware stores. To refresh your memory on these, re-read Chapter 4.

If the body is without floorboards or a firewall, you'll need a piece of 3/4-in. plywood big enough for one or both. Shop grade is OK, but a good grade of exterior or marine plywood is best. In any case, the plywood shouldn't have been stored outdoors at the lumber yard where it could absorb moisture. Moisture adversely affects the curing of resins.

You'll also need several 1 X 2-in. and 2 X 2-in. hardwood strips. It is best to buy a little more than you need, at least if you have return privileges on the surplus.

If the body has a built-in 'glass floorboard and firewall, it may be too flimsy. In these areas, it helps to add more structure. Because weight and additional thickness is often not a big consideration, some extra plywood stiffeners shouldn't be noticed.

In the earlier discussion of fiberglass products, I mentioned the thick, heavy sheet of non-directional spun glass fibers called *mat*, and lighter weight bi-directional *cloth*. Both can be used for supplemental reinforcement of repro bodies, but there's another type of fiberglass material—a paste-like substance called *adhesive/filler*—that's designed for bonding and filling fiberglass panels on Corvettes and the like. This non-flowing filler makes duck soup of otherwise difficult fiberglass-reinforcement jobs.

The quantity of fiberglass materials needed depends upon the degree of reinforcement necessary. When using mat or cloth, use about three times the surface area of the plywood panel to be bonded to the body. Also, use the heaviest mat and cloth available. Two gallons of resin will be adequate for a full-length floorboard and firewall.

Mix Resin—Follow closely the directions for mixing catalyst with resin. Recommendations vary from one manufacturer to another, and the exact percentage of hardener is important. If too much *catalyst* (hardener) is added, the mixture will *kick off* too quickly, possibly causing cracking. If too little is used, the result will be a sticky mess that may never harden. As in all 'glasswork, though, experiment until you find the exact amount of catalyst required for that day.

Those inexpensive cardboard paint containers sold by hardware stores are excellent for mixing resin, but only mix small quantities. Pie tins are favored by fiberglass workers as secondary containers for spreading resin.

On mild or warm days, it normally takes about 30 minutes for well-saturated mat and cloth to set-up. This provides the time needed to work out air bubbles and excess resin. It also allows you to shift the mat or cloth around if necessary.

Economy 'glass body can be a good buy if you are willing to invest additional time to the project. Installation of floorboard and firewall are two biggest tasks, with hanging of doors a close third.

Taken one step at a time, however, none of the tasks are that formidable. Lots of patience is required, first in laying out floorboard . . .

. . . and then laying it in. If you're building a channelled roadster, you'll find that the money savings justifies the additional effort.

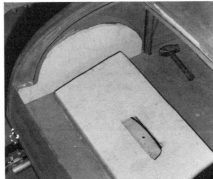

'Glass roadsters that will have rumble seats sometimes need more reinforcing than manufacturer provides. After plywood is cut to size, adhesive/filler is applied to floorboard . . .

. . . and plywood is set in place. Floor will now support two adults.

Beauty of working with fiberglass is ease with which it conforms to irregular patterns. Transmission tunnel is a perfect example. Lengths of welding rod makes a bridge on which 'glass mat and cloth is laid.

Don't forget that the batch of catalyzed resin in the can is kicking, too. It only takes one oversight for you to forever remember that you must apply catalyzed resin as soon as possible. As you gain experience, you'll quickly learn how much you can handle before disaster strikes in the form of a batch of hardened resin.

Get one gallon of acetone for clean-up. Acetone is both toxic and flammable, however, so use it with utmost care. Some folks simply cannot work with gloves, but if sensitive skin is a problem, wear rubber gloves when working with fiberglass.

The key to maximum strength when reinforcing a fiberglass body with wood is not how much or how thick the plywood is, but how well the mat and cloth is saturated with resin and the number of bonding layers used. In short, the more substantial the fiberglass lamination, the greater the strength.

INSTALLING 'GLASS FENDERS—If I had my way, all early-model street rods would be fenderless just like the original dry lakes jobs of the '30s and '40s. I admit, though, that some street rods benefit from the full-fendered "look"—in the Ford line, from 1935 on for certain. In fact, many feel that 1933—34 models don't look right without fenders unless they are channeled. Beyond cosmetics, of course, is the Motor Vehicle Code. Few states permit anything but the flyweights to run around fenderless.

Therefore, in the interest of keeping your car street legal, let's look at installing fenders. This is not much of a problem for "reel steel" guys, but sometimes a real headache for the 'glass bunch.

Fiberglass fenders, particularly the fronts, have a way of flexing and splitting on early models. The rears fit nicely on most cars because there's enough structure for attaching

A little supplemental reinforcing on new 'glass components pays off in fewer cracks, particularly in open cars. Corvette adhesive/filler is a favorite of many pro 'glassers for such work.

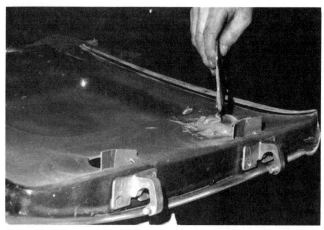

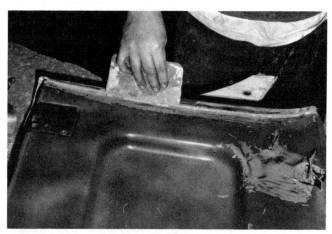

Adhesive/filler is excellent for adding much-needed reinforcement behind door hinges.

Adhesive/filler is also useful for additional bonding of 'glass panels that will take a beating. Doors certainly fall into this category.

them to. Also, the fenders are relatively light. On most early models, however, the front fenders are fairly heavy and all that weight is flopping around in the wind, largely unsupported. Although the quality of modern fiberglass fenders is vastly superior to those of the '70s and earlier, stress cracks eventually appear.

Unfortunately, there is no cure-all for the cracking problem. About all you can do is make sure that fender-attaching points are beefy. Some builders add a few layers of cloth on the inside of the body and the underside of the fender in attaching areas. Oversize nut plates or fender washers should always be used to distribute the load at the fender well. Of course, substantial stock-type fender braces—where originally used—are critical. And again, some builders add a second or third brace. Such braces are easily fabricated and can be designed so they follow the inside contours of the fenders. In short, anything that can be discreetly done to stabilize and support the front fenders will be worth the effort.

Just as with the body and doors, trim off any excess material and lightly sand the edges of the fenders and splash aprons with #220-grit paper.

The majority of fiberglass fenders, splash aprons and similar bolt-on components are not pre-drilled. They, too, have impressions or other bolt-hole indexes. You must take considerable care in first locating and then securing components to the body proper. In most cases, this is an advantage, for you can more precisely fit the part to your particular car, although it requires additional effort.

Mount Hardware—The first pieces to mount on a 1927—34 Ford based repro street

rod are the running boards—and splash aprons when used. These components are the least likely to be misaligned and, to a large extent, they determine the exact location of both rear and front fenders. Before they are installed however, be sure the support brackets are not kinked or bent.

It's almost impossible to properly install fenders and the like without some help, so don't try it alone. Depending on the mounting arrangements for your car and the as-delivered readiness of the components, several small C-clamps may also be needed to temporarily attach the running boards to frame or brackets. When clamping or bolting fiberglass, however, remember that it is brittle. Too much pressure will crack the 'glass.

Once the running boards are clamped or bolted in place, and repeated checking con-

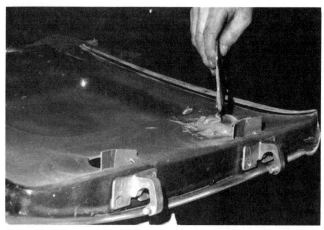

Another area that can benefit from additional beef is area below driver's seat. Again, sections of plywood can be 'glassed right in over existing 'glass floorboard.

firms that their location is correct, the rear fenders can be installed. Most rear fenders tuck up into the fender well. But, because fiberglass is much thicker than sheet metal, many interferences may be encountered. Match the fender as best as possible with the running board on one end and the rear of the body or rear deck panel at the back end. It may be necessary to locally grind or sand down the fender material to get a neat fit. Many manufacturers deliberately leave excess material just to make close-tolerance fitting easier. It's easier to remove material than add it when fitting a body panel.

Once you're satisfied that the fender fits and all seams and the like match, gently clamp the fender to the body and running board in as many places as possible. Again, be very careful not to over-tighten and fracture the 'glass.

Drill the first holes in the topmost mounting points using a sharp bit for a clean cut. Some rod builders drill two holes just big enough to secure the fenders with machine screws so they can back off and check fender alignment with the wheels and tires in place. (Yes, you should have your wheels and tires about this time.) At any rate, if something doesn't look right, new holes can be drilled and the extra small holes are filled or forgotten. No one will know.

Another method is to drill one oversize hole so you can wiggle the fender a little. Either way, once the fender is aligned to your satisfaction, the remaining bolt holes can be drilled. Before doing so, however, make sure the fender is secure to the body along its full circumference before drilling. Drill through both the body and fender at the same time. It is also much easier to drill from the inside of

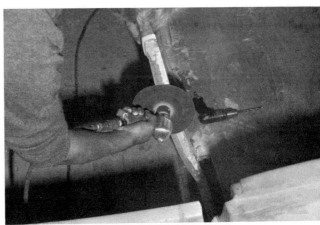

Great care must be taken when assembling fiberglass fenders. Overtightening a bolt will surely crack the fiberglass. Extra bracing should be used to support big, billowy fenders.

Hanging doors requires a lot of trial-and-error work to get things just right. Door hardware is available from antique-parts houses.

the body wherever practical. By the way, the final bolt holes should be somewhat larger than the attaching bolts. Fenders should never be bound in so tightly that there is no room for some shifting or installation of bead welting.

As just mentioned, the largest fender washers possible should be used behind the bolts. As for nuts, the best to use are the aircraft type with nylon locks. They won't back off even when they are not tightened. Remember, bolts in fiberglass should not be torqued as much as if they were in sheet metal. Otherwise, you'll crush the fiberglass.

When the running boards and rear fenders are securely mounted, install the front fenders. Mounting is essentially the same as with the rears, but using the wheels and tires as reference is doubly important, particularly if additional bracketry will be used. Not only should the wheels be centered in the fender opening, there must be no interference either from steering or suspension movement.

REDOING OLD FIBERGLASS

Before I close this chapter, following are some tips on how to deal with an older, previously owned fiberglass body that has endured several years of street duty. First, you'll probably find some mis-alignment and a few cracks, particularly in the floorboard area. There's no reason to suspect shoddy workmanship if everything else is reasonably sound.

The process of pulling an older 'glass body back into alignment is basically the same as with a new one. Unless badly out of shape, only a little more time and effort with the body jack and heat lamps is required. The floorboard, however, may take more work.

The floorboard is the only part of the body that fastens securely to the frame. The remainder of the body is secured to the floorboard along a single, highly loaded joint. This joint, therefore, is bound to crack eventually. Making this repair is basically the same as,

'glassing in wooden floorboard stiffeners, except for one or two extra considerations.

One section should be refinished at a time to maintain alignment, assuming it was right. And, the paraffin residue that frequently covers the surface of cured 'glass must be ground off to ensure a good bond for the bonding of the new 'glass.

As in any plywood-to-'glass operation, first inspect the wood for dampness. Trapped moisture will adversely affect resin set-up. Two layers of 1-1/2-ounce mat or one layer of 3-ounce mat in 4—6-in. widths around the perimeter of the floorboard will return sufficient strength to the joint.

If two layers of mat are used, both can be applied at the same time, but each should be saturated with resin. You can't "paint" resin on mat as you can with cloth. Lay the mat and squeeze out the air bubbles with a commercially available fiberglass roller. Let one side set-up while the other is worked.

26 Paint

Paint is the most visible product of a street-rod-builder's labors. It must be "perfect!"

If you're going to paint your car, look forward to three things: lots of hard work, learning based on trial-and-error, and personal satisfaction that no other aspect of rod building offers. For, the paint job, more than any other thing, is on public display. The audience may never get a glimpse of the engine if it's kept underhood, and they may never get to peak at the interior of the cockpit. Few will ride in the car, so how are they to be impressed with its power or handling? Few, in fact, will even appreciate the quality of the metal or 'glass work because they didn't see what you began with.

But, inside or out, day or night, rain or shine, all the world will get the chance to marvel at the perfection of your street rod's paint work. It is probably not thicker than the paper these words are printed on, but the *color coat* (topcoat) brings out the lines, contours and classic styling of that old car. It is the final touch of beauty to the eyes of all who behold your street rod.

I will not encourage you to do something that you don't want to do, but I assume that you would at least *like* to paint your car. So, plan on doing it right.

SELECT BASIC EQUIPMENT

The paint-spray equipment you choose for your home shop is, as always, dependent on what you can afford. Although you only need an air compressor, 12 feet of 5/16-in. hose, an air-pressure regulator and filter, and a top-quality spray gun, there's a wide variety from which to choose. Not only that, there are several other pieces of related equipment such as exhaust fans, buffing and polishing tools and the like that both enhance safety and make the job easier.

This doesn't mean you have to purchase new, professional equipment. Not at all. In fact, with the exception of the spray gun, moderately priced air compressors and filter/regulators available from large merchandising chains such as Sears and Montgomery Ward are more than adequate.

The compatibility of the equipment within the spray system and to the type of paint you select is more important. The first piece of equipment to consider is the most expensive: the air compressor. This is discussed at length in Chapter 6, so I won't repeat the same information. Just remember that air compressors are rated according to their volume

delivery in standard cubic feet per minute (scfm). Portable units suitable for the home shop run up to 8—9 scfm, which is adequate for most automotive painting projects. Air-storage tanks of about 20-gallon capacity are OK for uninterrupted spraying. Don't go smaller.

Other pieces of equipment are the pressure regulator, and oil and water extractor. A combination unit is usually the most practical. You can buy one that is compatible with your compressor where you purchase your compressor.

All other components being adequate, the key to a good paint job is the spray gun. There are two types used in automotive work. Professional painters prefer a gun that is attached to a remote *cup* or large-capacity paint pot on the floor. The gun is all that is held. The other type, and the one you are most likely to purchase, is the basic *nonbleeder* gun equipped with a one-quart screw-on cup. This gun uses air pressure to siphon feed and requires a 1—2-HP compressor delivering 4—9 cubic feet per minute (cfm), and 25—50-psi line pressure for minimum-quality automotive refinishing.

Work Area—More than one street rod has been sprayed right in the middle of a home garage or on the pad out in front of it. Most communities have local ordinances concerning painting and storing paint. You had best check them out before a neighbor complains. Beyond the legalities, overlooking obvious fire hazards such as the pilot light of a hot-water heater can be tragic.

Fresh air is not only essential to your health, but paint will dry quicker. A lack of ventilation can easily result in problems such as poor drying, dulling and wrinkling. So, if you can manage it, do your final painting in a rented spray booth, many of which exist in larger metropolitan areas. If you can't swing this, but still want to paint your car at home, double-check that there are no open flames in the work area, there's plenty of ventilation and several exhaust fans, entrances to the living quarters are sealed, and there are no clothes or other items in the work area that might be ruined by the inevitable overspray. If you can't move them easily, such as a washer and dryer, cover them.

Automotive Paints—All paints are alike in at least one way: They are composed of *pigments, binders* and *solvents*. Pigments are dry powders, white or colored, that give paints their colors. There are as many as there are color variations. Pigments also add to the durability of the paint.

A binder, a clear, syrup-like liquid, is the constituent of paint that allows it to adhere to a surface. There are thousands of varieties of binders. Pigment is evenly distributed throughout the binder during the manufacture of the paint.

The final component of paint is the solvent, or thinner. It's gives fluidity to the pigment/ binder mixture. Without some kind of thinning agent, the paint could not be applied with a spray gun—even a brush. The solvent, however, is a *fugitive* agent. The solvent begins to evaporate the instant the paint is sprayed on the surface. Depending on the type of paint used, complete evaporation takes from a few minutes to a several hours. Only the pigmented binder remains and that, of course, is the hardened paint film.

You, as the painter, will rarely be involved with formulating the pigments and binders, but not so with solvents. Although all solvents are similar in appearance, viscosity and smell, each has a dramatically different effect on the way the paint sprays, adheres, flows out and finally looks when dried. It also affects paint durablility.

That is why it is imperative that you stay within a brand line when dealing with automotive paints, and that you always follow the manufacturer's directions.

Automotive Undercoats—Although different manufacturers have pet names for their undercoats, such as *primers* and *primer/ surfacers,* and topcoats such as *enamel* and *lacquer,* and the never-ending synthetic variations, the old standby definitions are still needed to adequately outline what each is designed to accomplish.

Undercoats include the primers, primer/ surfacers, sealers, primer/sealers and putties that provide the base for the *color coats.* There are about 16 different varieties, but only a few of these concern us.

Primers are designed to grip the bare body surface and establish a secure foundation for all that comes later. They are typically applied in thin coats and *are not meant to be sanded or to fill in scratches or other imperfections.* Straight primers are usually lacquer-based.

Primer/surfacers, on the other hand, contain about twice as much pigment as do straight primers. They are designed to offer the good adhesive qualities of a straight primer—prepare bare surfaces for painting—but also fill in minor imperfections and scratches. Primer/surfacers can be sanded when dry, and the smoother their final coats, the more glossy the finished color coat.

Sealer is yet another type of undercoat. It is applied over a previous paint coat to improve the uniformity and gloss of the final color coat. A few, *but not all,* sealers are designed to stop color bleed-through from a previous paint job. This latter-type sealer should not be used unless bleed-through protection is specifically required.

Primer/sealers not only seal off old finishes and prevent lifting, they also prime bare surfaces. They are not designed for filling, however.

Putty undercoats are the final type. They are available in tubes and fill deep scratches and imperfections. Essentially, they are thick primer/surfacer pastes with a minimum amount of solvent. They are not sprayed on, but rather applied with a flexible plastic paddle or putty knife.

TYPES OF AUTOMOTIVE PAINTS

There was a time when the fledgling rod builder only had to learn the differences between automotive enamels and lacquers. Enamels were paints that dried slowly, but when dry were about as glossy as they would ever be. Buffing was not needed. Lacquers were similar in composition, but had an additional component called *nitrocellulose* that caused them to dry very quickly. And everyone knew that lacquers needed to be *rubbed out* to achieve a glossy finish. In the days when magazine-featured cars boasted the inevitable "20 coats of hand-rubbed, show-quality lacquer," no serious street rodder doubted what finish he wanted on his car. Enamel was for taxi cabs and Uncle Mert's stocker.

Finishes of 30 years ago hardly exist in their traditional form today. This is the age of synthetics and plastics. In fact, when my coupe was treated to its one and only candy-apple red paint job some 10 years ago—see *Street Rodder Magazine*, August, 1976—the legendary Stan Betz supplied the paint. Stan, a long-time supplier of custom paints to the West Coast trade, told me that he wouldn't be surprised if the true nitrocellulose lacquer and toners he dug up and mixed for me were some of the last in Southern California—I had better enjoy them while I could. Although fun, a scavenger hunt for paint is hardly what I recommend. So let's take a look at modern paints you can buy at any auto-paint store.

Acrylic Lacquer—Originally, true lacquer was made from the resinous secretions of the *lac bug* and *cellulose acetate,* another resin derived from plant tissues. Some years ago, however, paint manufacturers began to use acrylic resins (thermoplastic polymers) in lieu of the ancient ingredients. The result was a high-quality, but expensive, fast-drying, *user-friendly* automotive finish. It is relatively easy to apply, particularly in the home-shop environment.

When correctly thinned and sprayed, acrylic lacquers flow out nicely, hold up well when color sanded—still necessary to achieve high gloss—and, in general, are much more durable than the old-time nitrocellulose lacquers. Lacquers, both true and acrylic, dry from the inside out. Consequently, early color sanding shortens the drying time. Although acrylic lacquers haven't quite duplicated the depth—that ethereal, mirror-like dimension—of nitrocellulose lacquers, the trade-off has been a sound one.

Synthetic Enamel—Originally, enamels were made from the milky juice of the varnish tree. It was first used, of all places, in Libya. Modern enamel manufacture has also been revolutionized by thermoplastics.

Synthetic enamels are undeniably better than "true" automotive enamels used until the early '60s. Today, these very slow-drying finishes are the darlings of well-equipped commercial paint shops because of their low cost, excellent durability and high gloss—not to be confused with *depth*—when applied in a spray booth and baked in an infrared heat lamp oven. Without the latter, as much as 24 hours are required for complete drying. Considering other paint choices, synthetic enamels aren't practical for using in the home-based shop.

Acrylic Enamel—Acrylic enamels are somewhat less troublesome to spray than the old stuff or straight synthetics. They dry much more quickly, but often not quickly enough to avoid problems. In short, they require a completely dust-free environment for a superior job. Consequently, they are not practical for home-shop use. However, they are well suited for *hurry-up* work of a commercial shop with an oven.

Apart from drying time, the benefits of acrylic enamels are numerous. For instance, there's no need to rub out the last color coat; the finished product has a reasonably high gloss, and the durability of acrylic enamel is outstanding. Acrylic enamels have much to offer, and if you can get access to a spray booth and bake oven, and you've developed sufficient skill, you should consider using acrylic enamel. But, there's something better:

Catalyzed Acrylic Enamel—This, the most high-tech of all new enamels, incorporates a urethane catalyst. Urethanes are another of that long line of *esters* that so dominate modern industrial materials. In acrylic enamels the result is a beautiful, glossy finish extremely resistant to rock chips and scratches. Best of all, it can be touched up or recoated at any time. That's a real boon to the street rodder who drives his car on a daily basis.

189

Catalyzed acrylic enamels are available off the shelf in many colors, including a variety of candy colors, metallics (polychromatics), pearls and iridescents.

Bottom Line—There are other types of modern automotive paints, particularly the polyurethanes and acrylic urethanes, but acrylic lacquer or catalyzed acrylic enamel is the most practical for home-based use. If, after looking over the color and custom options, making a choice still presents a problem, let your work area make the decision for you. If you must spray your car outdoors, acrylic lacquer has the edge. If you are going to spray indoors, I recommend that you use catalyzed acrylic enamel. Both types of paint are reasonably forgiving in that application imperfections can be color sanded and rubbed out. Both can be touched up or modified if your mood shifts. And both can be endowed with enough gloss and depth to satisfy the soul.

Painting begins with sanding (lots of it) and stripping (lots of it) of *all* old finishes. Job is labor intensive, so be prepared to devote a lot of time to these preparatory phases.

THINNERS, SOLVENTS & REDUCERS

The number and types of automotive paints, while numerous, are at least manageable. The number and types of thinners, solvents and reducers, however, can boggle the mind . . . and would, except for the cardinal rule: *Always use the exact thinner or reducer recommended by the paint manufacturer.*

Reducers, by the way, are the *solvents* used in acrylics, synthetic and urethane enamels. *Thinners* are the *solvents* for lacquers.

You may have accumulated various thinners over the years. If so, you know they were expensive. Consequently, you may be tempted to do a little substituting because there can't be that much difference between them. Right? Wrong! Don't do it. There is no exception to the rule of compatible thinners. Use only what the manufacturer recommends.

The major differences between thinners are their evaporation rates—from seconds to days—and their ability to dissolve the binder. Some thinners won't dissolve certain binders at all. Not only that, you may not find this out until the paint is actually sprayed on the car. So, read the instructions on the can first.

Retarder, another type of solvent, is an agent that slows drying. There are two types, one for lacquers and enamels, called a *universal retarder;* the other is for urethane-based paints.

Friends In Need—Although most of what you need to know about paint is on the can, chances are you won't get very far without a question or two popping up. That's why you should develop a good working relationship with the fellows at the paint-supply store.

You'll be spending several hundred dollars at their establishment before you finish the job. Along with that expenditure can come a lot of good, solid advice . . . if you ask for it. Don't hesitate. They are more than willing to pass on, not only the vast array of printed information provided by paint manufacturers, but other pertinent information. Painters who squirt cars in year-round rainy climates do things a little different from those who paint in desert regions, so this "custom" information can be very important to you and your street rod.

RULES TO FOLLOW

Once you've picked your paint, work area and supplies, you can no longer avoid rolling up your sleeves and getting on with the program. However, please observe the following safety rules:

● There must be adequate ventilation and some means of removing the paint fumes; usually exhaust fans.

● Have at least one fire extinguisher within easy reach.

● Electrical equipment used must be in top-notch condition. Temporary hookups that could inadvertently cause a spark or static electricity must be strictly avoided.

● The work area, including the floor, must be clean and free of debris.

● All persons in and around the work area must observe the NO SMOKING sign.

● During spraying, wear an appropriate face mask. Provide observers with the same.

SURFACE PREPARATION

There can never be too much effort expended if you expect to achieve a lasting or successful paint job. Therefore, start by removing the old finish. Don't try to get by with merely sanding the surface. It's true that good-quality old paint is better than primer, but older rods that have seen any appreciable street duty invariably have been re-finished. There's simply no telling what lies under the existing paint. All too often, checks or cracks invisible or hidden to the eye exist. And that's doubly true when "custom" paint jobs have been previously applied. New paint will not hold up over checked film, no matter how smooth the sanding job feels. In short, *to the metal* is the only direction to take.

Strip Exterior—If the car doesn't need or hasn't been treated to the Redi-Strip process as described in Chapter 24, prepare the previously painted surface as follows: All exterior trim such as mirrors, radio antenna, accessories, all chrome or stainless-steel ornaments, bumpers and brackets, grille, headlight and taillight buckets and running boards must be removed. Unless it's a running car that is only being re-finished, remove all window glass and securely tape in sections of cardboard to prevent overspray from entering the passenger compartment.

Solvent-type paint remover is probably the fastest way to remove old finishes from metal cars. Rarely do the best of them get it all off, but most will lift the bulk of the paint film. Eye protection is a must, as are gloves. Protective garments will prove their worth the first time a glob of the remover lands on tender skin.

Unless your car is very small, the application of remover is a two- or three-day job. And often, there are stubborn areas that resist multiple applications of remover. At any rate, power sanding is next on the agenda. My favorite power sander for this type of work is a small 1/2-horsepower, hand-held pneumatic random orbit-finish sander that uses 3.5 X 9-in. strips of sandpaper. First passes over the body should be made with relatively coarse paper, or about #60 grit. Follow this with successively finer #80- and #100-grit paper to finish the metal and smooth scratches. The more you sand, and the finer you "grit down," the smoother the metal. Fanatics use steel wool for the very last go 'round.

As soon as possible following the last sanding, wash the entire car with a solvent-type cleaner. This will remove all wax, grease and dirt residues left over from the stripping and sanding. This is most important when solvent-wax type removers have been used. Don't be afraid to apply the cleaning solvent liberally. And use plenty of paper towels.

Blow out all the cracks, crevices and moldings to remove hidden dust or paint sludge. Caution: Always wear eye protection when using compressed air.

Next, wash down any recently soldered or leaded-in areas with ammonia, then thoroughly rinse with water.

Metal Prep—The last step in preparing the metal body is applying phosphate-type metal conditioner. Sometimes called *metal prep,* this mild acid not only removes all oil, surface rust and silicones, it slightly roughens or etches the metal surface. This ensures improved paint adhesion and greatly lessens rust renewal later. Reduce and apply the metal conditioner according to the instructions on the container. Leave it on for a minute or so. Wipe the conditioner off carefully with clean, dry paper towels. Finally, blow out the cracks and crevices again.

Primer/sealer should be applied within 30 minutes of a thorough drying. In the meantime, however, be very careful not to touch the bare metal with your hands or clothing.

Sanding—You will be sanding your car after every step from the time you strip it until you apply the last color coat. Power sanders are useful in the beginning, but eventually you must abandon them in favor of hand sanding. Surfaces sanded by hand require plenty of water, so a dribbling garden hose stationed nearby is a messy necessity. Great care must be exercised. More than one chip in fresh paint can be blamed on careless handling of a garden hose with its brass fitting still in place. Prevent this from happending to you and clip the fitting off the old hose and buy a new one.

Custom painters usually start with #320-grit paper for color sanding, changing to #400, and finally to #600. But, whatever paper you're using, remember to use a sanding pad, and to sand with light, uniform strokes. It is best to use parallel strokes in one direction only. Avoid dry sanding. Instead, use water to eliminate dust and leave a smoother finish. Sanding scratches that show up after the first coats of primer/surfacer are from using paper that's too coarse, pressing too hard, or not using a sanding pad. Sometimes it's simply from sanding the finish before it has dried adequately.

Masking—A street rod is not typical, simply because disassembly of the car is the rule rather than the exception. Nonetheless, you should know how to do proper masking. Careful masking provides sharp paint edges and avoids the sloppy appearance of painted edges of glass or trim.

Paint-supply houses carry rolls of inexpensive kraft paper for masking purposes. The few square yards you'll need won't cost much. Don't use newspaper for masking. The ink may dissolve in paint solvents and cause staining. Newspaper is OK for masking window glass or wheels. Spend a little more and get good-quality masking tape rather than trying to scrimp by with cheap, second-rate stuff that tears where and when you don't want it to.

Start by masking curved areas with 1/4-in.-wide tape. It's more flexible than wider tapes. Use 1- or 2-in. tape to extend the masking where necessary.

Prepare the Paint—Don't get careless when preparing primer or paint. The most frequent error of all is the failure to simply stir the paint sufficiently before pouring it into the spray cup. In fact, at least one paint manufacturer reports that the majority of primer/surfacer problems are from insufficient stirring.

Thorough stirring ensures a uniform mixture of pigment, binder and thinners. Undercoats, because of the heavier pigment content, require especially conscientious stirring. Add slowly the correct type and percentage of thinner while continuing to stir. Although the percentage of thinner should be monitored carefully, it's better to add a little too much thinner than not enough.

Finally, strain the thinned paint though a fine-mesh metal or cloth strainer. Undercoats are poured through a 50-mesh screen; topcoats through a finer 100-mesh. Most of the better spray guns have replaceable metal strainers, but strain all paints before pouring them into the cup.

Soft curves such as in this cowl area are the only places you can sand with your bare hands. Flat panels should be block-sanded.

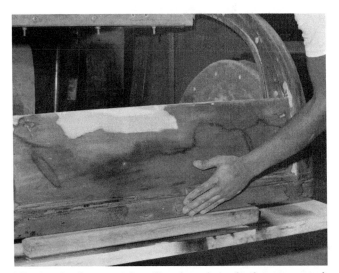

Whether in sheet metal or fiberglass, imperfections cannot always be seen. More often than not, they must be detected using an *educated* feel.

Using the Spray Gun—It looks so simple, the easy back-and-forth movement of the spray gun . . . in the hands of an experienced painter. Then you pick it up for the first time. It's heavier than you thought. You dry practice a few left and right passes. So far so good. Then you notice that you somehow dribbled a few drops on your hands and you know if that paint had fallen on the surface of the car it might have burned right through to the metal. Yeah, unsprayed paint is *hot*—it acts as its own solvent.

Practice is what makes perfect, but it shouldn't take years to develop the eye/hand coordination that will allow you to do a good paint job.

Paint spray guns are delicate, precision tools. Every one that leaves the factory has been tested for general operation and adjustment, for atomization, and for spray-pattern size and uniformity. It's neglect and carelessness that subsequent owners subject a spray gun to that causes the majority of spraying problems. And 90% of the neglect is related to improper cleaning of the gun.

There are two knobs on the back side of the spray-gun body. The top one is for air-pressure adjustment; the lower one is for fluid-flow adjustment. You know where the off/on trigger is. The rod that goes from the trigger into the body of the gun is the air-valve stem. The "business end" of the gun is the only part besides the cup that disassembles. The air cap unscrews to reveal a fluid tip. The tip slips off to further reveal the fluid needle. When replacing the fluid tip and air cap, make certain the cap is tightened securely in position.

Finger-Tighten Only!—Unless your spray gun is brand new, make sure it is absolutely clean. Ditzler and other paint companies make paint-gun-cleaning solvent that works best to keep the aluminum alloy parts in tip-top shape. Never immerse your spray gun in thinner because it will destroy the lubricant in the packings around the fluid needle. A few ounces of clean solvent placed in the cup and sprayed through the gun is fine, but the gun and cup should be wiped clean and dry immediately afterward.

Once you've familiarized yourself with the gun and its parts, mix some primer and thinner in the recommended percentages. Strain this mixture into the cup and make sure the regulator is set at the recommended pressure.

Obtaining the proper-width and shape of the spray requires nothing more than trial-and-error manipulation of the air and fluid adjustment screws. The air screw governs the shape of the spray. Turning it clockwise produces a round or conical spray; turning it counter-clockwise produces a fan shape. The fluid-adjustment screw, on the other hand,

governs the amount of primer—or paint—going through the gun. It must be regulated according to the type of material being sprayed. Remember, though, that as the width of the spray is increased, more material must be passed through the gun to get the same coverage.

When you are ready to start practice spraying, shoot a test pattern on a piece of cardboard. Check it and adjust the gun accordingly. Initial adjustments are made by backing off the fluid screw two or three turns from the fully-closed position. Make pattern corrections with the air-adjustment screw. Anything less than a perfectly uniform pattern—an elongated ellipse—with good atomization is cause for further adjustment.

If the fan-spray pattern is heavy in the middle or has a splatter effect, raise the atomizing pressure at the regulator. If you see a *split spray*—heavy on each end and weak in the middle in the shape of a peanut—atomizing air pressure is probably too high. Reduce it at the regulator. However, the split may be due to the material being too thin for the width of the spray. This can be corrected by turning the fluid adjustment counter-clockwise while, at the same time, turning the air-adjustment clockwise. This reduces spray width, but eliminates the peanut shape.

A tear-drop spray pattern—heavy and wider at either the top or bottom—usually means that the material has dried around the outside of the fluid tip and is restricting the passage of the atomizing air. A loose air cap is sometimes the culprit. If not, remove the air cap and fluid tip, and clean them with thinner. Do not use a wire, or anything hard to clean the air passage.

Spraying Technique—The temperature at which paint is sprayed and dried is critical to the smoothness of the finish. Painting at home rather than in the controlled conditions of a spray booth has its drawbacks. For instance, you'll have to pick a day when there is no hint of rain or high humidity. Not only must the shop temperature be just right—about 70—75F—so must the temperature of the sheet metal. Fiberglass bodies are usually at room temperature, but sheet metal can be 10F cooler. If a metal car is sitting outside before you shoot it, remember that direct sunlight will raise its surface temperature significantly. If you spray outdoors, you may have to use retarder to slow drying. Specifics such as these are best discussed with your paint-supply dealer.

Spray guns deliver their best performance at 8—12 in. from the work surface. Get too close and the high velocity of the spraying air will ripple the wet paint film. Get too far away and too much thinner will evaporate and you will get a good dose of dreaded *orange peel*.

Next, you must master the strokes and overlaps. If the gun is not square to the surface, the fan pattern will not be uniform. If it is swung in an arc, and the distance from the nozzle to the work varies, the paint will go on wetter where the spray is closer to the surface and drier where it is farther away. The gun must always be held square to the work and kept at the same distance, so watch your wrist motion.

Work to a wet edge by using approximately 50% overlap. Control this by directing the center of the spray fan to the lower or nearest edge of the previous stroke. Don't try to paint your way 360° around the car. Doing so is likely to allow drying, which will make blending difficult when you return to your starting point. This is particularly true if this is your first try at painting a car. Novices tend to work slowly. Instead, start with the hood area, then the left and right fenders. Next, do the top, then drop down to one entire side of the car, but not the rear. Move across to the opposite side and paint it. Paint the deck area last. If you apply the first coat without moving too slowly, no single section has been sitting with paint on it long enough to make blending troublesome.

Primer/Surfacer Application—Applying primer isn't difficult, but don't take it lightly. First off, don't forget that there are primers, primer/surfacers and primer/sealers.

Chances are, you'll need a primer/surfacer. Use a light-colored primer/surfacer when a light color coat will be applied, and vice versa. It's best to spray thin, wet coats of primer/surfacer and permit short, solvent *flash-offs* between coats. Applying heavy coats in one pass can lead to problems such as hard sanding, poor hold-out—where the topcoat is sucked in or absorbed—and pinholes. Beyond that, it is almost impossible to be much more specific because reduction and application vary considerably, depending on brand and type.

Putty Application—As mentioned earlier, putty is a paste undercoat used to fill deep scratches and rough spots—problem areas too big for a primer/surfacer to fill. But, it is *not* a substitute for further metal work or plastic body filler.

When applying putty, you must work as fast as possible to ensure a smooth, uniform film. Putties contain solvents that evaporate rapidly. So, *balling up* will occur if the putty isn't worked fast enough. Putties should be applied only to surfaces at room temperatures, and in thicknesses no greater than needed to smooth out the rough spots. Two or three thin applications with adequate drying time in between, is better than one heavy application. Thoroughly dried putty can be sanded with #320-grit paper or finer. If there

To obtain a measure of perfection in your paint job, spot primer . . .

. . . and block-sand dozens of times until you're satisfied with the surface of the body.

is a *cut-through* to bare metal, re-spray the area with primer/surfacer.

PREPPING 'GLASS BODIES

Most expensive fiberglass bodies available today easily justify their higher prices by the quality of their exterior. Budget body shells, however, often have wavy surfaces; considerable time and patience must be expended before they are ready for color. Regardless, if block sanding starts to get wearisome, remind yourself that the finished product will reflect your efforts in more ways than one.

Nevertheless, the preparation of a fiberglass body isn't all that different from a rod based on vintage tin. However, there are a few variations from what we have just discussed.

New fiberglass body will need a lot of sanding, no matter how much it cost. Start by sanding out imperfections such as mold marks.

Begin your preparation of a fiberglass body by carefully washing the entire body with a naptha-base degreaser to remove any remaining mold wax. Next, lightly sand the body with dry #220-grit paper to break the glaze and give the surface a *tooth* for the primer to adhere. Take pains not to sand off the gel coat. It separates the 'glass fibers from the surface. The best bodies will need little sanding. However, even with the best surface, lots of block-sanding is required for a perfect paint job.

Spray the first coat of primer/surfacer on wet. Although you shouldn't be careless, don't worry about runs, either. After a day or so drying time, spray on another, but not so heavy, coat of primer/surfacer. When that has adequately dried, start block-sanding with #220-grit paper in long, straight strokes. Dry sanding at this stage is better than wet sanding, but it does require more paper. Fortunately, sandpaper is not that expensive.

In general, three or four coats of primer/surfacer will do. But remember to allow sufficient drying time between coats. One day drying time is minimal because primer that shrinks can ruin any paint job.

You will get to know your street-rod body intimately after all of this contact. Consequently, you should find most imperfections. One way to speed things up, however, is to apply a *guide coat*. Spray on a coat of dark primer/surfacer followed by a lighter shade. When dry, block-sand again. Dark spots that remain after most of the light primer/surfacer has been sanded off are slight depressions in the surface. They need more attention.

Fill the low spots with a thin coat of glazing putty, but don't try to cover anything too deeply. If in doubt, plan to re-resin it.

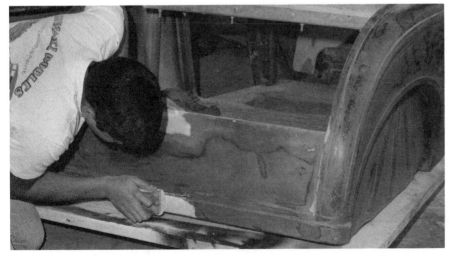

Block sanding with finer grits—#400 or #600—can be done wet or dry, but many painters like the dry method because it minimizes the mess.

When you think your fiberglass body is ready for color, wash it down completely with a commercial pre-wash solution such as Fin-L-Wash. It's sold in NAPA stores. This solution will evaporate in still air, but high-pressure air from your air hose will speed drying.

Before painting a full-fendered car, take one precaution. Spray a thick layer of rubberized undercoat on the underside of each fender. This will protect them from *stars*—dents from the underside—caused by small rocks thrown by the tires.

COLOR-COAT APPLICATION

Wipe the car down with a *tack rag* before spraying it with the color coat. You can get these at your local paint-supply store. Varnish in the tack-rag cloth will pick up small bits of dust or dirt.

The same spray techniques used for the primer/surfacer hold true for applying color coats. Don't let the paint dry between coats, and don't apply too many coats. That myth of 20 coats is just that, a myth. Depending upon the type of paint, three to six coats is plenty. Paint that's too thick will tend to crack. In fact, if you live in cold country, talk with some of the pros in your area to see what they do. Metal shrinks more than paint, so extreme temperature drops can damage paint.

Although it is not my intention to encourage you to attempt any exotic work first time 'round, I will mention the possibilities of applying *clears, pearls, candies* and all the other "trick"—for tricky to apply—topcoats

that are dealt with at length in HPBooks' *Paint & Body Handbook*. Some of these must be applied while the color coat is still wet; others are applied after drying. Depending on your level of painting skills, you may want to go "all out." If so, do your homework first, then do it. A careful study of the accompanying photo sequence will get you in the ballpark for most conservative paint jobs.

RUBBING COMPOUNDS, POLISHES & WAXES

Rubbing compound is designed to remove *orange peel* and produce a bright smooth finish. It consists of abrasive powder that is dispersed in water, solvent or oils. Compound for acrylic enamels is usually finer than that for use on acrylic lacquers.

For lows that are fairly broad, a paint stick makes a handy bridge for leveling putty. A paddle or scraper that is too small will drop into the area and remove as much putty as it will put in. Careful downward stroking is the recommended method of applying filler.

After the filler has hardened, block-sand the repaired areas once again. Continue to look for surface imperfections. When found, mark them. A small supply of fiberglass adhesive/filler kept handy on a paint stick can then be applied to the marked spots with a small plastic paddle.

Although manufacturer's recommendations take precedence over anything else, sprayed acrylic lacquers can be rubbed and polished within a day or so depending on the type of thinner used, the number of coats, and

weather. If, however, you get antsy and start rubbing or compounding too soon, you'll be rewarded with *hazing* or *dulling-back*.

Hand rubbing compounds should be applied sparingly on a clean, soft cloth, never directly. Gentle back-and-forth strokes are better than hard aggressive strokes, even though it takes more time. If you are using a power buffer, the compound can be applied to the work surface with a soft paint brush. As the buffing wheel moves across the work, it spreads the compound evenly to rapidly produce a bright, dry finish.

There is an inherent danger that goes with using compounds, particularly when applied with a power buffer. And that is the possibility of cut-throughs. About the only thing that can be done is don't work rubbing compounds too hard. Cut-throughs can bring a lot of grief in the form of difficult touch-ups.

Waxes and polishes are also designed to produce a glossy finish. But, unlike compounds that merely abrade the surface, these leave a supposedly protective film of wax, oil or silicone. The controversy of whether or not this is true rages on, but I must tell you, polishes and waxes sometimes can have harmful effects on custom paint jobs, such as water spotting, yellowing, dulling and even checking. At any rate, don't use a polish or wax on new acrylics—lacquer or enamel—until the paint has cured at least a month. In fact, many paint manufacturers, as well as professional painters, advise that the best paint care is frequent washing with plain, *warm* water.

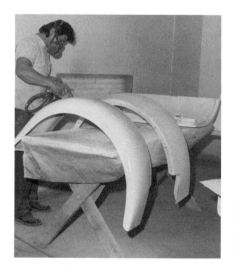

When all is said and done, painting in a spray booth is far better than outdoors.

Final art in application of custom paint is a custom rub-out. Careless slip with buffer will cut through to primer. So, if paint is not easily touched up, don't practice buffing on it.

Man behind sewing machine—in this case Jack Garrison—is who you should talk with when choosing materials for your car's interior. Upholstery shops specializing in street-rod work have seen it all, and are your best source of advice.

In terms of when it should actually be done, you should do your car's upholstery somewhere between wiring and painting. For in the natural order of street-rod building, that's where you should get serious about upholstery. In this chapter, I also include several other cosmetic topics.

Start thinking about whether or not you will do your own upholstery work. Don't scoff at the idea without at least giving it some thought. It could be beneficial. If done properly, an owner-upholstered car in a conservative pattern can save as much as $1000 in labor charges. Assuming you purchase moderately priced materials at retail prices, rent an industrial sewing machine, and buy a few handtools, total cost should be about half of the labor charges. And, you end up with some tools and experience in the process.

If machine rental drags on for a year while you practice, the cost will increase accordingly. You don't have to make a decision just yet; just keep the thought in the back of your mind.

Classic Upholstery Materials—First and foremost, consider the type and quality of materials for your street-rod interior. Pre-World War II Fords had a limited number of materials from which to choose. Quoting from a 1940 Ford sales brochure: "Choice of striped mohair or broadcloth upholstery. Antique finish genuine leather for seat cushions and seat backs of Convertible Club Coupe."

Mohair, striped or otherwise, is made from the hair of the Angora goat. Such luxury was hardly deemed appropriate for Henry Ford's lowest priced production cars. Although called *mohair,* a wool-based cloth in a pile weave with about 1/16-in. nap (fuzz) was used. Curiously, imitation mohair is not exactly cheap today.

Broadcloth, on the other hand, is a thick, closely woven wool-based fabric that is similar to mohair, but with a shorter nap. It is also stronger and more durable. For purposes of comparison, modern automotive-quality broadcloth is more expensive than the popular polyvinyl, but less costly than imitation mohair.

Leather, of course, needs no introduction. Imitations, synthetics, Polly, Esther and all their sisters may come and go as modern technology expands its scope. But genuine leather, a garment and upholstery material that reaches back to antiquity, always has and always will spell real class. Although there is hardly any shortage of leather—there are a million surplus dairy cattle in this country—

scientific methods of tanning have done little to reduce the cost of leather. Beyond that, leather is relatively difficult to work with, even for the professional.

The omission of any mention of carpet and headliner in the early Ford brochure is not an oversight. The buyer of a brand-new 1940 Ford didn't have any choice. Only prestige cars of the day had carpeting, and this was an expensive cut-pile wool. The front floorboards of the "low-priced three" were covered in wall-to-wall rubber mats, much like economy pickups of today. Rear-seat passengers, however, were treated to a little more class. They rested their feet on a rubberized pile horsehair mat.

The doors were usually upholstered in a special *sidewall material,* another cotton/wool blend similar to, but lighter than broadcloth. Headliner material in the low-priced pre-war car was a cotton/wool combination. Inasmuch as it suffered the least occupant abuse, it was a little lighter weight than sidewall material.

Modern Upholstery Materials—Leather, wool, and other time-honored organic materials began to price themselves out of the automotive market in the '30s. And that paved the way for synthetics, which today dominate the upholstery field by 98%.

Leatherette was the popular name for a material technically known as *pyroxylin,* a coarse cloth coated with a nitrocellulose compound. Although it was the first synthetic automobile upholstery material, developed in the '20s, it didn't appear in many production automobiles until the '40s. Even then, its use was primarily confined to door panels and the like because it did not stretch easily. *Stretchability* is an indispensable characteristic of upholstery materials used on seats.

Another significant addition to the now-growing roster of synthetic textiles arrived with the DuPont Company invention of *nylon.* Introduced in the mid '30s, it immediately found great favor everywhere in the industrial world except for automotive fabrics. It seemingly had everything going for it—it could be manufactured economically, dyed, stretched, and would last forever. But it wouldn't retain heat or absorb moisture and was, therefore, unpleasant to sit on for long periods. In time, however, combinations of nylon, cotton and *acetate*—still another synthetic fiber—overcame many of the short-

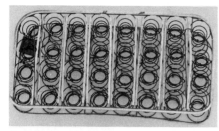

A potential problem when re-doing an original or reproduction interior is finding the correct seat cushions. If you're building a Model A Ford, you can get about whatever you need from reproduction folks.

Don Geisens rebuilt original springs and things in my coupe's seats. Forty-five years on the road took its toll.

Terry Berzenye built this stainless-steel framework for his roadster seat; upholsterer Larry Casas cushioned it with thick rubber straps before trimming.

Different trimmers use different pading and cushioning materials. Regardless, the "bottom line" is passenger comfort.

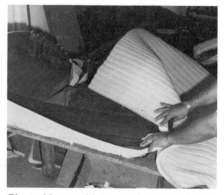

Pleated foam rubber—under several trade names—has become a staple of custom and street-rod upholstery shops.

comings. As a result, blends began to be accepted for a variety of automotive-upholstery applications.

The really big news in upholstery fabrics, however, was the discovery of *polyvinyl.* This synthetic material, manufactured by the *polymerization*—a chemical process that links natural and synthetic compounds together—of *thermoplastic resins,* made its automotive debut in the late '40s. But, it wasn't until the flexible plastic was backed up with a twill cloth that its utility was fully recognized. *Polyvinyl,* or simply *vinyl,* can truly be said to have revolutionized custom automotive interiors.

This is the first material you probably thought of when you began to ponder your street-rod interior. And no wonder: Fully 90% of all street rods completed since the '50s have had vinyl interiors. The most common brand, of course, is Uniroyal's *Naugahyde,* a registered trademark. Other brands of similar synthetics include Goodrich's *Koroseal* and General Tire's *Bolta.* Like nylon, fiberglass, and other trademarks that have lost their capitalization and become part of our language, *naugahyde,* to most of us, simply stands for any kind of automotive-upholstery vinyl.

Whatever it's called, there are several grades of automotive vinyl. One with only a twill or knit backing has relatively little elasticity. Better grades have a thin layer of foam rubber between the vinyl and cloth backing. Commonly called *expanded vinyl,* it is preferred for most custom interiors. Expanded vinyl has a pleasant, soft feel that adds a leather-like luxury to a seat.

If you are not aware of the hundreds of vinyl colors and surface textures available, you will be when the sales clerk spreads out samples on the counter. Choosing one is not an easy task. It is far more difficult, in fact, than choosing a paint color. Whatever, quality vinyl is stain resistant and *color-fast*—fade proof—in almost all cases. Even when

casually maintained, it will last for many years. It has, and will probably remain, the fabric of first choice for street rods.

There are modern automotive upholstery materials other than thermoplastics. You can see a fair representation in any new-car showroom. Those that are used in both production cars as well as show cars include all the aforementioned woven fabrics and their look-alike imitations. There's also a wide variety of wool, cotton and synthetic blends such as crushed velvet, velour, corduroy and even blue denim.

The primary advantage of these fabrics is that they better conform to irregular seat and cushion shapes than does polyvinyl, but most are not nearly as wear-resistant or stain-resistant as vinyl. Nevertheless, cloth, with its vast pattern, texture and color variety, has

a special luxury all its own. Also, the better grades are specially treated to resist permanent staining.

Patterns & Polyfoams—There was a time when every street rod simply had to have a pleat-and-roll, or tuck-and-roll, interior. Even today, the traditional look is still considered somewhat in style. An equal, if not greater number of interior designs, however, owe their origins to the multitude of patterns found in new cars. After all, both foreign and domestic manufacturers spend fortunes on the best artistic talent available in an effort to achieve a competitive edge. You could do worse than to draw a few ideas from their offerings.

Fortunately, a lot of the labor in building a complicated custom interior has been avoided with polyurethane foam "rubber," which is

196

Automotive upholstery involves more than seats. What you can't see is sound deadening provided by jute and felt padding under carpeting and trim panels.

Another type of sound deadener is easily applied in the home workshop—if you have an old spray gun. 3M's Body Schutz is a rubberized product that will go where nothing else can.

Terry Berzenye's Ford 351C has a healthy dose of chrome plating. And the highly polished stainless-steel firewall doubles the effect. Getting really good chrome isn't always easy.

available in several molded designs as well as a number of thicknesses and densities. In fact, Polyfoam—a trademark of General Tire—is the mainstay of most auto-upholstery shops. It is used for both structural and padding purposes. There's even an extremely dense variety that can be used in seat cushions without springs, and more than one builder of a channelled roadster or rumble-seated car has found it useful and reasonably comfortable. Horsehair and cotton, once the major automotive seat-padding materials, are seldom used, thanks to Polyfoam.

Carpeting—The final major material used in custom upholstery is that for carpeting. Quality street-rod interiors require "100% nylon." Although that percentage may be questionable, it is best for both beauty and long life. Two designs are typically available: loop pile, which has the edge with regard to durability, and cut pile, which many agree is the best looking. Both are available in various pile lengths and, as in the case of upholstery design, the ultimate choice is yours.

DO-IT-YOURSELF UNPHOLSTER?

What we put off before must now be dealt with—should you attempt doing your own upholstery? I must admit that I am more than a little hesitant about recommending that you do it, regardless of how much you study the accompanying photographs and text, pros and cons of the materials, or theory and technique of machine sewing. The need for skill and experience will become apparent the first time you try to pass a scrap of cloth through the sewing machine. Automotive upholstery is a skilled trade. A botched job will not only

reek of amateurism, material cost will be the same as for a top-quality job.

As this volume goes to press, however, I am reliably informed that HPBooks has another in its series of automotive handbooks in production . . . one on upholstery. Perhaps we should both suspend judgement until we've read it.

CHROME PLATING

Every experienced rod builder can sing at least one sad song when it comes to chrome plating. For instance, my die-cast hood ornament was misplaced; another's was dissolved. Still another fellow's coveted embossed grille guard had FORD buffed right out of the steel! Make no mistake about it, chrome work is tricky. Not just the electrochemistry of the plating process, but the handling and storage of small parts and, most importantly, what is done with the buffing wheel.

It should be obvious, therefore, that you should learn the in-and-outs of chrome-plating services. Not merely to forestall problems, as important as that is, but in order to avail yourself of all of the benefits.

Pick a Shop—If you want top-notch service rather than the lowest price, it's usually best to deal with a small, owner-operated shop. The man who has his pride invested in the product being turned out is most likely to give you the best work consistently. And when you get the bill, you can feel confident of getting the value you're about to pay for.

This is not to say that you can't get good service from big plating shops. But, it is true that day-to-day demands of a volume-production facility invariably puts them at

odds with the off-the-street, one-time customer who brings in a couple of bumpers and a bag full of old car parts. Their feeling about it is that your business isn't worth the effort in paper work.

In the final analysis, get opinions from street rodders in your area. Good will and word-of-mouth recommendations are what keep high-quality, low-volume shops in business.

The "Acid" Test—Before metal can be plated, it must be thoroughly cleaned. Grease is removed from the object by soaking it in a hot alkaline solution, then vigorously hand scrubbing it when removed. If the piece was previously chromed, it must be *de-plated*. It is placed in a special tank containing sulfuric acid that removes the old plating by drawing it off to a lead cathode when direct current is introduced.

If the part to be plated is rusty, another process is typically used—*acid pickling*. The part is immersed for a short time in hydrochloric acid. By the way, with all of the acids they use daily, chrome shops are under the close scrutiny of city and state environmental pollution-control agencies. And, as necessary as it is to the health of all concerned, meeting stringent governmental requirements has added to the cost of plating.

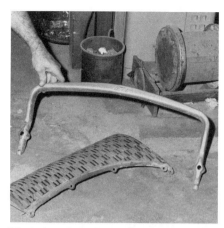

Most important step in getting good chrome—and saving rare pieces—is to discuss what you want and what you have with shop owner. Tell him you want that FORD script to stay as crisp as possible.

Man on buffing wheel is responsible for the health of your parts. His skill must be second to none.

Moment of truth is when parts are removed from chrome tanks. May all yours shine.

The use of acids brings several non-human concerns to mind, however. One is obvious—acids break down the molecular structure of most metals. Die-cast parts are particularly vulnerable. Although die-cast parts aren't pickled, no chrome shop can positively guarantee that an ancient grille or hood ornament will survive the basic plating process unscathed. So, when you bring in your die-cast jewels, be sure to impress the proprietor with the fact that they are die cast, and they are irreplaceable.

Hydrogen Embrittlement—Another problem not quite so obvious as a complete disappearing act is the dreaded *hydrogen embrittlement*. Part of the hydrogen released during the acid processes is absorbed into the steel, which causes brittleness in certain alloys. Spring steels are particularly susceptible. Other than short pickling times, most remedies—which consist primarily of oven baking—are not easily accomplished.

Decorative chrome is a fact of life for all street-rod builders, however, so a certain amount of risk is assumed. But based on some rather extensive aircraft research done a few years ago, I will repeat my oft given advice against chroming critical suspension and steering components such as springs and load-bearing shafts and arms.

Perils of Buffing—The greatest *cosmetic* hazard in chrome work is buffing a part prior to plating. Buffing metal to a glass-smooth, bright sheen is necessary for beautiful plating. The problem is that proper buffing of metal, steel as well as die-cast, is a tender, gentle operation that simply requires a lot of experience . . . and an operator who cares.

When checking out a plating shop, start by asking about the tenure and intelligence of the man or woman who will buff your part(s). Does that sound pompous? Too bad! Putting it bluntly, some shops are not cautious about the brain power of workers assigned to the polishing and buffing room. In such a place, you can take great pains to explain just how rare your hood ornament is and how important it is to you that its exact shape and design be faithfully retained. But, if your little speech doesn't filter through, you're wasting your time. Don't risk your part. If you're in doubt as to the savvy of the buffer, leave. If you don't, you may be sorry.

The Plating Process—Technically, electroplating is adhering a metallic coating to the surface of metal using direct electric current (d-c). The basic process in use today differs little from the one George and Henry Elkington patented in England in 1840. The Elkington system was designed for silver plate but, except for the different chemicals used in various plating baths, all electroplating processes are basically the same.

The plating tank is essentially a large electrolytic cell. It holds the electrolyte, which is an aqueous (watery) solution containing ions (electrically charged atoms) of the metal to be used for plating. The object to be plated is suspended in the electrolyte and acts as the *cathode,* or negative pole. A piece of plating metal also suspended in the electrolyte acts as the *anode,* or positive pole.

When the object to be plated is connected to the negative terminal of a d-c source and the plating metal is connected to the positive terminal, direct current flows in the cell. Ions

from the electrolyte are then drawn to the cathode, transformed to the metallic state, and deposited on the surface of the plating object. Gradually, the anode dissolves to provide more metal ions for the electrolyte. If a non-dissolving anode is used, fresh electrolytic solution must be added to the plating bath.

Triple Plating—Top-quality automotive chrome, like marine chrome, is a three-step process; thus, the term *triple plating*. The piece is first copper plated, then nickel plated, and finally chromium plated.

The copper plating bath contains a deadly witch's brew of cuprous cyanide, sodium cyanide and sodium thiosulfate. The operating temperature is held to 104F (40C) by thermostatically controlled heating coils. The anodes, which are usually arranged around the sides of the tank, are charged with d-c current.

The part being plated is suspended in the center of the tank. The thickness of the copper deposited depends on how long the part stays in the tank: 20—30 minutes is not uncommon if the piece is badly pitted or very porous and needs a thick coating of copper.

When, in the judgement of the plater, sufficient copper has been deposited, the piece is removed from the tank and given a good rinse to prevent deposits from drying on the surface. Then it goes back to the polishing room where it is buffed to a brilliant sheen and any surface defects are removed. This second polishing is the key to depth and luster in the finished product.

When you first see a part wearing a bright new coat of highly buffed copper, you might want to stop there; the richness of this color is

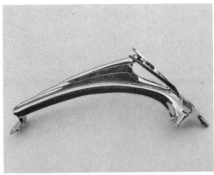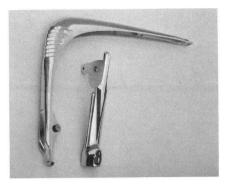

Much of the pleasure of owning a street rod comes from details the casual observer may not even notice—Vintique, Inc. hood ornaments and '40 Ford headlamp "door" for instance. Modern rodding wouldn't be the same without such high-quality parts.

nothing short of beautiful. Unfortunately, pure-copper plating quickly tarnishes and is too soft to be serviceable. It has, however, been used in custom-car interiors after it has been sprayed with clear lacquer. That's a little tidbit for the adventuresome to ponder, but for most purposes, the next step toward a long-lasting chrome-plated beauty is a dip in the nickel tank.

The *Watts composition* is the most commonly used nickel-plating bath. It contains nickel sulfate, nickel chloride and boric acid. Additional organic compounds are used to enhance the quality of the nickel deposit. When properly done, the plated object is simply removed from the tank gleaming brightly and in need of no further polishing. Indeed, polishing is not practical because the layer of nickel is no more than 0.001—0.002-in. (25—50 *millionths*) thick. Even so, it takes about 30 minutes for the deposit to build up. After one more rinse, the workpiece is finally ready for chroming.

Inert lead anodes are used in a solution of chromic acid and sulfuric acid. The chrome that is deposited on the part is replaced in the solution by adding more chromic acid. Believe it or not, only 30—50 *millionths* of an inch thickness is required for good corrosion resistance. A coating as thin as that only requires that the part be in the tank a short time, but not to worry. All chrome does is prevent the nickel from tarnishing. When the part is removed from the chrome tank, it is again rinsed and inspected for flaws.

Problems You May Face—As mentioned above, die-cast parts are the most delicate items you are likely to bring to the plating shop. If you are street-rodding vintage tin, and if quality reproduction parts are not available, you and the plater must take great care with them.

If the old chrome is badly pitted, expensive reclamation may be required. The trouble is, once started, pitting is extremely difficult to

Aluminum polishing is a "tender art." Metal is soft and gouges easily; parts street rodders bring polishing shops are full of tight curves, presenting quite a challenge.

stop. Die castings poured before World War II were made with low-melting-temperature alloys of zinc, tin and lead. Moisture that was unavoidably absorbed over the decades resulted in more pitting than meets the eye—it is also under the chrome plating. So, after stripping off the old plating, the part should be carefully inspected. If the pitting is not so extensive as to render it worthless, heavy copper plating and very careful buffing may save even marginal items. *Heavy-handed buffing of the pitted area before copper plating only results in dips and low spots.*

Often, previously chromed steel parts such as bumpers will require repairs. Careless welding of plated parts invariably captures some chrome in the basis metal. This will create problems during subsequent chroming. In short, repairs to steel parts scheduled for rechroming must be made *after* de-plating. That may mean two trips to the plating shop, but that's part of the price for quality work.

Finally, some fellows never get the message. Chrome plating is thin. A lot of good chrome has been ruined at home by polishing it with rubbing compounds, scouring cleansers and even mildly abrasive polish. Some of the so-called chrome cleaners are even abrasive. Most good chrome will easily clean up with ammoniated liquid window cleaners such as Windex, etc. Given gentle cleaning and the protection of non-abrasive carnauba wax, the luster and sparkle of quality chrome should last for years.

Metal Polishing—Although part of the chrome-plating process, polishing is a decorative process in and of itself. This is particularly true with regard to aluminum and stainless-steel components typically used on a street rod.

If you need a reason to justify metal polishing beyond just good looks, you need to look no further than the ease with which a once handsome intake manifold quickly takes on an unpleasant scuzzy appearance. Fresh cast aluminum is porous, so it inevitably gets stained from gasoline, oil and crankcase vapor. And, regardless of how diligently you apply the elbow grease and all the many scouring agents available at the supermarket, a manifold just never seems to come clean.

Polishing a new or recently sandblasted item such as an intake manifold may be too much to handle. Several specialized tools and a whole box full of supplies are required . . . plus a fair amount of experience. After all, aluminum is soft, and mistakes are commonly made by those who are considered experts. In short, first-time-around polishing should be left to a professional who cares.

This is not to say that once your parts have been professionally polished, that you couldn't, or shouldn't, re-polish them after a year or so of street duty. Sears and other retail-marketing chains sell metal-polishing kits and supplies. So, if you have a 1/4-HP electric motor and a flexible shaft with a

If it ain't one vat, it's another. Seems like much of what street rodding calls *attractive* requires a visit to a smelly old factory. Anodizing is no exception, but just as with pudding, the proof of what you get is in the senses.

Old timers painted dropped axles with a 10¢ can of Woolworth's best. If you want bright red instead of chrome on *your* axle, use baked-on epoxy powder paint. It'll outlast you.

chuck, you can easily bring back the good looks of that aluminum intake manifold. It just takes time and patience.

Another workshop task to take on is periodic machine buffing of the stainless-steel exterior trim with which early Fords are lavishly adorned. Just because they are "stainless" doesn't mean they won't lose some of their gleam over the years. However, their luster comes back after only two or so hours invested in removing and polishing them.

ALTERNATIVES TO CHROME

What's that you say? You're tired of everyday, belly-button chrome-plated ornamentation, and you want your street rod to wear something different? No problem. There are a number of other decorative treatments. Some are quite inexpensive, too.

Almost all of the options do, however, requir metal polishing. There's just no way to bring out luster on a rough surface. Admittedly, polishing is a labor-intensive operation, which means it's expensive or time consuming.

Copper & Nickel Plating—I've already discussed copper plating. Its rich, reddish gold color offers an alternative to chrome in a dry, protected environment such as the cockpit. I wouldn't recommend it for engine or exterior work, however. The same is true of nickel plating, with or without the copper underplate. Nickel will also tarnish, but it can be polished from time to time just like silver. And its silver-like luster can be an interesting addition to any interior.

Brass Plating—Speaking of luster, what about that old favorite of the Roaring Twenties—brass plate? You don't see much of it anywhere except on Fad T rods. That's a pity. Brass, an alloy of copper and zinc, is less costly than chrome, but requires more maintenance. In tasteful application, it just

might be what sets your car apart from the rest.

Cad Plating—Cadmium plating has a number of adherents among the more frugal street-rod builders. No wonder, a polished and silver-white cad-plated part costs only a fraction of what it would cost if it were chrome plated. Cad plating is available in two major varieties: silver-white (Type 1), and irridescent gold (Type 2). *Cad iridite,* (Type 2), has the edge with regard to corrosion resistance. For long plating life, ask for a *clear bright dip.*

Cadmium plating has an added advantage in that parts such as hood springs, which can be severely weakened by chrome-plate-induced hydrogen embrittlement, can be oven-baked to significantly reduce the problem. My admonition against any kind of electroplating on suspension springs still stands, however. They should only be painted.

Anodizing—Anodizing is a common term in street-rod parlance, although many rod builders don't quite understand exactly what it is.

Technically, anodizing is an invisible electrochemical process designed to obtain a controlled surface oxidation with a depth of a few thousandths of an inch. By itself, it is not decorative per se, but once anodized, the surface can absorb a special dye. Beyond that, anodizing provides an excellent barrier against corrosion. The confusion stems from the often overlooked fact that only aluminum alloys can be anodized.

Dyes for anodized aluminum are available in a wide variety of colors: black, blue, navy blue, bluish green, bronze, brown, olive brown, red brown, yellow brown, gold, orange, golden orange, red, fiery red, violet, red violet, blue violet, turquoise, yellow and brass yellow. And if that's not quite enough choice, anodizing is also a perfect

"primer"—it adds excellent paint-gripping characteristics to normally hard-to-paint aluminum.

Anodizing and color impregnation is a relatively inexpensive basic process. That, of course, does not include the cost of polishing, and for color with a mirror gleam, the part should be professionally polished. The "as-shipped" sandblasted finish of most cast-aluminum parts such as intake manifolds, will have a kind of dull, dark appearance after dyeing.

Unfortunately, die-cast aluminum parts such as valve covers sometimes do not accept the dye well. So, talk it over with the shop foreman or merely have them polished.

Incidentally, first-class anodizing shops will, upon request and at extra cost, spray the dyed part with a clear enamel—clear coat—and then oven-bake it. The extra cost is worthwhile if you want long-lasting good looks.

If you are contemplating one of the more exotic colors—tastefully applied, these can be striking—you should be aware that they are more expensive and that it normally takes longer to get them back. The process is not different, but no shop can mix an unusual dye bath just for your one part.

If you do decide to get something exotic, bring the part in long before you need it. When the shop schedules a commercial run of that particular color, your part can be more economically dyed.

Metal Spraying—Metal spraying has long been popular among street-rod builders for exhaust-system components. The process consists of passing a metal wire through a special torch where it is melted and sprayed under high pressure onto the surface of a metal component. The types of wire usually sprayed include aluminum (the most popular), brass, bronze, copper, lead, monel and

A bodyman once told me there are two things a driver looks at most: top of hood and instrument panel. Needless to say, instrument panel is a critical part of street-rod interior. Panel from Magoo's can be ordered with VDO gauges and sending units.

If it's high-tech you want: Valley Auto Accessories three-dimensional, fully machined aluminum, digital panels are available in two styles, ready to install, and complete with micro-circuit instruments. Sending units—except fuel—are included.

stainless steel. Note that sprayed stainless steel doesn't look as attractive as what you may be accustomed to seeing. It turns gray-black under the heat and pressure of the application process.

The only preparation required prior to metal spraying is sandblasting. This gets the part clean. Before you take your parts to the shop, however, grind off any casting or welding imperfections.

Most metal spraying is reasonably priced. If applied thickly enough, aluminum coatings can be polished. As is, aluminum will have a tendency to absorb oil and discolor, but sealers can be used to reduce this problem.

Porcelainizing—Porcelainizing has the ring of classic quality. And it should, for many classic cars of the '20s and '30s had porcelainized exhaust and intake manifolds for long lasting, easily maintained beauty. Porcelain is a translucent ceramic made of pure clay and is available in various colored fusible materials.

Not every locality will have a porcelain shop interested in street-rod work, but if you have access to one, it offers—at a cost roughly comparable to quality chrome—a handsome decorative coating simply not found on every rod that shows up at the drive-in on Cruise Night.

The best parts for porcelainizing are made of steel or cast iron. The process is not recommended for many stainless-steel alloys, nor will porcelainizing endure on aluminum, brass or bronze. High thermal-shock porcelain compounds in dark colors are recommended for most automotive components.

A part slated for porcelainizing is first oven-baked for several hours to drive out as much grease and carbon as possible. It is then sandblasted to eliminate the scale. When spotlessly clean, both inside and out, a thick porcelain coating is sprayed on. The part is then dried over a low gas flame before being subjected to oven-baking at 1400F for several

more hours. When the part has cooled, it will exhibit a smooth, glossy finish.

Powder Coating—Most decorative finishes so far described, in varying degrees, must be treated with respect. Some, such as porcelain, are downright delicate. But if you require maximum rough-and-tumble durability, baked-on epoxy finishes, often called *powder paints* or *powder coatings,* are for you.

The materials used in this process—special epoxy powders—are fine, free-floating "dusts" that are sprayed on with a special gun. The fancy name for this operation is *electrostatic deposition.* And, yes, it is similar to the phenomenon that permits a comb to attract a piece of paper. The powder adheres to the part after it's baked in an oven at 300F for approximately 30 minutes. During baking, it melts and flows out with almost as much gloss as porcelain.

Powdered epoxy coatings offer excellent resistance to most all routine abrasive mishaps and all solvents except ordinary brake fluid. The powders are available in a number of standard industrial high-gloss colors, including red, green, yellow, orange, black and white. In addition, in the past few years, such exotic hues as the candy-apple translucents have appeared.

The range of uses for powder coatings is nearly limitless with the obvious exception of nonmetal components or any assemblies that cannot be baked. Powder coatings have been successfully used on wheels, suspension components, entire street rod frames, window moldings, engine blocks, bumper brackets, and all manner of accessory items. It, too, is surprisingly inexpensive compared to chrome or even conventional painting.

ADD WARMTH
TO YOUR STREET ROD

Before I close this section, I think you should be aware that sometimes the decorative processes I've discussed are just a little

bit . . . well, for want of a better word . . . cold. Sometimes even austere. Chrome, in particular has a way of giving this feeling to those who don't have a true appreciation of engineering that goes beyond strict utilitarianism. This is not to say that chrome and the like, tastefully assigned here and there, doesn't add great beauty to any street rod. We all know better. These embellishments are, for the most part, best restricted to the engine compartment. Even though ours is obviously a mechanical hobby, the car doesn't have to be *all* nuts and bolts.

But how are we to put some warmth in the cockpit? Or add a splash of lighthearted zest to the exterior? Furry dice dangling from the rearview mirror or fuzzy dogs brainlessly bobbing their heads back and forth sure won't do it. It has to be a little more subtle and much less campy than that.

Well, one of the time-honored methods of adding warmth to the interior is through what is called *wood tones.* Wood tones can be classic wood-grained paint schemes or simply brown and tan colors on metal or plastic components. Or, a throwback to a grander era than this age of synthetics—real wood!

Your choice of interior color(s) is naturally one of personal taste and preference. But I sincerely hope that hold-outs for the early '50s imitation—or even genuine—zebra and leopard skin or checkered-flag patterns have long since abandoned street rods for mountain climbing or some other equally hazardous sport. Wood tones, however, do fit in with most modern street-rod-interior schemes.

The best areas for that bit of wood tone warmth is the dashboard and, to a lesser extent, steering column and wheel, window moldings, and window cranks and door handles. Walnut and mahogany are the favored furniture woods for automotive interiors. And the abundance of reproduction early-car dashboard and door hardware makes the task of attractive interior decorating much easier than it was a few years ago.

Softening & Highlighting the Exterior—Only slightly less important than the interior, when it comes to *deburring* the mechanical excesses of a street rod, is a touch of softness in exterior paint scheme and graphics. The best all around approach to that end is pinstriping. Your car shouldn't look like some automotive rendition of the tattooed man in the circus, but gentle accenting of the body lines and particular styling features can make even a chrome-plated brick look good. If you've found a local pinstriper talented enough to adorn your car, chances are his artistic judgement is astute enough to tell him when to quit. To determine this, have a look at some of his work. He should be able to show you several examples.

Metric Conversion Chart

Multiply:		by:		to get:	Multiply:		by:		to get:

LINEAR

inches	X	25.4	=	millimeters(mm)		X	0.03937	=	inches
miles	X	1.6093	=	kilometers (km)		X	0.6214	=	miles
inches	X	2.54	=	centimeters (cm)		X	0.3937	=	inches

AREA

inches^2	X	645.16	=	millimeters^2(mm^2)		X	0.00155	=	inches^2
inches^2	X	6.452	=	centimeters^2(cm^2)		X	0.155	=	inches^2

VOLUME

quarts	X	0.94635	=	liters (l)		X	1.0567	=	quarts
fluid oz	X	29.57	=	milliliters (ml)		X	0.03381	=	fluid oz

MASS

pounds (av)	X	0.4536	=	kilograms (kg)		X	2.2046	=	pounds (av)
tons (2000 lb)	X	907.18	=	kilograms (kg)		X	0.001102	=	tons (2000 lb)
tons (2000 lb)	X	0.90718	=	metric tons (t)		X	1.1023	=	tons (2000 lb)

FORCE

pounds—f(av)	X	4.448	=	newtons (N)		X	0.2248	=	pounds—f(av)
kilograms—f	X	9.807	=	newtons (N)		X	0.10197	=	kilograms—f

TEMPERATURE

Degrees Celsius (C) = 0.556 (F - 32)   Degree Fahrenheit (F) = (1.8C) + 32

```
°F   -40          32      98.6              212                          °F
          0    40    80    120   160  200   240   280   320
°C   -40   -20    0    20    40    60    80   100   120   140   160   °C
```

ENERGY OR WORK

foot-pounds	X	1.3558	=	joules (J)		X	0.7376	=	foot-pounds

FUEL ECONOMY & FUEL CONSUMPTION

miles/gal	X	0.42514	=	kilometers/liter(km/l)		X	2.3522	=	miles/gal

Note:
235.2/(mi/gal)=liters/100km
235.2/(liters/100km)=mi/gal

PRESSURE OR STRESS

inches Hg (60F)	X	3.377	=	kilopascals (kPa)		X	0.2961	=	inches Hg
pounds/sq in.	X	6.895	=	kilopascals (kPa)		X	0.145	=	pounds/sq in
pounds/sq ft	X	47.88	=	pascals (Pa)		X	0.02088	=	pounds/sq ft

POWER

horsepower	X	0.746	=	kilowatts (kW)		X	1.34	=	horsepower

TORQUE

pound-inches	X	0.11298	=	newton-meters (N-m)		X	8.851	=	pound-inches
pound-feet	X	1.3558	=	newton-meters (N-m)		X	0.7376	=	pound-feet
pound-inches	X	0.0115	=	kilogram-meters (Kg-M)		X	87	=	pound-inches
pound-feet	X	0.138	=	kilogram-meters (Kg-M)		X	7.25	=	pound-feet

VELOCITY

miles/hour	X	1.6093	=	kilometers/hour(km/h)		X	0.6214	=	miles/hour

Supplier's Index

Manufacturers of street-rod products are listed two different ways. First they are listed by company name in alphabetical order—then product groupings are listed alphabetically. If you are looking for a particular product, look first in the Product Index. The number behind each item refers to the number of the manufacturer(s) shown in the Suppliers Index.

Every year new street-rod companies are formed and a few go out of business. Therefore, don't consider this list to be the last word. If you want a complete and current listing of manufacturers supplying a particular street-rod component, refer to the advertisements in the latest street-rod monthlies. The following is merely a guide.

1. **Albrecht Towing Service**
   3107 Albrecht Avenue
   Akron, Ohio 44312

2. **Anderson Industries Incorporated**
   (Ai Fiberglass)
   6599 Washington Blvd.
   Elkridge, Maryland 21227

3. **Antique Auto Sheet Metal Company**
   14274 Amity Road
   Brookville, Ohio 45309

4. **A-T Chassis Design**
   1945 Grant St. Unit 4
   Santa Clara, California 95050

5. **B & M Automotive Products**
   9152 Independence Avenue
   Chatsworth, California 91311

6. **Ben Deiner Fabricating, Inc.**
   14190 S.W. 20th Street
   Davie, Florida 33325

7. **Bill Keifer's California Custom Roadsters**
   401 W. Chapman Avenue
   Orange, California 92666

8. **Bird Automotive**
   9140 W. Dodge Road
   Omaha, Nebraska 68114

9. **Bitchin Products**
   10707 Airport Dr.
   El Cajon, California 92020

10. **Bob Drake Reproductions**
    1819 N.W. Washington Blvd.
    Grants Pass, Oregon 97526

11. **Bow Tie Reproductions**
    132 S. Main Street
    Germantown, Ohio 45327

12. **Brizio Street Rods**
    263 Wattis Way
    South San Francisco, California 94080

13. **Bud Matthews Chassis**
    16392 Gothard "H"
    Huntington Beach, California 92646

14. **Butch's Rod Shop**
    10 E. Main Street
    New Lebanon, Ohio 45345

15. **California Metal Shaping**
    1704 Hooper Avenue
    Los Angeles, California 90021

16. **California Street Rods**
    17091 Palmdale
    Huntington Beach, California 92647

17. **Carlin Manufacturing**
    1250 Gulf Street
    Beaumont, Texas 77701

18. **Central Mass Antique Auto Parts**
    56 Franklin
    Finchburg, Massachusetts 01420

19. **Classic Manufacturing**
    2620 West M-8
    Lancaster, California 93536

20. **Chassis Engineering**
    RR2 Box 256A
    West Branch, Iowa 52358

21. **Currie's Enterprises**
    1480-B N. Tustin
    Anaheim, California 92807

22. **David Moell**
    1052 Mattingly Road
    Hinckly, Ohio 44233

23. **Dennis Carpenter Reproductions**
    P.O. Box 26398
    Charlotte, North Carolina 28221

24. **The Deuce Factory**
    424 W. Rowland Avenue
    Santa Ana, California 92707

25. **Don McNeil's Specialized Auto**
    Components (SAC)
    1815 C Orangethorpe Park N.
    Anaheim, California 92801

26. **Downs Manufacturing**
    11830 Shaver Road
    Schoolcraft, Michigan 49087

27. **Early Ford Reproductions**
    124 Maple Avenue
    Altamont, New York 12009

28. **The Early Ford Store**
    2141 West Main Street
    Springfield, Ohio 45504

29. **Engineered Components, Inc.(ECI)**
    P.O. Box 2361
    Vernon, Connecticut 06066

30. **Experi-Metal, Incorporated**
    6345 Wall Street
    Sterling Heights, Michigan 48077

31. **Ezra Welding Shop**
    Route 2, Box 309
    Winamac, Indiana 46996

32. **Florida Rod Shop**
    3019 Alt. Highway 19
    Palm Harbor, Florida 33563

33. **Gaslight Auto Parts**
    P.O. Box 291
    Urbana, Ohio 43078

34. **Gene Reese Chassis Parts & Components**
    11111 Ables 110
    Dallas, Texas 75229

35. **Gennie Shifter Co.**
    930 So Broadmoor Ave.
    West Covina, California 91790

36. **Gibbon Fiberglass Reproductions**
    P.O. Box 490
    Gibbon, Nebraska 68840

37. **Guldstrand Engineering, Inc.**
    11924 W. Jefferson Blvd.
    Culver City, California 90230

38. **Harold Looney's Vintique, Inc.**
    P.O. Box 65
    Orange, California 92666

39. **Hamilton Automotive Industries**
    7762 Gloria Avenue
    Van Nuys, California 91406

40. **Heidt's Hot Rod Shop, Inc.**
    3100 Swallow Lane
    Rolling Meadows, Illinois 60008

41. **Howell's Sheetmetal Company**
    P.O. Box 179
    Nome, Texas 77629

42. **Jim Meyer Street Rods**
    21176 Highway 99E
    Aurora, Oregon 97002

43. **Kugel Komponents**
    10821 Whittier Blvd.
    Whittier, California 90606

44. **Kurt's Hot Rod Shop**
    (Kurtco Manufacturing)
    105 S. 36th Street
    Phoenix, Arizona 85034

45. **Lloyd Arnold Rear End Covers (LAP)**
    Products
    8206 3/4 Sorensen Ave.
    Santa Fe Springs, California 90670

46. **Linken Manufacturing**
    1452 Wallace Road
    Oakville, Ontario
    Canada L6L 2Y2

47. **Magoo's Auto Shop**
    7630 Alabama Avenue, Unit 2
    Canoga Park, California 91304

48. **Minnesota Auto Specialties**
    (MAS Racing Products)
    2538 Hennepin Ave. South
    Minneapolis, Minnesota 55405

49. **Outlaw Performance**
    P.O. Box F, Rte. 380
    Avonmore, Pennsylvania 15618

50. **Patrick's Cars And Trucks**
    P.O. Box 648
    Casa Grande, Arizona 85222

51. **Pat Schreiber Specialties**
    P.O. Box 123
    Bethalto, Illinois 62010

52. **Paul Horton Street Rod Products, Inc.**
60 Woolwich Street N
Breslau, Ontario N0B IM0 Canada
(519) 648-2150
U.S. Mailing Address:
P.O. Box 100
Lewiston, New York 14092

53. **Paul Ellis**
Route 28
Knoxville, Tennessee 37290

54. **Pete and Jake's Hot Rod Parts**
8827 E. Las Tunas Drive
Temple City, California 91780

55. **Poli-Form Industries**
500 McQuade Drive - P.O. Box 191
Watsonville, California 95077

56. **Posie's**
219 N. Duke St.
Hummelstown, Pensylvania 17036

57. **Progressive Automotive**
125 W. Rome STreet
Baltimore, Ohio 43105

57A. **PSI Street Rod Components**
9113 East Garvey Ave.
Rosemead, California 91770

58. **RB's Obsolete Automotive**
7130 Hwy. 2
Snohomish, Washington 98290

59. **Redi-Strip Paint Sripping & Rust Removal**
9910 Jorden Circle
Santa Fe Springs, California 90670

60. **Rock Valley Antique Auto Parts, Ltd.**
Route 72 & Rothwell Rd.
Stillman Valley, Illinois 61804

61. **The Rod Factory**
2901 W. Thomas
Phoenix, Arizona 85017

62. **Ron Francis' Wire Works**
167 Keystone Road
Chester, Pennsylvania 19013

63. **Rootlieb, Inc.**
P.O. Box 1829
Turlock, California 95380

64. **Sanderson Headers**
202 Ryan Way
South San Francisco, California 94080

65. **Sbarbaro Hot Rod**
27690 Industrial Blvd.
Hayward, California 94545

66. **Southeastern Automotive Manufacturing**
1070 N.E. Terrace Street
Forth Lauderdale, Florida 33334

67. **Specialized Auto Parts**
7130 Capitol Street
Houston, Texas 77261

68. **Specialty Cars**
17211 Roseton Avenue
Artesia, California 90701

69. **Speedway Motors, Inc.**
P.O. Box 81906
Lincoln, Nebraska 68501

70. **Stewart-Warner Instrumentation Division**
1840 Diversey Parkway
Chicago, Illinois 60614

71. **The Streetrod Manufacturing Company**
7068 S. Lafayette Way
Littleton, Colorado 80122

72. **Super Bell Axle Company**
152 "M" Street
Fresno, California 93721

73. **Superior Glass Works**
16706 S.E. Taggart
Portland, Oregon 97236

74. **TCI Engineering, Inc.**
1416 West Brooks Street
Ontario, California 91761

75. **Technical Fabrications**
2132 Stall Drive
Harvey, Louisiana 70058

76. **Terry Berzenye's Specialized Auto Repair**
1075 North Harbor Blvd.
Anaheim, California 92801

77. **Total Performance, Inc.**
406 S. Orchard Street. Rt. 5
Wallingford, Connecticut 06492

78. **Transgo Performance**
2621 Merced Ave.
El Monte, California 91733

79. **TRW Automotive Aftermarket Group**
Replacement Parts Division
Cleveland, Ohio 44131-5582

80. **Ultimate Street Rods**
Rt. 1, Box 116
Woodward, Oklahoma 73801

81. **Valley Vintage Rods**
978 Collins Street
Oxnard, California 93030

82. **VDO Automotive Instruments**
980 Brooke Road
Winchester, Virginia 22601

83. **Vintage Chassis Works**
6145 Rt. 14 Bypass
Canfield, Ohio 44406

84. **Vintage Chevrolet Specialties**
P.O. Box 275
Macon, Illinois 62544

85. **Vintique Reproductions**
9318 24th Avenue East
Tacoma, Washington 98445

86. **The V-8 Shop**
7555 Bond Street
Glenwillow, Ohio 44139

87. **Walker Radiator Works**
694 Marshall
Memphis, Tennessee 38103

88. **Wescott's Auto Restyling**
19701 S.E. Highway 212
Boring, Oregon 97009

89. **Windsor Fabrications**
87 N. La Vista Blvd.
Battle Creek, Michigan 49015

PRODUCT INDEX
(Manufacturers and Custom Builders)

Brake Kits & Components
Airheart disc brakes: 32, 77
GM disc-brake kits: 14, 20, 24, 29, 32, 42, 46, 72, 77
Mustang disc-brake kits: 72, 77
FoMoCo disc-brake kits: 25
JFZ disc-brake kits: 43, 47
MoPar disc-brake kits: 14, 20, 42
Volvo disc-brake kits: 42, 54, 77
GM master-cylinder mounts: 20
Mustang master-cylinder mounts: 14, 16, 20, 24, 25, 42, 54, 74
Brake-pedal assemblies: 7, 12, 20, 24, 25, 42, 54, 57, 74
Rear disc-brake kits: 29, 69
Misc. brake-system components: 7, 12, 14, 16, 20, 25, 29, 32, 37, 42, 43, 44, 47, 52, 54, 57, 72, 74, 77

Cooling-System Components
Electric-fan kits: 47
Pressurized street-rod radiators/1917-48 Ford: 87
Pressurized street-rod radiators/1932-48 Chevrolet: 87
Pressurized street-rod radiators/1932-34 Dodge and Plymouth: 87

Engine, Transmission & Driveline Installation Kits & Components
4, 7, 8, 12, 14, 16, 20, 24, 25, 32, 34, 35, 39, 42, 47, 48, 52, 54, 57, 61, 68, 69, 74, 75, 77, 81, 83

Early Ford Front Suspension Kits & Components
Conventional radius-rod kits: 7, 32
Parallel radius-rod kits: 4, 14, 20, 24, 25, 42, 48, 52, 54, 77
Leaf-spring assemblies: 25, 48, 54, 56
Spring perches: 54, 72, 81, 83
Wishbone-splitting kit: 14, 20, 25, 54
I-beam and tubular axles: 20, 25, 32, 48, 72, 77, 83
Spindles and tie-rod arms: 72, 77

Electrical-System Components
GM alternator brackets: 6, 12, 14, 16, 42, 47, 77
Wiring harnesses/1932 Ford: 16, 62, 77
Wiring harnesses/all early cars: 62
Misc. electrical-system and wiring components, 5, 6, 24, 25, 34, 47, 52, 54, 62, 74, 77
Instruments and gauges: 70, 82

Exhaust-System Components
Big-block Chevy headers/Fad T frames: 64
Big-block Chevy headers/1932 Ford frames: 64
Buick V6 headers/1927-34 Ford, GM, MoPar frames: 64
Chevy V6 headers/1927-34 Ford, GM, MoPar frames: 64
Small-block Chevy headers/Fad T frames: 7, 32, 64
Small-block Chevy headers/1928-31 Ford frames: 20, 64
Small-block Chevy headers/1928-34 Ford frames: 16, 25, 34, 64
Small-block Chevy headers/1935-48 Ford frames: 25, 64
Small-block Ford headers/ 1928-48 Ford frames: 64
Ford Flathead headers: 50, 69

Fiberglass Reproduction Chevrolet Bodies & Components
1932 roadster: 66
1933-40 components: 73
1934 roadster: 49, 69

Fiberglass Reproduction Ford Bodies & Components
1923-25 Model T roadster: 2, 8, 48, 77
1926-27 Model T roadster: 2, 77, 88
1927 Model T Touring: 55
1928-29 Model A roadster: 2, 36, 55, 66, 88
1929 phaeton: 88
1929 roadster pickup: 36, 88
1930-31 phaeton: 36, 88
1930-31 roadster: 66, 69, 88
1931 roadster pickup: 88
1931 pickup: 88
1932 roadster: 26, 36, 69, 88
1932 phaeton: 88
1932 three-window coupe: 26, 66, 77
1932 five-window coupe: 26
1932 Victoria sedan: 26, 85
1933 Victoria sedan: 66, 89
1933-34 three-window coupe: 2, 36, 55, 66, 77, 89
1933-34 five-window coupe: 89
1933-34 phaeton: 36
1933-34 roadster: 36, 66, 69, 85
1934 sedan delivery: 89
1934 roadster pickup: 36
1934 Victoria sedan: 89
1935 pickup: 66
1939 convertible: 36, 88

Independent Front-Suspension Kits & Components
Pacer IFS/1935-40 Ford: 20
Jaguar IFS/1927-40 Ford: 25, 43, 77
Opel IFS/1928-32 Ford: 39
Custom design IFS/1928-40 Ford: 42, 43
Mustang II IFS/1928-48 Ford: 40, 57, 76

Independent Rear-Suspension Kits & Components
Jaguar IRS installation components and kits: 7, 25, 32, 42, 43, 46
Corvette IRS installation components and kits: 20, 34, 37, 42, 44, 57

Metal Reproduction Bodies, Components & Assembly Kits
1928-29 Ford roadster: 19
1928-29 Ford roadster: pickup 19
1930-31 Ford roadster: 19
1930-31 Ford roadster: pickup 19
1932 Chevrolet roadster: 30

Rear-Suspension Kits & Components
Rear axle installation kits: 8, 12, 20, 25, 32, 42, 43, 52, 54, 57A, 74, 77
Rear radius-rod kits: 8, 14, 25, 52, 54, 57A, 74, 77
Watts linkage kits: 8, 25, 43, 32 77 TP
Anti-roll-bar kits: 8, 12, 14, 16, 24, 54
Coil spring installation kits: 8, 57A 77

Rear Panhard rod kits: 14, 25, 52, 54, 74
Rear shock-mounting kits: 12, 14, 16, 20, 24, 25, 52, 77
Triangulated 4-link rear axle mounting kits: 16, 25, 57
Coil-over-shock suspension kits: 7, 12, 14, 24, 25, 52, 54, 74
Narrowed and centered Ford 8- and 9-inch rear axle Assemblies: 21, 69, 74, 76

Reproduction Chevrolet Frames & Frame Assemblies
1931-32: 57
1934-45: 49

Reproduction Ford Frames, Frame Assemblies & Repair Components
Fad T: 7, 8, 13, 32, 48, 52, 68, 75
1926-27: 13, 20, 32, 42, 52, 61, 75, 77, 80
1928-31: 7, 8, 12, 14, 25, 32, 42, 54, 57, 61, 68, 74, 75, 77, 80, 81
1932: 12, 13, 14, 16, 20, 24, 25, 34, 43, 47, 52, 54, 57, 65, 74, 75, 81
1933-34: 12, 13, 14, 25, 34, 52, 54, 57, 65, 74, 75, 77, 81
1935-40: 13, 25, 34, 49, 57

Reproduction Early Car Parts & Accessories
10, 38

Street-Rod Kit-Car Assemblies
Fad T roadster: 7, 8, 69, 77
1927 Ford Track roadster: 55, 69
1927 Ford roadster: 77
1929 Ford roadster: 77
1929 Ford High Boy roadster: 47
1929 Ford phaeton: 77
1932 Ford phaeton: 77
1932 Ford three-window coupe: 77
1932 Ford roadster: 77
1932 Ford lowboy roadster: 69
1932 Ford High Boy roadster: 77
1934 Chevrolet roadster: 69

Steering Installation Kits & Components
Corvair steering-gear mounts: 7, 8, 32, 42, 77
Econoline steering-gear mounts: 42
Vega steering-gear mounts: 8, 12, 16, 20, 25, 42, 74
Mustang steering-gear mounts: 14, 16, 20, 25 42, 54
Saginaw steering-gear mounts: 20, 25, 42, 54
Volkswagen steering-gear mounts: 32
Misc. steering components: 7, 8, 12, 14, 16, 20, 24, 25, 32, 42, 47, 54, 74, 77, 79
Rack-and-pinion-steering assemblies: 79

Reproduction Sheet-Metal Components
1923-27 Ford: 63
1928-31 Ford: 1, 3, 15, 17, 18, 19, 27, 31, 33, 41, 63, 67, 86
1932 Ford: 15, 16, 23, 41, 63, 86
1933-34 Ford: 15, 23, 41, 63, 86
1935-48 Ford: 15, 23, 63, 86
1929-33 Chevrolet: 11, 26
1934-35 Chevrolet: 58, 63

Index